D1738226

THREE IN ONE

Essays on Democratic Capitalism,
1976–2000

MICHAEL NOVAK

EDITED BY
EDWARD W. YOUNKINS

ROWMAN & LITTLEFIELD PUBLISHERS, INC.
Lanham • Boulder • New York • Oxford

ROWMAN & LITTLEFIELD PUBLISHERS, INC.

Published in the United States of America
by Rowman & Littlefield Publishers, Inc.
4720 Boston Way, Lanham, Maryland 20706
www.rowmanlittlefield.com

12 Hid's Copse Road
Cumnor Hill, Oxford OX2 9JJ, England

British Library Cataloging in Publication Information Available

Library of Congress Cataloging-in-Publication Data

Novak, Michael.
    Three in one : essays on democratic capitalism, 1976-2000 / Michael Novak ; edited by
Edward W. Younkins.
        p. cm.
    Includes index.
    ISBN 0-7425-1170-7 (alk. paper)—ISBN 0-7425-1171-5 (pbk. : alk. paper)
        1. Economics—Moral and ethical aspects. 2. Capitalism—Moral and ethical aspects. 3
Democracy—Moral and ethical aspects. I. Younkins, Edward Wayne, 1948- II. Title.

HB72 .N684 2001
330.12'2—dc21

                                                                    00-05335

Printed in the United States of America

∞™ The paper used in this publication meets the minimum requirements of
American National Standard for Information Sciences—Permanence of Paper for
Printed Library Materials, ANSI/NISO Z39.48-1992.

CONTENTS

Economics, Religion, and Morality

The Nature and Responsibilities of Business and the Corporation

ACKNOWLEDGMENTS

The author and editor would like to thank the following publications and organizations, where many of the articles included in this book appeared or were given as lectures:

Across the Board
American Enterprise Institute (AEI)
Centre for Policy Studies
The Christian Century
Christianity Today
Creative Living
Crisis
Directors and Boards
Dravo Review
Economic Affairs
First Things
The Franklin Foundation
Freedom at Issue

Humanities Foundation of West Virginia
The Institute of Economic Affairs (IEA)
  Health and Welfare Unit
Journal of Ecumenical Studies
Journal of Markets and Morality
Loyola Business Forum
Policy Review
The Public Interest
Public Opinion
This World
University of Notre Dame
Washington Post
Worldview

More detailed publication information is included at the back of the book.

Introduction

MICHAEL NOVAK'S CONTRIBUTIONS TO POLITICAL AND ECONOMIC THOUGHT

Edward W. Younkins

Michael Novak, one of the leading Catholic social theorists of our times, is the author of numerous monographs, articles, and reviews, and has written over twenty-five influential books in philosophy, theology, political economics, and culture. He holds the George Frederick Jewett Chair in Religion, Philosophy, and Public Policy at the American Enterprise Institute in Washington, D.C., where he also serves as Director of Social and Political Studies. He has lectured all over the world and has taught at Harvard, Stanford, Syracuse, and Notre Dame. During 1981 and 1982 he served as chief of the U.S. delegation to the United Nations Human Rights Commission in Geneva as a Reagan appointee with the rank of ambassador. His writings have appeared in more than a dozen languages. In 1994 he received the prestigious Templeton Prize for Progress in Religion for his service in defense of freedom and for his influential work in Christian social teachings on economics. Previous recipients of the Templeton Prize include Mother Teresa, Alexander Solzhenitsyn, Billy Graham, and Charles Colson. In addition, in 1999 Michael Novak was presented with the Francis Boyer Award for his status as an eminent thinker who has made notable intellectual contributions to improved public policy and social welfare. Some past recipients of this award are James Q. Wilson, George F. Will, Irving Kristol, Ronald Reagan, Jeanne J. Kirkpatrick, Robert H. Bork, Henry H. Kissinger, Paul Johnson, and Gerald R. Ford.

He once studied for the priesthood and for years was a democratic socialist. Novak at one time believed in socialism because its ostensible ethical system seemed superior. The son of Eastern European immigrants, he formerly thought that the communitarian religious ethic of his heritage was being attacked by the individualistic ethic of commerce. However, he was persuaded through observation of human affairs and intense reflection that he was mistaken. He recognized that capitalism is superior to socialism both in practice and in theory and that Judeo-Christian virtues not only survive but also flourish under democratic capitalism. Novak can now be considered a neo-conservative intellectual who believes passionately in a free society.

According to Novak, religious and cultural life is fundamental to all aspects of our lives—not just complementary. Religion and culture affect everything in people's lives, including their politics and economics. Throughout his writings, Novak has urged us to embrace a tripartite system of democratic capitalism including a market economy, a democratic polity, and a moral-cultural system that would nourish the values and virtues on which free societies depend.

During his life, Michael Novak has been a seminarian, a novelist, a journalist, a "new-left" political activist, a theologian, a philosopher, a publisher, and a diplomat. However, his crowning achievement has been to prepare the way for Pope John Paul II's 1991 social encyclical, *Centesimus Annus*. Novak accomplished this by being the first contemporary theologian to seriously inquire about the nature and morality of modern capitalism. His many years of in-depth theological and philosophical exploration have enabled him to develop a powerful moral and intellectual framework for democratic capitalism. He has shown that there is a great deal in Christianity's 2,000-year-old tradition of intellectual inquiry and that its accumulated body of knowledge can provide positive and profound insights into the nature of contemporary capitalism.

When the papal encyclical *Centesimus Annus* appeared in 1991, it was evident that Novak's writings had been favorably received by Pope John Paul II. In *Centesimus Annus*, the Pope views the free market as the most efficient instrument for utilizing resources and effectively responding to human needs, explains the moral foundations of the market economy, and repudiates the idea of a third way between capitalism and socialism. Of course, as in all things human, the Pope finds faults in the practice of capitalism, as Novak does, too.

Paul Johnson, the British historian and journalist, has written that Michael Novak has probably done more than anyone else since Adam Smith to promote the moral case for market economies. Novak has laid the intellectual and moral groundwork for embracing capitalism with moral seriousness and moral integrity. Since business is a morally significant field, it can be practiced morally or immorally, and the costs of moral failure are high, for the system itself as well as for individual participants in that system.

Novak maintains that economics is a branch of moral philosophy and the liberal arts as well as a science. He argues in the Aristotelian tradition that economics is part of a broader inquiry into ethics and politics. Moral philosophy, economics, and political science should therefore be studied as highly interrelated fields, each shedding complementary light on complex concrete realities.

He observes that economics grew out of moral philosophy as one of the moral sciences, but that at some point during the nineteenth century mainstream economics became detached from the moral sciences and ultimately from morality itself. This resulted from economists' attempts to assume the scientific methods of the natural sciences and mathematics; the adoption of positivism, which eliminated moral issues from consideration; and the academic movement toward specialization, which led to the fragmentation of knowledge.

Novak explains that Adam Smith and John Stuart Mill were wise to view economics as a branch of moral philosophy. Economics should be treated not only as a mathematical and a moral science, but also as a humanistic vocation. Every person is an acting subject, capable of reflection and choice, faced with scarcities inherent in nature, and sensing the call to barter, trade, create, and better their condition. Political economy is the study of human action—it is the branch of moral philosophy that studies what is right and what is wrong in dealing with scarcity and optimizing prosperity. Novak heralds the Austrian School of economics for its contributions to the restoration of economics as a field worthy of study by moral philosophers.

Michael Novak has painted a portrait of democratic capitalism and has thoroughly discussed a number of fundamental ideas and basic concepts that underpin democratic capitalism. Those ideas and basic concepts include, but are not limited to, the following: (1) the person as free, self-responsible, and accountable before God; (2) man as God's image-bearer, with the inalienable right and opportunity to share in the process of creating the future of the world; (3) to exercise the right to personal economic initiative is to fulfill the image of God inherent in every man and woman; (4) the tripartite nature of democratic capitalism including a market economy, a political democracy, and most importantly, a moral-cultural system based on respect for individual freedom; (5) the concept of person as distinct from and richer than the concept of individual—a person is capable of insight and love; (6) codefinition of person and community; (7) love as sought for the beloved; (8) charity as voluntary concern for one's fellow human beings; and (9) the communitarian individual.

In addition, Novak's basic principles include (10) the family as indispensible to republican government, democratic institutions, and the liberal tradition; (11) the individual as transcendent; (12) self-interest rightly understood; (13) ordered liberty as opposed to license; (14) stewardship; (15) men as flawed creatures—every human being sometimes sins; (16) a limited state based on the inviolability of personal rights, the skepticism of concentrated power, and man's innate sinfulness; (17) a constitutional government as an effective social system designed for sinners; (18) pluralism resulting in the diffusion of power into many associations to ensure freedom from tyranny; (19) the principle of subsidiarity; (20) mediating institutions based on freedom of association; (21) a crucial distinction between civil society and the state; (22) civil society as made up of freely chosen or natural associations through which citizens can govern themselves independent of the state; (23) the state as a man-made means of securing liberty and justice for all men alike; and (24) the common good as something achieved by the participation of all the citizens.

Then, too, there are (25) the doctrine of unintended consequences; (26) the veil of ignorance; (27) spontaneous order and catallaxy; (28) change as creative destruction; (29) the common good of civil society as larger, more fundamental, and more vital than the common good of the political community (i.e., the state); (30) the human mind as the cause of the wealth of nations; (31)

practical wisdom as ordered reason; (32) the Catholic Whig tradition; (33) the Catholic ethic that stresses the creativity, liberty, and responsibility of the individual; (34) private ownership as necessary for human creativity; (35) social justice as a social habit and personal virtue involving activism, organizing, and trying to make the system better; (36) recognition that a system that creates economic growth from the bottom up is the best way to help the poor; (37) the principle of human economic progress involving each person's God-given capacity to create more in a lifetime than he or she consumes; (38) positive-sum conceptions of man, nature, and wealth; (39) positive-sum transactions in which all parties to a transaction believe they will benefit (i.e., mutually beneficial exchanges); (40) power based on authority; and (41) the rule of law rather than the rule of men.

Other key components of Novak's thought include (42) the corporation as a mediating economic institution with specific and limited responsibilities that stands between the individual and the state; (43) the importance of incentives; (44) profit as a reward and as an indicator that a business is functioning well by properly employing productive factors and satisfying human needs; (45) honest competition through which competitors compel each other to cooperate better with the buying public; (46) the notion that human flourishing is the life-task of every individual; (47) business as a calling; (48) the cardinal business virtues of creativity, community building, and practical realism; (49) intellectual property laws; and (50) stockholders as the only true stakeholders.

Novak's achievement lies in his construction of a theory of democratic capitalism based on rational reflection about the world. He has identified the underlying ideas of democratic capitalism. Although virtually all of his writings contribute to the portrait he has painted of democratic capitalism, the readings included in this anthology make his case especially well. This book has several purposes: to introduce readers to Michael Novak's systematic explanation of democratic capitalism; to invite readers to study his works in their entirety; to provide a background for individuals who wish to examine Michael Novak's ideas in greater depth and detail; and to make available in one place provocative articles by Novak in various publications, often not widely known to the general reader.

Michael Novak's writings on democratic capitalism grew out of a long self-education process as described in "Controversial Engagements," included in this volume. In addition, his political and economic thought has matured over the more than twenty years since he made his first tentative steps away from his belief in socialism and his criticisms of many aspects of capitalist reality.

Although Novak's body of work has grown to immense size, many of his best articles and lectures, published in leading journals such as *Crisis, First Things,* and *The Journal of Markets and Morality,* or delivered as lectures and conference papers in Europe and Latin America, as well as throughout the United States, have not yet appeared in book form. Novak often uses scheduled lectures to begin developing ideas that will appear later in a more mature form in his books. The works selected for this volume represent an attempt to present a concise introduction to the essentials of Novak's thinking.

The essays and lectures selected for this anthology both paint a coherent portrait of democratic capitalism and illustrate the growth and maturation of Novak's writings about political economy. To accomplish both these ends, this collection is divided into the following six sections: The Idea of Democratic Capitalism; Free Persons, True Communities, and the Common Good; Economics, Religion, and Morality; The Nature and Responsibilities of Business and the Corporation; The International Scene; and An Autobiographical Afterword. In order to instill an appreciation of the evolution of Novak's thought on democratic capitalism, the articles within each section will be presented in chronological order. This book is the only place where a reader can go to see how Novak's thoughts on political economy have developed from their hesitant beginnings in 1976, through their first full unfolding in *The Spirit of Democratic Capitalism* in 1982, to the more advanced positions of the end of the 1990s. In addition, I've included a "Reader's Guide" to Novak's writings in the area of democratic capitalism for readers who want to study his ideas in greater depth and detail.

I'd like to thank Michael Novak for permitting me to pursue this project. In addition, I am in debt to his research assistant and secretary, Cornelis (Kees) Heesters and Cathie Love, for their assistance with this undertaking. Most of all, I am indebted to my own secretaries at Wheeling Jesuit University, Carol Carroll and Carla Cash, for their most capable and conscientious help in bringing this book to print.

Edward W. Younkins
Wheeling Jesuit University

THE IDEA OF
DEMOCRATIC CAPITALISM

"Democratic capitalism is not just a system but a way of life. Its ethos includes a special evolution of pluralism; respect for contingency and unintended consequences; a sense of sin; and a new and distinctive conception of
community, the individual, and the family."

1

A CLOSET CAPITALIST CONFESSES

The day I heard Michael Harrington say that most liberals are "closet socialists," I knew by my revulsion that I had to face an ugly truth about myself. For years, I had tried to hide, even from myself, my unconscious convictions. In the intellectual circles I frequent, persons with inclinations like my own are mocked, considered to be compromised, held at arm's length as security risks. We are easily intimidated.

The truth is there are probably millions of us. Who knows? Your brother or sister may be one of us. The fellow teaching in the class next to yours; the columnist for the rival paper; even the famous liberated poetess—our kind, hiding their convictions out of fear of retribution, lurk everywhere. Even now we may be corrupting your children.

We are the closet capitalists. Now at last, our time has come. The whole world is going socialist. Nearly 118 out of 142 nations of the world are socialist or statist tyrannies. A bare 24 are free-economy democracies. We are the world's newest, least understood and little loved minority. It is time for us to begin, everywhere, organizing cells of the Capitalist Liberation Front.

I first realized I was a capitalist when all my friends began publicly declaring that they were socialists, Harrington and John Kenneth Galbraith having called the signal. How I wished I could be as left as they. Night after night I tried to persuade myself of the coherence of their logic; I did my best to go straight. I held up in the privacy of my room pictures of every socialist land known to me: North Korea, Albania, Czechoslovakia (land of my grandparents) and even Sweden. Nothing worked.

When I quizzed my socialist intellectual friends, I found they didn't like socialist countries, either. They all said to me: "We want socialism, but not like eastern Europe." I said: "Cuba?" No suggestion won their assent. They didn't want to be identified with China (except that the streets seemed clean). Nor with Tanzania. They loved the *idea* of socialism. "But what is it about this particular idea you like?" I asked. "Government control? Will we have a Pentagon of heavy industry?" Not exactly. Nor did they think my suggestion witty, that under socialism everything would function like the Post Office. When they began to speak of "planning," I asked, who would police the planners? They had enormous faith in politicians, bureaucrats and experts. Especially in experts.

"Will Mayor Daley have 'clout' over the planners?" I asked, seeking a little comfort. "Or Congressmen from Mississippi?" My friends thought liberal-minded persons would make the key decisions. Knowing the nation, I can't feel so sure. Knowing the liberal-minded, I'm not so comforted.

Since they have argued that oil companies are now too large, I couldn't see how an HEW that included Oil would be smaller. My modest proposal was that they encourage monopoly in every industry and then make each surviving corporation head a Cabinet officer.

Practical discussions seemed beside the point. Finally, I realized that socialism is not a *political* proposal, not an *economic* plan. Socialism is the residue of Judeo-Christian faith, without religion. It is a belief in community, the goodness of the human race and paradise on earth.

That's when I discovered I was an incurable and inveterate, as well as secret, sinner. I believe in sin. I'm for capitalism, modified and made intelligent and pubic-spirited, because it makes the world free for sinners. It allows human beings to do pretty much what they will. Socialism is a system built on belief in human goodness, so it never works. Capitalism is a system built on belief in human selfishness; given checks and balances, it is nearly always a smashing, scandalous success. Check Taiwan, Japan, West Germany, Hong Kong and (one of the newest nations in one of the recently most underdeveloped sectors of the world) these United States. Two hundred years ago, there was a China and also a Russia. The United States was only a gleam in Patrick Henry's eye.

Wherever you go in the world, sin thrives better under capitalism. It's presumptuous to believe that God is on any human's side. (Actually, if capitalism were godless and socialism were deeply religious, the roles of many spokesmen in America would be reversed in fascinating ways.) But God did make human beings free. Free to sin. God's heart may have been socialist; his design was capitalistic hell. There is an innate tendency in socialism toward authoritarianism. Left to themselves all human beings won't be good; most must be converted. Capitalism, accepting human sinfulness, rubs sinner against sinner, making even dry wood yield a spark of grace.

Capitalism has given the planet its present impetus for liberalism. Everywhere else, they are hawking capitalist ideas: growth, liberation, democracy, investments, banking, industry, technology. Millions are alive and living longer because of medicine developed under capitalism. Without our enormous psychic energy, productivity and inventions, oil would still be lying under Saudi Arabia, undiscovered, unpumped and useless. Coffee, bananas, tin, sugar, and other items of trade would have no markets. Capitalism has made the world rich, inventing riches other populations didn't know they had. And yielding sinful pleasures for the millions.

Six percent of the world's population consumes, they say, 40 percent of the world's goods. The same 6 percent provides more than 50 percent, far more than it can consume. No other system can make such a statement, even in lands more populous, older and richer than our own. As everybody knows, hedonism requires excess.

Look out, world. The closet capitalists are coming out. You don't have to love us. We don't need your love. If we can help you out, we'll be glad to. A system built on sin is built on very solid ground indeed. The saintliness of socialism will not feed the poor. The United States may be, as many of you say, the worthless and despicable prodigal son among the nations. Just wait and see who gets the fatted calf.

2

THE CLOSET SOCIALISTS

Seldom have 1,200 words of mine generated so much attention as "A Closet Capitalist Confesses" *(Washington Post,* March 14, 1976). Bruce Douglass's temperate and reasoned reply in the *Century's* pages ("Socialism and Sin," December 1, 1976) provides a rare opportunity for discussion. On grand themes like "capitalism" and "socialism," much passion is generated. Arguments are theological rather than empirical, for the reality of any economic system is larger than the universes of empirical fact. When "systems" are in conflict, there is pitifully little room outside them where one can find a vantage point of neutral observation.

Douglass was wise to suspect at first that I was "putting us on—that it was all tongue-in-cheek"; but upon mature reflection he was also perceptive enough to see that I *"was* serious." I have difficulty believing in socialism; I cried out in the dark for help. Douglass thinks the 1970s an inauspicious time for capitalism; my weak faith found these years inauspicious for socialism. The spectacle of Great Britain's becoming less than great, the terrors of the Gulag Archipelago, Ingmar Bergman's problems with the Swedish tax bureaucracy, the disastrous socialisms of the Third World, the flight of economic resources from socialist-leaning Quebec, the perfidy of political planners in New York City, efficient tyrannies from Cambodia to Czechoslovakia—these do not inspire me with confidence in the practice of socialism. As a religious vision, socialism has my respect. As a practical way of arranging human political and economic affairs, it evokes my skepticism. I find that even candles burned to St. Michael Harrington (my socialist patron saint) fail to quicken sluggish faith.

I

On reflection, I realized that I had never read an intelligent description, let alone a defense, of democratic capitalism. Persons trained in the humanities, history and sociology—my usual contacts in the literary and intellectual worlds—tend to speak disdainfully of capitalism, profits, business and Detroit. They tend also to be as economically illiterate as I am, who long could not read a balance sheet, do not understand "the dismal science," find business a foreign world. The only *theoretical* materials I ever encounter are socialist.

So it hit me: Socialism—to play on the Volvo slogan—is the thinking man's economics. They go together, socialism and intellectual life. Capitalism is abandoned to practical men and women of affairs. Democratic capitalism as we experience it in the U.S. has no "manifesto," and pitifully scant theoretical interests. There are many fundamentalist preachers of the creed—in Rotary clubs, at the AMA—but there is no serious theology accessible to the ordinary reader. All the fashionable theoreticians—John Kenneth Galbraith, Robert Lekachman, Michael Harrington and a scattering of others—are socialists and review each other's books.

According to the prophetic tradition, one ought to warn oneself to think against prevailing winds. It is one thing to be a nonprofit thinker; nonprophet thinking is worse indeed. It is not really very "radical" for a theologian to promote socialism; it is the expected niche. In *A Theology for Radical Politics* I did not urge forms of socialism, but only those forms that strengthen rights and properties and extend our own tradition. No doubt our own form of democratic capitalism has accepted many socialist elements over the generations; Peter Drucker's work on the effects of "pension-plan socialism" is only one such evidence. It is an advantage of our system that it is subject to continual modification—"creeping socialism," as some call it.

Intellectually speaking, a theologian should be critical of both capitalist and socialist tendencies. It is by no means plain from the historical record that all virtue and truth reside on one side. Among businesspeople, one would perhaps want to raise one set of reflections; among socialist-inclined intellectuals, another. In recent years the balance of highly respected public rhetoric has plainly tipped toward the socialist side. Wisely? Critically? Or in "bad faith"?

The wisest course for a theologian today, I believe, is to be suspicious of the two ideologies—of, as Peter Berger puts it, those twin *Pyramids of Sacrifice*—and to start thinking carefully about one's own economic experience. It is necessary to begin reading economics. As I argued in *Ascent of the Mountain, Flight of the Dove,* economic systems are the most profound institutional enforcers of the prevailing "sense of reality." Economic institutions are more basic than political institutions. Sophistication in "political consciousness" must give place to sophistication in "economic consciousness." But economic consciousness is not to be gleaned solely from books of propaganda. Experience is a more reliable criterion by far. We must move from "political theology" to "economic theology." We might even speak of "the economy of salvation," if liberation theology had not already made that particular connection. But in launching out in these directions the greatest weakness of us theologians is how little we know about economics.

II

Douglass's defense of socialism is unusual for its modesty and pragmatism. His essay is one of the best I have read on the subject. One can sense his care to submit to the evidence, not to be stampeded by desire. Still, one need not look at the evidence from within his horizon. Looked at from another standpoint, his evidence does not help a doubter.

Douglass really has only two points to make, and one of them confirms the central point of my essay. He says it best: "Democratic socialism still remains, therefore, much more a vision than a demonstrated possibility." It *is* a vision. One must approach it as one approaches a religion. Even its claims—as Douglass correctly reports them—are religious: it will generate a new type of human being, more rational, people who "acquire only what they truly need." At stake in the choice between democratic capitalism and democratic socialism "is a fundamental *moral* distinction" [italics added]. Dr. Douglass resists my phrase "secular religion" in order to rebut the "secular" part; it was the "religious" part that caught my attention.

"Under socialism," he writes, "no one goes hungry; everyone who is able works; those who work receive benefits commensurate with their social contribution; and there are not the radical disparities in wealth and opportunities characteristic of capitalism." My own minimal travels abroad teach me no such facts about the practice of socialism. Do most persons in, say, Czechoslovakia meet U.S. minimal standards of nutrition? By our definition, are they above the poverty line? As for unemployment, forced labor can end that anywhere. I believe I have seen evidence of "radical disparities of wealth and opportunities" in every socialist nation I have visited, even independently of reading Yugoslav social critic Milovan Djilas. As for social cooperation, here is how Soviet MIG-25 flyer Viktor Belenko, who defected to Japan, described American crewmen at work on a carrier: "I've never seen men work with such proficiency and coordination." They moved so casually, he marveled, "without ever being given an order and without anyone shouting at them."

The problem is that socialism is now several generations old; it is no longer merely a vision or a dream; it has a historical record and is embodied in actual systems—scores of them around the world. Characteristically, intellectuals deal with *ideas* and *visions* when writing of socialism—and then suddenly become ruthlessly concrete when describing the capitalism they know. This hardly seems fair, until one recognizes that democratic capitalism lacks the texts, theories and visions that might be compared point for point with those of socialism. As a body of ideas, socialism has a coherent beauty and the elaborate casuistry theologians love. That alone makes me believe that it is too good for this frail, sinful world—that it is lacking in practice and is too beautiful by half to supply a useful guide to actual human behavior.

III

Still, one tries to believe. Wouldn't it be wonderful if an economic-political system delivered *everything*: not only productivity sufficient to alleviate poverty, disease and ignorance, not only freedom for science and intellectual pursuits, but also citizens tutored to "acquire only what they truly need"? My experience with socialists suggests that they are anybody's equal as consumers, connoisseurs of good foods and expensive foreign cars (built by multinational corporations), and not detectably less greedy than the capitalists I have known. My hunch—ingrained cynicism, perhaps—is that the coveting of goods antedates capitalism and outlives socialism. In addition, my limited international experience (both travel and reading) does not indicate that socialist systems are more "rational" or even more "humane" in the allocation of resources than capitalist systems.

As a vision, socialism encourages my longing to believe. As a system well advanced in historical experience, it prompts me to ask myself: Would I want to live under such a system? Would I like for the U.S. to become one? Until a better apologist gets to me, I will have to confess, shamefaced (since this confession proves me less humane, less just and less visionary than those with faith), that my flesh and my experience will not let my spirit soar so high.

Temporarily, therefore, I confess as a matter of considered judgment that democratic capitalism is not only a more humane and rational economic-political system than socialism has yet produced but also the most advanced human form of liberty, justice and equality of opportunity yet fashioned by the human race. When a better system comes along, or when genuine internal improvements are imagined for it, I will most happily support such. For ours is obviously a deficient human system. Nonetheless, actual socialisms are, without exception, worse.

IV

I have even formulated some reasons for this dreadful conclusion, to which my head, despite the heart's yearnings, forces me.

First, *liberty*. Democratic capitalism "is indeed flexible," to cite Douglass once again. It is endlessly reformable. Freedom of ideas prevails, private initiatives are encouraged, and practicality has great weight. "As Michael Harrington keeps insisting," Douglass warns us, "as long as the means of production remain in private ownership, there is a fundamental structural obstacle to the realization of socialist objectives"—and also, it might be added, to total state tyranny.

I seem to lack the necessary confidence in bureaucrats, political leaders and state ownership. On reflection, I prefer a world in which private ownership is both possible and effective. I prefer the liberation of private spheres of economic activity, so that economic and political orders are kept in tension.

It's ideologically impure of me, I know, but it does seem that "socialist objectives" may not be worth destroying that tension for, and that they could not survive its disappearance. In a word, the socialist dream seems not only unworkable in practice but also deficient in theory. Countervailing forces in the economic order are indispensable.

Second, *equality.* Recently I heard civil rights spokesman Bayard Rustin ask an audience (predominantly black) which nation of the world a black would rather be living in now. Is there more opportunity for self-realization for a young black—or Hungarian, or Indian, or Dominicano—in any other existing system? The American ideal is not, of course, equality of results but equality of opportunity; but even in the (humanly unrealizable) sphere of equality of results, what system in existence draws as many immigrants year by year, or counts as "poverty" annual incomes unparalleled elsewhere? (The *average* grant to a welfare family in Harlem last year was $6,100.)

Last summer I watched a bicentennial parade in Cresco, Iowa, a town just over 100 years old. The earliest farm implements were resurrected. Three generations ago, one saw vividly, America was an underdeveloped nation. No tractors, no power machines. Then, in this same midwest, industrial invention flowered as nowhere else. (My wife's grandfather himself invented the extension ladder, the grubbing machine—for pulling up stumps—and a special lightning rod.) A great historical miracle occurred. Democratic capitalism nourished it. The whole world now has new horizons.

Disparities of wealth and power, within the United States and outside it, cannot by any means be understood simply as evidence of "oppression" or sins against "equality." The subject is a complicated one. Some use inequality of results as prima facie evidence of inequality of opportunity on the one hand, or of "oppression" on the other. Would that life were so simple. Equality of results is neither a natural, nor a virtuous, nor a creative, nor a free condition. Egalitarianism is, in practice, egalityranny; it must be enforced. Its social costs—in inventiveness, initiative and creativity—are exceeding high.

Third, *justice.* I fail to see any practicing socialist state whose schemes of justice exceed those of democratic capitalism. Justice is never fully achieved by human institutions, but in no land known to me—or to former militant Eldridge Cleaver—does the steady advance of justice have as creditable a track record as in ours. The demands we Americans characteristically make on our social institutions are both extraordinary and exorbitant. We even expect them to make us happy. Justice in Czechoslovakia? Forget it.

V

And so on. Perhaps it is best, by way of conclusion, to show how Dr. Douglass's second point—the irrationality and inhumaneness of capitalism, so disappointing to our academic socialists—fails to help my lack of faith.

1. *Detroit's automobiles.* Dr. Douglass can buy a car of virtually any size from Detroit, or from any other auto-producing nation. Has any socialist a wider range of choice than he? I do not share his enthusiasm for mass transportation; neither the Long Island Railroad, nor the Bay Area Rapid Transit, nor New York City's subways, nor the Paris Metro, nor Eurail, nor any other system can quite match the liberty of action and distribution of costs of the personal automobile. Social costs of various sorts will force us to live differently in the future. You and I will pay for them.

2. *Food production.* The problem is not one of underproduction, for no economic system in the world is so productive, but one of international distribution. One need not buy foods containing additives; the fastest-growing group of food stores is the "independents" catering to the advanced and purified tastes of (among others) intellectuals. Our artificial foods do not seem to lead to shorter life-spans than those of our ancestors.

3. *The energy crisis.* Having discovered oil and its uses, we will now have to find other cheap sources of energy, and live differently. Socialist nations will no doubt suffer even more than we from higher oil prices.

4. *The consumption ethic.* The most highly educated Americans—who happen to be the most affluent—provide the best markets by far for consumer goods. Who else has so much discretionary income? My socialist friends drive expensive foreign cars and have habits in consumption that are not quite so "conspicuous" as to be vulgar, but are actually even more expensive. In a society like ours, there is also freedom *not* to consume. One can teach such restraint to one's children and one's students, if one practices it. One need not care too much about the sinfulness of one's neighbors. Some like consumption, some pornography. Let them.

5. *"Public penury."* Douglass's comment about "underpaid teachers, policemen, firemen and social workers" is probably intended ironically, so far as New York is concerned; but even in Washington federal salaries are notoriously high. In any case, the public pays. Government is not an efficient provider of many services. Where there is government, there is corruption—and also high motivation, well, to shrug.

Douglass wants "a rational plan" rather than "the whims of investors." Look at this meaning of "rational." Would you be satisfied with someone else's "rational plan" if you had a better idea? Investors are rather more careful about their own money than the word "whim" suggests. It seems to me more intelligent—and vastly more creative—to develop and utilize our productive capacities on the basis of the intelligent self-interest of investors than on the whims of planners (to invert a Douglass sentence). Socialist planning has not become the laughingstock of socialist citizens for nothing.

Douglass would like a world without economic accountability: "If you choose to do something which does not lead to profits and which requires substantial financial support, your chances of being frustrated are rather high." Such chances are high in any case in this imperfect world. But the amount of money available for nonprofit work, with substantial financial support, in this nation of all nations in history is astronomical. Dr. Douglass and I draw remarkable salaries from nonprofit universities, for example. Has any civilization ever paid so many so well for being nonproductive?

VI

There is scarcely a sentence of Douglass's modest defense of socialism and calm attack upon capitalism which—much as I admire it—does justice to the complex facts of my own experience of democratic capitalism. Capitalism "builds upon and in fact encourages selfishness"—but also extraordinary generosity, a sense of service, voluntarism, giving. "A capitalist environment naturally inclines us to believe that people *must* be addicted to a greedy, competitive individualism." But how, then, explain the extraordinary innocence and moralism of Americans, so many of whom seem to believe in the essential goodness of humanity and are so deliciously outraged by each example of "greedy, competitive individualism" they encounter in the news? Dr. Douglass argues from what the socialist books say Americans *must* be like—not, I think, from the way his friends and associates regularly behave.

A very large proportion of Americans do *not* seek upward mobility; are content to stay at the salary level they have attained; do not work in order to consume; are not greedy, or even competitive; nourish their families and like their neighbors. The top 10 per cent, the ambitious, of course, do otherwise—and pay the high personal costs. The democratic capitalist conviction is that such individualists will—subject to the checks and balances of our society—do more good than harm. The record seems to support this rather optimistic assessment of human liberty, this method of "harnessing human egoism." As to "cultivating a better human nature," those of us who are Christian leave this slim possibility to the miracle of divine grace and meanwhile do not set too much store by the chance of its happening in history.

Dr. Douglass makes the best case against capitalism and for socialism that I have yet encountered. His vision sounds noble, moral, heroic even. At night, faith wavering, I still thumb through pictures of Sweden, Albania, China, Yugoslavia, Nigeria, and other socialist experiments, trying to awaken a dying light. How fortunate are those who still believe.

3

AN UNDERPRAISED AND UNDERVALUED SYSTEM

Socialism, it appears, is like the Volvo: the thinking person's ideology. It is, according to Irving Howe in *World of Our Fathers*, the vital inheritance of Jewish immigrants. It attracts many dissidents of Catholic origin, like Michael Harrington, Garry Wills, Rosemary Ruether, and the busy workers at the Center for Concern. According to Henry Ford II, it has come to dominate in the bosom of the Ford Foundation. On television shows corporate tycoons and small businessmen are invariably corrupt, and on the television news—that lucrative portion of one of the most profitable of all industries—profits in other industries are reported on with faint whiffs of moral disapproval.

The attraction of socialism, there is no doubt, arises from its humanistic vision. "We are united in the affirmation of a positive belief," announced the first issue of *Dissent*, the Democratic Socialist journal edited by Irving Howe and Lewis Coser, in 1954, "the faith in humanity that for more than one hundred years [has] made men 'socialists.'" And a little later in that first issue: "*Socialism is the name of our desire*. And not merely in the sense that it is a vision which, for many people throughout the world, provides some sustenance, but also in the sense that it is a vision which objectifies and gives urgency to the criticism of the human condition in our time." It is a lovely desire, a delicate vision, this socialism. It is an ethic and a vision more fundamental than the economic or political theorems it from time to time enunciates, tries, discards.

How I would like to march in when the Socialist saints come marching in! How noble they are, unswayed by the "tepid liberalism" of the rest of us. So true to brotherhood, sisterhood, compassion, egalitarianism, justice. Even in their reluctant commitment to the flawed Democratic party, made on the grounds of grudging realism, our Socialists trail clouds of moral glory.

Yet each time I look lustfully at the argument for socialism (God knows I do, and forgives me for it) actual people, faces, and experiences leap from memory. I could live in a dream of ideology if hard experience did not awaken me. But economic systems require humble scrutiny. To judge them one must examine plumbing, sanitation, heat, power, light, water, fuel, paper, pen, typewriter, telephone, copier. One must examine things, things, things. Things so humble one may easily use them and never notice, purchase them and never feel the pain of choosing *not* to have some other. Amid abundance one forgets mean scarcity. Freed by affluence, one soars above materialism.

God knows I have tried to soar. Government planning, government spending, government responsibility—and distrust of freedom, distrust of individuals, distrust of free markets, contempt for profits—all these I have favored.

When the government puts buzzers on my seat belts, however, flesh rebels. When I stop to make my ideology concrete—when I ask, "Who *is* this government?"—I squirm. Those who make decisions far away from me constitute no eternal form of truthfulness, decency, and justice. When I have met them—decent folks at HEW, well-meaning missionaries of the Civil Rights Commission, poverty lawyers, publicists for government departments, aides to famous senators and congressmen, organizers from the Peace Corps, and the rest—their uplift leaves me in depression. Ideologues—kind-hearted, decent, soft-spoken, sensitive, compassionate propagandists: What else can one say? They have a mission. They wish to make us better.

At first, agreeing with their liberal values, I'm glad *we're* in the government. But then I find *us* a little too missionary, holding out, as it were, brassieres to natives, making the world to fit our image. It is so depressing to be told (and to tell others) to be good. I haven't the discipline to be a Socialist. I want to take my chances with the liberties of others and with my own.

When I read learned articles on "planning," my inner eye immediately begins to imagine the faces of the planners. Who will appoint them? Which constituencies will they represent? What types of individuals will find fulfillment in such jobs? It strains credulity to believe that "planners" will be more representative than the Congress is, or than the market is. The class of people most likely to be recruited as planners is not precisely the class to put most trust in. Neither do I see very clearly the checks and balances to be placed against these planners. What standing will they have in our Constitution? Will control surrendered to them in any way come back into possession?

I am not a Platonist about planners. They will be men and women of flesh and blood, like you and me, with interests and positions to protect. They will be insulated from electoral control. They will impose unpopular commands. Planners, one thinks suspiciously: philosopher-kings! No more to be trusted than in Plato's time.

And so the thought has recently become insistent in my doubting mind: If I no longer believe in democratic socialism, is there a form of democratic capitalism I must trust in more? Is there a theory of democratic capitalism not invented yet, beyond the manifestoes of socialism or the classic texts of capitalism?

There are three items in the creed of democratic capitalism I must devoutly believe in: (a) individual freedom and the methods of trial and error; (b) the innate selfishness and corruptibility of every human being; and (c) the capacity of a system of checks and balances to transform selfishness and corruptibility into a modicum of creativity, virtue, efficiency, and decency. These, as I uncover them, are the essential inner form of democratic capitalism. Their indispensable core is contained in (b), which may be stated thus: "Do not trust anybody." On this humanistic pessimism is our Constitution founded. For popular consumption, and put in the more optimistic mode of Anglo-Saxon hopefulness, the maxim is more clearly put: "In God we trust." That is, in no one else.

We trust no president, no court, no senator, no congressman, no governor, no sheriff, no public sentiment, no popular mandate—on every source of power that has been the wit of humankind to invent our Constitution commands us to place checks and balances. It so commands us, not from resentment, but from a long-experienced, wise, and irreformable pessimism about the human race. No human being, whether in solitude or in mass assembled, should be entirely trusted. No lesson of experience speaks more clearly, more credibly, to me. It is *unfair* to human beings to place full trust in them; none can bear such weight. Everyone sometimes fails. Inerrancy, infallibility, impeccability—no proper human aspirations, these. *Errare humanum est:* Such wisdom is not new. Even in so intimate a relation as marriage, forgiveness is a necessary grace; no one sustains a total trust. *A fortiori* in the governance of states.

Democratic capitalism is not a system to be trusted; so it announces. This is its intellectual advantage. It does not demand to be acclaimed as the best, most perfect system. In addition to providing the basic goods of life in abundance, cheaply and efficiently, it alone of all the world's known systems generates an entire industry of well-rewarded critics. So eager is it to breed reform and change—and make a buck on it—that no system is in fact more radical. Pell-mell it overturns the habits, traditions, and cultures of the past. Under its tutelage and leadership world process has been accelerated as never before. Conservative? Inertial? Which capitalist of your acquaintance lives in a world like that of a generation ago? Democratic capitalism undermines all historical traditions and institutions (even itself).

To announce support of democratic capitalism it is not necessary to hold that paradise has thereby, or will someday, be reached. It is not necessary to assert that democratic capitalism is a *good* system. It is certainly not a Christian system, nor a highly humanistic one. It is in some ways an evil, corrupt, inefficient, wasteful, and ugly system. One need only assert that it is better than any known alternative.

Socialism, meanwhile, no longer has the status of a dream or an ideal. It has been realized in something like fourscore regimes. Comparing like to like—actualities to actualities, dreams to dreams—it is not clear to me that democratic capitalism is inferior in performance or in dream to socialism. The defense, "Democratic socialism has never yet been fully tried," sounds like a classical apologetic for Christianity. Mind grasps it, doubt remains. Socialism is inherently authoritarian. Its emphasis upon democracy is inconsistent with its impulse to plan and to restrict.

Compared to the democratic capitalist the Socialist is twice born: born first into faith that the individual can be liberated from the present institutions of society; born again into the faith that the individual, so liberated, will be no slave to self but only to the common good. Socialism believes in the saintliness of human individuals under better social forms, democratic capitalism believes in their flawed self-interest under all.

The problem for a person weak in socialistic faith, like myself, is that he finds few allies in present dialogues. I cannot assent to the authoritarianism explicitly in the work of Robert Heilbroner and implicit in the work of John Kenneth Galbraith, Robert Lekachman, Michael Harrington, George Lichtheim, and Irving Howe. Many other defenders of "socialism," of course, are not serious; for them "socialism" functions merely as an expression of resentment about their own role in the scheme of world events. It expresses their hostilities toward themselves and toward the system on which they blame their own deficiencies. They do not truly intend to support the system they would put in its place.

I see few allies either among those who speak for capitalism. Those who publicly defend it often make it worse. Corporate executives and Rotarians use a vocabulary so hoary, so culturally limited, that not even they, one must assume, can believe it, save on ritual occasions. They celebrate themselves, so to speak, in obsolete English—in that classic, dry and dated style of Locke, Smith, Ricardo, and Mill, enlivened by Ayn Rand, stiffened yet again by Milton Friedman. Not very heady stuff. Relics in a cathedral dusted off; rubbings off old tombs.

In ideological warfare democratic capitalism is hopelessly outclassed. Those ads paid for by Mobil Oil on the Op-Ed pages of the *Times* (and other papers) are more deadly in their prose than the editorials surrounding them. I look to them for light, find disappointment. The reason probably is that capitalists have not been trained to think—have, indeed, been tutored *not* to think, *not* to theorize, *not* to dream—rather, to be practical. The radical impulse of capitalism is to set schemes and speculation to one side in order to detect some practical detail that might modify the technology of mouse traps. Socialism's dreams are the soul's response to capitalism's practicality.

Democratic capitalism seems willing to lose any number of ideological battles, provided only that it win the franchise for producing, delivering, and getting paid for goods or services. It will build cars in Kiev, deliver Pepsi to Leningrad, teach computer technology to engineers in Moscow—anything for dollars, no ideology attached. The self-confidence of capitalists is, however, shallow. They believe that what the world wants is goods. They leave the Good beyond their caring—leave it to priests, poets, propagandists. That is why they are losing everywhere. Lenin predicted that capitalists would sell socialism everything necessary for the latter's triumph—socialism could never hope to equal capitalism, but capitalism would destroy itself.

The point is not that democratic capitalism carries no ideology, depends on none. Most certainly it does. Democratic capitalism depends upon a disciplined triumph of the human spirit. Yet it resists reflection upon its own presuppositions. Democratic capitalism can function successfully only in certain types of cultures, in which high values of individual responsibility, social cooperation, and the voluntary spirit have for centuries been nourished. Its severe disinclination toward philosophy allows poisonous effects: (a) the spiritual life of its own citizens is slowly starved; and (b) it cannot compete with socialism on the plain of ideological warfare—it cannot explain itself. It is one of the choicer ironies of history that the economic system most dependent upon, and most supportive of, liberty of spirit should present itself to the world as brute and inarticulate, mute in the language of the spirit.

To be sure, democratic capitalists display an openness and practicality far beyond those of Socialists. They find it easier to borrow shamelessly from Socialist systems—"creeping socialism," the more resistant capitalists call this process—than Socialists from them. Faced with a choice between an elegant theory and successful practicality, democratic capitalists prefer the latter. They prefer what works to what inspires. In the ideological struggle to inspire those millions on this planet who are neither Socialist nor capitalist, this preference, too, is damaging.

Disdainful of their own intellectual task—and disdainful of the intellectuals, symbol-makers, and publicists who might execute it—corporate leaders show no respect for words, images, or critical ideas. Texaco and trust? Paper mills and conservation? Americanism and automobiles? The corporate sector, one comes to believe with despair, is philistine, its leaders not worthy of the system their creativity makes possible.

For generations corporate leaders seemed to think they did not need a theory or an ideology, that all they had to do to prove their case was to produce. They are learning now, perhaps too late, that the realm of ideas has power and attraction of its own. Traditional religion, on which they implicitly relied, has been undercut by Oldsmobiles, expressways, TV sets, suburban barbecues. Whoever says "capital" says dollars; while Socialists seem to feed humanistic, even religious, aspirations. Capitalists seem so materialist. Sensitive souls, repelled, flock elsewhere. "Not by bread alone" is a harsh word for producers.

Here Daniel Bell's much neglected thesis in *The Cultural Contradictions of Capitalism* requires meditation: Democratic capitalism depends upon the life of the spirit, which its practice undercuts. Bell pleads (with some despair) that democratic capitalism must tap again its religious and humanistic sources. It is ironic that capitalism should turn out to be more "godless" than socialism; that its narrow empiricism should undermine the religious spirit more deeply than socialism does. Socialism offers a holistic vision of the self in society, gives history a point, and establishes before the human heart the image of a nonalienated and brotherly way of being. It opposes religion, but on the terrain of religion. Capitalism, indifferent to the spirit, seems acquisitive and shallow.

In a word, democratic capitalism suffers from a lamentable intellectual failure. It does not grasp its own identity. It carries with it, and depends upon, a vision of the responsible individual; moral autonomy; social cooperation and fellow feeling; intellectual and artistic freedom; creativity beyond alienation; religious liberty; many-faceted pluralism; inalienable human rights. In its dreams it is at least the equal of the dreams of socialism. Not by accident do great artists and unfettered intellects, saints and "constituencies of conscience," voluntary associations of many sorts, and initiatives, inventions, and creativities of all kinds multiply in democratic capitalist societies. Why, then, do the proponents of "the free enterprise system" blather about the economic system merely? Why, alarmed by threats to their "free markets," do they invoke an obsolete rhetoric, mainly defensive, narrowly construed, which must repel even those who might in the main agree with them?

For democratic capitalism is not only an economic system; it is also a political system. Indeed, apart from a long institutional history under capitalist tutelage, it is very difficult for a people to be democratic. Without certain economic freedoms, political freedoms lack institutional support. Without a free economy, the idea of the independent individual does not emerge. As Socialist planners acquire political clout, becoming commissars, so, inversely, the trial-and-error of the free market inspires citizens to individual initiative, risk, and self-realization. A Ralph Nader opposing General Motors is conceivable under democratic capitalism. Were the auto industry "democratically" controlled by the state, a Ralph Nader would be a "counterrevolutionary," "reactionary" agent, a "traitor against the people." In "popular democracy" totalitarianism lurks.

The religio-humanistic revival pointed to by Daniel Bell requires no return to Jimmy Carter pietism. It calls for an intellectual deepening. In an earlier book, *An End to Ideology*, Professor Bell seemed to praise intense commitment to the practical and the expedient. These, in his latest book, he has diagnosed as a fatal limitation in our system. But there is another sense in that expression, "an end to ideology"—an end to *merely* ideological thinking, to sloganizing, to mindlessly taking sides. Many today hunger for something better than socialism, better than capitalism, something we have not yet articulated for ourselves.

For ours is not a system of "free enterprise" merely, nor a "free market system" only, nor a "nonideological" system. Our system is a political system, a democratic system, based upon both a Constitution and practicing institutions that incarnate a "bill of rights." It is, moreover, a philosophical and spiritual system, nourishing and shaping and developing a specific human type, divergent from other human types. It is a moral and cultural system.

There are, indeed, three ways to destroy our system. (1) One can destroy its economic genius. (2) One can destroy its political genius. (3) One can destroy its cultural genius. To attack any one of these is to attack the other two. Too foolishly do some believe that changes at any one of these will leave the others sound.

4

ON THE GOVERNABILITY OF DEMOCRACIES: THE ECONOMIC SYSTEM

The Evangelical Basis of a Social Market Economy

"The industrial regime inherited from Europe has now become unrecognizable in this country. It has been superceded by new economic structures which are still in the making, and in a state of fluidity, but which render both capitalism and socialism things of the past. Free enterprise and private ownership function now in a social context and a general mood entirely different from those of the nineteenth century. . . .

"You are advancing in the night, bearing torches toward which mankind would be glad to turn; but you leave them enveloped in the fog of a merely experiential approach and mere practical conceptualization, with no universal universal ideas to communicate. For lack of an adequate ideology, your lights cannot be seen."

Jacques Maritain, *Reflections on America*[1]

The world is entering yet another age of economics. Virtually all the major problems which preoccupy governments are economic problems—problems of growth and limits, food and fuel, employment and inflation, productivity and expanding populations, development and justice. The official documents of the churches since *Rerum Novarum* (1891) seem more and more preoccupied with economics. Yet there is hardly a less developed area in the tradition of Christian thought, whether in philosophy or in theology, than the relation of Christianity to economics.

Only rather late in Christian history, in fact, did there develop an exposition of the evangelical roots of democracy. In his little classic *Christianity and Democracy* (1948), Jacques Maritain has shown once and for all the consonance between democracy and Christianity.[2] He showed how Jewish-Christian conceptions of the individual, the community, and sin led over time to the state of mind and practice—to the *ethos*—that made the recognition of the inalienable rights of individuals practicable in the worldly polity. Thus, in that book, Maritain dealt with two of the three fundamental and coordinate systems of a modern, fully differentiated society: its political system and its moral-cultural system. At that stage of his development he was not ready to deal with the third significant system, the economic system. Since the most grievous problems in the governability of democracies today appear to arise in the economic system, it seems necessary to carry Maritain's thought further at precisely this point. We may well be encouraged by Maritain's brief but penetrating chapter on the transformation of capitalism in *Reflections on America* (1958).[3]

In his earlier period, Maritain had asked about the political systems with which Christianity is compatible. Specifically, he asked whether democracy is a natural expression of the Christian ethos. By analogy, we must ask with which economic systems Christianity is compatible. Specifically, we must ask whether an economic system based upon markets and personal incentives is a natural expression of the Christian ethos. We may also ask a further question. With which economic systems is *democracy* compatible? Is capitalism the natural economic expression of a democratic polity?

There is implicit in these questions a triune concept of social order, which makes systems of the democratic type different from all traditional or socialist societies. In traditional and socialist societies, the social order is unitary. One authority is granted powers over political, economic, and moral-cultural matters. In fully differentiated societies, these three systems are kept distinct, autonomous, interdependent but separate. So our underlying question has a very general nature first. Is it a natural expression of the Jewish-Christian tradition that a society ought to be differentiated into three distinct systems, united and yet distinct? My answer to this question is affirmative. It is impossible to offer reasons for this proposition here.[4] We shall simply assume its truth, while inquiring into the evangelical roots of one of the three systems: the economic system. Does an economic system based upon markets and incentives have evangelical roots?

In my own intellectual life, as in that of Maritain, I was early led to believe that democratic socialism or social democracy was more in tune with Christianity, at least in the order of ideals, than capitalism. Few themes are more common in Western intellectual history than the denigration of capitalism.[5] Among "the despised and abject" things of this world (Isaiah 53), capitalism ranks high. The reasons why this is so are multiple. First of all, of course, capitalism has many faults, distortions, and ill effects (as do all rival systems). Secondly, as Maritain has pointed out, it lacks a theory, in particular a moral theory.[6] Its theory has been left predominantly to economists, whose professional concern lies less with the political system and the moral-cultural system than with the economic system alone. Even there, economists tend to overlook the political and moral-cultural dimensions of economic realities, confining themselves as narrowly as they can to merely economic dimensions. In abstractions, such a narrow focus may be useful. In real life, it distorts understanding. In practice, capitalism has political and moral-cultural dimensions of greater intellectual significance than any existing theories about it have articulated.

Philosophers and theologians have yet to study capitalism with the close attention to real experience which it deserves.

In the third place, the intellectual history of capitalist ideas suffers from two internal flaws and sources of distortion. Unfortunately, the theory of capitalism was first developed in the Anglo-Saxon intellectual context of individualism and utilitarianism. In some ways, this context was favorable to economists. But it led to serious misunderstandings among humanists. The distinctive social organism produced by capitalism is not individualistic at all. It is a corporate organism, the business corporation. In addition, the inherent motive of capitalism as a system is not the well-being of the individual. It is the well-being of the entire human race. This underlying motive is expressed in the title of the most important document in the history of capitalism, Adam Smith's *An Inquiry into the Nature and Causes of the Wealth of Nations* (1776). As its title plainly states, the intention of democratic capitalism goes far beyond the question of individuals, beyond the question of Scotland or Great Britain; it aims to assist all nations. Adam Smith is the inventor of the idea of sustained economic development. His point of view embraced the entire world in all its cultures. His book on the economic system must, moreover, be read in the context of his earlier book on the moral-cultural system, *The Theory of Moral Sentiments* (1769), and his work on the political system which he left unfinished at his death. The triune intention was present from the beginning.[7]

Regrettably, the tradition of individualism and utilitarianism in Great Britain prevented these larger perspectives from becoming better known. Capitalism grew up together with democracy in Great Britain and the United States, in an ethos heavily saturated with Jewish-Christian pluralistic, humanistic values. Its practice was, therefore, more complex and far richer than the individualist, utilitarian theory in which it was embedded. In addition, after 1870, the ignominious tradition of Social Darwinism—"the survival of the fittest"—did immeasurable damage to the theory of capitalism. It was the transformation of capitalism beyond the bounds of individualism, utilitarianism and Social Darwinism, in fact, which so surprised Maritain in America and arrested his attention. In practice, capitalism is not what these early cocoons in which it was embedded had led him to believe that it is. It is a practice in search of an accurate theory. Maritain appealed urgently for such a theory. Yet, aside from a few brief notes, he did little to supply it. One may note a similar evolution in the thinking of the great American theologian, Reinhold Niebuhr.[8] It will be the task of our generation to carry these tentative beginnings to fruition in a theory worthy of the actual practice. Then, in that light, reformers may lead the system to a larger fulfillment of the dreams of liberty, equality, and justice.

I propose to proceed in three steps. First, it is important to reflect upon the larger human dimensions of economic systems. Second, we must climb upon the shoulders of Maritain (and others) so as to take advantage of what they have already accomplished. Third, we may begin the actual inquiry into the evangelical roots of a social market economy which makes use of personal incentives. It is to be hoped that younger scholars will carry these beginnings through to completion.

1. THE ECONOMIC SYSTEM

It is a typical mistake to think of capitalism as an economic system merely. Analogously, it is a typical mistake to think of an economic system apart from its *political* and *moral-cultural* dimension. In actual life, each one of us is an economic agent. But each is also a citizen. Each of us seeks God, follows conscience and the pursuit of truth and understanding. In the concrete, we are all three of these at once. Human beings are simultaneously economic animals, political animals, moral-cultural animals. On the other hand, it is often useful, in Maritain's phrase, *distinguer pour unir,* to distinguish in order to unite. This is true for intellectual inquiry, in which one must proceed step by step; one cannot do everything at once.

It is also true in the proper organization of concrete social life. One of the great discoveries of modernity is the possibility—even the necessity—of differentiation in social institutions. It is a social *good* to practice a certain separation of church and state, to empower a free press, to maintain universities free from state control: that is to say, to differentiate the *political system* from the *moral-cultural system*—to allow each a certain autonomy, while recognizing that each system in a sense depends upon the other. In the same way, it was an important social good when human beings began to separate the economy from state controls and to protect the state from control by economic interests. It is as important to separate the *economic system* from the state as to separate the church (and other moral-cultural institutions) from the state. Like the political system and the moral-cultural system, the economic system, too, is entitled to a certain autonomy, even while we must recognize that it, too, depends upon the other two systems, as they depend upon it. It is good for human beings to have a trinity of systems, each distinct from the other two even when united with them to form a single social order.

Each of these three systems has its own institutions, rituals, procedures, social base, and social strength. Each has characteristic tendencies, ambitions, achievements, and distortions. Each for its own well-being requires the health of the other two. Each requires a certain balance and coordination with the other two. Each has a tendency to seek its own aggrandizement at the expense of the other two. Each needs to be watched closely—and checked—by the other two.

It is sometimes pointed out that a healthy democratic polity depends upon the *separation of powers* (executive, legislative, and judicial). Analogously, a healthy and fully differentiated social order depends upon the *separation of systems* (political, economic, and moral-cultural). As it happens, different personality types are commonly attracted to each of these different systems. In this way, each type develops, as it were, a psychological interest in checking the other two, a kind of native suspicion and hostility to the type of persons involved in the other two. Thus, it often happens that poets, priests, philosophers and literary intellectuals cherish no excess of admiration either for men of commerce and industry or for politicians; and the reverse.

In a healthy society, then, there are, in effect, three different routes along which the will-to-power may be exercised. Some individuals move to the top of the economic system; a different type (generally speaking) to the top of the political system; and a third type (again generally speaking) to the top of the moral-cultural system. It is a rare human being, indeed, who moves confortably in all three spheres. This systematic diffusion of the will-to-power is accomplished, in the long run, for the good of society. Each type of person, summoning up the powers of his or her own sphere of accomplishment, has both external and psychological interests in preventing persons of other types, representing other bases of power, from wholly dominating society. History affords many sad examples of domination by one sector only. The case of Iran under the Ayatollah Khomeini and the mullahs is a recent instance. Domination by emperors, popes, and ideological parties in other times and places affords other instances. The differentiation of systems is intended to prevent such unitary domination, through the checks and balances of the three relatively autonomous systems.

No thinker has been as clear about the structural distinctions to which I am pointing than Daniel Bell, who in his major studies, *The Coming of Post-Industrial Society* (1973) and *The Cultural Contradictions of Capitalism* (1976), has decisively broken with all merely unitary or holistic schemes of social theory.[9] Human life, Bell notes, cannot be understood within a single scheme or on a single plane merely. Three quite different systems, operating with different rhythms and in different frames of time, affect every human being. The economic system is focussed along an axis of *utilitarian or functional* rationality. The political system, according to Bell, has now come to be focussed along an axis of *equality* and *entitlements* (often group entitlements). The cultural system is focussed along the axis of the *self.* From Bell's point of view, it is an error to try to think of social systems along one of these axes only. Furthermore, each of these axes points in a rather different direction from the other two. They are, therefore, both for society as a whole and for individuals fraught with "contradictions." Each axis in some respects contradicts and frustrates the other two. So far as individuals go, each in his or her own twenty-four-hour days is pulled first one way, then another, by the contradictory demands of the three systems within which all live. The search for self-fulfullment is not easily conducted when one's attention must be fixed upon the functional tasks of one's economic position. Nor can a political system concerned with equality and entitlements easily be reconciled with the imperatives of economic rationality, or even with the manifest differences in the personality, efforts, desires and demands of each individual self.

There are many questions to be raised about the exactness of Bell's definitions and concepts. I would have several important criticisms to make of particular points. Yet for our present purposes his scheme is quite helpful. For Bell stresses the different "rhythms" and time-spans involved in each of these axial imperatives. At times, the imperatives of self-discovery and self-fulfillment are instant, spontaneous, and immediate. In another sense, they span an entire lifetime and occupy those many private and personal hours of the day on which the political system and the economic system make relatively little, if any, impact. The time-horizon within which political leaders work (in democracies, at least) is notoriously different from the time-span of industry and commerce. Politicians are tempted to seek immediate benefits, whose costs other politicians in later administrations may have to pay. The question politicians regularly meet from voters is "What have you done for me lately?" The demands made by economic systems often cut across personal desires and inclinations and respond poorly, if at all, to political manipulation. The three axial systems, in other words, affect individuals in different ways and with different effects.

One essential point may be drawn from these reflections. No economic system represents the whole of life. An economic system may be as autonomous as the moral-cultural system and enjoy its own proper liberty and separation from the state. Still, the individuals who work within it are subject to imperatives that arise from axial principles, whose origin lies outside the economic system itself. They are subject to imperatives arising from political life and to others arising from moral-cultural life. In the concrete, there is no such thing as "economic man," and no economic system lives (or can live) in a vacuum apart from a political system and a moral-cultural system. When we speak of an economic system, therefore, we must take pains to speak of its concrete, living connections with the political system and the moral-cultural system in which it is embedded.

In this respect, one cannot speak of "capitalism" solely as an economic system. Historically (and inherently) it grows up in concert with the imperatives of a democratic polity. Its own imperatives are not identical to the axial principles of democracy. Yet the two feed upon and require each other in fascinating ways. Similarly, as Max Weber pointed out, the rise of capitalism is inconceivable apart from the power of a specific moral-cultural system, an *ethos,* which gives it shape, meaning, and motivating force. One may disagree with Weber's exact diagnosis of that *ethos;* it was, clearly, far less Protestant, far less Calvinist than he thought.[10] But he is surely right in seeing that buying and selling, which are immemorial economic activities as ancient as the Mediterranean civilizations and the desert caravans of Biblical times, did not constitute "capitalism" until a specific moral-cultural system had reached a certain level of development. An economic system must always be studied in conjunction with the political system and the moral-cultural system in which it is embedded.

Let us, for a moment, concentrate upon the interplay between an economic system based upon markets and incentives and a moral-cultural system based upon Jewish-Christian understandings of liberty, the individual, the community, sin, and the like. Throughout history, most economic systems were relatively stagnant. Few showed sustained growth. All experienced cycles of prosperity and famine. The very concept of sustained economic development was lacking. The figure of the miser represented a certain quintessential evil, for in a no-growth economy anyone who hoarded gold or other goods subtracted from the common store. In order for sustained economic development to become possible (or even conceivable), individuals needed to believe that they could alter the future—indeed, had an obligation to do so. The techniques for releasing their economic activism needed to be invented. The formation of a new economic system depended upon changes in the moral-cultural system. Individuals had to begin to believe that they could improve their own economic position. They needed liberty. They needed law and stability. They needed patterns of social cooperation. They needed systems of long-term accounting. They needed new institutions in which risks could be shared and enterprises larger than those sustainable by single individuals might be launched. They needed to be willing to defer present gratification, to invest and to labor for the sake of future rewards. They needed to concentrate upon small savings and small gains, cumulatively recorded. Many parables in the gospels express some of the required attitudes of good and wise stewardship (even while pointing out that Christianity, as a more than thisworldly religion, imposes still more stringent axes of judgment). Sustained economic development, therefore, rests decisively upon moral-cultural values of certain sorts.[11]

In some ways, then, economic systems are dependent upon moral-cultural systems. Where certain attitudes, habits, beliefs, aspirations, and exertions are lacking, economic development is unlikely to occur. Inversely, even among peoples who lack material resources or favorable natural conditions, strong moral-cultural traditions of certain sorts may give rise to amazing economic developments. To some extent, such phenomena seem to have appeared in Japan, Hong Kong, Taiwan and elsewhere. The ethos of particular peoples is of exceeding—perhaps primary—economic significance.

On the other hand, economic systems impose demands upon moral-cultural systems. At times, cherished magic, taboos, beliefs, customs and attitudes must be set aside, or else an economic system of the modern, developing sort simply cannot take root. An economic system is necessarily a teacher and reinforcer of some moral virtues, and utterly dependent upon the strength and vitality of others. Where pecuniary dishonesty, bribery, and corruption are a way of life—where even economic reporting and accounting are unreliable—economic systems are penalized as they are not where opposite qualities are more common. (Such virtues are never perfectly and universally practiced.) Where individuals lack initiative or a talent for self-starting enterprise, the economic situation is quite different from one in which opposite talents frequently appear. Moral-cultural systems are not equal. Economic systems are much affected by such variations. The axial imperatives of a new form of economic system often evoke cultural resistance from those who live by other imperatives.

Thus economic systems are not *merely* instrumental. They carry some moral imperatives of their own, and these are often rather different from those which prevail in the moral-cultural institutions to which they are joined. Some philosophers or theologians tend to think that the moral-cultural system defines the kingdom of ends, while economic systems play a lowly instrumental role in the kingdom of means. This is not quite true. An economic system, too, necessarily incarnates certain goals and purposes. These goals and purposes are not merely materialistic. Thus, a people that would choose as one of its social goals sustained economic growth is choosing not solely an increase in the abundance of material goods but also a set of moral disciplines, habits, and activities—a way of life. Such a way of life may have among its specifications a love for liberty, for noble behavior, for highly developed character, for justice and compassion, and the like. The economic system of the Greek city-state, for example, had among its purposes, at least for its elites, such ideals as Aristotle set forth in the *Nicomachean Ethics*. Some analogous qualities are compatible with an economic system of sustained economic growth; some are not. Sustained economic growth does not consist solely in material abundance; it springs from and it continues to demand the exercise of moral character of certain sorts. Should such character disappear, so would sustained economic growth. A hedonistic, narcissistic culture is not likely to invest in its own future or to make the necessary sacrifices for its own posterity.

There is a further matter. From the point of view of the concrete individual, one's participation in an economic system does not exhaust the whole of one's life nor is it merely a means to an end. Work is not merely a means for "making a living." Work is in itself a mode of living, and may even be a mode of praying. Perhaps like you, I have worked at many "menial" jobs, including mass-production jobs, and tedious farm jobs. Every sort of job "takes something out of you." One's substance passes into it. The job affects one's being. Much is written about the alienation in modern work, capitalist or socialist. More ought to be written about the alienation in *every* form of work (writing a paper, for example); and also, about the contribution of every form of work to one's own being. Many writers suggest that not having any work is even worse than having "alienating" work. Philosophers, theologians and others need to grasp the extent to which working is living, and hence not merely a means. On the other hand, work is not the whole of life. No human is defined by his or her economic activities alone.

A similar point must be made with regard to wealth. Wealth is neither an end in itself nor solely a means. The medieval maxim runs: *Radix malorum cupiditas.* This maxim blames *cupiditas*, not money. By contrast, the modern version runs: "*Money* is the root of all evil." The latter version is not true to experience. Power also corrupts—man being seldom so innocently occupied, Dr. Johnson has written, as in the getting of money. The roots of evil cannot really be said to lie in money. Indeed, the moral meaning of wealth lies not in its *possession* but in its *use*, in the passions and interests it serves. To have wealth is to exercise a more ample liberty than is available without it. One's moral hazards are thereby magnified. ("It is easier for a camel to pass through the eye of a needle than for a rich man to enter into the kingdom of heaven.") To use wealth wisely and well may be to make of it a moral good, but to use it badly is to call down upon oneself harsh moral condemnation. Neither poverty nor wealth guarantees virtue; neither suffices for salvation. The wealthy, however, have greater obligations than the poor. On the other hand, wealth is in itself a good of liberty, which it much enlarges. "The wealth of nations" is to be esteemed, not for its own sake, but for the misery it may alleviate and for the liberties it may enlarge.

Thus, economic systems are properly to be judged not only in the light of how much wealth they produce, although that is in itself good, but also in the light of *how* their wealth is *used*. There are not an infinite number of economic systems within the historical experience of the human race. One may recount the chief types in a few lines: slavery, barter, trade, feudalism, mercantilism, capitalism, socialism, communism. Alternatively, one may speak of economies based upon hunting, fishing, agriculture, land, exchange, industry, state control, intellect and services, and other characteristics of this sort. History may reveal new forms of economic life, as it often has. But we should not become bemused by fantasies of limitless possibility. The ways are relatively strait and few—as compared, for example, to languages and cultures.

Who can doubt that the major field of interest for governments and peoples today lies in this relatively narrow sphere of economics? Between 1900 and 1950, the population of the world doubled. Since 1950, it has doubled yet again. This planet must now be made to yield more food, clothing, building materials, medicines, school books, and all the other instruments of our complex life than ever before in history. The primary problem facing the human race is a problem of production. But it is followed by problems of distribution, scarcity, and, in certain directions, limits. Yet we must not lose sight of the preeminence of the problem of production.

From ancient times, the primary emphasis in philosophical and religious thought has fallen upon *distributive justice*. The problem of *productive justice* was understandably neglected, even though it has obvious priority, both logically and in reality. For this truth did not acquire force until Adam Smith invented the possibility of sustained economic development. Once it is shown that human beings with intelligence, organization, and effort have the capacity to unlock riches of creation never imagined by the ancients—oil, chemicals, alloys, foods, even the silicon of the sea—and once it is clear that millions (indeed, billions) of persons remain in need, then (and only then) does the responsibility to produce what can be produced become a clear moral imperative. Thus, only in modern times has the moral imperative of production come to precede the moral imperative of distribution and to be grasped as its necessary precondition.

In the centuries before 1800, famine visited the peoples of the world, on the average, once every fifteen years, and the earth supported a bare 890 million persons.[12] Today, enough is known to make famines unnecessary and to render famines no longer God's responsibility but man's.

Governments can govern today only insofar as they meet the exigent material needs of their peoples. Given the new historical possibilities, the economic policies of governments will be rejected if their peoples cannot glimpse the real probability of a future better than the past. Governments depend upon the productivity of their economic system. More than philosophers and theologians have recognized in the past, the promise of democracy depends upon high levels of economic productivity.

What, then, have Christian philosophers and theologians to say about the available economic systems? There already exists a rather large body of Christian reflection upon socialism, particularly in Latin America and in Europe. Ironically, even in the United States we already have a big book by a Jesuit, *Marxism: An American Christian Perspective* (1980),[13] but we do not yet have a single examination by a theologian or philosopher of democratic capitalism. Indeed, in *Reflections on America*, Jacques Maritain confessed his own biases against the images conjured up in his mind by the word "capitalism." There is no denying that, rhetorically, it is easier to stand before the intellectual class as a socialist. In many circles, it is almost unforgiveable to declare oneself to be in favor of capitalism. Yet this situation is odd. There are, as yet, no examples of socialist states becoming democratic. All existing democracies depend upon a large component of economic liberties. How can we properly defend democracy, if we overlook its inherent relationship to capitalism? How can democratic governments govern, unless they have a compatible economic vision?

It is not necessary for a people or a culture to be Jewish or Christian in order to develop a market economy. But a market economy is inherently, by its nature, open to persons of every culture, faith, race and philosophical point of view. It is altogether fitting that such a system should have been first invented and given spiritual legitimation under the impulse of the Old and New Testaments. Such a confluence of cultural currents occurred rather late in European history. It occurred first among the Erasmian Christians, both Catholic and Protestant, and among Jews and others described by Hugh Trevor-Roper.[14] It occurred in the visions of Adam Smith and James Madison.[15] It occurred gradually in the social systems of perhaps a dozen or a score of the nations on this planet. Jacques Maritain was the first to see the need for a new theory about the transformation of capitalism. Let us learn from him first.

2. CHRISTIANITY AND DEMOCRATIC CAPITALISM

"Democracy is linked to Christianity and . . . the democratic impulse has arisen in human history as a temporal manifestation of the inspiration of the Gospel. The question does not deal here with Christianity as a religious creed and road to eternal life, but rather with Christianity as leaven in the social and political life of nations and as bearer of the temporal hope of mankind . . . as historical energy at work in the world."

Jacques Maritain, *Christianity and Democracy*[16]

Reflect on these words of Maritain. Cannot an analogous claim be made about capitalism—*about the economic system* based on respect for the rights of the individual, on markets, and on incentives? This is, after all, the economic system which grew up stride by stride alongside democracy in Great Britain, the United States, and then a score and more of other nations after 1776. To be sure, in the annals of social revolution, democracy has long carried a favorable reputation (so favorable that even the least democratic of nations insist upon calling themselves by the name which most condemns them). By contrast, capitalism has almost everywhere been held in disdain.

When Maritain first came to America during World War II, he came with a European intellectual's negative judgments on capitalism. To him, capitalism connoted unchecked greed, atomistic individualism, and a merely mechanical view of human relations in the marketplace. The reality as it was actually lived surprised him. Transformations must have occurred within the American economic system, he thought, during recent generations.[17] He described these as revolutionary in import. They startled him by their depth and scope. He believed that a "new reality" had appeared, for which there was yet no suitable name or even an adequate theory.

In too many people's minds, Maritain noted, capitalism "stands for the primitive economic system of the nineteenth century." But something new had appeared. The new system, too, remained "imperfect, but always improving, and always capable of further improvement." In this new system, "men move forward together, working together, building together, producing always more and more, and sharing together the rewards of their increased production."[18]

"This new social and economic regime," Maritain wrote in 1958, "is still in a state of full becoming, but it has already brought human history beyond both capitalism and socialism." This "new social and economic regime is . . . a phenomenon which gives the lie to the forecasts of Karl Marx, and which came about not by virtue of some kind of inner necessity in the evolution of capitalism which Marx has overlooked, but by virtue of the freedom and spirit of man, namely by virtue of the American mind and conscience, and of the American collective effort of imagination and creation."[19]

Maritain had always been a great believer in human experience, in obscure ways of knowing, in "creative intuition," and in that wisdom which is barely if at all articulate in its profound workings. So it is not surprising that he was able to discern more at work in humble reality than anyone before him had discerned. He wrote: "Here we have a decisive fact in modern history; and this fact is a considerable success of the experiential approach dear to the American mind." He called the chapter in which his reflections on this theme unfolded: "Too Much Modesty—The Need for an Explicit Philosophy," and was explicit: "But now I return to my point, namely to the need for an adequate ideology, or philosophy. And I ask: who in the world is aware of this decisive fact which we have just discussed?" He saw the necessity of a new name for this misunderstood system, and proposed, among others, "the new capitalism," "democratic capitalism," "economic democracy," "mutualism," "distributism," "productivism." He himself preferred "economic humanism,"[20] as a term "more pleasing to the ear, and more accurate."

Let us assume for the moment that Maritain had his facts correct; that there has been, in fact, an inner transformation in the very nature of capitalism, not only in the United States but around the world. He traced the roots of this transformation to "the freedom and spirit of man" in "the American mind and conscience." But this "American" mind and conscience has profound Jewish and Christian roots. Despite its reputation for secularism, pollsters and scholars have long observed that the United States is perhaps the most religious country—in its practices and explicit attitudes—of any modern nation. Is democratic capitalism in its transformed state, then, like democracy itself, evangelical in its roots? Democratic capitalism cannot be understood apart from an ethos of a specific sort; in some cultures of the world it would make no sense, could hardly be realized. A market economy may be as much an expression of the Jewish-Christian "historical energy" in the economic order as democracy is in the political order. Indeed, democracy itself may not be able to be realized apart from a market economy and personal incentives.

Until now, democratic socialists and social democrats have tried to capture the moral *élan* of democracy in order to steal it away for socialism. Socialism has many attractive moral qualities. But as the governing philosophy of a social system it has three grievous difficulties. First, it runs a very great risk of recreating the ancient patterns of state tyranny. Second, even in its democratic forms, it runs the risk of endowing collectivities, especially the best organized ones, with excessive power at the expense of individual liberties. (This is a real threat in all welfare democracies.) Third, paying too little attention both to markets and to incentives, it runs the risk of slowing productivity and raising the level of inefficiencies, thus reducing societies to a zero-sum game, within which factionalism and other forms of discontent multiply. Social democracy has had a relatively long period of trial in Western Europe. Its successes are many. Yet it has fallen short of the dreams of its founders. It can go forward toward socialist ideals only at great peril to its liberties. Are there not, then, other ideals? Is there no alternative to "democratic socialism"?

It seems intellectually useful and even urgent at the present time to look with fresh eyes at the experience of democratic capitalism. Christian thinkers have for many years now emphasized the connections between Christianity and democracy. But they have neglected the connections between Christianity and capitalism. Yet questions of economics are of urgent concern to governments today. What ought governments to expect of economic systems? How ought democracies to govern their economic systems? Above all, what have Christian ideas, values and inspirations to say about economic systems?

It is important to note that capitalism and socialism are not symmetrical concepts. Under the theoretical framework of democratic capitalism, there are three distinct systems, each with its own autonomy and yet each also in part dependent upon the other two: an economic system, a political system, a moral-cultural system. By contrast, socialism is unitary. It tends to collapse these three systems into one. Socialism fuses the economic system and the political system into one, under the aegis of a single, collective moral-cultural system. Socialism is more like a religion or a moral vision than capitalism is. Socialism proposes to produce the "new man" who will spring forth (like Venus from the sea) under "socialism with a human face." Capitalism has never been so morally pretentious. Morally, it has spoken of itself with what Maritain describes as excessive modesty. By and large, it has left moral visions to the poets, the philosophers, the archbishops. It thinks of itself as only one of three systems. These three systems are relatively autonomous. Each is *coordinate* with the other two. None is *subordinate* to the others.

In this respect, capitalism is not an alternative to democracy or to a Judaeo-Christian culture. It is not so pretentious. It plays only one of three roles. It is compatible with democracy, on the one hand, and with the Judaeo-Christian tradition, on the other. But it does not exhaust either the democratic or the Judaeo-Christian ideal. The coalescence of all three systems into one unitary system, as in the socialist model, may at first seem to be in keeping with the Jewish-Christian ideal of social harmony and social unity. It certainly attracts a certain type of person. But unitary systems are especially vulnerable to tyranny, whether by a majority or by the seizure of collective powers by a small elite.

Democracy is based upon the *separation of powers* (executive, legislative, and judicial). A truly differentiated and fully humane social system is based upon the *separation of systems* (political, economic, moral-cultural). Democratic capitalism is such a system of systems. The warrant for this separation of systems is found in Judaeo-Christian views of the nature of the individual, of social life, of history, and of sin.

3. EVANGELICAL ROOTS

Aleksandr Solzhenitzyn has argued that Western ideas of progress and revolution took a "wrong turn" at the time of the Enlightenment.[21]

He attributes to secularism and to materialism modern beliefs in progress (especially material progress), the legalism of democratic life, the free press, the cult of the individual, narcissism, and other modern vices. He holds an ancient Russian Orthodox view of the sinfulness of human beings. In this view, dreams of progress are doomed never to come true. Solzhenitsyn places his trust in

Christian virtue—in the power of such virtue in the lives of rulers and among whole peoples who follow in the ways of justice, charity, and peace. He seems at once too pessimistic and too optimistic.

One sympathizes with the great Solzhenitsyn's intentions. Yet his views on the relation of democracy and Christianity are not historically correct. As Maritain shows, it is not the Enlightenment which is the yeast that made the democratic idea grow. It is not the Enlightenment which, as Robert Nisbet has shown in *History of the Idea of Progress,* taught the West that the future may be different from the past.[22] It is not the Enlightenment which instructed Adam Smith, James Madison, Thomas Jefferson, Benjamin Franklin and others about the sinfulness of every human being. It is not the Enlightenment which counselled the invention of checks and balances against every form of tyranny, even the tyranny of "good" rulers, "benevolent" dictators, and "philosopher kings." It is not the Enlightenment which taught that one must not trust even the virtue of the common people.

Without by any means intending to do so—exactly when trying not to do so—the great Solzhenitsyn, in wishing for a regime of virtuous Christian leaders, apart from democratic constraints, may be paving the path for a regime all too like that of the fabled Grand Inquisitor. In compassion for men, one may seek to make men virtuous by depriving them of liberty. There are too few protections in Solzhenitsyn's vision of the future to protect humankind against the tyranny of virtue.

Thus Solzhenitsyn, like many others, in seeking the true ground and origin of democracy, attributes too much to the Enlightenment, too little to Christianity. Yet, like democracy, so capitalism grew out of specifically Christian soil. Its preconceptions are also Jewish-Christian. Its ethos is in some substantial measure—but not entirely—Jewish-Christian. Its roots are in significant particulars evangelical. Time is brief, but we may at least suggest a few themes for further study.

(1) *The communitarian individual.* The characteristic social invention of democratic capitalism in the economic sphere is the corporation. The corporation is a social construct, which springs, however, from individual initiative. Virtually every economic corporation of the present day is founded upon an invention or, at least, upon an organizing idea. In all cases, the idea originated in the mind of a single human individual or a small team of individuals. Around this idea, such persons gathered colleagues, pooled investments, organized enterprises, and risked such resources as they thus invested. The risk was in every case a social risk. One individual alone would have been powerless. Founders of corporations necessarily rely upon cooperation, trust, covenants, and compacts. Usually, the corporation is independent of the state. It is a collective of individuals who "incorporate themselves" and place at risk, not public funds, but their own funds.

The history of the communitarian individual thus generated by the institutions of capitalism has not yet been written. Such an individual is a new social type. We are accustomed to think of such persons as "robber barons," thus imagining them to be like an *old* social type—that of the feudal aristocracy. We thus omit from consideration precisely what is new about them. When historians one day turn to examining the communitarian individual, however, they will have to turn to the emphasis which Adam Smith placed upon *benevolence, sympathy, fellow feeling,* and the spirit of *fair play* which he explored in his pregnant book, *The Theory of Moral Sentiments* (1759) which set the stage for his invention of the economics of development. The founder of a corporation does not rely, like a baron, on troops of his own enlisting. He does not seek military adventure or glory. He relies upon persuasion, legal compacts, and the productivity of an idea realized in an economic enterprise.

The fundamental nature of capitalism as Adam Smith expressed it in the beginning, and as has been realized before our eyes in history since his time, is *not* "the wealth of individuals," nor yet "the wealth of Great Britain," but "the wealth of nations"—*all* nations, without exception. The driving force of capitalism is social, indeed universal. (Smith would have been cheered, one thinks, by the immense successes of Japan—and even of OPEC—since World War II, and the "economic miracles" of Germany and Italy. The world has been transformed by the driving force he liberated.)

Moreover, capitalism proceeds even in particular localities only through the organizing of collaborative efforts. It is true that the ideas and initiatives of the individual are important. But the individual alone is not a corporation. Buying and selling are activities as ancient as the human race; they do not constitute capitalism. What constitutes capitalism is an organizing ethos, a corporate enterprise, a collective effort. Capitalism is far more social in character than its enemies—or its friends—have yet grasped. The growth of organized labor, of collective management, of profit-sharing and pension plans (the transformations which so struck Maritain) have been implicit in the ethos of capitalism from the beginning. It is true that these advances were won only through struggle, but so were those of democracy and many important victories in the history of Christianity, too. They could be won in relative peacefulness and with internal consistency, however, precisely because they were inherent in its inner logic. If, for example, a wage contract is conceived of as a voluntary exchange, both parties to it are entitled to renegotiate it constantly. The original historical weakness of the position of labor was bound, over time, to become a position of strength. The idea of "contract" remains intact as the contract becomes more favorable to labor, as well it ought. Future transformations in the relation of capital and labor are also likely.

(2) *The social nature of man.* British utilitarianism provided a limited intellectual framework for understanding the true import of capitalism. Social Darwinism, which followed utilitarianism by nearly three-quarters of a century, led understanding still further astray. Nonetheless, the early conception of "economic man" was self-consciously designed to be an abstraction, not so much in order to deny the existence of "political man" or "moral-cultural man," as to

allow analysts to concentrate upon one aspect at a time. The economic system was never imagined to be coincident with the whole of human social nature. Capitalism was designed to be for the economic system what democracy is for the political system, and what the family, churches, universities, presses and other media are for the moral-cultural system. Since it is part of human nature for human beings to require one another's assistance, capitalism was designed to be a complex system in which there is a division of labor, a division of purposes, and a division of talents. It was conceived as a vision of interdependence—not only at the work-site, but in an entire world of "free trade." Adam Smith, James Madison, and others argued explicitly that a world made interdependent through commerce, trade and industry would, of necessity, become more law-like and pacific.[23] They showed no particular respect for, or trust in, men of commerce and industry; quite the opposite.[24] But they observed that both in their typical temperament and in their typical self-interests (to which they attached more importance) such men were unlike the military rulers, clergymen, and feudal lords of the past, all of whom delighted in and benefited from abstract causes, adventures, and conquest. Sinful and of the lower classes as men of commerce and industry might be, the entire scaffolding of their activities depends upon systems of law, stability and predictability. Lenin would one day taunt capitalists for selling the communists rope for their own hanging. It was precisely this ideological indifference of the men of commerce and industry which Smith, Madison and others found hopeful. The interests of such men lie in interdependence, not in barriers or in strife.

Similarly, an economic system based upon markets and personal incentives seemed to them singularly apt as a companion to a system of democratic pluralism. No test of faith or metaphysics is required for entrance into markets. None is appropriate for a pluralistic democracy. This does not mean that faith and metaphysics are matters of indifference. Rather, it means—as Maritain pointed out—that practical cooperation among men of good will does not need to wait upon prior resolution of all philosophical or theological disputes.[25] In order for democracy to function, it is not necessary for all to become converted to the same vision of reality. In order for a capitalist economy to function, it is not necessary for all who take part in it to share the same faith or metaphysics. Indeed, the notion that each *person* should be free to make his or her own decisions of economic agency is intended to reinforce the ideal of personal integrity in every sphere. This notion in the economic sphere matches that in the moral-cultural sphere which defends each person's conscience, and that in the political sphere which defends each person's human rights.

To be sure, liberty is dangerous. Any free society will give plenty of evidence of sinfulness. Some persons will use their liberty as saints, others as sinners. A market system protects their economic liberties as democracy protects their political liberties. Alas, their moral liberties will be used as humans will use them.

It follows, furthermore, that political liberties without economic liberties are empty. Totalitarianism may be just as effectively enforced through complete controls over economic transactions as through police surveillance.[26] If presses must depend upon state allocations of newsprint, numbers of copies printed, and systems of distribution, such presses are not free. Political liberties require economic liberties. Moral-cultural liberties depend upon both. Thus religions whose essence lies in the free acts of individual conscience—as do narrative religions like Judaism and Christianity—require as their natural expression in human social life systems of political liberty and economic liberty alike.

(3) *Emergent probability.* Some thinkers have held that human progress is illusory, since history is inevitably caught in cycles of eternal recurrence. Others have held that human history is determined by forces beyond the liberty of individual human beings. Judaism and Christianity teach a quite different vision of history. Bernard Lonergan has described it in abstract philosophical terms as a vision of "emergent probability."[27] In this vision, human history is open to new futures, yet the sequences of any one future depend upon the fulfillment of prior conditions in preceding sequences. Human liberty may affect the fulfillment of such conditions. Thus, choices made by humans today affect future probabilities. Humans may fulfill the necessary and sufficient conditions for a future development Y, or fail to fulfill them. They are partly responsible for the emergence or non-emergence of Y in the future. At times, even a single individual may invent new possibilities or set in motion new sets of occurrences which dramatically alter the probabilities faced by others. The world which humans face is, therefore, open, uncertain, not perfectly stable, subject both to progress and to decline. Ideas count. Moral energies count. For want of them, whole societies may perish. Especially gifted societies may flourish in unprecedented ways. The Lord of History thus respects the liberty of his creatures in the long disorderly pilgrimage of history.

Both democracy and capitalism were invented as experiments. Their founders were not certain that either experiment would endure. Such founders recognized many hazards. They were obliged to argue against heavy opposition. They succeeded, at times, only through the force of arms. Their own sins and failings at times place the entire experiment in which they were engaged at jeopardy—as Abraham Lincoln observed during the terrible Civil War in the United States from 1861–1865. Every market democracy has experienced the risk of failure or collapse, in one form or another, since its founding. Nothing in the stars guarantees the survival of either democracy or capitalism. Both are creatures of liberty. Both are subject to laws of emergent probability.

(4) *Sin.* Perhaps the most important contribution of Judaism and Christianity to democratic capitalism is a theory of sin. According to this view, no human is without sin. In social systems, the most destructive expression of human sin is the will-to-power. Democracy is founded upon a theory of sin which holds that, because of the dangers of tyranny, all forms of political power must be diffused. Political power is more dangerous than economic power, since it has at its disposal the coercive powers of the state. In order to attain other social goods, however, modern democracies have judged it necessary to expand the powers of the twentieth-century state beyond those of the nineteenth-

century state. The dangers of tyranny are growing once again. On the other hand, it is the inevitable tendency of economic agents to expand and to solidify their economic power. As Adam Smith warned from the beginning, society and state alike must be ever vigilant to prevent economic monopolies, however irrepressible the tendency toward them. Modern technology and mass production have dramatically expanded expanded the scope and economic power of the largest corporations. The contest between the expanded powers of the central state and those of the corporation—often operating in an international framework—bears the closest scrutiny. Those concerned to protect human liberty must worry both about the corporations and about the state. Both are creatures of sin, like all things human.

The theory of sin invites us to be vigilant about our liberties. It suggests that the wrong solution to our perplexities would be to increase further the power of either one of these giants in the effort to contain the other. This is why the socialist solution appeals less and less to thinking persons today. If the eleven major oil companies of the United States, for example, are already too powerful, the creation of a single U.S. government agency to subordinate all of them hardly seems to diminish that threat.

4. CONCLUSION

My aim has been to extend the work of Jacques Maritain, who showed that democracy has its roots in the Jewish-Christian leaven active in Western history and now in the entire world. I have wanted to propose an hypothesis for further investigation. This hypothesis is that capitalism—an economic system based upon markets and incentives—has, like democracy, evangelical roots. Both democracy and capitalism breathe vital air from a moral-cultural system based on powerful ideas about the communitarian individual, the social nature of human life, emergent probability, and sin. Much else could be said. Perhaps what has been said may contribute to enlarging the discussion. In any case, democratic capitalism, such as the world has until now experienced it, is not yet at the end of its pilgrimage nor in the final stages of its testing. We will need all the energies our religious traditions offer to us, and all the clearsightedness and courage of which we are capable, if we are to be as inventive as our predecessors were. We have much to do.

NOTES

1. Jacques Maritain, *Reflections on America* (New York: Charles Scribner's Sons, 1958), pp. 101, 118.

2. He summarized the thesis of the book: "But the important thing for the political life of the world and for the solution of the crisis of civilization is by no means to pretend that Christianity is linked to democracy and that Christian faith compels every

believer to be a democrat; it is to affirm that democracy is linked to Christianity and that the democratic impulse has arisen in human history as a temporal manifestation of the inspiration of the Gospel." *Christianity and Democracy,* trans. Doris C. Anson (New York: Charles Scribner's Sons, 1948), p. 37.

3. See the chapter entitled "Too Much Modesty—The Need for an Explicit Philosophy," *Reflections on America,* ibid., pp. 101–120.

4. I will offer such reasons in my forthcoming book, *The Spirit of Democratic Capitalism,* scheduled for publication in 1982.

5. Among the small but growing literature on the intellectual biasses against capitalism, I cite the following: F. A. Hayek, ed. *Capitalism and the Historians* (Chicago: Univ. of Chicago Press, 1954); Ludwig von Mises, *The Anti-Capitalistic Mentality* (South Holland, Ill.: Libertarian Press, 1972); Michael Novak, ed. *The Denigration of Capitalism: Six Points of View* (Washington, D.C.: American Enterprise Institute, 1979), especially the chapter by Edward R. Norman, *Denigration of Capitalism: Current Education and the Moral Subversion of Capitalist Society.*

6. Concerning the need for a theory of the American "transformation of the economic system," Maritain wrote: "This country should never, and will never, give up the experiential approach, which is a blessing for it; but . . . it would be quite beneficial for it to develop, at the same time, an adequate ideological formulation, an explicit philosophy, expressing its own ideal in communicable terms. This does not mean, of course, that it would be advisable to manufacture an ideology for the sake of propaganda, God forbid! It means that the development of a greater general interest in ideas and universal verities is a presupposed condition without which no genuine possibilities of intellectual communication can emerge." *Reflections on America,* ibid., pp. 101, 118.

7. See especially William Letwin, *Adam Smith:* Re-reading *The Wealth of Nations, Encounter,* March 1976; Garry Wills, *Benevolent Adam Smith, The New York Review of Books,* February 9, 1978; Irving Kristol, *Adam Smith and the Spirit of Capitalism,* in *The Great Ideas Today:* 1976 (Chicago: Encyclopaedia Britannica, 1976); Jacob Viner, *Adam Smith, International Encyclopedia of the Social Sciences;* Thomas Wilson and Andrew S. Skinner, ed. *The Market and the State: Essays in Honour of Adam Smith* (London: Oxford Univ. Press, 1976).

8. See the chapter, "From Marxism to Democratic Capitalism," in my forthcoming book, *The Spirit of Democratic Capitalism.* For Niebuhr's mature view of socialism, see especially *The Children of Light and the Children of Darkness* (New York: Charles Scribner's Sons, 1944), ch. 3; "Why is Communism So Evil?" in *Christian Realism and Political Problems* (New York: Charles Scribner's Sons, 1953), pp. 33–42; *Our Moral and Spiritual Resources for International Cooperation* (New York: U.S. National Commission for UNESCO, 1956); *Biblical Faith and Socialism: A Critical Appraisal,* in *Religion and Culture,* ed. Walter Leibrecht (New York: Harper & Bros., 1959), pp. 44–57. On Neibuhr's abandonment of socialism, see John C. Bennett, *Reinhold Niebuhr's Social Ethics,* and Arthur Schlesinger, Jr., in *Reinhold Niebuhr: His Religious, Social, and Political Thought,* eds. Charles W. Kegley and Robert W. Bretall (New York: Macmillan Co., 1956), pp. 46–77; John C. Cort, *Can Socialism Be Distinguished from Marxism? Cross Currents,* Winter 1979–1980, pp. 427–28.

9. Daniel Bell, *The Coming of Post-Industrial Society* (New York: Basic Books, 1973), see especially pp. 12–13; idem, *The Cultural Contradictions of Capitalism* (New York: Basic

Books, 1976), see especially the Introduction. Bell writes: "Against the holistic view of society, I find it more useful to think of *contemporary* society (I leave aside the question of whether this can be applied generally to the inherent character of society) as three distinct realms, each of which is obedient to a different axial principle. I divide society, analytically, into the *techno-economic* structure, the *polity*, and the *culture*. These are not congruent with one another and have different rhythms of change; they follow different norms which legitimate different, and even contrasting, types of behavior. It is the discordances between these realms which are responsible for the various contradictions within society." *The Cultural Contradictions of Capitalism*, p. 10 (italics his).

10. For the best treatments of Weber's famous thesis, see: H. R. Trevor-Roper, *Religion, the Reformation and Social Change*, in *The European Witch-Craze of the Sixteenth and Seventeenth Centuries and Other Essays* (New York: Harper & Row, 1969), pp. 1–45; David Little, *Religion, Order, and Law* (New York: Harper & Row, 1969). Also among the classic secondary literature: R. H. Tawney, *Religion and the Rise of Capitalism* (New York: Harcourt, Brace & Co., 1926); Ephraim Fischoff, *The Protestant Ethic and the Spirit of Capitalism: The History of a Controversy, Social Research*, 11 (1944): 53–77; Anthony Giddens, *Max Weber, and the Development of Capitalism, Sociology*, 4 (1970): 289–310.

11. "An economy consists of people whose performance determines its material advancement. Economic achievement depends primarily on people's aptitudes and attitudes (e.g. interest in material success) and their social institutions and political arrangements (e.g., in encouraging people to take long views). Societies, groups, and individuals differ widely in these matters. . . . Differences in these human determinants largely account for differences in economic achievement and rates of progress." P. T. Bauer, *Foreign Aid, Forever? Encounter*, March 1974, p. 17.

12. See Henry Hazlitt, *The Conquest of Poverty* (New Rochelle, N.Y.: Arlington House, 1973; Gary H. Koerselman and Kay E. Dull, ed., *Food and Social Policy I* (Ames, Iowa: Iowa State Univ. Press, 1978). On population, see Colin Clark, *Population Growth and Land Use*, 2nd ed. (London: Macmillan, 1977), table III. i.

13. Arthur J. McGovern, *Marxism: An American Christian Perspective* (Maryknoll, N.Y.: Orbis Books, 1980).

14. See Trevor-Roper, *Religion, the Reformation and Social Change*, ibid.

15. See Adam Smith, *An Inquiry into the Nature and Causes of the Wealth of Nations* (New York: Modern Library, 1937); cf. James Madison, *The Federalist*, no. 47, and Marvin Meyers, ed., *The Mind of the Founders* (Indianapolis: Bobbs-Merrill, 1973).

16. Maritain, *Christianity and Democracy*, ibid., p. 37.

17. Maritain described transformations in the unions, the corporations, the political system, and the beliefs of individuals in *Reflections on America*, pp. 105–11.

18. Maritain, *Reflections on America*, pp. 112–113; he is here quoting the words of William I. Nichols, in *Wanted: A New Name for Capitalism, This Week*, March 4, 1951.

19. Maritain, *Reflections on America*, ibid., pp. 114–15.

20. Ibid., pp. 113, 115–16.

21. Aleksandr Solzhenitsyn, *A World Split Apart* (New York: Harper & Row, 1978), pp. 47–51. See also Ronald Berman, ed., *Solzhenitsyn at Harvard* (Washington, D.C.: Ethics and Public Policy Center, 1980).

22. Robert Nisbet, *History of the Idea of Progress* (New York: Basic Books, 1980).

23. See Ralph Lerner, *Commerce and Character: The Anglo-American as New-Model Man, The William and Mary Quarterly* 36 (January 1979): 16.

24. Lerner, ibid., quotes Adam Smith's characterization of this "man of spirit and ambition," who is depressed by his situation; for whom escape from the mediocrity of his station is paramount; whose virtues are not those of the great but are closer to those of "the inferior ranks of people" (pp. 15–16).

25. Addressing the Second International Conference of UNESCO in 1947, Maritain remarked: "How is an agreement conceivable among men . . . who come from the four corners of the earth and who belong not only to different cultures and civilizations, but to different spiritual families and antagonistic schools of thought? Agreement . . . can be . . . achieved . . . not on the affirmation of the same conception of the world, man, and knowledge, but on the affirmation of the same set of convictions concerning actions." *Man and the State* (Chicago: Univ. of Chicago Press, 1951), p. 77.

26. See my *A Lesson in Politish Economics, Washington Star,* December 15, 1979.

27. See Bernard Lonergan, *Insight,* rev. ed. (New York: Philosophical Library, 1958), especially pp. 121–28.

5

THE VISION OF
DEMOCRATIC CAPITALISM

"You are advancing in the night, bearing torches toward which
mankind would be glad to turn; but you leave them enveloped in
the fog of a merely experiential approach and mere practical conceptualization, with no universal ideas to communicate. For lack
of an adequate ideology, your lights cannot be seen."

Jacques Maritain, *Reflections on America*

Public opinion polls regularly uncover two odd facts. First, Americans report
a high sense of their personal well-being but pessimism about the nation.
Second, the values, beliefs and attitudes of the nation's elites are remarkably different from those of the general population—rather less religious, and of a
rather different moral vision. Such facts as these suggest that we are in Maritain's fog, lacking an active public idea about our nation, a coherent moral vision about ourselves. *Privately,* all may be well; *for the nation,* there is confusion.
The visions of our *elites* do not inspire our *people.*

Yet some have observed that the Reagan administration is one of the most
"ideological" in memory. Others note that it is also one of the most "intellectual" in memory. Its chief spokesmen and supporters are trying hard to establish a new national vision. Above all, President Reagan, David Stockman, and
others plainly show for democratic capitalism as powerful a moral passion as any
socialist ever had for socialism. In this, they are supported—for the first time in
generations—by a small but growing band of intellectuals. It is time that critics
took this new vision seriously. The debate it opens is bound to affect the nation for decades.

For years, defenses of our system have rested for the most part on pragmatism. "Democratic capitalism works." No use arguing about faith and
metaphysics. If someone needs a better drill bit, they'll have to buy it from us.
But pragmatism isn't going to wash any longer—not as a philosophy with
which to interpret the American experiment. Two things have changed in our
world today which undermine mere pragmatism. To be practical today one

must deal: (1) with instant international communications and symbolic war-fare; and (2) with morale and spirit here at home and among our friends. There's an old political maxim, "You can't fight somebody with nobody." In the same way, you cannot fight a powerful set of symbols with no symbols.

A comprehensive defense of democratic capitalism as an economic, moral-cultural and political system has yet to be offered to the world. Lacking it, we have been losing the war of ideas and symbols.

Consider a map of the world. Among the approximately 160 nations, per-haps three dozen can be called "developed." Nearly all these have a "mixed" po-litical economy, composed of (1) *an economic system* based on markets, incentives, and private property; (2) *a political system* in some measure based on rights, the pursuit of individual happiness, and institutions of due process; and (3) *a moral-cultural system* based on pluralism and liberal values. A huge swathe of the map is covered by Soviet-style socialism (the USSR, Eastern Europe, Afghanistan, Cuba, Ethiopia, Vietnam and others), the Marxism of China, regimes more or less imitative of the Soviet model like Libya, Iraq and Syria, and Africa's self-declared socialist republics.

EDUCATING SOCIALISTS

For more than a hundred years, beginning about 1820, socialism existed chiefly as an idea in books. There was no instance of it among the world's political economies. Since 1917, and especially since 1945, all this has changed. A majority of the world's political economies are described by their own elites as socialist.

Thus during the past thirty-five years, socialism (in the Marxist-Leninist and other variants) has acquired an empirical record. Socialism is no longer merely an idea in books. It has been put to the test of reality. Symbolically, so-cialism is supposed to stand for democracy, equality, justice, fraternity, and pros-perity. Its strong suit has been its moral claims. It is supposed to produce greater brotherhood, equality, and cooperation than democratic capitalism. Does it ac-tually do so? The record lies open for inspection.

Until recently, U.S. intellectuals who think of themselves as "liberal" or "pro-gressive" have tended to embrace in a non-ideological way the methods and vi-sions of "social democracy" or "democratic socialism." To lapse into shorthand for a moment, those of us nourished in the Democratic party during the past gener-ation have been, for the most part, concerned with strengthening the *political* sys-tem, often at the expense of the economic system. We thought the goose which laid the golden eggs was invulnerable. We may not have been out-and-out social-ists, but we certainly saved our most bitter jibes for the fat cats, multinational cor-porations, industrial giants, conglomerates, and just plain "business." We champi-oned "people over profits." We seldom had an affirmative word for economic activists. We preferred to be political activists and favored our kind. We did all this by a kind of rote. We had been *educated* to think of business as an alienating, philistine, reactionary, and possibly fascist force. We may have been too pragmatic to be ideological socialists, but our hearts were "on the left."

THE WITHERING SOCIALIST IDEA

The evidence of their senses, however, has led a significant new band of intellectuals—whom Norman Podhoretz describes as "The New Defenders of Democratic Capitalism"—to question their own socialist past. This questioning has proceeded in three stages. The first stage consisted in trying to rescue the *ideal* of socialism from the dreadful record of Soviet-style "scientific socialism." This attempt to broaden the ideal of socialism drew attention to the mixed record of "socialist" countries like Great Britain and Sweden. It began to seem that every existing democracy contained large components of capitalism—private property, enterprise, markets, incentives—and that democratic socialism no more than communism alleviated the alleged ills of the modern world—"alienation," "the dissatisfaction of the working class," and so on. The third stage arose from the conclusion that "capitalism" and "socialism" were obsolete categories and that the decisive distinction lay not in economics but in politics: the key ideal is "democratic" as opposed to "nondemocratic."

Slowly, then, the socialist ideal, put to multiple tests of reality, has evaporated. For some, it remains a piety—the more it fails in practice the more fiercely it is idealized.

The record is plain. Socialist practice in its many manifestations has never yet lived up to socialist theory. There is not a single example of a socialist state which has abandoned totalitarian claims in order to become democratic. Purely socialist economies stagnate in mammoth inefficiencies and vivid inequalities. Nonetheless, the failure of democratic capitalism to develop its own *moral* theory allows socialism to boast superior moral claims, despite its failures in practice. Idealists still tend to believe that socialism, even if it hasn't worked so far, offers a more attractive *moral* ideal than democratic capitalism.

No one who has served in the various organizations of the United Nations can fail to note that international rhetoric, premises, and arguments are, in virtually every respect, socialist. Almost no one dares to argue the premises of democratic capitalism. From one side, an unceasing din. From the other, silence.

At stake in such arguments is the fate of billions of human beings, especially the poor. If socialism did deliver what it promises, this circumstance might be tolerable. But if socialism is essentially an impractical, nostalgic, and inherently authoritarian idea, the universal din in its behalf bodes desperate ill for the world's peoples. It is bad enough that socialism deprives its citizens of liberty. Some might be willing to accept this outcome if the system served at least to produce sufficient bread and a rough form of equal distribution. The empirical record, however, is no more promising about the production of bread than about the development of liberties.

In 1800, this planet supported—usually in great misery—some 800 million people. Today, thanks largely to medicines and technologies developed in a relatively few nations, this planet supports nearly 4.5 billion persons. On a worldwide scale, the need for a truly productive economic system has never been more acute. The era is past when fundamental errors about political economy were relatively cost-free. The proven inability of socialist systems to produce enough even for their own needs (not least in agriculture) is an international disaster of major proportions.

Thus, the most unnoticed event of the past fifty years has been the death of the *idea* of socialism. To be sure, in the absence of a rival idea, socialism continues to attract adherents. But the original idea has suffered death by a thousand qualifications. Skeptical intellectuals have begun to raise questions about it as they used to question capitalism. Who can be in favor of nationalized industries which go broke, results in shortages and long lines, and have the effect of putting everyone on the public dole? Today, nearly all sophisticated socialists are also opposed to traditional socialism. They, too, abhor the gigantic bureaucracy of state-owned industry. They, too, scorn the welfare state, and want to lead local revolutions against it. The new battle cries of democratic socialism are "community" and "participation." Democratic socialists kick and scream against the twentieth century. Their causes are anti-modern: "no growth," "environmentalism," "small is beautiful," and town meetings in every factory and on every common of every village of the land. Socialism, invented in the nineteenth century, and failing in the twentieth century has sought refuge at last in the myths of the eighteenth century.

A NEW THEORY

Until recently, alas, it has been the misfortune of democratic capitalism that practically the only intellectuals interested in defending its intellectual bases have been economists. Democratic capitalism is not merely an economic system. It is also a political system and a moral-cultural system. Without a political system of a certain sort, and without a moral-cultural system of a certain sort, its economic system cannot function. Apart from free capitalist economic systems—"mixed economies," to be sure—there are on this planet no examples of free political systems. A state in total control of economic life is a state in total control of political and moral-cultural life.

Purists argue that there is no purely "capitalist" state and, as yet, no purely "socialist" state. (Most Western socialists deny that the Soviet Socialist Republic represents the true dream of socialism or even of Marx.) But the purist objection misses the point. The sort of system which has grown up in the United States, Japan, and the other relatively few Western democracies—the system designated by the name "democratic capitalism"—is, and has always been, three systems in one. It has *always* been a "mixed" system. One can show this in the writings of Adam Smith. One can show it in the historical record from generation to generation. It is not the fault of the economists that they have concentrated their professional attention on their own part of the system. The failure to consider the role of the other two systems—the political system and the moral-cultural system—must be laid at the feet of our political theorists and our humanists. The system as a whole, in its interdependent three systems, is better than any theory we have of it. Humanists have long been accustomed to kicking capitalism around. It is not easy for them, suddenly, to give it three cheers. Yet, considering the alternatives, they have begun to see in it certain powerful virtues.

THE ECONOMIC CASE FOR DEMOCRATIC CAPITALISM

It is a typical mistake to think of capitalism as merely an economic system. Analogously, it is a typical mistake to think of an economic system apart from its political and moral-cultural dimension. In actual life, each one of us is an economic agent. But each is also a citizen. Each of us seeks God, follows conscience, and pursues truth and understanding. We are all three of these at once: simultaneously economic animals, political animals, and moral-cultural animals. On the other hand, it is often useful, in Maritain's phrase, *distinguir pour unir*, to distinguish in order to unite. This is true for intellectual inquiry, in which one must proceed step by step; one cannot do everything at once. It is also true in public policy. Each of the three systems requires thought, nourishment and care.

The new writers who defend "democratic capitalism" are doing more, then, than defending "free enterprise." They recognize that the primary case to be made is political and moral-cultural. Moreover, they do not regard democratic capitalism—the three systems in one—as a substitute for religion or morals. It is a this-worldly system they defend, a human contrivance. It may, indeed, be the best humans have ever invented, but it is by no means "the Kingdom of God." Moreover, they expect and intend to see it develop further in the future, to reform itself, to progress. For these reasons, they are willing to give two cheers for democratic capitalism, not three. They remain skeptical.

Note, for example, the interplay between an economic system based upon markets and incentives and a moral-cultural system based upon Jewish-Christian understandings of liberty, the individual, the community, sin, and the like. Throughout history, most economic systems were relatively stagnant. Few showed sustained growth. All experienced cycles of prosperity and famine. The very concept of sustained economic development was lacking. The figure of the miser represented a certain quintessential evil, for in a no-growth economy anyone who hoarded gold or other goods subtracted from the limited common store. In order for sustained economic development to become possible (or even conceivable), individuals needed to believe that they could alter the future—indeed, that they could improve their own economic position. They needed liberty. They needed law and stability. They needed patterns of social cooperation. They needed systems of long-term accounting. They needed new institutions in which risks could be shared and enterprises larger than those sustainable by single individuals might be launched. They needed to be willing to defer present gratification, to invest and to labor for the sake of future rewards. They needed to concentrate upon small savings and small gains, cumulatively recorded. Many parables in the gospels express some of the required attitudes of good and wise stewardship (even while pointing out that Christianity, as a more than this-worldly religion, imposes still more stringent axes of judgment). Sustained economic development, therefore, rests decisively upon moral-cultural values of certain sorts.

In some ways, then, economic systems are dependent upon moral-cultural systems. Where certain attitudes, habits, beliefs, aspirations, and exertions are lacking, economic development is unlikely to occur. Inversely, even among peoples who lack material resources or favorable natural conditions, strong moral-cultural traditions of certain sorts may give rise to amazing economic developments. To some extent, such phenomena seem to have appeared in Japan, Hong Kong, Taiwan, and elsewhere. Such examples show that democratic capitalism is open to nations far beyond those in the Jewish-Christian tradition. That relatively few cases arise shows that not all systems of morals and culture can support a democratic polity and a capitalist economy. The ethos of particular peoples is of exceeding—perhaps primary—economic and political significance.

On the other hand, economic systems impose demands upon moral-cultural systems. Sleepy habits of older times must yield to new disciplines. Cherished magic, taboos, beliefs, customs, and attitudes must be set aside; otherwise, an economic system of the modern, developing sort simply cannot take root. Iran under the Mullahs appears to have rejected democratic capitalism as a body rejects a heart transplant. An economic system is necessarily a teacher and reinforcer of some moral virtues, and utterly dependent upon the strength and vitality of others. Where pecuniary dishonesty, bribery, and corruption are a way of life—where even economic reporting and accounting are unreliable—economic systems are penalized as they are not where opposite qualities are more common (though such virtues are never perfectly and universally practiced). Where individuals lack initiative or a talent for self-starting enterprise, the economic situation is quite different from ones in which opposite talents frequently appear. Moral-cultural systems are not equal. Economic systems are much affected by such variations. The imperatives of a new form of economic system often evoke cultural resistance from those who live by other imperatives.

Thus economic systems are not *merely* instrumental. They carry some moral imperatives of their own, and these are often rather different from those that prevail in the moral-cultural institutions to which they are joined. Some philosophers or theologians tend to think that the moral-cultural system defines the kingdom of ends, while economic systems play a lowly instrumental role in the kingdom of means. This is not quite true. An economic system, too, necessarily incarnates certain goals and purposes. These goals and purposes are not merely materialistic. Thus, a people that would choose as one of its social goals sustained economic growth is choosing not solely an increase in the abundance of material goods but also a set of moral disciplines, habits, and activities—a way of life. Such a way of life may have among its specifications a love for liberty, for noble behavior, for highly developed character, for justice and compassion, and the like. Sustained economic growth does not consist solely in material abundance; it springs from and it continues to demand the exercise of moral character of certain sorts. Should such character disappear, so would sustained economic growth.

THE MORAL AND POLITICAL CASE

The moral-cultural case for democratic capitalism, then, comes down to the virtues it produces and favors. Among many others, the new intellectuals single out four: community, broad distribution, productive improvement for all, and pluralism. A few words are useful on each.

(1) *Community*. Adam Smith did not call his book *An Inquiry into the Nature and Causes of the Wealth of Individuals*, or even of *Scotland* or *Great Britain*, but of the *Wealth of Nations*—all nations, all humankind. The fundamental imperative of democratic capitalism has been the welfare of the entire human community. Furthermore, the distinctive social invention of democratic capitalism was not the individual but the *voluntary association*, registered in law as the *corporation*. For economic tasks are larger than one man alone can perform, and their time frame is larger than the life of a single generation. Thus, an institution was needed that bound human beings together cooperatively across time and space—and bound them voluntarily. The new form of community is more likely to be voluntaristic, mobile, and urban.

Whether in the making of a movie, in scientific work, among managers of a corporation, or among workers, solidarity of many new sorts is both possible and necessary, admirable and satisfying, in the modern world. Many new television sit-coms, it will be noted, deal with comradeship which modern persons create on the job, in the workplace, as well as in the family. Most persons, polls show, *like* their jobs, their fellow or sister workers, their firms or companies. They enjoy one another's company. And they have sufficient social skills to mix in many different kinds and types of social worlds.

Democratic capitalism has been done a disservice by the British intellectual tradition of individualism and utilitarianism. More attention ought to have been paid to less explicit virtues—highly notable in Great Britain—of sympathy, fellow-feeling, benevolence, fair play, and conscience. These are social virtues of a very high order. Without them, the functioning of either democracy or capitalism is inconceivable.

(2) *Broad distribution*. Marx predicted that capitalism would "impoverish" the working class. He seriously misunderstood its dynamics. In fact, it raises

every group in society both materially and in boundless upward mobility. It made the working class a middle class—brought about its *embourgoisement* so thoroughly that today socialism is far more decisively a movement of the intellectual professional class than of any other.

Furthermore, comparative empirical studies tend to show (1) that the chief glory of democratic capitalism, as opposed to Soviet-style socialism, is its habit of sharing the fruits of development broadly among the entire population, not primarily elites; (2) that the gap between the richest portions and the poorest parts of the population is less in the former; and (3) that the poorest under democratic capitalism are considerably better off than the poorest of the latter. Socialism has not fulfilled its claims of achieving greater equality—certainly not of opportunity, but also not of result.

(3) *Productive improvement for all.* Most premodern treatments of justice speak solely of distributive justice. This was because the idea of economic development had not even been invented until Adam Smith. Today, with a swollen world population, the moral imperative of sufficient productivity to care for all these billions is not only possible of fulfillment but morally obligatory. Socialism has not solved the problem of productivity. It no longer suffices for the hopes and needs of the world. The *moral* argument for "supply side" economics is even stronger than economic arguments. More schools, clinics, clothing, food, electric lights, refrigerators, potable water, sanitation facilities, and other goods and services are now needed by the world's population than ever before in history. The ethics of justice have shifted decisively from distributive to productive justice. Both are essential, but the latter is the precondition of the former.

(4) *Pluralism.* It is true that democratic capitalism represents but one historical ideal, and that not all sorts of moral-cultural conditions or political conditions are compatible with it. Any people that desires to concentrate some energy upon economic development will have to adopt moral-cultural practices and political practices consistent with such development. One cannot have both instant gratification, for example, and savings and investment, or complete political irresponsibility and self-government. It is simply not true that for democratic capitalism, in the moral-cultural order, "anything goes." As Milton Friedman likes to say, there is no free lunch. Certain moral-cultural demands must be met.

On the other hand, democratic capitalism is not a surrogate for religion. It does not impose one rule of conscience upon all. It is based upon the primacy of conscience, on the one hand, and on strong communities of traditional moral commitments, on the other. It is not only a quite naturally pluralistic system; it utterly depends upon pluralism of conscience for its self-correction and hopes for moral progress. It is based on the lesson Montesquieu, Madison, Tocqueville, Smith and many others learned from studying all other forms of political economy: human life is too precious to be entrusted to the conscience of one person or one group alone. This wisdom is embossed on U.S. coins: "In God We Trust"—meaning "Nobody else!"

There is always a danger under democratic capitalism that such radical pluralism will lead to moral anarchy and to the destruction of the system from within. Yet human beings are perfectly capable of learning by experiment. In recent years, for example, millions of Americans have experimented with "the new morality"—with "open marriages," the glorification of "me," the pursuit of each vagrant instinct or fad—and have begun to observe the consequences. The widespread revulsion against the observable results of these experiments is, on the whole, the vindication of the good sense of our people. If individuals cannot govern themselves, the very basis of "self-government" collapses. The survival both of democracy and capitalism depends on the strength of critical moral-cultural commitments.

CONCLUSION

The new intellectuals have discovered, often to their surprise, that a new public vision of democratic capitalism entails an unprecedented examination of its moral and cultural foundations. Spiritual capital, too, can be squandered. The life of the spirit also has its "supply side." This discovery comes late to a culture born in the heat of the religious wars of the seventeenth and eighteenth centuries, a culture not eager to rend itself apart over disagreements in metaphysics or faith. It is coming not a moment too soon.

Democratic capitalism and socialism, then, are not symmetrical concepts. Under the theoretical framework of democratic capitalism, the three systems— the economic system, the political system, and the moral-cultural system—are distinct; each has autonomy, yet each is also in part dependent upon the other two. By contrast, socialism is unitary. It tends to collapse these three systems into one. Socialism fuses the economic system and the political system into one, under the aegis of a single, collective moral-cultural system. Socialism is more like a religion or moral vision than capitalism is. Socialism proposes to produce the new man who will spring forth (like Venus from the sea) under "socialism with a human face." Capitalism has never been so morally pretentious. Morally, it has spoken of itself with what Maritain describes as excessive modesty. By and large, it has left moral visions to the poets, the philosophers, the archbishops. It thinks of itself as only one of three systems. These three systems are relatively autonomous. Each is *coordinate* with the other two. None is *subordinate* to the others.

In this respect, capitalism is not an alternative to democracy or to a Jewish-Christian culture. It is not so pretentious. It plays only one of three roles. It is compatible with democracy, on the one hand, and with the Jewish-Christian tradition, on the other. But it does not exhaust either the democratic or the Jewish-Christian ideal. The coalescence of all three systems into one unitary system, as in the socialist model, may at first seem to be in keeping with the Jewish-Christian ideal of social harmony and social unity. It certainly attracts a particular type of person. But unitary systems are especially vulnerable to tyranny, whether by a majority or by the seizure of collective powers by a small elite.

Democracy is based upon the *separation of powers* (executive, legislative, and judicial). A truly differentiated and fully humane social system is based upon the *separation of systems* (political, economic, moral-cultural). Democratic capitalism is such a system of systems. The warrant for this separation of systems is found in Jewish-Christian views of the nature of the individual, of social life, of history, and of sin.

In the view of many, therefore, the Reagan administration has already done very well to focus public attention upon the moral and philosophical bases of our way of life. What is at stake here is not only the fate of one administration, but a pluralistic, many-sided debate on the nature of the distinctively American vision of political economy. If it is true that our predecessors have unlocked for all humankind the basic secrets of liberty and development, the task before us is immense. The entire world has need of this knowledge. And we ourselves need know that our daily work in developing the system we have received to yet new heights is of immense spiritual and material significance to the entire human race. For the destiny of the race is our destiny. The least we must do is to be faithful to our our own genius—to understand our own system thoroughly, to cherish it, and to make it work for the good of all humankind.

Our commerce and industry serve purposes of liberty and justice. They themselves do not pretend to represent an ideology, a religion, an obligatory vision. But they do help to establish the material conditions not only of liberty, but also of those plural visions that feed our souls. Long enough we have tried merely to be practical, content as Maritain says, "in the fog of a merely experiential approach." We ourselves need more light than that now. The world, too, wants to know: "Who are you, you Americans? What sort of vision have you?"

Arguments about how best to answer that question are the deepest and best arguments of all.

6

THE SPIRIT OF
DEMOCRATIC CAPITALISM

I am happy to have an opportunity to talk with you this afternoon, and, above all, to have a question and discussion period afterwards, which is the part I look forward to the most. I would like to add that I am an alumnus of one of the universities of this state. A good many years ago I was awarded an honorary degree from Davis and Elkins College. I have always thought very fondly of West Virginia and felt part of you since that time.

One of the privileges of teaching at Stanford was that, from time to time, you had the occasion to sit around the swimming pool with your students. Once I was there with a small group including one of the more attractive young women in one of my classes who was flipping her nose plugs which slipped out of her hand and into the pool. The young men got up to fetch it for her. She said, "No, I want Professor Novak." That impressed me a great deal. I said to her, "Why me?" She looked me cold in the eye and said, "Because nobody I know can dive down deeper, stay down longer and come up drier."

I say that by way of warning, because my task is to ask you to reflect a little bit more philosophically, even theologically, upon the nature of our system than we commonly do. It's a very practical system, this system of political economy in the United States. It was founded by people who wanted to be very practical. They had come out of their religious wars. They didn't want to create a system with such a high metaphysical threshold that only a few people could enter into it. They wanted a system in which you wouldn't argue philosophy and metaphysics. You would just concentrate on doing what needs to be done. Sign a contract to do A, B, C or D, and do it, and let's not argue about why you are doing it and why I'm doing it and what we have in view. That's another matter.

It's a marvelous, marvelous insight—the notion that human beings could be one in practice without being one in theory. Most of the world doesn't understand that. There's a story out of Poland from last summer about the potential solutions to the Polish crisis, one realistic, one miraculous. The realistic solution, so this story goes, is if our Lady of Czestochowa would suddenly appear with all the angels and saints and solve the Polish crisis. The miraculous solution would be if the Polish people could learn how to cooperate to solve them.

The secret of cooperation is very rare. It's very rare in the Arab world, it's rare in Ireland, it's rare in Poland, it's rare everywhere. But it was a fundamental secret to the founders of this country that you could create a practical system of compromise, of adjustment, and not need to spell out all the philosophical foundations. The practical system worked very well, without very much theory. But only under certain conditions.

When I was studying the history and philosophy of religion at Harvard, my father-in-law, a lawyer in Iowa, used to refer to me as his son-in-law, the celestial physicist (and I think with affection). He used to tell me at least twice a year, "Michael, if you can't do it, teach it." I always thought that put things rather well. It's a country built by practical people, a country which wants metaphysics and poetry and so on as a kind of ornament. But it wants to keep first things first. People with their feet on the ground first. That's the way the world was, but the world, even in our lifetime, has changed. More and more, ideas inhibit men and women of action. People know what they should do or ought to do, but they can't do it, because public opinion or a set of going ideas, or whatever, won't allow them to do it. You meet many business executives who will tell you that they spend most of their time asking first of their lawyers "What can we do?" rather than their business people deciding what we ought to do.

Decisions are made to an extraordinary degree not for business reasons, but for reasons of a productive economy. But, first of all, under constraint. There may or may not be good reasons for that; I'm not going to argue that point at the moment. I'm only trying to say that the world has shifted since the days when my father-in-law spoke to me as he did. You see, since 1949, 110 new nations have come into existence around the world. There are now a little over 160 nations; new experiments in political economy. It would be wrong to say these were chosen, because people in most places haven't had much voice in what has been chosen. On the other hand, the vast majority of them have not imitated our example at all. In fact, they don't seem even to have considered the historical record very much. They don't seem to be concerned about what works and what doesn't work. Again and again you've seen nations making choices about which you can predict that this is going to end in poverty and tyranny. There isn't a country in Africa which is now growing as much food as it did twenty-five years ago. When Hitler occupied the Ukraine or Ukrainia, he did so because it was known as the breadbasket of the world. It had always been a net exporter of wheat. Since the Socialist Revolution, there have now been 63 straight years of bad weather, and Ukrainia doesn't even feed itself. Thus, in a peculiar way, the world seems more to be led by symbols and ideas than by reality itself. That's the point I want to underline.

In that circumstance, a system whose strength is building a better mouse trap and not arguing ideology suddenly finds itself handicapped. I often meet not only business executives, but distinguished Americans from every walk of life, whose children come home from the university talking about evil corporations and obscene profits. The parents don't believe the arguments made by their children, but, not reading the same books or the same articles, they don't know how to reply to them either. They are not satisfied with their own responses, so while they are not persuaded, they feel they haven't persuaded their children, and in the process they lose self-respect. When you take self-respect from people you have taken a great deal away from them. One does find all around the country a certain bad faith on the part of a great many people who were not persuaded about the moral value and moral importance of what they are doing. It's not so much that they doubt it. However, one thing they do know is they can't defend it, not even to their own children. Now, you can ask, "Why are we doing such a bad job in the world as a whole?" Begin with the front living room and the kitchen. If we can't explain it even to our own children, then how can we explain it to others?

The difficulty is, I think not that we lack a theory. There is a theory, but it has largely been implicit, because the system was built, constructed to be so practical, and most of us have concentrated most of our energies on the practicalities of it. That's entirely proper, until you find yourself in a world situation in which there are mass medias. Symbols and ideas become as common as the morning and evening news all around the world. And symbols may or may not have anything to do with reality. Thus you find, it seems to me, political economy after political economy making choices that you can almost guarantee are going to lead to hunger and will certainly lead to tyranny. Yet these choices are being made almost every day in Nicaragua, in Iran, in Angola and so forth around the world.

If you go to the United Nations or to any international forum, you would discover that nobody speaks for our system. There are only perhaps twenty nations in the world which are like us—free nations, democratic in polity, capitalist in economy, pluralist in culture—the three characteristics of our system. Somewhere between twenty and thirty (depending upon how tight your criteria are) out of 160 nations. But even our allies never defend the capitalist part of the system of the mixed economies. They defend the democratic part.

One thing you learn in fact if you are a United States representative at the United Nations (as I had the privilege of being twice for six week sessions in Geneva at the Human Rights Commission) is that there is hardly a leader or intellectual of Africa, Asia or of Latin America who will speak in favor of our system, in favor of the capitalist part in particular. The democratic part is easier for them. They are not necessarily socialists, but almost universally anticapitalist. It's extraordinary!

In November I visited Bangladesh, a poor country, but it has a good shot at becoming a very healthy country. It has a marvelous water and sun situation. Three or four harvests a year are possible, could even be five if they had agriculture. At any case, in 1972 in the revolution they turned to America for help to get a grant from the Ford Foundation to bring in some advisors from MIT and Harvard. What do they propose as a new economic plan? First of all, the very notion that they would propose a plan is extraordinary. But they did, and, of course, they proposed to nationalize all the industries. Planned development in a efficient way. If you visited in 1982, as I did, what would you expect to have happened by 1982 from 1972? You are absolutely right. They've got a barrel full of national industries, every one of which is losing money, and the government is desperate to sell them off to somebody who can make them work. They didn't get that advice from Moscow. They got that advice from MIT and Harvard. That's the point I'm trying to make. It is extraordinary what is happening in the real world around us.

Now if you ask yourself why that happened (and we come a little bit deeper coming to my second point now and get right on to the subject of the humanities and the business culture) you begin to recognize that the intellectual tradition of our country for two hundred years, especially in the humanities and in the social sciences, has been anti-capitalist. There was William Blake writing about those dark Satanic mills and the novels of Dickens and Coleridge, Ruskin, Carlyle, Matthew Arnold, all of them anti-capitalist. In the social sciences, Marx thought that he was simply applying social science. Socialism was simply social science applied. When the assumption is that society is like nature, it can be analyzed by experts and put back together again in a more intelligent way. It's an almost perfect model of the socialist spirit if not necessarily the socialist theory: a rationalized society put together by experts. This is so true that even our conservatives tend to be anti-capitalist.

Just a couple of months ago Russell Kirk had another of his annual long articles attacking the corporations and capitalism in *National Review*. My good friend George Will, the columnist, writes his anti-capitalist column about every three months. You just watch for it, a regular routine. George calls himself a stained glass conservative. I call him a rose trellis conservative, because he really does seem to believe that Great Britain and New England were lovelier places when there was a rose trellis over every rural cottage of the land, which had no floors, no privies, no glass in the windows, but, on the other hand, no asphalt, no credit cards, no massage parlors either. He really does think that since the eighteenth century it has been down hill.

You will find hardly a voice in favor of capitalism from our conservatives. If, in the humanities, anywhere in the tradition, by anybody nowadays who has absorbed the tradition in school, someone would say of one of you, "You have aristocratic taste," that would be a compliment. You ought to feel rather good about that. But if you are told you have bourgeois taste you ought to know you've been insulted, or you would have been. Isn't it extraordinary that it is simply class language, nothing but sheer class prejudice, absolutely contrary to fact incidently, because everything the aristocrats have to exhibit their good taste was made by bourgeois craftsmen. They didn't do it themselves. The one thing an aristocrat is not allowed to do is work. They practice the liberal arts. I was wondering, what is liberal arts? It means the liberating arts, and I was thinking, follow this through, what are you free from when you finally master the liberal arts? It hit me with the force of a single word—work. You know, the liberal arts are the non-industrial, non-commercial arts, and there's been an implicit antagonism between the liberal arts and the business schools and the industrial departments. They have almost nothing to do with one another in most universities.

In 1982 I was at Notre Dame University for the first meeting in a University founded in 1842 jointly held between the Theology Department—important at Notre Dame—and the business school—even more important at Notre Dame. They had been on the same campus for 140 years, but they had never had a meeting. Now they invited me to speak on the following subject: Can a Christian work for a corporation? I refused to speak on that subject. They said, "You've got to come and you've got to speak on that theme. Treat it any way you'd like." I said, "I won't do it unless I can ask it in the tone of voice which says 'Can a Christian be a Bishop?' or 'Can a Christian teach in a university?' or 'Can a Christian be a dean?'" I said, "If I can put it in that context I guess I'll do it." They said, "Handle it any way you want." Well, I told this to my friend Irving Kristol, and Irving gave me a marvelous solution. So when I arrived I said, "You asked me to address the question 'Can a Christian work for a corporation?'" I said, "My answer to that is no, only Moslems and Jews." There was a sudden frightened silence in the room, because, of course, what they wanted me to say was yes, and feel guilty.

Now if you ask yourself why that has come about we could go down a long detour and that would be hard to prove one way or the other. My own thumbnail description of what happened is that in Great Britain, as everywhere else on earth, there was a more or less unitary society in which most of the big decisions were made by the Crown over many, many years. Decisions were slowly pulled from the Crown by the Parliament and elsewhere, but only over time. Even as late as the eighteenth century a business corporation in Great Britain was not always, but by and large, a monopoly grant from the Crown, a favor granted by the Crown in return for services rendered. You see relics of this still on British products like biscuits and tea and coffee, "by appointment of Her Majesty." You were given the right, as if it were owned by the Crown, to practice a business trade—the Falkland Islands Company, the East India Company, and so on were examples of this in the overseas field.

In the United States in the year 1800, with only four million people strung out along the Eastern seaboard—and from the point of view of California Easterners are strung out along the Eastern seaboard—there were already more business corporations than in all of Britain combined, in fact, in all the world combined. Of course, that is in part because there were so many fewer lawyers in the year 1800. Nobody knew what you couldn't do. If you wanted to get together and start a business, or open a mill, or a lumber yard, you just did it. But there were in fact more business corporations in the United States in the year

1800 than anywhere in the world. Now as this system began to spread back to Britain, a new class became powerful and important to the Crown made up of people who worked, nobles or aristocrats who weren't well born, no silver spoons in their mouths, not even a good accent. All they could do was produce things and sell them. But it turned out if you wanted to raise an army or you wanted to build highways or you needed a dam the Crown was turning away from the aristocracy and more and more to the rising commercial and industrial class which hadn't existed before, at least in any numbers. As the aristocracy declined, the humanists who tutored their children and ornamented their court (and that was the usual employment of the humanists) declined with them. These crass, unlettered, not well-born persons, whose only claim was competence, vulgar competence, rose in esteem and attracted a certain loathing. They didn't have aristocratic pretenses, but those in the liberal arts do. I can't help but think about an aristocracy of the spirit to match the aristocracy of the blood, and think about nobility of spirit in aristocratic images because of the history of three thousand years. Well in any case that's speculation. I'm trying to understand why the emotional clash is present between the humanities and the commercial and industrial arts, the work-a-day arts of ordinary life.

A business civilization makes its central class not the aristocracy, and not the clergy, and not the land holders, and not the military—and those were the classic alternatives—but a new class, inventors and producers of commerce and industry. There is hardly a voice celebrating that, although the advent of that class produced the enormous liberty and enormous benefits. Where is the novel; where is the poetry; where are the dramas which even consider that subject in the neutral tone of voice, let alone celebrate it? Hardly a one. Almost unbroken hostility. That is a fact I think that needs explanation, someway or the other.

Now what I'd like to do in the time remaining to me is say just a few words about the nature of the system itself, and then pick out two or three qualities of that system which we ought better to understand, both for the sake of our own morale and for the sake of explaining ourselves better to the world, for no one guaranteed that this experiment which we are living will succeed. There is every prospect that it will destroy itself. And its great weak spot, as everybody has seen, is not its economy, which has many, many faults and troubles until you compare it with the alternative, or its politics, which is absurd. You only have to watch the Congress of the United States wrestle to pass a budget which will oblige them to pay for what they want to spend rather than having it postponed for their children to pay for it. It is almost impossible for the self-governing Congress, it seems, to be willing to do that, to be willing to govern itself in that respect. So it's a horrible political system, until you compare it to the alternatives. What everybody sees as the great weakness in our system is our own ideas about it. Failing to understand and appreciate ourselves what we are doing, we shall lose our morale about it, and be unable to commend it to other people of the world who need it because it is the only known source of producing bread and liberty.

Adam Smith wrote a book in the year 1776, he published it in that year having written it for over twelve years, which was the first one in history to ask the right question. That question is still not being asked in the Departments of Sociology all across this country. I keep reading articles by the hundreds called "The Causes of Poverty." Wrong question. I mean, supposing somebody figured out the causes of poverty. So now that you know how to make poverty, who wants it? I mean it is absolutely the wrong question. It is just an insane question.

But if there is one thing clear in the human race it is that the vast majority of people of all times and places have been poor. In the year 1800 there were only 800 million persons on this planet. Hobbes described their life in Great Britain as solitary, poor, nasty, brutish, and short. Sounds like the name of a Charleston law firm actually. In France, Victor Hugo described the life of many as *Les Miserables*. These are in two developed countries. And in Paris and in London, until the 1780's almost every ten years, plague, disease or famine would kill as many as 10,000 people in a couple of weeks. The average age at death of the oppressed sex in France in the year 1800 was twenty-seven.

In this circumstance, Adam Smith asked the right question, an inquiry into the nature and cause of the wealth of nations. He was the first one to perceive that the *wealth* of the world is not static and finite, that history is not a series of seven lean years and seven fat years, or it need not have been, and it need not be. It was not an endless series of cycles, always the same. There is nothing new under the sun. He realized that the miser was imagined as the great villain. Remember all the stories about misers as the great villain in every village? Well it makes sense that the miser is a villain if there is a zero sum because if he sits in his counting house counting up his money, all the money he has is subtracted from the common store. That's all there is. And while he is looking at it, feeling it, and touching it, other people don't have it. It's a cruel way to live. Adam Smith began to see how, if you invest that money, in order to produce more money, the miser is no longer the villain. He's a damn fool, and he disappears from literature. Balzac tells the last story about a miser.

In short, there was a tremendous transformation of values, a whole transformation of culture and, above all, a transformation of perspective. Ethics changed its fundamental meaning. If you read Aristotle three hundred years before Christ, or Thomas Aquinas twelve hundred years after Christ, or any of the writers then, the great theme of ethics, when you are talking about political life, is distributive justice—justice and distribution. If the world is a zero sum there is no problem except how to distribute it. Beginning with Adam Smith there is a whole new ethical problem. If you face the world of 800 million people, most of them poor and hungry, and ridden with disease and ignorance and the rest, and you *can* produce new wealth, then you *must* produce new wealth. There is born a new moral obligation, what I would call, for want of a better word, productive ethics—the ethics of production. If you can do it, you must, given the widespread poverty of the world. That's why he called his book *The Wealth of Nations* not the wealth of individuals, and not the wealth of Scotland (which he dearly loved, more than he loved Great Britain) and not the wealth of Great Britain, but the wealth of nations because the vision he had was of an entire planet for the first time imagined as one, imagined as developed, that there would be a sound material base put under every human being on the planet. That's what he meant by the wealth of nations, so there wouldn't be such penury and disease and ignorance.

The fundamental motive of the system he imagined, that I want to underline, was a *social motive*. He was talking about a social system which would attain social justice by feeding all the hungry of the world and by doing it in a pacific way, law-like way. He figured this task could not be done by the clergy, because if you attempt to unite the world through the clergy they will in fact divide the world, as we've seen in Iran and Iraq and elsewhere. Religious passions run too deep for unity. And it can't be done by the generals because they will seek victory. And it can't be done by the aristocracy because they will seek glory. The only way it will be done, he argued, is by those people we don't terribly much like. They don't have the right accents or the right schooling, and so forth. They are people who depend on the law, because essential to their work are contracts for the long term. They will have to start doing things today for which they won't be paid until five years out, or ten years out, or twenty years out, and they can only do that if there is a structure of law to reinforce contracts. Therefore it is in the nature of their interests that they will want the world interdependent based on trade, pacific, peaceful, and law-like. They won't have any great beautiful visions of all this, and that's an advantage. If they had great beautiful visions they would be tempted to kill those who don't have the same visions, but since all they want are decent commercial and industrial relations and for this they need a structure of law and peace, the chances of building one world are very high for the first time in history. It's a marvelous vision.

As Adam Smith wrote he looked toward the New World and saw two experiments taking place, one in South America and one in North. Of the South American experiment he remarked that they had far more wealth than North America, many more natural resources—gold, silver, lead. In North America the soil along the Eastern seaboard was thin, producing corn, tobacco, cotton, fur, and that's it. Even the people of South America, he thought were of a superior cut. Many more conquistadores, nobles, and generals who were rewarded for services to the Crown. In North America, there were many more lower class dissidents, criminals even, and very few nobility or high born. Whether you look at natural resources or at people you would say Latin America is going to do better. He didn't say so; neither did Jefferson nor Madison. All three predicted that South America would end in poverty and tyranny. Why? Because of the idea by which South America was founded. They were recreating the Holy Roman Empire with its great land and estates based on land holders, the military, and the clergy. And we had had, they wrote, 1,500 years of the Holy Roman Empire. What had it ever done for the poor?

In North America, by contrast, though the land looked poorer and less rich in resources, and though the people looked of a lower cut, Smith argues that they would produce unparalleled prosperity and unprecedented liberty because of the idea on which they were founded. Jefferson sees this point and put on the seal of the United States (which you can still see on the dollar bill, and you really ought to look at it) "Novus Ordo Seclorum," the new order of the ages. It's an *ordo*, an idea, a system, an order, that is the heart of the North American experiment. They understood it. From a distance, Smith recognized that this is something new in history. What was new? Two steps in it were new. First principle—you can not trust politicians (I could almost stop there) to make decisions of conscience or of ideas or of information. Therefore, you must separate the church from the state. Take it away from politicians. Take the press away from the politicians—information. And take the universities away from politicians—ideas. And it's not because of the evil of politicians, but the sort of power that comes with the state. You must take it away from state power, no matter how good the politicians are.

This separation of church and state and ideas wasn't so new because Geneva and other free cities had already experimented. The second insight was more original. You can not trust politicians to make all economic decisions. You must free the economy from the state in an unprecedented way. You can't do it completely. It's impossible to do it completely. The state has to guarantee the value of money, for example. It will need to do some infrastructure things, such as roads, airports (well, airports weren't even thought of at that time) but harbors and other sorts of things. They would have to set some other rules of the game, so you can't separate them completely, but more than had ever been done before to separate the two. This was original. No state had so legitimated and separated the economic sphere as did the fledgling United States.

Thus what was created in the United States was a three-legged system, a trinitarian system, if I may put it that way—a polity with its own institutions and rules and leaders and lifestyles; an economy with its institutions and leaders and lifestyles in the unions, in the corporations, in the small businesses, in the farmers. It's a very complicated set of institutions in the economic sphere. And the churches, their institutions, their leaders, the press, the universities. Now I spend most of my time in a third of these systems, the universities, the writers, the intellectuals and so forth, and I can tell you I think, and I think I am being fair about this, a great many of my colleagues can not interpret for you the financial pages of the *Wall Street Journal*. That is, they don't understand what all the symbols mean or what makes the numbers move one way or another. I'm not sure anybody understands that completely, but they understand even less. But the point I want to underline is they lead perfectly happy lives. You don't have to understand the economic system to lead a perfectly happy life in the United States. In fact, it is required of politicians that they not understand the economic system.

These are three fairly diverse systems and characteristically people who move from one of them into either of the other two don't do so well at it. They have to learn a new set of rules. You put business men in politics and they almost always create disasters for a while. They don't much understand why politicians act the way they do. They haven't learned all the mistakes you can make or all the ways you can be burned, and it takes them a while. Characteristically politicians know they have to listen to professors and experts and they invite them in for lunch and, after some pleasant conversation, when you get down to business, you can hear the gears change into expertise and the politicians' eyes go to the ceiling. There is not a great deal of love between intellectuals and politicians, if I have to say, in all fairness. I mean, they need each other, but it would be wrong to say they totally admire one another.

It is the point of the whole system, if you follow my thought here, that you would develop three systems in which people of quite different psychologies and learned skills over a lifetime don't like the people in the other two very well. It is supposed to be that way. This division of systems is the fundamental notion of our system. It is based on the principle "don't trust anybody." This wisdom is all summed up on the motto eventually embossed on our coins "In God We Trust," meaning we trust nobody else. The whole notion of protecting our liberties is divide power—divide economic power from political power from the power of ideas.

By the old ancient, ancient Jewish and Christian notion of original sin, everybody sometimes sins. There is no person who doesn't sometime sin. Therefore don't put your trust in one person making all these decisions. You'll be disappointed. It can't work, and it is unfair to that person. So don't let anybody have too much power. Divide the powers, or more accurately, divide the systems. We constantly divide powers everywhere we can because we believe in original sin. The second part of the doctrine of original sin goes like this: most people, most of the time, are good, decent, generous and responsible. These two principles go back to back. The first one makes democracy necessary. The second one makes it possible. The first one makes capitalism necessary. The second one makes it possible. The first one makes pluralism necessary. The second one makes it possible.

All the philosophers of history said it couldn't work. If you want to have an economic order, the best thing to do is have a few people plan it out. Intuitively it is obvious. You are in a new nation. You want to develop as quickly as you can. The best thing to do would be to have a plan. Sit down and figure it out so you don't waste anything, so some people aren't doing this and other people taking it away as fast as they build it. It is the obvious thing to do. Sit down and plan it out. It is counter-intuitive to come to the conclusion that it doesn't work. It should work. It is obvious that if you use your head and plan it out, it will work. The only problem is it never does. That's a counter-intuitive judgment. Capitalism is a counter-intuitive system. Socialism is an intuitive system. The younger you are the better you like it. It takes a bit of experience to understand the counter-intuitive views of democracy and pluralism.

Well, I've now gone to the third part of my remarks, and I've really established the first point in them as I wanted to, that one of the fundamental ideas of our system, which we don't realize and therefore we don't defend very well, is its sense of sin, to put it in religious language, or its sense of fallibility, to put it in secular language. Divide power. It's a marvelous, marvelous lesson of political economy. If only Utopian revolutionaries could grasp that. If only people around the world would realize that just because you have a revolution you're not necessarily going to make things better. Everything depends on what happens the day after the revolution. Revolutions are fun, but the crunch comes the day afterward. Now how do you divide the power to make sure nobody gets too much? It is such an important idea, and it is almost universally absent. Everywhere around the world countries are relapsing into the ancient unitary model of one person making all the big decisions. Take Iran. Now the Ayatollah decides how much oil they are going to pump, makes all the big economic decisions. He decides what the punishment for adultery would be. He makes all the moral decisions. He decides who is going to do this and that. He makes all the political decisions. The classic pattern of most of the world.

I want to touch on a second idea, very important to democratic capitalism, this triple system. We are usually accused by our enemies, and our friends often boast of the fact that ours is a system for individuals, rugged individuals. Absolutely wrong. That's just not true. What's mistaken about democratic capitalism is the kind of community it builds, not the village community or the small town community that our grandparents knew, but the sort of community we have in this room where people come voluntarily and are here for a certain purpose together. We don't give 100 percent of our lives to one another in this room, but there are certain things we want to accomplish and we want to do them together, so we give enough of our lives to this sort of cooperation. I'm willing to bet you tomorrow and tomorrow and tomorrow you'll be going to more meetings.

I asked a friend of mine in Italy, "Why did you go to America?" He said, "To make money." "Then why did you come back to Italy?" "To live. You know," he said, "you get a shave and a haircut that will last two hours, dinner for five hours. In America, you all work too hard. Everybody works forty hours a week, and then goes to forty hours of meetings. I couldn't do it. I give up."

Smith—I want to make three points about community, very quickly—called his book, as I mentioned, not an inquiry into the wealth of *individuals*. Ours is a *systemic* view. What we are trying to create is a world system which puts a sound material base under every human being on this planet. That's the first notion of community which capitalism represents. Second, the distinctive institution of democratic capitalist history is the invention of the corporation. Now I know every business man thinks that he is a rugged individual, and there's a good reason for it. I saw it on a little sign down in Georgia in a motel that I stayed at once. My wife actually doesn't like me to use this story, but I love it. It said behind every successful man there stands a lovely little woman telling him he's wrong. Now every person who has built a business, man or woman, has had the experience of asking advice of others and everybody tells them it can't be done. Everybody says if it could be done somebody would have done it. Thus everybody who does something original and well invariably goes through the Biblical saying, unless you are willing to reject your father, your mother, your brother and sister and others for My namesake, you are not worthy of Me. At the end of this you can understand why every businessman thinks, "By God, I did it myself," because he can remember when nobody else agreed with him. On the other hand, if you watch what he does, the first thing he has to do is get a good lawyer, and a good accountant, and a good work force, maybe a good partner. In other words if you watch the way a successful corporation actually grows, even a small one, it depends on good people. It is not a one-person operation and it can't be, and if somebody wants to run it as a one-person shop it is going to be in deep trouble.

My point is the insight behind democratic capitalism is that the economic tasks are too large for one individual, first. Second, they are too large for any generation. You need a new social form which is corporate, communal, and which outlives the life of anybody. Business corporations had never existed before. The law on which they were based was the law of monasteries. The Benedictines were the first multi-national corporations. No, really, they were the first ones to sell wine, cheese and honey all over Europe and the world. They also did it, interestingly enough, by being the first to be so efficient at it that they could live above subsistence. They lived on their own profits. They were such good farmers that they could give seven hours to prayer a day. They could work seven hours and pray seven hours because they were efficient businessmen and they sold across many nations. Corporate law developed out of monastic law because it was the only model for something that lived longer than any individual and it was given to something more than subsistence living.

The third point I want to make under this heading of community is the psychology we create. I would argue that democratic capitalist societies create the most social minded people of anybody on this planet. Take my daughter, the youngest. When she was only eight she already belonged to more different organizations, took part in more different activities, and went to more different kinds of meetings than both my wife and I could drive her to. We do not bring up our children to be rugged individualists. We bring them up to know how to do lots of different things. We expect them by the time they are eighteen (if you can push them out the door at eighteen. With all my friends there doesn't seem to be any generation gap. The kids are still bringing the laundry home at twenty-eight. All my friends are dying for a generation gap) to go out to Iowa or New Hampshire or some state where they've never been during an election time with their tennis shoes and their peanut butter sandwiches and within twenty-four hours have a statewide organization going. Nobody giving orders, no authoritarian business, knowing all their friends by their first names (I've discovered nobody knows anybody's last name) and know what to do and how to do it. It's an extraordinary range of social skills. They are not individualists. Even the bumper stickers now they put on their cars, usually foreign made imports, say "Smile." It's a different sense of community than the human race has ever seen, but it's quite extraordinary, and quite powerful in its range of social skills.

The last point I want to make is this. The answer to Adam Smith's question, the cause of the wealth of nations, was the head, intellect. That's the cause of wealth. All the things which we today call resources, virtually all of them, didn't even exist in Adam Smith's time. They were yet to be invented. He got the idea from John Locke, who said if you took the best developed field in all of Britain by nature—right inclination, right sunlight, precipitation, soil quality—and counted up at the end of one year the harvest of strawberries or alfalfa or whatever it was, produced by nature, and then in the following year applied the best agricultural science, even of the seventeenth century, you would discover you could produce not twice as much as nature, not ten times as much, but one hundred times as much. Therefore, Locke concluded, the earth is far wealthier than we have imagined. It is not a zero sum. Every acre of it is infinitely rich. The Creator made it that way, and it is the task of human beings to use their intellect to become co-creators to discover the secrets which the Creator has blessedly hidden everywhere, and to bring out from the earth what the Lord implanted there. I'm putting it in theological terms because I think most people in the era I'm speaking of thought religiously. That's why Max Weber says that capitalism developed precisely in Jewish Christian culture. Buying and selling is as ancient as the human race, but capitalism isn't. There's been lots of buying and selling, but that's not the same as imagining a world that has unlimited wealth. That's something different.

Now the point I want to emphasize is to what an extent the founding fathers grasped this. When they opened up the West it was the Congress of the United States that enacted the Homestead Act. They didn't want the West to become another Argentina, or El Salvador, with the few landed families. They wanted as much ownership as possible. The idea was democratic capitalism, multiply ownership. Second, they wanted to be sure that the source of wealth was respected, and so they established land-grant colleges. West Virginia University is a land-grant college. It still leads in agricultural research, both here and overseas, and they all do. The notion of the founding fathers came right out of Adam Smith; the source of wealth is intellect. It is not the back of the farmer, or the strength of the horse, but the use of the noggin that makes the difference and creates wealth. And so every state must look around its university as the source of its wealth. It was a brilliant idea. And then the state came in and built dams, rural electrification, the highway act, from the beginning this has not been a laissez faire idea, it has not been a free enterprise nation. It has been a nation based on what I call democratic capitalism. The polity has a strong role to play in developing the economy, in promoting the general welfare. The state plays a role. What it doesn't do is manage. The democratic capitalist idea is different from the democratic socialist idea insofar as the democratic capitalist state like the Homestead Act, the land-grant colleges, the rural electrification, and so forth, promotes the general welfare by doing things to empower people, and then letting them do for themselves. The democratic socialist idea is somewhat different. It ends up creating state agencies to make the decisions, and to do things. There is a strong difference there, although sometimes subtle in practice as to which and I think you decide in practice by which works.

And then, finally, creativity. We are of all the systems of the world, although we are now losing it to the Japanese, the system which has most constructed its life to promote intellect, to promote invention, and to bring inventions as soon as possible to the service of the people. It is not only that we actually develop more inventions than anybody else, we do, though we are beginning to lose the edge on that. But, even better than that, we get the new inventions to the market faster than anybody else and that's quite an extraordinary feat, and on that is what all our wealth is based. I've gone on much too long, and I do apologize for that. But I wanted to lay out as best I could a way I've begun to try to think about our system. If we don't think about its novel strengths it could then happen that this experiment will blaze through history like a meteor that lasted two hundred years, and then will be destroyed, not so much by its enemies, but by a loss of faith in itself.

FREE PERSONS,
TRUE COMMUNITIES,
AND THE COMMON GOOD

"The very purpose of a true community is to nourish in its midst the full development of each person among its members. Conversely, it is in the nature of the human person—an originating source of knowing and loving—to be in communion with others, who share in his or her knowing and loving."

"The relation between free persons and the community is reciprocal. In one sense, free persons are ordered to the common good. Citizenship requires attention to the common institutions that secure personal liberation and help them to flower. In another sense, common institutions are ordered to the full development of free persons. Reciprocally, communities are judged by the degree to which their members develop to their full human possibilities, and persons are judged by how they create, nourish, and develop communities and institutions worthy of free persons. The free person is ordered to the building up of the common good, the common good is ordered to the fulfillment of free persons."

7

MEDIATING INSTITUTIONS

The Communitarian Individual in America

A new public policy is emerging, one which may turn out to be as fruitful for Democrats as for Republicans. Indeed, there are reasons for believing that both major parties in America are in the grip of necessities larger than their prior intellectual conceptions. The competition seems to concern which party will better succeed in grasping the new necessities and successfully mastering them. Neither can wholly return to the outdated and unworkable habits of the past.

Succinctly stated, the emergent public policy begins by facing squarely the existence of recalcitrant social problems, and by recognizing that tried-and-true Republican conceptions of "trusting the individual" are as insufficient as the hoary Democratic conceptions of "leaving it to the state." The public policy thinking of Republicans is becoming less individualistic, more social; and the public policy thinking of Democrats is becoming less statist, more willing to look to other social agencies.

The meeting place of these two trends, which questions of cost and humaneness make virtually inevitable, lies in the concept of mediating structures. Since this new concept depends on two assumptions about the actual character of the American social system, we must reflect on the personality type actually promoted by the American system and on the character of that system itself. Ethics begins in politics, Aristotle teaches us; the *ethos* is shaped by the *polis*.

Self-knowledge, for polities as well as persons, is always an intention, not a finished achievement. Self-discovery entails the rejection of earlier self-images. Two common misunderstandings about the United States, often shared by Americans themselves, represent images to be rejected. The first is that we are a nation of individualists, weak and fractured in our communities. The second is that ours is, on the one hand, a "free enterprise" economy or, on the other hand, a pale imitation of "mixed" social democratic economies like those of Great Britain and West Germany.

The emergent public philosophy is based on quite different assumptions. Two of these may be succinctly stated: (1) The secret to the psychology of

Americans is that they are neither individualists nor collectivists; their strong suit is *association,* and they freely organize themselves, cooperate, and work together in superb teamwork. (2) The social system of the United States is constituted of three independent, yet interdependent, systems of institutions, organized along different axes and even different values: a political system, an economic system, and a moral-cultural system.

This second assumption needs some explanation. The intellectual tendency inherited from Europe of dividing analysis into pairs—liberal vs. conservative, right vs. left—has encouraged us to misapprehend our own threefold structure. Dualistic thinking leads us to imagine that one must prefer either the state or the individual, either the political system or the economic system. In actual practice, all three parts of our social system play important roles in strengthening and restraining each other. In particular, the political system has as one of its central tasks to "promote the general welfare." Its role in promoting commerce and industry, and in empowering associations of citizens, is critical. The role of the economic system in fulfilling the material aspirations of all citizens, and in freeing them for aesthetic, religious, and moral pursuits, is indispensable to the legitimation of the political system. The American system is neither statist nor laissez-faire. It is a system of *political economy* rooted in a powerful and historically original *idea; novus ordo seclorum,* as the founders put it. From the beginning, the state has undertaken tasks essential to the promotion of commerce and industry, but in a special American spirit. For the most part, the state has not tried to *control* or *manage* economic activities. Rather, it has actively provided all of the indispensable infrastructures and preconditions which the economic system can scarcely provide for itself.

This, then, gives rise to the central question in American political economy: How, in practice, ought the American political system address itself to the notable American capacities for free association and the building up of mediating institutions? Individualism alone is not sufficient, and it is not in the American grain. Free enterprise alone is not sufficient, and neither is an omni-activist state.

ASSOCIATIVE COMMUNITY

Frequently, in discussions of community, scholars accept as the primary model for community a form of life, either that of family kinship or that of the agricultural village, characteristic of pre-modern societies. This enables them to speak of "the breakdown of community," for it is clearly true that in a postmodern society earlier forms of community are fractured and opened up. It does not so clearly follow, however, that the earlier ideal of community represents the highest form of community, or that all forms of community ought to be measured by it. Much depends upon selecting as one's ideal the most relevant and telling concept of community.

When I contrast, for example, the village community of my great-grandparents in the Tatra Mountains of Central Europe with the forms of community known to their great-grandchildren in the United States, I am not fully persuaded that that earlier form of community was in all ways superior to the later. Similarly, when I reflect on the strong family life that earlier generations are said to have experienced, I am not fully convinced that it was in all respects superior to the sort of family life known to our generation. If not everything new has been gain, neither has everything been loss.

Not to wander too far afield, I would like to sketch at least some components of an ideal type of community, drawn more from modern than from premodern experience. It is true that primordial ties of blood (I suppose today we ought to say genetics), familial dependence, shared faith, shared tradition, and shared cognitive horizon retain a more powerful force in human affairs than a merely individualistic, atomic theory of human life properly expresses. Still, forms of community based upon blood, family, kinship, shared faith, shared traditions, and shared cognitive horizon exhibit quite remarkable human weaknesses. If it is too much to regard such communities as universally unenlightened, narrow, bigoted, unsophisticated, and unfree, it is not too much to observe their real limitations.

Consider the family. Even in the relationship between husband and wife, the role of election and free choice, although in some societies not prominent, has long been codified in Christian and Jewish marriage liturgies. Free will is of the essence; coercion renders the marriage contract invalid. Thus, in this primordial form of community, the role of contract or covenant has long been recognized. Children do not, of course, choose their parents. Still, it is regarded as a good that children should come to love their parents not only out of dependency but also, as it were, as chosen friends—responding to freely given love with freely given love in return.

Without appealing to an image of human relations which implies that each human person is solitary, atomic, and entirely rational and voluntaristic in his or her self-approbated behavior—without, that is, appealing to various schools of rationalism, voluntarism, and radical individualism—one may still hold that in communal relations an elective contract or covenant represents the highest form of human dignity. Proximity, instinct, affection, similarity of background, and many other "non-rational," "non-voluntaristic" factors may be involved in human communities. There may never be (or only rarely) a "purely" rational or voluntary choice. Still, a measure of freely chosen compact plays a significant role in the ideal of human community. One of the founding images of the American sense of community lies, accordingly, in such documents as "the Mayflower Compact." A long and hallowed literary and liturgical tradition employs the image of God's covenant with His freely chosen people and their acceptance thereof as the original model for this idea. The Jewish and Christian God first loves humans, and then is loved freely in response. The ideal of community between God and humans, based upon free election on both sides, came in this way to inform the classic American ideal of human community.

Compared to the traditional societies of "the old world," it is no doubt true that the communities of "the new world" experienced conditions of uprooting, mobility, and voluntariness of a unique sort, unique at least in their frequency and massive social character. Immigrants had to "break" from their communities of origin, at least in part (certainly in the geographical ties of imagination and sensibility, in their love for their native mountains, plains, towns), in order to rebuild new communities in a new land. But they *did*, in almost all cases, build communities, not only on the frontier but in city neighborhoods. True enough, the initially distinct American experience of emphasizing the right of each individual to pursue personal happiness led to a new exhilaration on the part of individuals, who in large numbers were taught to depart from the bosom of their families to "make their way in the world." Perhaps because ancient communal ties were so strong, great symbolic energies had to be unleashed to encourage young persons to "break" from their homes and to "strike out on their own." Thus, the cowboy, even the gangster, the outsider, the loner, the "Marlboro man," became powerful and distinctively American symbols. Simone de Beauvoir recounts in her memoirs how she, Jean-Paul Sartre, and others in their circle first came upon the images of the existentialist hero in American movies of the 1930's.

THE "NEW WORLD" COMMUNITARIAN

This symbol of the lonely individual was embodied often enough in reality to be credible, for it was involved in the decision of succeeding generations of American children to try new ways and to seek out new places, apart from the horizons of their families. Still, this symbol tells only a small part of the American experience. Characteristically, the outsider or adventurer or inventor built a new community, a new family, a new set of associations, a new corporation, even a new industry. And many Americans remained "at home" in their communities of birth. Apart from myth, the American individualist is remarkably communitarian; our favorite sports—baseball, football, basketball—are liturgies of teamwork and association.

Few cultures in the world, I think, promote in their young as many habits of cooperation, sympathy, teamwork, organization, and other social virtues as the American. Tocqueville already noticed this trait in 1836, a trait, perhaps, required by the necessities of settling a new continent. Nearly all tasks were too large for one man or family alone; cooperation was indispensable to survival. The associative ethos of Judaism and Christianity reinforced its importance. Is there an American village or city without its annual "Brotherhood" awards? In fraternity and association, Americans were not violating an ethos but fulfilling it, and not only for physical but also for psychical survival. American philosophers like Josiah Royce and John Dewey are preeminent among philosophers of the world in their astute and detailed reflections on the centrality of community to human life.

The American ideal of community, however, has never been collectivist or state-centered or all-encompassing. If, on the one side, Americans are not individualists, neither do they admire belonging to one institution alone. There is no one overarching religion to which all subscribe. Although the English language and the heritage of British political institutions have given the nation the backbone of its common culture, there is no strictly enforced ethnic or particular cultural horizon, and the common culture itself is shaped by the continuing contributions of many cultures. The continental size of the United States makes for disparate regional interests, experiences, and perceptions. As Madison and Hamilton prescribed in *The Federalist,* the promotion of commerce and industry further divided the nation into diverse and competing values and interests. The number of associations to which many citizens belong is quite staggering. Organizations as diverse as the Veterans of Foreign Wars, the Lions Club, Parent-Teacher Associations, the Boy Scouts, the Girl Scouts, athletic leagues, and all the multitude of voluntary associations embraced under the United Way and all the committees, organizations and activities promoted by a multitude of churches, keep many Americans almost as busy attending meetings after school or work as they are during the average work week.

Between individualism and collectivism, there is in America a third way. Between the individualist and the collectivist there is the communitarian individual—the individual whose life is given substance by the many communities and associations in which he or she participates. The American way of overcoming individualism is not through an all-consuming attachment to the state or any other collective, but through the building up of many diverse associations and communities. Undoubtedly, there are individuals who are left out, truly lonely and perhaps forgotten ones, as there are, indeed, true individualists who choose to remain outside as many associations as they can. Yet, as there is a full literature on the lonely American, there is another on the American as a joiner, organization man, conformist. (The adversarial intention in much American literature and journalism—intending to blame Americans for every opposite failing—can hardly escape attention.) The empirical truth, then, is rather complex, but the ideal of community is clear. The spectrum of reality in America is broad, but a great many Americans live quite rich communal, associative lives, both in their families and at work, among friends they choose and among others with whom fate has conjoined them. Even strangers are remarkably friendly to one another, as travellers from many lands have often observed. Americans commonly chide one another to be yet more open, ecumenical, understanding, cooperative, helpful—even to "smile." It is not an American ideal to be self-enclosed, indifferent to others, hostile, or cold. Even such volumes as *Looking Out for Number One* and *Assertiveness Training* have as their premise that learning such things is against the ordinary grain.

POLITICAL ECONOMY UNDER
DEMOCRATIC CAPITALISM

These two general concepts, concerning the associative character of American life and the special ideal of a coordinate political and economic system, set the stage for new practical experiments in political economy. Given their social skills, Americans are in a position, in addressing social needs, to go beyond individualism and beyond statism. Given the mutual respect of the economic system and the political system, each with its own strengths and weaknesses, Americans are in a position to maintain an activist government without establishing government as the chief agency for managing and administering vast social programs. This large conceptual framework is important, but not sufficient.

The general principle, however, is plain. A swollen government must be taught to divest itself of as many activities involving its own managerial administration as possible. Simultaneously it must catalyze other social agencies and offer them the necessary support to perform the necessary tasks better and more efficiently. Some examples give hope. As often as possible, users should pay the costs—the airlines for air traffic controllers, for example, as is done in Switzerland and elsewhere. For some public services, like sanitation, contracts to private companies have proven to be less costly than a governmental agency. In other areas, however, like welfare, the complexities and perplexities are intimidating. One hardly knows, at first, which techniques to recommend.

The principle is to empower individuals through local agencies to achieve their own independence. Yet, in many cases, government must do the empowering. Without government, many important social energies cannot be released. Thus, the American ideal of political economy depends upon the wisdom and undergirding strength of an activist government, which must remove impediments, lend assistance, and through positive actions release the manifold energies of the private sector. A do-nothing political system would fail "to promote the general welfare." A do-everything political system smothers it. Finding the techniques that actually empower citizens is at the heart of wise political economy.

Historically, the American political system has attempted to empower families to own property and has provided assistance which private services could scarcely provide. Consider the Homestead Act, the land-grant colleges, rural electrification, the federal abolition of slavery, civil rights acts against discrimination based upon race, the provision of social security and unemployment insurance, and many other indispensable governmental activities. Our political and economic systems are not identical, but go together in mutual modification, and are both further modified by our common moral-cultural institutions, habits, and values.

Thus, the distinctively American conception of political economy is not that of a free economic system alone, nor that of an omnicompetent state. In the American model—more fully realized in practice than in abstract theory— the political system is distinguished from the economic system, but is interdependent with it in many ways. Utility companies represent a form of semi-private, semi-public business. Some corporations—port authorities, the Tennessee Valley Authority, the Post Office, and many others—have a uniquely public character while remaining somewhat insulated from direct day-to-day control by the political system. Furthermore, without governmental regulation, competition would lack the common rules without which a fair game cannot be played. To list all the ways in which the political system modifies, supports, and regulates private industries of extremely diverse sorts would take us too far afield. But it is important to notice that, in practice, the relations between the American political system, in its many diverse parts, and the American economic system, in its own baffling diversity, are extremely complex.

Even in the pages of *The Federalist,* Madison and Hamilton properly understood that one of the chief tasks of political leadership is to create conditions for a flourishing and diverse economy. Correspondingly, one of the chief tasks of business leadership is to nourish the sorts of prosperity, economic progress, fairness, and sense of community which are essential to a democratic polity. Neither politics alone nor economics alone is sufficient. Democratic capitalism is neither socialist nor laissez-faire in its conception; it is a form of *political economy,* a set of coordinate, not subordinating, systems. At one extreme, the state does not attempt to absorb into itself and utterly to subordinate to itself the entire economy. At the other extreme, no business or industry is without political responsibilities expressed by sanction of law, by custom, and by self-restraint.

It is difficult to draw exact lines in any purely theoretical way marking off the precise limits of the political system, on the one hand, or of the economic system, on the other. Yet industry by industry, case by case, adjudication of rights and responsibilities is constant. Errors at either extreme are relatively easy to spot, even if partisans at the extremes may strenuously argue their positions. What cannot be denied is that, equally, the political system and the economic system each has its integrity and assigned turf even as particular cases and the general proportions of the playing field are passionately debated.

It is common to express this consensus by describing the American system as a "mixed" system, neither purely capitalist nor purely socialist. Yet there are reasons for thinking that this common expression is seriously misleading. It is absurd to think that government, which after all has responsibility for currency, can be wholly insulated from indispensable activities in the economic sphere. That is why thinkers such as Adam Smith, Madison, and Hamilton thought in terms of *political* economy. In actual practice, moreover, especially in an economy of continental size, crossing sovereign state lines, neither the political system nor the economic system can avoid intersecting with the other at many points, not least in the lives of all citizens who participate in both. The ideal of the American system is not properly described, then, as a "mix" of capitalism and socialism. It is more accurately described as a "mix" of a vital political system and a vital economic system. Each system depends, in part, on the vitality of the other. (The experience of other nations in which one or the other is comparatively weak and is virtually swallowed by its stronger partner illustrates the need for mutual vitality.)

For this reason, and parallel to the expression "political economy," I prefer to describe the American system as "democratic capitalism." The ideal of democratic capitalism is not that of a purely independent free enterprise system or laissez-faire, nor is it the ideal of democratic socialism. Democratic capitalism is not a halfway house between socialism and laissez-faire. It is, in its own right, a quite distinctive ideal. There is a tendency in democratic socialist thought to grant the state, or at least the political system, ultimate and final power over the economic system. There is a tendency in libertarian or laissez-faire thought to subordinate the state to the economic system, and the social texture of actual life to the solitary individual. By contrast, the ideal of democratic capitalism is that of two coordinate systems, in some respects independent of each other and in some respects interdependent, but neither subordinate to the other.

There is one set of problems, however, which since about 1955 has tipped the American system closer to the socialist ideal. These are the problems of "the safety net," gathered under the rubric of "the welfare state." Typically, faced with a social problem, one set of critics has turned to the individual, while another set has turned to a state agency. From social security programs to aid for families with dependent children, from assistance for the handicapped to unemployment compensation, the argument almost always has been settled by increments of state activism. For social problems are, by their nature, beyond the capacity of solitary individuals. Does it follow, however, that they are best addressed directly and in a managerial way by the state? This conclusion would follow if the only form of social agency were the state, but this condition is not met.

THE ROLE OF MEDIATING INSTITUTIONS

Undeniably, a large society faces problems that may overwhelm solitary individuals. Undeniably, the solutions to social problems must also be social. It does not follow that the state is the only, or the most effective, or the cheapest, or the most sensitive social agency. Besides the state, there are many other social agencies, some already existing, and some perhaps yet to be imagined.

The dimensions of the sudden growth in the social welfare sector of the federal budget are spectacular. In 1955, federal entitlement payments to individuals stood at approximately $20 billion or 21 percent of the federal budget. By 1970, these sums had grown to approximately $70 billion or 31.8 percent. By 1980, they had grown again to $270 billion or 46 percent. Since these entitlements have become automatic, projections for 1984 come to just over $400 billion or 52.7 percent of the budget, and no end to uncontrolled escalation is in sight.[1]

Many entitlement payments do not, of course, go only to the poor. All retired senior citizens are entitled, for example, to the social security payments they have been conscientiously foregoing during their working years. Still, when $300 billion has been spent to eliminate poverty during 1981 alone, citizens may well ask why eliminating poverty costs so much. Are cheaper, more effective methods not available?

Suppose, for example, that one accepts an admittedly extreme estimate of 25 million Americans who would, without transfer payments, be living below the official poverty line for a non-farm family of four ($8,450 per year). How much ought it to cost to see to it that all poor persons received cash sufficient to bring them above this line? For the sake of simplicity, let us divide the number of poor individuals into household units of four each. That makes 6.25 million poor households. To transfer cash payments of $8,450 to each such household directly would cost about $50 billion (much less if we include income the poor already receive). Poverty—in this strictly mathematical sense—should be eliminated at a fraction of what is currently being expended. It is by no means clear, then, that current federal strategies for eliminating poverty—an admirable aim—follow the most direct, effective, and cost-efficient path.

There is, indeed, a certain contradiction in much recent thinking about the elimination of poverty. On the one hand, poverty is most easily and commonly described in monetary terms: so many dollars for a non-farm family of four. On the other hand, government entitlement payments are chiefly designed to meet specific *crises* in which individuals may be involved. Thus there are programs for medical assistance, food stamps, families with dependent children, rent supplements, and many other specific cash and non-cash transfer payments. Each of these programs has its own criteria, paperwork, administrative apparatus, and self-policing functions. Two problems arise here. First, measuring the non-cash benefits, especially medical care, is extremely difficult. As the *Times* piece already cited explained, "Medical benefits do not improve the economic well-being of a household as much as cash would." Secondly, the overhead involved in all the many administrative agencies may be, cumulatively, far more costly than direct cash payments to the poor. Given the cash themselves, the poor might better select—and with far less dependency—their own priorities.

The social problems of poverty are clear enough. So also are the responsibilities of society to meet these problems. Two arguments have so far been addressed, however, against choosing the federal government as the agency through which to meet those needs. One is the constant escalation of costs. The other, related but not identical to it, is skepticism about the efficiency of government as the superior practical agency of the good society. The factor of cost imposes the reality principle. Something must be done to control costs. It is the second factor, however, which gives rise to the search for other agencies besides those of government to meet the necessary tasks.

Most everyone agrees that a good society ought to provide a "safety net" for its less fortunate citizens. Programs for direct cash transfers to the poor—a guaranteed annual income—have more than once been proposed in the Congress. This direct approach has so far failed of adoption. A third idea has, therefore, come under consideration. If direct cash transfers through some form of guaranteed annual income are not adopted, and if the strategy of multiple governmental agencies to meet multiple specific crises gives rise to uncontrollable costs, are there not other social agencies which might properly meet undeniable social needs? There are, in any society, many other social agencies besides the state. Because these social agencies mediate between the individual and the state, and mitigate the vulnerability of individuals left to themselves, such agencies have come to be known as "mediating" or "mitigating" institutions. Among them are the churches, schools, unions, fraternals, neighborhood organizations, and other voluntary associations of every sort.

Is it possible that social needs can be met more efficiently, more cheaply, and with greater effect through social agencies in the private sector? Furthermore, might not costs to government be reduced if the government used its own funds to strengthen these non-governmental organizations, rather than to attempt to meet all social problems itself?

EXPERIMENTAL PROGRAMS

In the pragmatic context of American life, such programs are liable to begin piecemeal, as small experiments. No grand architecture is yet in place, even though the basic conception seems to be gaining adherents. Let us simply list, then, some examples of how this new approach might work.

(1) Consider a family with a retarded child. If the child is hospitalized in a governmentally funded hospital (and in some cases this may be necessary), the costs may run to $30,000 or more per child per year. If, on the other hand, the family would be willing to care for the child at home, then either a cash transfer or a tax credit of, say, $2,000 per year might so empower it. Invested over ten years, such funds might pay for special facilities in the home such as a whirlpool or other therapeutic devices. The savings to the government would seem to be great. In at least some instances, individual churches or other groups have sponsored programs for the retarded and the handicapped in their localities. At a fraction of the cost of total institutionalization, such programs have been able to provide a daily environment, sometimes including income-producing work suitable to those involved, of remarkable human quality. Such churches or other local agencies might well require some federal subsidy to meet their costs. Even if such a subsidy reached as high as $4,000 per year per handicapped person it would be far less than the cost of total institutionalization.

(2) A bill (S. 1581) is before the Senate Labor and Human Resources Committee to allow taxpayers the choice of a tax credit or a deduction for each household which includes a dependent person who is at least 65 years old. This bill encourages families to maintain their care for grandparents and other elderly relatives. It also gives the elderly the satisfaction of contributing a significant share to family income through the tax credit or deduction. Not all the

elderly would be covered by such a provision, but a significant number would be. To the profound human value of a multi-generational household would also be added an empowering incentive. (Not to be neglected is a source of some child care for some fortunate families.)

(3) Another bill (S. 1582) would exempt from taxation certain trusts established for the benefit of elderly parents or handicapped relatives, and would provide a deduction for contributions to such trusts. While not universally applicable, this possibility might relieve pressures on social security for at least some millions of retired persons.

(4) Another bill (S. 1579) would allow corporations, large or small, to deduct all contributions made to a joint employee-employer day care facility. A variation of this provision was enacted in the Economic Recovery Act of 1981.

(5) The Economic Recovery Act of 1981 also permits working spouses to invest the first $2,000 of earnings in a tax-exempt Individual Retirement Account. Accumulating over a working lifetime at compound interest, such a fund would provide a substantial sum (easily $100,000 or more) available at retirement. This provision has two important social effects. Since over half of all married couples now have two incomes, a great many households may be stimulated to add substantial sums, tax-free, to the national pool of investment capital. Savings will thus be encouraged. Furthermore, sole reliance upon social security payments will be reduced. Both spouses will be accumulating substantial retirement accounts.

(6) In every community, rural and urban, there are private associations or networks involved in feeding the elderly, in developing supervised activities for teenagers, and the like. In times of stress, it has been found, individuals in trouble turn first and most often to these personal, local networks for assistance. Last of all do they turn to governmental agencies. Furthermore, they report higher rates of satisfaction when they turn to persons already known to them among their neighbors, in their churches, in groups with which they are affiliated, and the like.[2] A measure of governmental subsidy to such local networks and associations, already in place and functioning with affective ties of many sorts, would seem to offer an effective use of such funds. Costs would seem to be far less than for governmental duplication of local capacities.

(7) Two decades ago, teenage unemployment among whites was higher than such unemployment among blacks. Currently, the problem of teenage unemployment among blacks is considerably greater. The figure is often announced in percentages: "Forty Percent [or Fifty Percent] Black Youth Unemployment." In hard numbers, however, the scale of the problem is more readily apparent. Fluctuating monthly, the figures from the Department of Labor tally just under 400,000 black youth unemployed.[3] Considered simplistically, at the minimum wage of approximately $6,000 per year, the total financial cost of employing all 400,000 of these young persons comes to $2.4 billion annually. It does not seem beyond the reach of Americans to invent ways for making at least part of the required wage costs available through local institutions, which might

put such youngsters to productive work. Some might be able to produce more goods and services than is represented by their wages. Even if some did not, the investment would seem to be of large future productive benefit.

Missing has been the link between work to be done and the unemployed who wish to do it. The fastest growing sector in the American economy has been the service sector and the many small businesses that are mushrooming in the service sector. Many such businesses are uniquely suited to young employees. Over 80 percent of all new jobs in the U.S. are supplied by small businesses.[4] I do not have in mind the precise mechanism that would expedite the hiring of larger numbers of currently unemployed black youths, yet appropriate tax credits or deductions to small businesses precisely for such employees seem likely to increase their numbers substantially. Combined with a reduction of paperwork so onerous for small business, and especially with respect to a work force that is demographically and vocationally quite volatile and temporary in its commitments (many are either in school or in those various forms of transition common to late adolescence), incentives designed for this purpose seem promising.

Institutions like churches, libraries, and voluntary organizations should be drawn directly into the task of designing employment for teenagers. Adult guidance seems even more important for *attitudinal* training than for training in specific job skills. The technical question is how to empower such institutions to furnish sound employment, of which most of them, involving labor-intensive work, are much in need. The problems of the Comprehensive Employment and Training Administration (CETA) programs, which attempted to do something like this but with a very heavy governmental overlay, are well-known. The amount of money spent seems disproportionate to the actual number of employees put to work and to the amount of wages actually paid. Significantly, the philosophy of CETA involved a high degree of governmental management. A policy which placed greater reliance upon local mediating structures, while drawing upon governmental resources as a catalyst, would entail a technically different design.

ASSISTING MEDIATING INSTITUTIONS

The involvement of many citizens in meeting local needs is a good to be desired. How can the government stimulate, and financially catalyze, such involvement? Instead of thinking of the state as the agency of first and full responsibility, can we learn to think of it as an empowering agency—neither administering nor doing so many tasks, but helping to stimulate other social agencies to do them?

One suggestion that may have some merit is offered by Stephen Roman and Eugene Loebl in their stimulating book, *The Responsible Society*.[5] Self-consciously, they try to conceive of government as a catalyzing rather than as a managerial agent. One device they recommend is that the government create a fund for certain types of socially necessary activities, from which private institutions may borrow at greatly reduced interest rates. (Such programs are already in operation for agricultural purposes.) As such institutions repay these loans, the fund is replenished. The burden falls upon such institutions to make such employment as they offer financially productive. Imagine, for example, that a local church or benevolent organization would borrow from this fund sufficient capital to employ ten youngsters as plasterers, painters, carpenters, and repairmen, under supervision and at something above the minimum wage, in the repair and restoration of local housing. In many neighborhoods, there is visible work to be done, and some in the community would be willing to pay at least modest sums to have it done. It is likely that local enterprises might succeed where governmental agencies have not, and at lower public costs.

Another suggestion is to turn more seriously to the churches of America. There is virtually no local community, no village, without its church. Most of these churches are already involved in social action of various sorts. It is said that the churches cannot undertake to meet vast and expensive social problems alone; they cannot collect sufficient funds; they do not have all the necessary forms of expertise; they cannot properly manage functions which are not properly their own. No one, of course, thinks of the churches as the only, or even as the primary, social agencies of the land, yet they are a critical resource, drawing upon the ideals and energies of more than 100 million Americans. How might we arrange our national approach to social necessities so as to make it possible for the churches to extend their activities more efficiently and further than they already have, and to do so better, and with greater humaneness, than government can? There will always be tasks which government alone can do, and some which government does best. Still, how can the expensive overload in government be lessened so that funds available to government might be used with greater effect and deeper affect? Society is larger than the state, and churches are an important part of our national social life. The present generation of ecumenism and cooperation, bridging many ancient sectarian chasms, offers a fresh opportunity to the nation. Habits of cooperation nourished now for some twenty years place these institutions in a new light in American society. Things before impossible now seem at least possible. Can we not take advantage of the moment?

A great deal of technical skill will be required, on a more practical level, to bring activist government support to private social agencies. The technical difficulty lies in the fact that when government acts it tends to overpower and otherwise to weaken less powerful agencies. Secondly, since government is not disciplined by market forces or market costs or other forms of private restraint, it must regulate and police its own actions. Hence, government can scarcely move without great and cumbersome administrative machinery. In establishing welfare agencies, for example, government typically establishes eligibility requirements which are exceedingly difficult to administer, regulate, and police. Thus, the technical skill required to use governmental power in ways as simple and direct as possible, without generating a vast bureaucratic workload, is of a very high order. It is higher than that to which a mere philosopher or theologian may aspire.

GOVERNMENT AS ACTIVIST CATALYST

The republic is not where it was twenty years ago. New things are possible. One universal public policy for a nation of continental size, of tremendously varied climates, economic bases, and local cultures, carries within it the seed of local abuse and local ridicule. By contrast, a public policy rooted in local communities, but catalyzed and assisted in its necessities by a vigilant national administration, more closely fits the texture of reality. Public policy must increasingly embody the common sense law that high morale depends disproportionately on local satisfaction, for local reality is cut closer to the human scale. To discipline local communities to national ideals, there exist potent national media, and national government upholds the constitutional law binding upon all. But national government itself cannot manage a national community.

The ideal of democratic capitalism is to bring the three independent, interdependent systems—the political system, the economic system, the moral-cultural system—into harmonious collaboration. Moral-cultural institutions like the churches, the schools, families, and the press cannot meet our social problems alone. Economic institutions like the great corporations, the unions, and small businesses cannot meet them alone. Political institutions like the agencies of government cannot meet them alone. If it was an earlier error to rely solely upon individuals, and a later error to rely too much upon the state, self-knowledge suggests a new approach to public policy through empowering other social agencies besides the state. Adopted step by step and pragmatically, sorting out what works from what does not work, this approach may carry the American experiment forward in ways at once original and also consistent with its founding ideal. In its view, government must remain activist, but in a catalyzing, rather than in a managerial, way. Its philosophy is not to ask what government can do for its citizens, but how it can empower them, in strong local communities, to do for themselves. It is neither individualist nor collectivist, neither socialist nor laissez-faire. *Annuit coeptis:* It is a new beginning.

NOTES

1. Robert Fear, "War on Poverty Is Difficult to Call Off," *The New York Times,* November 29, 1981.

2. See the work on mediating structures, by Peter L. Berger and Richard John Neuhaus, *To Empower People: The Role of Mediating Structures in Public Policy* (Washington, D.C.: American Enterprise Institute, 1977). See also: Robert L. Woodson, *A Summons to*

Life: Mediating Structures and the Prevention of Youth Crime (Washington, D.C.: American Enterprise Institute; and Cambridge, Mass.: Baltimore Pub. Co., 1981); Brigitte Berger and Sidney Callahan, *Child Care and Mediating Structures* (Washington, D.C.: American Enterprise Institute, 1981); Lowell S. Levin and Ellen L. Idler, *The Hidden Health Care System: Mediating Structures and Medicine* (Cambridge, Mass.: Ballinger Pub. Co., 1981); John Egan, et al., *Housing and Public Policy: A Role for Mediating Structures* (Cambridge, Mass.: Ballinger Pub. Co., 1981); David Seeley, *Mediating Structures and Education* (Cambridge, Mass.: Ballinger Pub. Co., 1981); Robert L. Woodson, ed., *Youth Crime and Urban Policy: A View from the Inner City* (Washington, D.C.: American Enterprise Institute, 1981); Robert L. Woodson, ed., *The Urban Crisis: Can Grass-Roots Groups Succeed Where Government Has Failed?* (Washington, D.C.: American Enterprise Institute, 1981).

3. On minority employment see Walter Williams, "Government Sanctioned Restraints That Reduce Economic Opportunities for Minorities," *Policy Review,* no. 2 (Fall 1977), pp. 7-30; and Peter Germanis, "The Minimum Wage: Restricting Jobs for Youth," *Backgrounder* No. 147, July 1, 1981 (Washington, D.C.: The Heritage Foundation).

4. See David L. Birch, "Who Creates Jobs?" *The Public Interest,* Fall 1981.

5. Regina Ryan Books/Two Continents Pub. Group, Ltd., 1977.

8

FREE PERSONS AND THE COMMON GOOD

One of the achievements of the U.S. Catholic Bishops' economic pastoral is its restoration to a place of honor of the classic Catholic concept of the common good. This step alone marks a reconnection of Catholic social thought to its Thomistic origins, at a moment in history in which certain themes of Thomistic thinking are more concretely verified in history than in times past. The fact that the contemporary imagination easily grasps the image of "the global village" (a metaphor first recreated by the Thomist-trained Marshall McLuhan) establishes, e.g., the imaginative context of natural law: a way of thinking about all human beings related to one another in a universal framework of mutual independence and mutual vulnerability. The twentieth-century impact of relativism, stressed by historian Paul Johnson in *Modern Times*, is diminishing. It is not the *in*dependence of cultures and moral systems that now most fascinates humans as their *inter*dependence.

The danger in natural law thinking (and in the concept of the common good) has been thought to be twofold: (1) that it is static and nonhistorical; and (2) that it is incompatible with pluralism and liberty. These accusations have a *prima facie* validity, since the concepts of natural law and the common good were first articulated in the environment of the relatively static and undifferentiated authoritarian societies of the ancient and medieval Greco-Latin world. Yet even Aquinas and his colleagues were acutely aware of the differences between Pagan Athens and Rome and Christian Europe. They were aware, too, of national differences, as the pattern of *nationes* at the University of Paris suggests.

Furthermore, in the twentieth century, leading democratic theoreticians such as Jacques Maritain and Yves Simon (followed in the practical order by Sturzo, de Gasperi, Adenauer, Schumann, Malik, Erhard, and others) brought these medieval concepts into the conceptual networks of democracy, pluralism, and personalism. It would be unhistorical not to observe the transformations such thinkers wrought in the classic notions, which in any case were theoretically open to such development. In their hands, it became clear that human beings are historical animals, whose nature is dynamic, inquiring, and open to the new demands and possibilities of history—including error, conflict, and tragedy. These thinkers wrote, after all, in the maelstrom of the First and Second World Wars. Maritain's work in helping to articulate the Universal Declaration of Human Rights of the United Nations illustrates both the power of the tradition of which he was the most able spokesman and the contemporary fertility and openness of his mind. Here, indeed, on the levels of the human spirit, lay the beginnings of the interdependence now widely celebrated, as it has become more concrete and visible through magnificent inventions in the transport and communications industries and through international trade, commerce, and finance.

Nonetheless, the concept of the common good remains uncommonly vague. For the past twenty years, even Catholic scholars have neglected it. References to it in various indices of periodicals during this period are virtually nil. How one can square the common good with personal liberty and cultural pluralism is most unclear.

In practice today, the common good is most often invoked in the context of economics. It is employed chiefly with reference to the condition of the poor, both within particular societies and in the relation between economically successful and unsuccessful nations. Concern with the creation and the distribution of wealth, and with some relative equality among the members of the human family, leads many to appeal to the common good as a device for inspiring individuals to attend to the condition of the less fortunate. How to produce economic development from the bottom up is itself a complex subject. It is something of a short-cut—increasingly recognized to be both a dangerous and a counterproductive one—to hold that the condition of the poor can better be raised, and thus the common good better served, by entrusting matters to the paternalistic administrations of state authorities.

In the medieval period, the church had not been adequately differentiated from the state; institutions of political democracy and human rights had not yet been established; markets were primitive and other institutions of free and dynamic economic development had not yet been put in place; and the routine of cultural and moral life had not yet been institutionally liberated from censorship and other authoritarian controls. In those days, care for the common good was invested in the authorities of church and state, ideally working in mutually respectful concert, but in practice often in deadly combat with one another. For such reasons, the concept of the common good carried heavy symbolic overtones of paternalism. The concept, moreover, was excessively simple. It was imagined that the common good could be easily known, almost by inspection, and efficiently secured by authoritative administration.

Many of the same symbolic overtones now attach to socialist schemes of the common good. It is helpful here to distinguish between classic authoritarian socialism and contemporary democratic socialism. The tendency of all socialist thought is to deprecate individualism ("bourgeois individualism"), private

interests, private property, and "unbridled" markets. Classic authoritarian socialism supplies as an alternative the authority of government over all aspects of
economic life. By contrast, contemporary democratic socialism is eager to defend both democracy in political life and democratic, decentralized methods in
all spheres of economic life. Classic authoritarian socialism, concerned to check
the error of individualism, tends to trust the wisdom of authorities of the central state. Contemporary democratic socialism resists such trust in centralized
authorities. It wishes to check the error of individualism by mandatory schemes
of democratic cooperation among all participants in economic activities.

Manifestly, classic authoritarian socialism exerts more concentrated discipline than the mere paternalism of the undifferentiated medieval society. But
even contemporary democratic socialism seriously underestimates the chilling
effect of decisions by committee and by worker sovereignty. Democratic methods are time-consuming and inflict underestimated knowledge-costs. Besides,
the dynamics of political decisionmaking bring into economic calculation many
inefficient externalities.

These objections, of course, are pragmatic rather than principled. Based
solely on them, one may allow many experiments to go forward. However, the
record of socialist experiments of many kinds suggests that socialist ideals consistently founder on rude facts of human personality and aspiration. In this
sense, many persons formerly inspired by socialist ideals have come to the conclusion that socialist ideals are, even in principle, based upon false premises. This
objection is principled, but it, too, is not incompatible with patience regarding
continued socialist experimentation. Call this the objection of skepticism.

Just the same, invocations of the common good in the economic sphere
are commonly aimed at "correcting" liberal individualism. J. Philip Wogaman,
in a paper called "The Common Good and Economic Life: A Protestant Perspective," writes for example that the "common good at least means the repu-
diation of any purely individualistic conception of the common life." Historically, this is not quite true. The common good was highly respected in history
long before the individual was, and long before institutions emerged to protect
the liberties of the individual. Indeed after the eighteenth century, societies that
respect individual rights came to be thought more historically advanced than
those that did not. In referring his definition of the common good to the individual, however, Dr. Wogaman suggests an important point. Jacques Maritain
demonstrates in *The Person and the Common Good* that one cannot understand
the classic concept of the common good without understanding the concept of
the person.

As every tree in the world is an individual with its unique location in space
and time, and with a shape all its own, so it is with every member of every
species of plant and animal. To speak of the individual in this sense is to speak
of what can be physically located, observed, seen, and touched. In this context,

the common good would be either the sum of the goods of each individual member or "the greatest good of the greatest number." A purely materialistic conception of the individual is compatible with a high valuation on each individual. But it is also compatible with the view that the whole is greater than any part and ought to take precedence over any part. It is this latter view that George Orwell satirized in *Animal Farm*. In this view, the human being in the social body is like the steer in the herd, the bee in the hive, the ant in the colony—an individual whose good is subordinated to the good of the species.

A person is more than an individual. As the concept of *individual* looks to what is material, so the concept of *person* looks to intellect and will: the capacities of insight and judgment, on the one hand, and of choice and decision, on the other. A person is an individual able to inquire and to choose, and, therefore, both free and responsible. For Aquinas, the person is in this sense made in the image of the Creator and endowed with inalienable responsibilities. The good of such a person, who participates in activities of insight and choice (God's own form of life), is to be united with God, without intermediary, face-to-face, in full light and love. The ultimate common good of persons is to be united with God's understanding and loving, the same activities of insight and choice coursing through and energizing all.

Analogously, on earth and in time, the common good of persons is to live in as close an approximation of unity in insight and love as sinful human beings might attain. Since this requires respect for the inalienable freedom and responsibility of each, and since human beings are imperfect at best and always flawed in character, it is by no means easy at any one historical moment either to ascertain the common good or to attain it. In order to solve both these problems, even approximately, persons need institutions suitable to the task.

But what sorts of institutions are likely to raise the probabilities of their success in identifying and achieving the common good in history? These must be invented and tested by the hazards of history. They are not given in advance. Human beings proceed toward the common good more in darkness than in light.

Two fundamental organizational errors are ruled out, however, by an accurate judgment about the requirements of the human person *qua* person. The specific vitalities of the person spring from capacities for insight and choice (inquiry and love). From these derive principles of liberty and responsibility, in which human dignity is rooted. The human person is *dignus*, worthy of respect, sacred even, because he or she lives from the activities proper to God. To violate these is to denigrate the Almighty. On the one hand, then, it is an error to define individualism without reference to God and without reference to those other persons who share in God's life. A self-enclosed, self-centered individualism rests upon a misapprehension of the capacities of the human person, in whose light each person is judged by God, by other persons, and by conscience itself (whose light is God's activity in the soul). The person is a sign of God in history or (to speak more accurately) participates in God's own most proper activities, insight and choice. The person is *theophanous*: a shining-through of God's life in history, created by God for union with God. This is the impulse in history, guided by Providence and discerned by the authors of the U.S. Declaration of Independence, when they spoke of human persons as "endowed by their Creator with inalienable rights," and strove to invent institutions worthy of human dignity.

On the one hand, then, a self-enclosed individualism falsifies the capacities of the human person. On the other hand, so does any vision of the common good as a mere sum of individual goods (or the greatest good of the greatest number). Even if it were true (in some dreadful utilitarian calculus) that a hundred persons would experience more pleasure from torturing one person than that person would experience pain, such an action would be an abomination. The person is never subordinate to the common good in an instrumental way. Persons are not means but ends, because of the God in Whom they live and Who lives in them. The common good of a society of persons consists in treating each of them as an end, never as a means. To arrange the institutions of human society in such a way that this happens without fail is by no means easy. The human race has so far only approximated the achievement of such institutions. The road not yet traveled is long. Over most of the planet's present surface, including most of the world's peoples, persons are still conceived of as means to the ends of the state. Their personal liberty is not respected. Every form of collectivism, in which each member is treated as a means to the good of the state, violates the dignity of the human person.

SYSTEMS AND INSTITUTIONS DESIGNED FOR THE COMMON GOOD

Since nothing else in history evinces the capacities of the human person for insight and choice, a social order worthy of human persons is not likely to resemble any other order in nature. A merely mechanical or procedural order, for example, is likely to miss the most crucial component of all, human character—that is, the complex of moral and intellectual skills through which each person slowly fashions his or her unique capacity for insight and choice. Even if one lists all the observable descriptions of individuals on file cards, and even if two (or more) individuals by some chance were represented by identical sets of such file cards (however long), still, these descriptions, as Gabriel Marcel pointed out, would fail to predict the differences between such individuals that would emerge as soon as one began working with them in close colleagueship.

In this sense, each person is an *originating* source of insight and choice, irreplaceable, inexhaustible, beyond even an infinite set of descriptions. (Even at the end of a long life together, husband and wife remain elusive and prove inexhaustible one to the other.) A person's character, as one comes to know it, does provide grounds for predicting behavior ("in" character or "out" of it); but a lively sense of inquiry and choice ceaselessly allows persons to grow in character and to be converted in finally unpredictable ways. No one responsible for choosing personnel for specific tasks will doubt how great differences among persons can be, how unpredictable success is, and how misleading *curricula vitae* and references can be. Human persons are alive with possibility, both for good and ill.

How, then, can we imagine a system designed according to the capacities of human persons? The most sustained treatments of this problem, approached in this way, have been advanced by F. A. Hayek in *Law, Legislation and Liberty* and in *The Constitution of Liberty*. Hayek's work has been sorely neglected by Catholic social thinkers. To comment further on it here would overburden this essay, for significant space would have to be assigned merely to exposition. But I would be delinquent if I did not at least mention that the consonance (and disagreements) between Hayek's work and such works of Jacques Maritain as *Man and the State* and *The Person and the Common Good* cry out for systematic attention.

The first point to stress is that the problem of the common good has three sides. (1) How can free persons come to know it? (2) How can it with highest probability (nothing in history being other than contingent and probable) be achieved? (3) Through which complex of institutions may it be pursued with maximal respect for human persons?

Since recent discussions of the common good arise most often in the context of economics, it is proper here to concentrate upon the economic system best suited to achieving the common good of free persons. In a fuller treatment, much more would need to be said about political systems and institutions, and about systems and institutions in the moral and cultural order (churches, universities, associations of writers and others, the media, families, civic groups, and the like). Let us discuss each of the three questions above in order.

(1) *The Veil of Ignorance.* It is not so easy to know the common good of free persons. There are three reasons for this. First, even in trying to determine one's own economic good—in the full context of one's own political, moral, and cultural goals—one often feels confusion and uncertainty. Should one buy this house? Take this position? Accept this contract? All such decisions are made in ignorance of the future. Not all the relevant contingencies can be known, and many that can be known are not certain to fall into place. Choice falls in the realm of uncertainty and practical wisdom, not in the realm of logic and certainty. It follows that it is no easier to know the economic good even of one's best friends and nearest neighbors.

Secondly, each of us is necessarily ignorant about the economic good of those in trades, professions, industries, technologies, and circumstances of which we have no experience.

Third, the economic good of the entire nation—on a high level of abstraction from particular persons or groups—may be easy enough to sketch in a "wish list": low inflation; low unemployment; steady growth; credit available at low cost; a stable currency; gains in productivity; a proportionate improvement of the national environment as compared with environmental damage; the steady advance of the poor out of poverty; care for those unable to care for themselves; and the like (almost *ad infinitum*). Yet the sustained investigation of the trade-offs among these many competing goods has won the historical sobriquet of "the dismal science." One can easily imagine the reasons why this is so. The phrase "the common good" sounds simple and clear. But upon inspection this good turns out to consist of many goods. And these are not only not in natural harmony with one another but often in direct conflict. Moreover, it is not easy to rank these goods in a preferential order. One person's set of preferences is not likely to be the set freely chosen by all others.

It is tempting to cut this Gordian knot by abolishing freedom and imposing a single view of order, according to someone's plan for the common good, in accordance with that person's scheme of social justice. Short of that, each person is free to try to persuade his fellow citizens that some scheme of preference, some vision of the common good in ordered rankings, is superior to others. Even so, however, the veil of ignorance is not ripped away. However beautiful any scheme may appear in theory, it may result in practice in declines in so many of the goods anticipated that the entire scheme falls into disrepute. The appeal of Catholic schemes of the common good would be far higher, for example, if the actual practices of Catholic nations had led to more admirable results. The prestige of socialist schemes has suffered from the deficiencies apparent in actual socialist experiments. And so forth.

The fundamental point, however, is that once one introduces the good of personal liberty among the social goods to be included in the common good, it becomes clear that "the common good" is a concept of a special heuristic kind. Free persons typically have pluralistic visions of the common good. The scheme of one differs from the scheme of another, neighbor's from neighbor's. Free persons conceive of the good in often mutually incompatible ways. Human ignorance is such that it is virtually impossible to settle such disagreements even on the theoretical plane. And even if they could be settled on the plane of theory, it is not certain that any one settled vision would be treated kindly by historical reality.

Therefore, if we were to accept the ideal of the common good as a general ideal, and even if we were to agree upon a particular vision of the common good, we would still be operating in considerable darkness and uncertainty. Whatever the common good is, it is not easy to know.

(2) *Achieving the Common Good.* Those who use the notion of the common good frequently exhort their fellows to "attend to" it, to "intend" it, and to "aim" at it. This conception no doubt goes back to Aristotle, who thought of all things in nature and history as "in motion," tending to an equilibrium that is their natural fulfillment or place of rest. Indeed, he defined "the good," in the

most generic and unspecified sense, as that to which each natural thing aims. He conceived of a human person, for example, as an animal in motion toward self-realization, at whose (always incomplete) achievement such a person would be able to act well in such uniquely human capacities as inquiry, insight, choice, and decision. In their childhood, Aristotle observed, humans are moved to action by pleasure and pain, feeling, emotion, memory, and passion. The impact of these influences never fades, but gradually the fully developing person comes to order them under the gentle (even "democratic") sway of persuasive insight and self-directed choice. Through self-knowledge, one comes to self-mastery and fluid, easy, satisfying possession of all one's powers. Since most humans do not achieve this, one must be patient with them. In the *polis*, Aristotle wrote, one must be satisfied with "a tincture" of virtue.

Yet in Aristotle's Athens, as in the Paris, Rome, and Orvieto in which St. Thomas Aquinas reconceived Aristotle's notions to meet an entirely new context, city-states were only small towns and the many functions and institutions of modern societies had not yet been differentiated. In those ancient and medieval contexts, one person, in effect, could paternalistically "see to" the common good. Often this meant little more than defending the citizenry from hostile attack, improving productive assets such as the supply of water, passing reasonable laws, and caring for the poor. "Golden ages" of prosperity and peace came properly to be celebrated. Yet all this was not incompatible with a fairly rigid set of fixed inequalities, in which resignation to their own lot and station was thought to be a high civic good for the lowly and underprivileged. Compared to the surrounding rudeness of primitive life in the countryside, such small city-states shone out with civilized beauty. Nonetheless, rivalries among the privileged nobles within them were brutal, conspiratorial, and murderous, as one learns from Machiavelli and, considerably later, from Shakespeare. In addition, the *vox populi* was relatively mute, and state and church controlled virtually all channels of commerce, industry, and economic advancement. It was against such *anciens regimes*, Max Weber points out, that the "free cities" and "city republics" of the early modern era began their revolt.

Slowly, an important idea entered human consciousness. One did not need to think of the "common good" as a vision "aimed at" or "intended" or imposed by a singular ruler or set of rulers. One had to think of it also as something *achieved* through the participation of all citizens. On the way toward this achievement, sustained thought proceeded through three realizations. First, the state had been the agent of excessive taxation, torture, censorship, and repression. Second, government to be just must be based upon the consent of the governed. Third, citizens retain inalienable rights, endowed in them by their Creator, upon which the state could not by any means trespass. Made in the image of God, persons capable of insight and choice are worthy *(dignus)* of a sacred respect. In this way, the idea of the limited state, based upon the inviolability of personal rights, slowly emerged in human thought. Thus, as Maritain puts it, the long centuries of Jewish and Christian teaching about the dignity of the human person, working like yeast in the dumb dough of history, sought fruition in institutions worthy of that dignity.

This development posed a radical challenge to notions of the common good. First, the freedom and dignity of human persons (made in the image of God) became a primary criterion for any social order truly ordered to the common good. Second, the advent of personal liberty destroyed the simplicity of the concept of the common good. Now each human being was held responsible for forming his own conception both of his own good and of the common good. Traditionalists feared that such radical pluralism would end in anarchy. This was not necessarily so. It would have been so if the concept of the common good depended upon a unity of moral aims, intentions, and purposes. Instead, the concept of the common good was radically transformed. It no longer meant an aim, intention, or purpose. The common good came to represent, on the one hand, a social achievement and, on the other, a benchmark.

It is one thing to aim at, to intend or to make one's purpose the common good. It is another thing actually to achieve a social order in which free persons have opportunities to pursue their own visions of the good, both personal and communal, both private and public. The liberals of the late eighteenth century set in motion the sorts of institutions that would with high probability realize such an achievement. Because of the veil of ignorance mentioned above, they came to the insight that free persons could not be expected to agree in advance about common intentions, aims, or purposes. A society respectful of the freedom and dignity of persons would have to forebear any direct and conscious effort to produce the common good. Under conditions of pluralism, that citadel could no longer be taken by frontal assault. On the other hand, it could with high probability be taken by an indirect, less paternalistic route. The order proper to subservient humans is one thing. The order proper to free men is another. The former can be an order ordered by an orderer. Formed in the mind of one, it can be made to "inform" the actions of all. The latter must be allowed to emerge from the free rationality of many. Arising from the intelligent decisions of many, from decisions taken in matters closest to their own hands, such an order can achieve a far higher quotient of practical intelligence than was embodied in any prior order.

How can this be so? We have already seen that it is difficult for any one person to be certain even of his own personal economic good. It is in principle impossible for any one person to comprehend all the concrete economic transactions that render the common good alive and vital in every nook and cranny of the economy. It is even impossible for any one person to comprehend all the goods that must be intended by the phrase "the common good" in a modern economy, even on a high level of abstraction. Economists do their best to do so. Yet even they will be the first to insist that they can tell you, from their science, probable gains and losses from particular courses of action, but that they cannot tell you which, of the many goods society might want to pursue, it *ought* to pursue, or how to rank them.

Yet all these testimonies to unavoidable human ignorance do not entail that a human economic order must be devoid of practical intelligence. On the contrary, under certain institutional arrangements and according to a set of rational rules derived from much experience, societies of humans that use such institutions wisely and obey their rules (amending them as experience teaches) can suffuse their own economic order with levels of practical intelligence never before attained. While we must doubt that any human economic order can be fully intelligible, designed as it must be for daily use by imperfect, highly fallible, and sinful persons, nonetheless, existing societies do differ markedly in the quotient of practical intelligence that infuses their daily economic life. For practical intelligence is infused into economic transactions in every corner of society by persons employing their own practical intelligence to the maximum degree possible. Social systems differ in their openness to the practical intelligence of individuals.

Here a brief digression may be clarifying. In a classic passage, Adam Smith pointed out in 1776, in the most revolutionary book ever written (whose full effect upon China, the USSR, and the Third World awaits the twenty-first century), that he had never known persons who said that they intended the common good ever to do very much to advance it. He made plain that he was speaking from observation. Such observation made him doubt the prevailing ideology, in which to seek one's own interest was held to be immoral. To the contrary, he observed—again, as a matter subject to empirical testing—that when persons diligently pursued their own interests, about which they were relatively quite knowledgeable, the sum of such actions cumulatively recorded on a national scale demonstrably raised the common good of the nation.

In this passage, in my opinion, Smith injured a powerful insight by speaking of "interests" rather than of practical intelligence. To block the path of a merely exegetical argument here, I will not assert that Smith *intended* to say "practical intelligence," or even that the logic of his argument in that context requires that he *should* have said it. In another context, one might well make that textual argument. To take a short cut here, however, I will merely assert that the word "interests" is incorrect and should be rejected. One should not make the claim that when each person seeks his own interests, then, as if by an invisible hand, his successfully achieving those interests adds to the common good of all.

On the contrary, the more accurate analysis is that when each citizen acts with the maximal practical intelligence that he can bring to bear upon the economic activities in which he is engaged, he adds to the degree of social intelligence available in his environment. When all other economic activists conduct their affairs with equivalent practical intelligence, then the entire social texture is rendered more luminous by the cumulative effect of all such acts.

There is a further factor at work. Of all forms of human life, economic activities are perhaps the most universal examples of human interdependence.

Almost no one today can live in total self-sufficiency and self-enclosure, like Robinson Crusoe, totally independent of exchange with others. The farmer does not build his own combine or drill for and refine his own gasoline, does not weave his clothes or build his own television set, and does not even grow the tea, coffee, spices, oranges, or other foodstuffs upon which his family relies in his own home. For this reason, virtually every economic good or service passes through physical places of exchange, governed by rules that allow for maximum convenience and minimal expenditures of time; in short, through markets.

I said earlier that the concept of the common good has been translated from the realm of aim, intention, and purpose to the realm of practical achievement. The common good must be achieved; but the best way to achieve it has been discovered to lie not in intending it directly, but rather in establishing institutions and rules that encourage citizens to maximize the practical intelligence with which they infuse their daily tasks. Thus, by an indirect route, citizens of practical intelligence help to build up the social intelligibility of the whole. In this intelligibility lies the common good: an achievement of practical intelligence throughout the whole.

But I said that the concept of the common good also names a benchmark against which the common good as practical achievement is measured. Permit me to elaborate.

It may well be that in the economic sphere the rule-abiding institutions of the market maximize social intelligibility and that their practical fruits in prosperity, progress, and an orderly, cooperative spirit are indisputable. Nonetheless, many other social pathologies and problems may rise into view: the problems of those with little or no income, the disabled, the unemployed, and others who can scarcely enter into markets. The concept of the common good, in this sense, obliges us to lift our heads to confront the social whole again, in order to discern where some citizens may be being excluded, where needs are unmet, where fresh and unforeseen problems are arising.

The modern market system arises from impulses of the Jewish and Christian inheritance of the West, which instructed our forefathers that the dignity of every human being is beyond price. That insight led to the liberation of economic activities from the repression common to traditionalist states and to the vindication of the creative economic energies of free citizens. Analogously, a market system functioning within a Jewish, Christian, and humanist culture will always be subjected—quite properly—to claims of a transcendent sort, obliging citizens to attend to the full dimensions of human life both within and outside the economic sphere. The common good as benchmark reminds us that no contemporary achievement of the common good has yet met the full measure of legitimate expectation. The human race is a pilgrim race. At no point can we ever say, "We have attained sufficient liberty for all," "We have attained sufficient justice for all," etc. The ideals to which we are bound always demand that we do still better.

Therefore, it is not wrong to appeal to the common good as benchmark in order to find the current achievement of the common good still inadequate. The concept of the common good is thus like a pincers. One of its grips focuses our attention upon the concrete achieving, the other upon tasks yet to be met. There is a moral dynamism within us, in our own culture and in our souls, the living legacy of Judaism, Christianity, and the humanism they have nourished. Our hearts are restless until the destiny that draws us is fulfilled. That destiny always measures us and levies fresh demands upon us. We come, thus, to the third question concerning the common good.

(3) *The Institutions That Serve the Common Good.* Once we cease thinking of the common good as a substantive account of what the world ought to look like when all our work is done, and try to think of it as a form of concrete achieving and a benchmark, our minds are led naturally to the institutions through which we can realize this achieving in a concrete, practical, regular, reliable, and routine way. Fresh impulses in human life come usually with passion and emotion; abiding impulses find shape in institutions. "*Politics begins in mysticism,*" Charles Peguy used to say, "*and mysticism always ends in politics.*"

Those who first called themselves liberals—and were called liberals—had in mind three liberations (which helps to explain why the appropriate liberal flag is always *tricolore*). They intended, first, to liberate humans from tyranny and torture; second, to liberate humans from poverty; and, third, to liberate humans from censorship and other oppressions of conscience, intellect, and art. For each of these three liberations, they invented appropriate institutions: *in the political order*, limited and conditional government, institutions of human rights, representative democracy based upon checks and balances, and free political parties; *in the economic order*, the relatively free market, patent laws and copyrights, labor unions, corporations of many sorts, ease of credit and business formation, the stock association, and the business company; *in the moral and cultural order*, religious liberty and the separation of church and state, the free press, rights and practices of free expression, and the independence of universities, the media, and other private associations, from the state.

Each of these institutions was designed to protect the pluralism appropriate to free persons. Each was also designed defensively, not so much to define the common good substantively for all, as to secure for all, against the encroachments of others, the right and the opportunity to pursue the good as each saw fit; and to construct checks and balances against the mighty. The first liberals were well taught, and undoubtedly confirmed through experience, the practical bite of Jewish and Christian teachings about the sinfulness, folly, and unreliability of humankind. They feared utopianism and fanaticism from any quarter. In a sense, they trusted reason, but not the reason of any particular man or party. They wished to assure a hearing for all, and to block a *dictat* from any.

The great liberals were in two important senses not ideologues. First, they trusted experience, observation, and experiment. Second, they were by temperament and choice conservatives, although decidedly not traditionalists. That is, they had great respect for the *tacit* knowing that accompanies experience, habit, tradition, and practical judgment. They were skeptical of "men of ideas" and "the idea class." They did not believe that their grandparents were less wise than they, but they did not fear to carry forward the work their grandfathers bequeathed to them. To their right, they opposed traditionalists, Tories, and the *ancien regime*. To their left, they opposed the socialists, the Diggers, and the Luddites. While they were acutely aware that theirs was a new party, representing a profound revolution in the affairs of humankind, they gladly identified their roots in ancient ways of thought from Aristotle through Aquinas ("the first Whig"). Indeed, most were for a time identified with the Whig tradition; Edmund Burke, Alexis de Tocqueville, Lord Acton and others belonged to this company. To recite some of their names—Montaigne, Montesquieu, and Bastiat in France; Adam Smith, Cobden, and John Stuart Mill in Britain; Madison, Jefferson, Franklin, Hamilton, and Lincoln in the United States—is both to fulfill a duty and to enjoy a privilege. In recent times, their tradition has been extended by F. A. Hayek and Ludwig von Mises; by Raymond Aron and Jean-Francois Revel; by Paul Johnson, Irving Kristol, Robert Nisbet; and by many others.

Because the liberal party is not utopian; because it does not offer a simple picture of paradise on earth; because it is preoccupied with checks and balances to shortsightedness, folly, and vice; because it patiently awaits the outcome of experiments and monitors unintended consequences—for all these reasons, the liberal party forms a view of the world more suited to the middle-aged mind than to the youthful mind. The artistic and the literary intellectuals have sought and found more dramatic materials elsewhere. In ideological combat all this proved for many decades a disadvantage. Today, however, in the closing years of our century, the harvest of forty years of frantic ideological experimentation is coming in. It is a harvest of many bleached bones, lying upon dry fields that echo with the cawing of crows. It is no wonder the liberal party is enjoying an international rebirth. It is always an autumn party, looking to the spring.

Just the same, there are three themes still incomplete in the liberal intellectual inheritance, one in each of the three liberal orders. In the political order, the popular desire for security, as contrasted with the desire for liberty, has proved stronger than anticipated. Throughout the democracies, electorates have been wooed by the promise of governmental subventions, subsidies, and securities. Vigilance, the price of liberty, has not been exercised. The story of the Grand Inquisitor suggests that, ideally, human beings want liberty but, when they have it, grow irked at its responsibilities and insecurities. There are only recently belated signs that the public is beginning to awaken to the costs and dangers of Leviathan.

Yet it is natural enough that families, provident for their future, desire under modern conditions the sort of security that rural living once afforded. It is not mean of them to do so. But the provision of universal security does choke liberty, innovation, and advance. As parents who overprotect their children reap unintended consequences, so some forms of compassion reduce citizens to a dependence upon the state not altogether different from serfdom. The liberal party cannot only speak of liberty. It must distinguish rigorously among the legitimate and the illegitimate desires for security. The liberal state is certain to be to some extent a welfare state. The limits to that extent await defining.

In the economic sphere, the liberal party has thought too little about the dilemmas of the underdeveloped countries. Caught between cold-blooded traditionalist economies and hot socialist ideologies, many educated persons in the Third World hardly know of liberal ideas and institutions, except as these are reflected in Marxist and socialist literature. They do not recognize that the liberal order begins from the bottom up, from universal property ownership, from open entry into markets, from ease in incorporating small businesses, from the extension of credit to the poor, and from the awakening of economic creativity and activism in every sector of the population. Institutional realities that could be taken for granted in early North America and in Europe are novel to those still living in societies whose institutional traditions antedate the modern era.

The liberal party must think through the small steps, the tacit knowing, and the accumulated wisdom by now taken for granted in their own historical achievements. The virtues, habits, attitudes, and aptitudes appropriate to a traditional society are not identical to those needed to make liberal political and economic institutions function as they ought. "Remembering the answers" to questions long ago socially resolved requires sustained, empathetic work. It is easy to forget how much blood and bitter learning went into our own habit-building and institution-building. Still the liberal hypothesis is that liberal institutions express a system of natural liberty, open to all cultures everywhere. The hypothesis is universal in its range. But, as for that other Kingdom, so in this world also, the gate is narrow and the road is strait. Not down every cultural path can free and creative economic development acquire momentum.

In the moral and cultural order, the liberal party in its youth rebelled against a repressive *ancien regime*. Now in its maturity the liberal party faces a far more deadly foe of liberty: relativism, decadence, hedonism, nihilism. In its early phase, the liberal party tended to concentrate upon the illegitimate restraints imposed by authorities from without. In its maturity, it must now concentrate its fire upon an illegitimate *absence* of all restraints from within. The Statue of Liberty, presented to the United States by France a century ago, is a symbol of true liberty: a woman, not a warrior, bearing in one hand the torch of enlightenment against darkness, and carrying in her other hand a tablet of the law. This Lady, unmistakably purposive, disciplined and serious in countenance, is a proper symbol of liberty, as the neon-lit pornography shops in mid-town Manhattan are not. Were moral decadence to become the symbol of liberal societies, liberty were lost. It is not necessary to be Puritan—there is ample room for sensuality and pleasure in the liberal view—to grasp that liberty is primarily an attribute of spirit, of intellect, of light, of reasoned law. Liberty is primarily an *idea*.

That, in the end, explains why liberty must always be rediscovered by every generation afresh, particularly as each in its maturation works its way through the passions and enthusiasms of youth. How a social order can be designed simultaneously to serve the common good and to respect the conscience and intellect of every free person is not an insight given by unaided nature. The institutions that make that achievement possible, and the ideas upon which such institutions rest, must be thought through again by every generation in a fresh environment. For it is by thinking that such ideas perish or survive.

Politics does, in fact, begin in mysticism. And mysticism must, in fact, end in politics. Human beings live in institutions as fish live in the sea. Only through certain institutions can free persons exercise their liberties. To understand and to invigorate these institutions is the best—the only—way to realize a common good worthy of free persons, and to push ever higher the benchmarks of what a free people may together accomplish.

9

THE FUTURE OF CIVIL SOCIETY

ATHEISM V. ATHEISTS

The foundational error of communism—the error that led Leo XIII to predict in 1891 that communism could not and would not work, that it was not only evil but futile—was its atheism. More exactly perhaps, its dialectical materialist atheism. For one can imagine an atheist who is not a materialist but a humanist. Such atheists have a sense of irony and tragedy, and an instinct for community and compassion; and they grasp and defend the rules of right reason.

Still, atheism is a fundamental error about the possibilities open to humankind. Like a guillotine, it cuts off horizons that are in fact open. It foreshortens the human perspective. The religious impulse is as universal and deep in humans as the love for music—even deeper. At the same time, it is possible for humans, even those who love music, not to have an ear for it, not to be able, on their own, to carry a tune accurately. Similarly, it is possible for those who respect religion, and know its power and its rightful place, not to have an ear for it, as Friedrich Hayek confessed in *The Fatal Conceit* that he, alas, did not.

For reasons such as this, it is important for believers not to pass judgment on the state of soul of professed atheists. Some of them may in the depths of their consciences be as faithful to the light of honesty, compassion, and courage as it is given to them to be. With such light as they have, they may be in God's eyes more pleasing in their fidelity than those to whom religious faith is given, but whose actual fidelity is less concrete.

In trying to force humans to believe that they are no more than random and temporary unities of matter, destined for oblivion, communism was obliged to deny far too many daily experiences. All around us, as the sociologist Peter Berger has put it, are "rumors of angels." To be on constant guard against these in-breaking intimations of the infinite requires a fierce discipline—and, in the end, one that is as self-mutilating as that imposed upon youthful Spartan militants of old or, in our own century, on the Nazi extermination units inured to the cruelty commanded of them.

Let me put this in another way. Among many of those confined to the prisons and torture chambers of the twentieth century, who entered prison as atheists or agnostics, there were not a few who decided at a certain moment not under any circumstances to continue cooperating with the lie. Such persons learned through terror the difference between the lie and truth, and no matter the consequences entrusted themselves to truth. In such truth, they found shelter against injustice, cruelty, and brutal power. And many came to believe, in Solzhenitsyn's words, that one word of truth is more powerful than all the arms of the world.

In 1989, that miracle year, so truth proved to be. And in this agonized way many came to the threshold of hope. In the experience of many, no God appeared to them in the darkness. And yet they knew, at last, what it is like to believe in God—to trust in the light, against the lie.

Thus, in trying to cut humans off by force from the transcendent origin of their own knowing and loving, Communism undid itself. Its project was futile from the first. In its very prisons and torture cells, it turned itself inside out. Its official materialism forced into evidence a nonmaterial love for truth, as opposed to the enforced official lies. And this, in turn, awakened silent reflection on the human significance of the indestructible instinct for truth in the human heart, no matter the material consequences. Why would anyone do something so lacking in pragmatism as to remain faithful to that instinct? What does that instinct say about the nature and existence of man? Despite itself, communism awakened wonder.

After establishing beyond the shadow of a doubt that atheism is like a snake's skin, unable to contain the bursting dynamism of the human mind, communism made one other thing clear: that a city organized solely as a state is bound to be tyrannical, airless, suffocating, and doomed to debility. Thus there was awakened at the heart of Europe a spontaneous outcry for the air and oxygen of "the civic forum."

CIVIL SOCIETY

As has been recognized since the time of Adam Ferguson in Scotland (1723–1816), civil society is a larger, more supple social reality than the iron rods and stiff, formal structures designated by the term "state." Civil society is constituted by conversations among free persons, associating themselves in a thousand inventive ways to accomplish their own social purposes, either with or entirely independent of the state. Civil society is the Internet that self-governing citizens construct for themselves over time, sometimes tacitly and unself-consciously, at times with full explicit purpose and deliberate voluntary choice.

But civil society is not an unambiguous term. Under the Austro-Hungarian Empire, for example, it sometimes connoted an informal network of aristocratic and other hereditary powers, who exercised considerable political authority behind the veils of state power. In other words, civil society was a euphemism for informal power parallel to, undergirding, and sometimes actually directing, the exercise of an often weaker state power. Civil society in this sense was a cover for real power. To it and to its hereditary and often tacit laws, the emperor himself frequently bowed.

The Habsburg talent, it has often been said, lay in forging informal consent among the disparate parts of the empire, chiefly through leaders whose authority derived from tradition. These the emperors did not so much command as gently herd toward tacit consensus, for their own mutual self-interest, and in the name of the practical common good of their subjects. That there was good faith and practical wisdom in these arrangements is evidenced by their longevity, and also by the relative loyalty they evoked in their subjects over many generations.

Nonetheless, such a regime was necessarily less meritocratic than suits modern ideas of liberty; less permeable by upward mobility than satisfies subjects longing to become citizens; and less open to the ideals of a new sort of city, the democratic city, which Tocqueville observed Providence bringing about in America. These new democratic ideals, Tocqueville predicted, would later move the souls of Europeans and others around the world. He was at least partly right. From the ashes of the *ancien regime* left by World Wars I and II, a regime more in tune with "the system of natural liberty" has everywhere been struggling to be born. Accurate emphasis falls upon "struggling."

Thus, we must be careful to point out that what we mean by civil society today is not the civil society of the old Habsburg era, the civil society of the *ancien regime,* but a civil society conceived of after the American model. The ideal we seek need not be (should not be) exactly like the American model, but should certainly be closer to it than to the past of the *ancien regime.*

But what is the American model? Many commentators, especially those on the continent but also those Americans infected with continental ideas of a socialist, Rousseauian, collectivist cast, think that what dominates the American imagination is the individual, the lonely cowboy riding carefree on the prairie, the free and unconnected atomic self, the do-as-he-pleases outlaw on the frontier beyond the laws of the city. By contrast, Europeans, a visitor observes, tend to fear the independent individual; they visibly prefer people tied down by a thousand gossamer Gulliver's threads of tradition, custom, and unquestioning willingness to do things as they have always been done.

A specter haunts Europe still—the specter of the free individual questioning the rationality of custom, tradition, and habit; the individual who is communitarian, but not wholly defined by his community.

Nonetheless, despite its reputation, the American character is not the exact opposite of the European character—is not purely individualistic—but communitarian without being intensely communal. The true inner heart of America, as Tocqueville grasped right at the beginning, is the art of association. In

America, fifty years after the ratification of the Constitution of 1787, Tocqueville observed thousands of associations, societies, clubs, organizations, and fraternities invented by a self-governing people unaccustomed to being told by the state (or even by custom) what to do and when to do it. At the time of the revolution in France, he wrote, there were not ten men in all of France who were capable of practicing the art of association as most Americans practiced it.

In the new science of politics, Tocqueville added, the art of association is the first law of democracy. This art does not belong to Americans only. It is rooted in the social nature of man. Its source does not lie in the authority of the state (as in France) or of the aristocracy (as in Britain), but in the capacity of all citizens to originate cooperative activities with their fellows, without being commanded from above. The American is not the individual par excellence, but the practitioner of association par excellence. The American is through and through a social being. Virtually nothing significant gets done in America apart from free associations, of a virtually infinite number of kinds. In this view, the primary agency of the common good is civil society; the state is secondary.

In America, even the churches come to be conceived of as associations, formed out of the decisions of individuals either to associate themselves with historical communities or to form new sects never seen before. In practice, this conception of churches as associations has gained considerable plausibility, even for Catholics and Jews, who did not historically think of their communions in so individualistic a way. After all, when immigrants arrived in America, they could choose whether or not to continue in the faith they brought with them in the habits of their hearts. A great many chose not to. Nonetheless, probably a majority of both Christians and Jews elected to recreate communities of faith in the New World, in continuity with their fellows in Europe.

FOUR CHARACTERISTICS OF CIVIL SOCIETY

The American conception of civil society, meanwhile, may be outlined swiftly in four propositions:

1. Civil society is a larger and deeper concept than state. Civil society is a moral reality conceptually prior to the state. To devolve power from the state to civil society is at the heart of the experiment in self-government. Self-governing citizens try to meet their social needs first through creating their own social organizations, and only as a last resort, when all else fails, through turning to the state. Turning to the state is considered a morally inferior, although sometimes necessary, way of proceeding—a falling away from the project of self-reliance and self-government.

2. The primary social institution of democracy is religion. "The first political institution of democracy," Tocqueville wrote, "is the churches and synagogues." The reason for this is twofold:

First, as Vatican Council II stressed, freedom of conscience is the first of all freedoms; it lies deeper than, and beyond the reach of, political institutions. The inner forum of conscience is beyond the reach of the political power, and morally prior to it. That is the meaning of the two American maxims: "One nation under God" and "In God we trust." Even for atheists, the term "God" in these public maxims is intended as a sentinel protecting the realm of conscience (including the consciences of atheists) from the power of the state.

Second, as the historian of liberty Lord Acton noted, the concept and practice of liberty are in historical fact coincident with the history of Judaism and, even more so, Christianity. The decision of the Council of Jerusalem to baptize the Gentiles, without demanding that they first be circumcised, cut the link between birth as a son of a Jewish mother and faith, therefore invoking liberty of spirit as the primary condition of faith. The ideal of liberty in its full range, from liberty of conscience to liberty of speech, and including civil and political liberties, does not appear in Muslim, Hindu, Buddhist, Confucian, Shinto, or animist cultures.

Thus, to weaken the churches and synagogues is to dilute the source of convictions about personal liberty from which the concept and practice of civil society flow. Here, surely, is one reason why the communists were determined to destroy the churches and synagogues. Judaism and Christianity depend on, and defend like tigers, liberty of conscience.

Another reason why church and synagogue are central institutions of civil society is that they encourage their members to take up their social responsibilities in other civic institutions.

3. The separation of church and state, yes, but also the inseparability of politics and religion. As the twenty-first century approaches, after the experience of communism, one urgent need is as clear as Bohemian crystal: the need for a limited state, under the rule of law, with multiple checks and balances, and also other protections to rein in the power of the state. Among these protections is the disestablishment of the churches. The power of the state should not be enhanced by its identification with religion. Churches need to be free from state power.

Nonetheless, the separation of the coercive power of the state and the spiritual/moral power of the churches, as institutions does not mean that the concrete human being should become schizophrenic. It would be a violation of integrity for a human person to be split between being a political animal on one side and, in a separate compartment, a privatized spiritual/moral animal. The separation of church and state does not entail sealing off, in the minds of individuals, watertight compartments between religion and politics. On the contrary, the deepest motives for loving liberty, respecting the dignity of the person, and feeling identification with the life of the earthly city are religious. Psychologists find that religion is rooted more deeply in the psyche than politics; most people change their religion much more reluctantly than their politics. Religion is a matter of conviction; politics, a matter of practical judgment.

On its many levels of consciousness, the human soul ought not to be divided against itself.

Therefore, public policies that affect both the polity and religion stir the souls of individuals in complex ways. Whether the issue is abortion, euthanasia, sex education, family life, or a host of other difficult questions, the intelligent person is likely to struggle with two different sets of criteria—moral and religious, on the one side, and political or social, on the other side.

It is wise, of course, not to confuse political reasoning with religious reasoning; even in the same person, these two modes are not the same. But the person of integrity cannot abandon either one. There are cases in which practical wisdom demands that one or the other must be given precedence. It is always a mistake, however, to simplify one's decision-making simply by cutting one side of one's mind out of the discussion and ramming through a partially considered decision.

4. Religion has a rightful place in the public square. Religion and politics do not meet only in the privacy of the heart; they also meet—and sometimes clash—in the public square. Here both the Protestant and the secular (libertarian) points of view sometimes fail to do justice to the realities involved. In many cases, it is imagined that religion is a mostly private matter, best confined within the closet of the individual's soul. In this view, the liberal society depends upon a bargain: Religion will be tolerated, even respected, but only so long as it agrees never to enter the public square.

For Jews, Catholics, and others, this type of liberalism is oppressive, for in their understanding religion has a social and public dimension, just as each human being has. True religion does not consist solely in prayers conducted in private, but also in helping the widow, feeding the hungry, caring for the poor—and building up the city of man. Religion requires action in the world. Religion requires vitality, civil argument, and cooperative action in the public square. The individualistic and privatizing understanding of religion, whether of certain Protestants or of some libertarians, is too cramped and narrow. Religion ought not to be established; but neither ought it to be confined in merely private places. Religious persons must be free to express their arguments in the public square, and to take part in public actions. They ought to do so with conspicuous civility, but they ought to do so.

The public square should not be naked or empty. It should ring with civil argument about how a free people ought to order its life together. In that argument, religious people ought to have a voice—in practice, many voices.

THE GREAT REVERSAL

One of the weaknesses in recent church-state relations is the assumption that religion belongs in the closet of privatized sentiment—not of conviction, but only sentiment; not a fruit of the critical mind, but only of the feelings. Actually, in this formulation, two mistakes are intertwined: first, that religion is a merely private internal matter; second, that religion is relativized, has nothing to do with mind or truth, but only expresses a preference or a feeling, without grounding in a judgment about reality.

At the founding of the democratic experiment, toward the end of the Enlightenment, democracy seemed strong and religion weak. Democracy commanded that religion accept certain demands: Religion would be tolerated if it agreed to be individualized, privatized, and relativized. Not only on pragmatic grounds, but for serious reasons of its own (having to do with the dignity of persons and an ideal of charity—caritas—as the form of human community), the Jewish and Christian communities agreed to play by the rules democrats prescribed.

But what has happened? Within two centuries, as the French philosopher Pierre Manent has argued, democracy has been diminished into a contest among special interests and a formalism of correct procedure. Democracy says little or nothing about man. It lacks a vision or even a clear statement of the criteria that any vision of a good society for free women and free men would have to meet. By affirming that it is sovereign over human nature and that it is, little by little, its own creator, with no plan laid down in advance, democratic humanity basically declares that it wills itself, without knowing itself. As Manent has observed, however, religion has conformed itself to all of democracy's demands; democracy can make no complaints against it. But democracy's silence on the question of man's destiny has left the Jewish and Christian religions with a decisive advantage in that they offer such a teaching. In Manent's words, "the relation unleashed by the Enlightenment is today reversed. No one knows what will happen when democracy and the Church become aware of this reversal."

Finding the proper relation between state and civil society, and especially between the state and the church, is still a work in progress. No country seems to have gotten it quite right, just yet. But there is no question, compared with the youthful pride of two hundred years ago, that the arrogance of the democratic state has been curbed. Cynicism regarding politicians grows. The social assistance state and its budgetary resources are in crisis. Public and private morals tumble into decline.

The free society is a noble cause, but it is maintained only through constant vigilance. And such vigilance depends upon a firm idea of the possibilities and duties of humankind, the conditions demanded by natural liberty, and a commitment to distinguishing lies from truth. No one may "possess" the truth, but all must be committed to pursuing evidence wherever it leads; in that sense, all must remain open to truth. Truth is as necessary to liberty as air to fire.

In one of history's sweetest ironies, it is today a pope, Pope John Paul II, who publicly defends reason and the idea of truth in the face of deconstructionists, postmodernists, and other children of the Enlightenment, who are nowadays renouncing both reason and truth and basing themselves on a metaphysic that recognizes only raw interests and disguised power. The pope defends reason, which the enlightened scorn. The pope speaks for truth discernible by reason, while the enlightened deny the possibility of truth, and clothe themselves in the interests of class, race, gender, and power. Speaking for reason and truth, John Paul II writes:

> If there is no transcendent truth, in obedience to which man achieves his full identity, then there is no sure principle for guaranteeing just relations between people. Their self-interest as a class, group or nation would inevitably set them in opposition to one another. If one does not acknowledge transcendent truth, then the force of power takes over, and each person tends to make full use of the means at his disposal in order to impose his own interests or his own opinion, with no regard for the rights of others.

In summary, it appears that Tocqueville was right in saying that without belief in a Creator to Whom everything that is is intelligible, because He understood it before He created it, and everything is graced and good because He loves it, the foundations of democracy are weak and likely to fail. It has not yet dawned on democratic humanists that the ecology of liberty rests upon a certain limited range of understandings both about human nature and about "the system of natural liberty." Without a concept of truth, people cannot reason with each other or converse with each other in the light of evidence. Without a commitment to truth, reason is irrelevant, only power matters. Religions, certainly those that speak of the Creator and Final Judgment, keep alive in consciences standards of truth beyond personal preferences.

10

THE JUDEO-CHRISTIAN FOUNDATION OF HUMAN DIGNITY, PERSONAL LIBERTY, AND THE CONCEPT OF THE PERSON

THE IMPACT OF RELIGION ON ECONOMICS

The great sociologist of economics Max Weber (1864–1920) demonstrated to the scholarly world that religious convictions alter economic systems. Against the Marxists, Weber showed that profound currents, stirring deeply in the human spirit, shake human beings from their bodily torpor in remarkably different ways, with notable effects upon economic systems. Although he is most famous for *The Protestant Ethic and the Spirit of Capitalism* (1904), Weber examined the interplay of religion and economics in many books on the history of various cultures.[1] Because of the abundance of literature available today on "the clash of civilizations"[2] and the real-world consequences of different formations of the human spirit through religion and culture, Max Weber's work may be more influential than ever.

Indeed, Weber's work suggests an important perspective for approaching the topic of human dignity. Empirical research led Weber to the hypothesis that Christianity (in one of its forms) and, behind Christianity, Judaism shaped human expectations in ways favorable to economic development. Stated in this general way, Weber's hypothesis has been solidly confirmed by a century of further research, although modified in important ways by other findings. For example, Professor Randall Collins has shown how, from about A.D. 1100 to 1350, the international system of Catholic monasteries produced several important characteristics of a capitalist economy: an explosion of economically useful inventions, the rule of law, a rationalized system of responsibilities, among others.

> These [Cistercian] monasteries were the most economically effective units that had ever existed in Europe, and perhaps in the world, before that time. The community of monks typically operated a factory. There would be a complex of mills, usually hydraulically powered, for grinding corn as well as for other purposes. In iron-producing regions, they operated forges with water-powered trip-hammers; after 1250 the Cistercians dominated iron

production in central France. Iron was produced for their own use but also for sale. In England, the entire monastic economy was geared toward producing wool for the export market. The Cistercians were the cutting edge of medieval economic growth. They pioneered in machinery because of their continuing concern to find laborsaving devices. Their mills were not only used by the surrounding populace (at a fee) for grinding corn but were widely imitated. The spread of Cistercian monasteries around Europe was probably the catalyst for much other economic development, including imitation of its cutthroat investment practices.[3]

In my own work, on the conceptual rather than the empirical level, I have attempted to demonstrate that the theological category of *imago Dei* (which affirms that every single human is made in the image of God) implies a specific kind of "calling" or "vocation" that Weber oddly neglects, the vocation to be creative, inventive, and intellectually alert in a practical way, in order "to build up the kingdom of God."[4] It is not so much the asceticism of biblical teaching as its call to creativity and inventiveness that accounts for the dynamism of Jewish and Christian civilization, including economic dynamism.

Most economists accept the principle that "ideas have consequences." Nonetheless, it has been a convention ever since the Enlightenment to regard as less than consequential the immense explosion of theological ideas during the era A.D. 1100–1350, an explosion that erupted in the breakthrough mentioned above. This is a serious practical error. Scores of thousands of men and women entered monasteries and launched highly rationalized and disciplined economic ventures. Moreover, at least five concepts crucial to the theme of human dignity and human liberty were brought to light during that period: the concepts of *person, conscience, truth, liberty,* and *dignity.* Although some shadow of each of these terms can be found in the pre-Christian period, no full understanding of any of them existed that would enable a fashioning of a new practical order, a new civilization, the new "city on the hill" that the medieval *civitas* was taught to emulate. It was the work of the medieval schoolmen that can be credited with developing these crucial tools.

In recognition of this achievement, Nobel laureate Friedrich Hayek (1899–1992), following Lord Acton, called one of these monks, Thomas Aquinas (1224–1274), "the First Whig," that is, the founder of the party of liberty in human history.[5] Many commentators have also noted that in *The Divine Comedy,* one of the greatest works of poetry in any language, Alighieri Dante (1265–1321) created both a dramatic rendition of the Thomist vision and a testament to the high importance an entire civilization attached to human liberty. Dante had wholeheartedly accepted the fact that every story in the Bible, Jewish and Christian, gathers its suspense from the free choices that confront every human being. How humans use their liberty determines their destiny; how we use our freedom is the essential human drama. Liberty is the axial point of the universe, the point of its creation. That is the premise of *The Divine Comedy* and the ground of human dignity.

HUMAN DIGNITY

What, after all, is human dignity? The English word *dignity* is rooted in the Latin *dignus*, "worthy of esteem and honor, due a certain respect, of weighty importance." In ordinary discourse, we use *dignity* only in reference to human persons. (But, of course, in the Bible it is also used of other special persons or "spiritual substances," that is, beings capable of insight and choice such as God, angels, and demons.) Both Aristotle and Plato held that most humans are by nature slavish and suitable only to be slaves. Most do not have natures worthy of freedom and proper to free men. The Greeks did not use the term *dignity* for all human beings, only the few. By contrast, Christianity insisted that every single human is loved by the Creator, made in His image, and destined for eternal friendship and communion. Following Judaism, Christianity made human dignity a concept of universal application. "Inasmuch as ye have done it unto one of the least of these my brethren, ye have done it unto me" (Matt. 25:40). Christianity made it a matter of self-condemnation to use another human as a means to an end. Each human being is to be shown the dignity due to God because each is loved by God as a friend. Each has God as "a father."

Obviously, many students of economics are neither Christians nor even believers in God. They, therefore, do not hold such things or look at the world in precisely this way. Nonetheless, as a matter of intellectual history, it is of great utility to discover the origin of concepts. Conventionally, intellectual history has been undertaken from the point of view of the Enlightenment, with a certain insouciant dismissal of what went before (as part of the "darkness," over against which the "enlightenment" is placed in contrast).[6] But this is to gloss over too many deeply buried presuppositions and hidden premises. Today, as the Enlightenment recedes ever further back in history and as its own limitations and failures become clearer, the intellectual arrogance of its early generations has dissipated. Its own inadequacies, too, are under judgment.

In particular, the partisans of the Enlightenment have not weathered well the assaults of nihilists, relativists, and post-modernists, especially in the last two decades. Reason, it sometimes seems, is inadequate for its own defense. In Western universities, those who loathe the Enlightenment as an expression of "white male hegemony"—"phallic," "patriarchal," from the "right side of the brain," and "oppressive"—seem to outnumber, or at least to intimidate, those who remain reason's supporters. Even many supporters of reason today express their commitment to it, not as a self-confident assertion of truth as of yore but as a personal preference; they speak in the language of faith. Partisans of the Enlightenment were successful in pushing aside religious people—which they neatly did by changing the rules to "Religion within the bounds of reason alone." But they have not been successful in meeting the assault on their other flank from those who do not share any faith in reason at all.

It is both fascinating and frightening in our time to watch the high priests of the Enlightenment being unceremoniously disestablished and mocked;

fascinating because so they once treated the earlier establishment; frightening because the twentieth century began with the abandonment of reason (in nazism and socialism) and one does not wish the twenty-first century to repeat the twentieth.

Among the figures of the Enlightenment, Immanuel Kant (1724–1804) is probably the one who most clearly spoke to the concept of human dignity. He did so in the light of a categorical imperative that he discerned in the rational being, and he made famous this formulation of the principle of human dignity: "*Act so that you treat humanity, whether in your own person or in that of another, always as an end and never as a means only.*"[7] This is not, of course, a description of the way in which humans always (or even mostly) treat other human beings. It is, in the Kantian scheme, a prescription, an imperative, a duty. Whereas, in other schemes, it might appear as an aspiration, a good to be pursued, an ideal for which to strive.

Still, it is not difficult, I think, to see in Kant's formulation a repetition in non-biblical language of the essential teaching of Judaism and Christianity: "*Thou shalt love thy neighbor as thyself*" (Lev. 19:18). "*And this commandment have we from him, That he who loveth God love his brother also*" (1 John 4:21). This interpretation of Kant seems correct for two reasons: First, the ancient philosophers of Greece and Rome, before the contact of those regions with Christianity, did not reach this principle. Second, one must note the quiet but strong culture of German pietism in which Kant grew to maturity.

From the point of view of modern history, of course, it seems absurd to say that humans are not means but only ends. In the twentieth century, more than a hundred million persons in Europe alone died by violence, often in a way they could not have foreseen even in their worst nightmares. In our century, history has been a butcher's bench, and the words *human dignity* have often sounded empty.

From the point of view of modern astronomy, too, it seems absurd to imagine the human being as the center of the drama of creation. The earth is far from being the center of the known universe; not even our solar system seems to be at the center, or even to be a major system among the almost innumerable galaxies (such as we see in the Milky Way) already known to us, not to mention many others whose existence we have reason to suspect.[8] To many, it seems likely that there are other forms of rational life—beings capable of insight and choice—in other galaxies, although no such creatures have actually been detected. What seems beyond doubt, however, is that the human race is tiny and seems insignificant and highly perishable in the vastness known to modern physics. As a secular friend of mine puts it, the cockroaches or even simple bacteria may be more important in the scheme of things than we—and outlast us. So where does modern science leave human dignity? Regrettably, I must refrain from discussing here the "Anthropic Principle" advanced by some physicists who hypothesize that from the very first "Big Bang," so many fundamental contingencies had to be in place for humans to have emerged, as we in fact have emerged, that a consistent pattern of improbable happenings in favor of human life is apparent.[9]

LIBERTY AND TRUTH

Jews and Christians explain human dignity by pointing to human liberty. For Christianity and Judaism, human liberty is an absolutely fundamental datum of God's revelation to humanity—or, if you prefer, an absolutely central datum of Jewish and Christian philosophy. It is less central to Islam because key Islamic philosophers of the early Middle Ages, such as Avicenna (980–1037) and Averroes (1126–98), developed concepts from Aristotle in a way that gave God total initiative and power over the human intellect, and thus, over the human will; they pictured the will of Allah as all-mastering. The essence of their theory was that in human understanding it is not the human subject who understands but, rather, the one Agent Intellect in creation, that of the Almighty.[10] This seemed plausible since we often experience as a surprise and a gift an insight that we have for a long time struggled to attain.

In the thirteenth century, many Christian philosophers and even theologians at the university of Paris and elsewhere first encountered Aristotle through these Arab philosophers (many of the original Greek manuscripts had been lost for centuries) and were swayed by the Arab interpretation. Not Thomas Aquinas. He understood immediately that human liberty was at stake. He was also fortunate to have in his hands, through his teacher Albert the Great of Cologne (Albertus Magnus, 1200–80) fresh Latin translations from the original Greek. The fifteen-year struggle of Thomas against the Averroists—who wanted him driven out of Paris—was a decisive event for Christian humanism and for the cause of liberty in the West.[11] It fully earned Thomas the title of "the First Whig," first given him by Lord Acton and later by Hayek.

Because the teaching of the Gospels is intended for Christians in every sort of culture, political system, and time, Christian philosophers are first of all concerned with an understanding of the *interior* act of liberty, only in the second place with liberty as a political and economic act. Confronted with any proposition—of fact, principle, theory, or faith—humans are responsible for the assent or the dissent they give to it. They are responsible for gathering the evidence necessary to make such judgments wisely, for struggling to understand the necessary materials, and for disposing themselves to judge such evidence soberly, calmly, and dispassionately. When they declare a proposition to be true or false, they assert what is true and real. In so doing, they open themselves to counter-argument and challenge from others, in the light of the evidence, over which no one person has total control. In this way, each person is called to be open to the truth of things, to the whole of reality, and each is subject to criticism from those who may be more penetrating, or less one-sided, than they. When human beings reach a judgment, they reveal a great deal about themselves. They are, in effect, under judgment by reality itself, as mediated by the community of inquirers who seek the truth of things.

Thomas Aquinas further noted that in every human act there are two moments. In the first place, human consciousness is open to everything around us—to, as the Harvard philosopher William James (1842–1910) called it, the whole "blooming, buzzing confusion" of present sensory impressions, memory, emotion, passion, imagination, concept, idea, and expectation. Human understanding cannot focus on all of these things at the same time, at least not directly. Thus, the first human liberty is the liberty of human understanding to *focus* (like a searchlight in the dark chaos) on one thing rather than another. Aquinas called this the liberty of *specification*.[12] Then, as the human understanding focuses on the many materials relevant to its consent or its dissent, another liberty becomes apparent: the liberty involved in reaching a determination that sufficient evidence is at hand for reaching a judgment, and the decision not to evade the evidence but, rather, to be faithful to it—to go ahead and make the judgment. This last step is not to be taken for granted. Often, we dread the evidence mounting before us or the consequences of what we are about to decide. At such times, we are tempted to take evasive action. Aquinas calls this second moment of liberty, the liberty of *exercise*. Thus, even within the inner realm of the soul there are already two moments of liberty.

In the prison literature of the twentieth century, there are many witnesses to the inner drama of these two internal acts of liberty—in the prison reflections of Mihailo Mihailov and Nathan Scharansky, for example, but also in many others. Even when all other external liberties are taken away, even in prison and under torture, the human mind and will retain the power to perform these two acts of liberty. Those who, when all else is lost, cling to the ideal of truth-seeking retain their liberty of specification. They retain their liberty of exercise by being determined not to be complicit in lies. "Purity of heart is to will one thing," Soren Kierkegaard (1813–55) wrote. To will to be perfectly faithful to the truth of things is to live by purity of heart and to act as a free man or woman even in the most extreme of circumstances.

To move from this profound concept of internal liberty to a projection of the sort of political, economic, and cultural institutions that make pure human liberty of this sort frequent in human lives is a very long step. It requires many generations of social experimentation. It is not to be imagined that the way to building a city of true liberty is a purely rational, abstract, conceptual achievement. Hayek quite rightly calls this "the fatal conceit."[13] That conceit was the chief engine of the murderous ideologies of the twentieth century.

THE CONCEPT OF CONSCIENCE

In conjunction with his defense of the interior ground of human liberty, Aquinas also formulated, for the first time, the concept of conscience. *Conscience* is not a term of the ancient Greeks or Romans. Neither is it, exactly, a biblical concept, although many texts in the Bible show the inner conflicts that gave rise to the need for such a concept: "*And it came to pass afterward, that David's heart smote him, because he had cut off Saul's skirt*" (1 Sam. 24:5); "*The spirit indeed is willing but the flesh is weak*" (Matt. 26:40); and "*For the good that I would I do not: but the evil which I would not, that I do*" (Rom. 7:19). After Kant, it has become common for modern people to think of the moral life as a matter of duties to be observed—a kind of obedience. But in earlier Christian ages, the moral life was thought of rather as a way to be walked, a set of paths to follow (with the lives of the saints as pathbreakers), an archetype (Christ) to model one's life upon, an image of a life to be lived out: "*Whosoever will come after me, let him deny himself, and take up his cross, and follow me*" (Mark 8:34).

For Thomas Aquinas, the first practical problem of the moral life is to find out what to do in the unique circumstances in which you, a unique, irrepeatable person, now find yourself. The moral life taxes our capacities for practical knowing. Even when we know the model or ideal we are pursuing, the right thing to do now is not always clear. Besides, we sometimes wish to evade clear knowledge, or we prefer to let passion drive us. Afterward, following an act of passion or evasion, we sometimes see clearly what we ought to have done, and feel the bite of remorse. This bite, too, comes from our faculty of practical knowing. Conscience, then, is the habit of practical knowing by which we discern the right thing to do in immediate circumstances, and by which we blame ourselves when we have turned away from this discernment—that is, failed to use the light within us. By frequent failures to use it, and by deliberate abuse of it, we can dim this light and all but extinguish conscience.[14] We can also deceive it, and some of the stratagems by which we deceive our own consciences are so classic that the great Oxford writer C. S. Lewis (1896–1963) set them forth vividly in *The Screwtape Letters*.[15]

THE PERSON

Finally, it is useful to mention that the concept of person also entered Western thought by way of sustained reflection on the Bible. For one thing, a concept was needed to name the special kind of spiritual substance capable of acts of insight and choice, such as the human being is—but not only the human being, but also God and the angels. Physicists speculate these days about whether in other galaxies there is also personal life capable of insight and choice that is not of the human species. In fact, the Bible describes creatures of that sort—many different genera and species of them—and calls them angels and archangels. The idea of many other living species is not unbiblical.

In another context, the concept of person was also needed to express the dual nature of Jesus Christ, who, according to the Bible, has both a human and a divine nature that remains the same. In other words, what is the principle that unites these two natures? This is the historical genesis of the concept of person. Its utility lies in designating what exactly it is in humans that is the ground of their dignity and the source of their free acts of insight and choice. A person is a substance with a capacity for insight and choice and an independent existence as a locus of responsibility. The fifth-century Christian thinker Boethius (c. 480–524) was the first to codify the definition: A person is a *substantia rationalis subsistens*. This concept of the "person" adds a significant new note to the concept of the "individual." A cat or a dog may be utterly individual and even manifest (in an extended sense) a distinctive personality. Still, cats are not held responsible for their acts, never have to choose a vocation, or a career—i.e., do not qualify as persons. Human beings are persons, as other individual animals are not. "The problem with animal rights," a friend of mine once said, "is getting the animals to respect them."

Acquiring this concept of the person was a crucial step for the modern age, for it led directly to the first declaration of human rights in history, when the Spanish missionaries argued that the Indians encountered in the New World were persons of full human dignity, not some inferior species. The missionaries argued that it was sinful before God and contrary to natural law to offend the dignity of the Indians, as many of their compatriots were obviously doing. They pressed their case at the Spanish Court, urging the monarch to rule accordingly.[16] The suit was argued successfully by theologians of Salamanca, the same school of theologians to whom Joseph Schumpeter (1883–1950) and Friedrich Hayek have given credit for many of the pioneering insights into the distinctive features of economic action, as well.[17]

This successful lawsuit helps to explain why outside the United Nations building in New York there stands a statue of one of the greatest of these theologians, the founder of international law, Francesco de Vitoria (1486–1546). The public recognition that oppression of the Indians was sinful, and the public declaration of their rights, alas, did not prevent terrible abuses. This is another indication of the power of the observation by James Madison (1751–1836) in the United States that mere declarations of rights are not enough. Rights are never sufficiently defended by "parchment barriers,"[18] but only by internalized *habits* and *institutions* that incorporate *checks and balances*.

CONCLUSION: THE NEW ECONOMICS

The civilized world is already beginning to celebrate the imminent arrival of the third millennium after the birth of Christ. Since the crucial civilizing ideas of human dignity, liberty, truth, conscience, and person have been slowly developed over the first two millennia after Christ's birth, and since their development was given a powerful impulse by Christ's teaching, it is perhaps not at all unfitting that we should take note of these contributions at this crucial time.

One of the most important contributions of the New Economics is to have focused attention on the primary importance of human capital. The concept of *human capital*, as Nobel Laureate Gary Becker makes clear, includes personal and social habits, as well as the slowly and experimentally developed social practices and institutions that are decisive for economic development.[19] On the role of social trust and others of these social practices, the recent book by Francis Fukuyama and earlier ones by Laurence Harrison are highly instructive.[20]

A second important contribution of the New Economics is to have focused on *human action* and the *human subject*—that is, on the human person and human liberty.[21] A third contribution of the New Economics is to have focused on the central role of *choice*—personal choice and *public choice*—in the dynamics of economic life.[22]

It is my hope that on all of these important contributions of the New Economics the present reflections have shed some historical and conceptual light. Helping to ground the New Economics in an accurate representation of human history and culture, and thus to engraft it into larger movements of culture, is the distinctive contribution I hope this essay furthers.

NOTES

1. Cf., for example, *The Theory of Social and Economic Organization*, trans. A. M. Henderson and T. Parsons (New York: Oxford University Press, 1947); *General Economic History*, trans. F. Knight (New York: Collier-Macmillan, 1961); and his unfinished masterpiece, *Economy and Society*, ed. G. Roth and K. Wittich (New York: Bedminster Press, 1968).

2. See Samuel P. Huntington's controversial book, *The Clash of Civilizations and the Remaking of World Order* (New York: Simon & Schuster, 1996) and the lively polemic touched off by Pierre Hassner's review "Morally Objectionable, Politically Dangerous" in *The National Interest* 46 (Winter 1996/97): 63–69, with Huntington's response, "Hassner's Bad Bad Review," 97–102.

3. Randall Collins, *Weberian Sociological Theory* (Cambridge: Cambridge University Press, 1986), 52–58. Collins also singles out the Cistercians for other economic innovations:

> The Cistercians were innovative in numerous respects. They were the first highly centralized organization, following a deliberate plan of expansion throughout Europe. They also established a new form of hierarchy within their organization, a division between the fully ordained monks and a second class of monastic laborers. The latter took oaths of celibacy, poverty, and obedience, but remained illiterate and were ineligible for advance to full monastic rank. The Cistercians were thus divided into a managerial class and a class of manual laborers, both working under religious incentives and subject to a strong asceticism.

Collins, discussing the Catholic Church's role in promoting the rule of law, continues:

> If we concentrate on the Church, however, as the "real" government of medieval Europe, the citizenship elements are much wider. For the organization of the Church itself was permeated by the rights and duties of legal citizenship *in that body itself.* To be sure, these citizenship rights were not uniform throughout its ranks. But almost everywhere there was some degree of participatory rule under law. The Pope himself was chosen by election, initially by the people and clergy of Rome, later by a restricted body of cardinals. Similarly, each monastic order elected its own general, or head, and many instituted safeguards in the form of a council of overseers who watched against abuse and had the power to turn him out of office. At a lower level, cathedral chapters elected their own bishops and monasteries their abbots. There was also a strong conciliar tradition within the body of the Church as a whole, which may have been manipulated by strong autocratic Popes but, nevertheless, represented the tradition of collective responsibility for legislation. Powers of election and appointment shifted over time, with lay people becoming excluded and the powers of the Pope increasing. (50)

The Church also played a part in securing a crucial institutional precondition for the mass market: "security from robbers and military predators."

The Church held the doctrine that it was a sin to kill a fellow Christian in secular battle, and attempted to confine military action to Crusades against foreign enemies and domestic heretics. This ban was not very effective, and sins of violence were usually commuted upon payment of penances. But in the 1000s and 1100s, just as the medieval economy was beginning to develop, there was a widespread movement to establish peace. Certain days of the week and times of the year were declared "God's Truce" in the wars among the nobility. More significantly, bishops took the initiative in organizing "peace associations," whose members swore to abjure private violence and also acted to put down robber barons and brigands. Monks and especially wandering friars took the initiative in ending local vendettas. These efforts were only partially successful, and there is no doubt that the volume of trade was kept down by the unsafe conditions that prevailed. But the peace associations and the friars did pave the way in settling the atmosphere of violence, and their gains were consolidated for a while in the 1200s by the strengthening of major secular states. (56)

4. Michael Novak, *The Catholic Ethic and the Spirit of Capitalism* (New York: The Free Press, 1993), 1–14, 222–37; *Business As a Calling* (New York: The Free Press, 1996), 18–40, 117–59; and *The Spirit of Democratic Capitalism* (Lanham, Md.: Madison Books, 1991), 36–48.

5. Friedrich A. Hayek, *The Constitution of Liberty* (Chicago: University of Chicago Press, 1978), 457, n. 4. Hayek notes: "In some respects Lord Acton was not being altogether paradoxical when he described Thomas Aquinas as the First Whig." Acton defined the Whigs as "defenders of liberty who defended it for the sake of religion," *Selected Writings of Lord Acton*, vol. III, ed. J. Rufus Fears (Indianapolis: LibertyClassics, 1988), 536; Aquinas, he observed, provided "the earliest exposition of the Whig theory of the revolution," *Selected Writings of Lord Acton*, vol. I, ed. J. Rufus Fears (Indianapolis: LibertyClassics, 1985), 34.

6. The sociologist Robert A. Nisbet noted that:

When we come to the Enlightenment, especially in France, it is fair to say that amid all the diversities of opinion and value in that complex age, there was one conviction on which all the *philosophes* found unanimity: disdain for revealed or institutionalized religion of any kind. . . .

There were, to be sure, differences among the *philosophes*, but they were united by the conviction that revealed religion is a collection of superstitions supportable only so long as man remains ignorant of the truths vouchsafed by modern science and philosophy. The *philosophes* did not see religion as a force proceeding from the very nature of the soul or, for that matter, from the nature of society. They saw religion solely as a set of intellectual propositions on the universe and on man; and since these were manifestly false propositions, their eventual liquidation could be confidently prophesied (and helped along!) through the propagation of faith in reason.

The Sociological Tradition (New York: Basic Books, 1966), 222–33.

7. Immanuel Kant, *Foundations of the Metaphysics of Morals*, trans. L. W. Beck (New York: Library of Liberal Arts, 1959), 428–29. For Kant, "man, and, in general, every rational being, exists as an end in himself."

8. As the physicist Paul Davies underscores:

If we *are* alone in the universe, if the earth is the only life-bearing planet among countless trillions, then the choice is stark. Either we are the product of a unique supernatural event in a universe of profligate over-provision, or else an accident of mind-numbing improbability and irrelevance.

"Physics and the Mind of God: The Templeton Prize Address," *First Things* (August/September 1995): 35.

9. On the "Anthropic Principle," which holds that "it's only a very special universe, a universe in a trillion, you might say, which is capable of having had the amazing fruitful history that has turned a ball of energy into a world containing human life," see John Polkinghorne, "So Finely Tuned a Universe: Of Atoms, Stars, Quanta, and God," *Commonweal*, August 16, 1996, 14.

10. For selections, see Ralph Lerner and Mushin Mahdi, *Medieval Philosophy: A Sourcebook* (New York: Cornell University Press, 1972).

11. An accessible treatment of this struggle can be found in G. K. Chesterton, *St. Thomas Aquinas: The Dumb Ox* (New York: Image Books, 1956), 66–96. For a more recent treatment, see Ralph McInerney, *Aquinas Against the Averroists: On There Being Only One Intellect* (Purdue: Purdue University Press, 1993).

12. On the distinction between specification and exercise, see Saint Thomas Aquinas, *Summa Theologiae* (London: Eyre & Spottiswoode, 1963), Ia2ae, Q.24, a.6.

13. See *The Fatal Conceit: The Errors of Socialism*, ed. W. W. Bartley III (Chicago: University of Chicago Press, 1988), 21, 27, 49, 75, 83. Hayek defines the fatal conceit tersely as "the idea that the ability to acquire skills stems from reason." In fact, Hayek argues, "it is the other way around: our reason is as much the result of an evolutionary

selection process as is our morality," 21. Hayek is seeking to undermine what he calls the "constructivist fallacy":

> The errors of constructivist rationalism are closely connected with Cartesian dualism, that is, with the conception of an independently existing mind substance which stands outside the cosmos of nature and which enabled man, endowed with such a mind from the beginning, to design the institutions of society and culture among which he lives.

Law, Legislation and Liberty, vol. I (Chicago: University of Chicago Press, 1973), 17.

14. On the Christian understanding of conscience, see Eric d'Arcy, *Conscience and Its Right to Freedom* (New York: Sheed & Ward, 1961). Brian Davies describes Aquinas' teaching on conscience:

> First, he says, we start with principles grasped by virtue of *synderesis*. Then we add judgments about what sort of actions we are thinking about on any given occasion. We might, for example, judge that such and such an act is a case of theft. Finally, we draw a conclusion concerning the goodness or badness of the act in question. This drawing of the conclusion is what Aquinas means by "conscience" *(conscientia)*. For him, therefore, conscience consists of applying general principles to the case in hand and with recognition of what kind of action we are dealing with. The work of conscience is to use principles grasped by *synderesis* to determine what is to be done, or whether what we have done is right or wrong.

The Thought of Thomas Aquinas (Oxford: Clarendon Press, 1992), 235. For Aquinas, conscience could even tell us to deny Christ, yet still must be respected:

> Not only may what is neutral take on the character of good or bad, but good can take on the character of evil, and evil the character of good, and all this because of the way an object is apprehended by the mind. Take an example: to avoid fornicating is good, yet the will is not set on this course save insofar as it is recommended by reason as good. If a mistaken reason presents it as bad, then the will pursues it as wearing the aspect of evil. The act of will, then, will be bad, since it is willing evil, not indeed what is evil in itself, but what is evil by another factor, namely, the reason casting it in that part. Take a similar example: to believe in Christ is good in itself and necessary for salvation; all the same, this does not win the will unless it be recommended by reason. If the reason presents it as bad, then the will reaches to it in that light, not that it really is bad in itself, but because it appears so because of a condition that happens to be attached by the reason apprehending it. That is why Aristotle speaks of a man being directly incontinent when he abandons right reason and being indirectly incontinent when he abandons reason even when it is wrong-headed.

Summa Theologiae, 1a2ae, Q. 19, a.5.

15. New York: Barbour & Co., 1985.

16. Arguing vigorously to the Spanish Court for the humane treatment of non-Europeans faced with forced conversion, the Spanish missionary Bartolomé de las Casas (1474–1566) wrote:

What love, affection, esteem, reverence, would they have, could they have, for the faith, for Christian religion, so as to convert to it, those who wept as they did, who grieved, who raised their eyes, their hands to heaven, who saw themselves, against the law of nature, against all human reason, stripped of their liberty, of their wives and children, of their homeland, of their peace?

"Human Dignity before Hobbes and Locke: A Condemnation of Abuses against Natural Law," *Crisis* (May 1994): 38. This text was drawn from Bartolomé de las Casas, *The Only Way*, ed. H. R. Parish, trans. F. P. Sullivan, S.J. (New York: Paulist Press, 1992), 208.

17. See Joseph Schumpeter, *History of Economic Analysis*, ed. E. B. Schumpeter (New York: Oxford University Press, 1954), where the author notes: "The very high level of Spanish sixteenth century economics was due chiefly to the scholastic contributions," 165; Hayek, in turn, observes that the tradition of "liberty under the law"

by the end of the sixteenth century . . . had been developed by some of the Spanish Jesuit philosophers into a system of essentially liberal policy, especially in the economic field, where they anticipated much that was revived only by the Scottish philosophers of the eighteenth century.

New Studies in Philosophy, Economics and the History of Ideas (Chicago: University of Chicago Press, 1978), 123. See also Douglas A. Irwin, *Against the Tide: An Intellectual History of Free Trade* (Princeton: Princeton University Press, 1996), 21–25, and Alejandro A. Chafuen, *Christians for Freedom: Late Scholastic Economics* (San Francisco: Ignatius Press, 1986).

18. Evoking the need to respond with institutional protections to the "encroaching nature" of power, which, if unchecked, tends to concentrate into an "overruling influence," Madison writes in *Federalist* #48:

Will it be sufficient to mark, with precision, the boundaries of these departments in the constitution of the government, and to trust these parchment barriers against the encroaching spirit of power?

James Madison, Alexander Hamilton, and John Jay, *The Federalist Papers*, ed. I. Kramnick (New York: Penguin Books, 1987), 309.

19. For Becker, consult *Human Capital* (Chicago: University of Chicago Press, 1993). There he offers this definition:

I am going to talk about a different kind of capital. Schooling, a computer training course, expenditures on medical care, and lectures on the virtues of punctuality and honesty are capital, too, in the sense that they improve health, raise earnings, or add to a person's appreciation of literature over much of his or her lifetime. Consequently, it is fully in keeping with the capital concept as traditionally defined to say that expenditures on education, training, medical care, etc., are investments in capital. However, these produce human, not physical or financial, capital because you cannot separate a person from his or her knowledge, skills, health, or values the way it is possible to move financial and physical assets while the owner stays put.

In his 1992 Nobel lecture, Becker picked up the theme again:

> Human capital analysis starts with the assumption that individuals decide on their education, training, medical care, and other additions to knowledge and health by weighing the benefits and the costs. Benefits include cultural and other nonmonetary gains along with improvement in earnings and occupations, whereas costs usually depend mainly on the foregone value of the time spent on these investments. The concept of human capital also covers accumulated work and other habits, even including harmful addictions such as smoking and drug use. Human capital in the form of good work habits or addictions to heavy drinking has major positive or negative effects on productivity in both market and nonmarket sectors.

"Nobel Lecture: The Economic Way of Looking at Behavior," in *The Essence of Becker*, ed. R. Febrero and P. S. Schwartz (Stanford: Hoover Press, 1995), 640.

20. See Francis Fukuyama, *Trust: The Social Virtues and the Creation of Prosperity* (New York: The Free Press, 1995), as well as Lawrence E. Harrison, *Who Prospers: How Cultural Values Shape Economic and Political Success* (New York: Basic Books, 1992), and *Underdevelopment Is a State of Mind: The Latin American Case* (Lanham, Md.: University Press of America, 1985).

21. See the great work of Ludwig von Mises, *Human Action: A Treatise on Economics* (New Haven: Yale University Press, 1949).

22. On public choice, a representative work is James M. Buchanan, *Cost and Choice: An Inquiry in Economic Theory* (Chicago: Markham Publishing, 1969). Michael Beaud and Gilles Dostaler define public choice in a recent survey of economic thought:

> As the theory of human capital had done for the choices of the individual in his private life, the theory of public choice uses microeconomic tools to study the behaviour of individuals in administration and in political life, as citizens and decision makers, and to analyse public finances and public economics. As in the goods market, agents (who may be interest groups) for example, meet in a political market, each trying to maximize their private interests, here with governmental means.

Economic Thought Since Keynes: A History and Dictionary of Major Economists (Aldershot, England: Edward Elgar Publishing, Ltd., 1995), 121.

11

HAYEK: PRACTITIONER
OF SOCIAL JUSTICE

"Social Justice Properly Understood"

INTRODUCTION

It may seem odd to open this celebration of the great achievement of Friedrich Hayek by mentioning two insights that he fell just short of making explicit, even though he made great contributions by exercising them in practice.

First, Hayek never quite announced that the free society has a three-sided shape, since it institutionalizes at once three different kinds of liberty: economic, political, and spiritual (moral, cultural).[1] For most of his life, Hayek seemed content to be known as an economist, and the Nobel Prize was awarded him for his originality in economics. However, at crucial points the principles in whose light Hayek proceeded included extra-economic principles; for instance, principles of law and representation, on the one side, and on the other, principles of morality, truth, and justice. Thus, although he is most widely known for his originality in discovering the theory of the free economy, some of his most important work regards the *constitution* of liberty, and matters of *law* and *legislation*.[2] Beyond that, having fought manfully in the war of ideas across most of the breadth of the human spirit, in history, philosophy, religion and social thought, Hayek was a fierce warrior in the third, quite different, realm of cultural liberty.

In brief, without having raised to the theoretical level the observation that there *are* three realms, as Daniel Bell has, and that each of these is organized around a very different *intellectual principle,* Hayek was in all three an accomplished practitioner. It was this three-sided skill, perhaps, that led the Committee on Social Thought to recognize in Hayek a special genius, when others did not.

The situation is much the same with regard to *social justice.* Hayek is famous for his sustained and animated put-down of most of the usages of that term to be found in public speech during the middle of the twentieth century. He ripped the concept as it is usually deployed to tatters.[3] Indeed, he stressed its fundamental contradiction: Most authors use the term, they assert, to designate a *virtue* (a moral virtue, by their account). But, then, most of the

119

descriptions they attach to it appertain to impersonal states of affairs; "High unemployment," they say, for instance, or "inequality of incomes" or "lack of a living wage," is a "social injustice." They expect the economic system to attain every utopian goal, as though all such goals are easily within reach and mutually compatible. They imagine that all social systems are under the command of identifiable persons, or should be, and they intend to find those persons and hold them responsible for outcomes of which they do not approve. Their main concern is to indict an entire *system* and its central institutions.[4] For decades they seemed to hold that socialism was a superior economic system, toward which "history" was moving. Their diagnosis, methods and remedies belong to specific intellectual traditions, socialist, social democratic, or Catholic.[5] They seem not to analyze the failures of the systems they prefer.

Hayek's critique lays out a multitude of objections to prevailing modes of thought. But his main thrust goes to the heart of the matter: Social justice is either a virtue or it is not. If it is, it can properly be ascribed only to the reflective and deliberate acts of individual persons. But most of those who use the term do not ascribe it to individuals but to states of affairs, as when they assert that this or that state of affairs—unemployment, low wages, deplorable working conditions—is "socially unjust." It is usually the "impersonality" of these that they decry, not the calm and discrete choices of individuals. They seldom attempt to change minds and hearts, one by one. Instead, they use political muscle to change the laws and to coerce massive compliance. In this respect, they are using the term "social justice" for a regulative principle of order, not a virtue, and by their own lights this is an illegitimate use. They are not appealing to "virtue" but to coercion. In addition, they are not overly scrupulous about the personal habits (virtues) of those who deploy political muscle, or the graft and corruption inherent in all uses of political power. In brief, their focus is not virtue. It is power. "Social justice" is a term used to incite political action for the sake of gaining political power.

> What I hope to have made clear is that the phrase "social justice" is not, as most people probably feel, an innocent expression of good will towards the less fortunate, but it has become a dishonest insinuation that one ought to agree to a demand of some special interest which can give no real reason for it. If political discussion is to become honest it is necessary that people should recognize that the term is intellectually disreputable, the mark of demagogy or cheap journalism which responsible thinkers ought to be ashamed to use because, once the vacuity is recognized, its use is dishonest.[6]

Social justice! How many sufferings have been heaped on the world's poor under that banner! How malevolently it rolled off the presses of Lenin, Stalin, Mussolini, and Hitler. It is no wonder Hayek loathed it so.

Hayek alludes to a second defect of twentieth-century theories of social justice. Whole books and treatises have been written about social justice without ever offering a definition thereof.[7] The term is allowed to float in the air as if everyone will recognize an instance when he sees it. This vagueness seems both studied and indispensable. For the minute one begins to define social justice—as a virtue, for instance, related to the classical Aristotelian virtue of justice—one runs into embarrassing intellectual difficulties. For most of those who use the term do not intend to raise the worldwide quotient of virtue. They employ "social justice" as a term of art (whose operational meaning is "We need a law against that"). They employ it, that is, as an instrument of ideological intimidation, for the purpose of gaining the power of legal coercion.

I have never yet encountered a writer on social justice, religious or philosophical, who directly confronts the criticisms of Hayek.[8] I know of only one theoretical statement, as we shall see, that comes through the gales of his withering analysis intact.

HAYEK AS PRACTITIONER OF SOCIAL JUSTICE

All this being said, the thesis I wish to propose on this happy anniversary of Hayek's birth is that, astonishing as it may seem, Hayek was in his own life a marvelous practitioner of the virtue whose theory he never found adequately articulated.

For there is a use of the term *social justice* that does name a new virtue needed by the new type of society of the last two hundred years, the free society.[9] Friedrich Hayek's own virtuous practices throughout his lifetime provide a perfect illustration of it. But so, too, do the virtuous practices of some persons whose political and economic views Hayek would certainly have argued against. To the extent that the competition of ideas is essential to the free society, the practice of social justice in the free society ought to be ideologically open to those of divergent points of view. Indeed, its relative indeterminacy is what makes the term *social justice* indispensable to the free society in all three of its spheres: political, economic, and spiritual liberty. We need to ask, happily echoing Tocqueville's question about "individualism rightly understood," What then is social justice rightly understood?[10]

Before continuing, we must note two ironies in what we are undertaking. First, Hayek's demolition of false understandings of social justice was necessary before a better concept could come to light, a concept he himself lived out in practice before it could be thematized. (Hayek would have enjoyed this primacy of practice to theory.)

Second, Hayek's love of theory qua theory more than once led him to make bold claims which seemed at the time wildly at variance with observable phenomena, and for which he was often mocked and made fun of. Let me mention but two: first, that socialism was epistemically blind and, therefore, could not possibly produce rational outcomes on a consistent basis, and must eventually falter on its own ignorance.[11] (For how could state bureaucrats, obliged each day to make up thousands of prices, possibly know how badly multitudes of individuals might want *x* or *y*, or how much sweat and effort they would be willing to expend to purchase it?) Again, Hayek argued that the power and permanence of the nation state in the twentieth century were greatly overestimated, and that (for instance) the state's power to control money would eventually slip out of its grasp. Hayek predicted, when it seemed farfetched, that at some future time private entities in an open market, not governments, would become more reliable guardians of the value of currencies, and that the monopoly power of governments over money would in this way be broken. Today's internet markets seem to be confirming his point, for through them today's profligate governments are being disciplined by freely acting international entities.

Hayek made many predictions, based upon purely theoretical findings, that were later vindicated. I believe, therefore, that he himself would have enjoyed the claim that on a clearer theory of social justice than any he had found in the literature, he himself might be said to have been a practitioner of social justice. That claim will only stand, however if we first seize the root of Hayek's objections to the most common construals of social justice.

SOCIAL JUSTICE WRONGLY UNDERSTOOD

Hayek began by noting an anthropomorphic tendency in human thought—an itch to understand all processes, however different in kind, in terms of human agency.[12] Consider the human animation and psychology given in all ages to animal life, from Aesop's Fables to the Grimms' Fairytales to Mickey Mouse and Bugs Bunny, the Three Little Pigs and the Big Bad Wolf. Consider, too, the tendency of humans to understand the general rules by which societies are run in the light of individual psychology and individual ethics. Even today many project onto the politics and economics of modern complex societies the same expectations as their ancestors who lived in simple tribes; they personify all outcomes, as if some all-powerful individual *chose* them, or could have altered them at will. Initially, Hayek hypothesizes, the term "social justice" was invented to make sense of the complex networks of causation in modern societies.[13]

The term "social justice" was first used in 1840 by a Sicilian priest, Luigi Taparelli d'Azeglio, and given prominence by Antonio Rosmini-Serbati in *La Costitutione Secondo la Giustizia Sociale* in 1848.[14] John Stuart Mill gave this anthropomorphic approach to social questions almost canonical status for modern thinkers in 1861 in *Utilitarianism:*

> Society should treat all equally well who have *deserved* equally well of it, that is, who have deserved equally well absolutely. This is the highest abstract standard of social and distributive justice; towards which *all institutions,* and the efforts of all virtuous citizens, *should be made in the utmost degree to converge.*[15]
> [emphasis added]

At the head of his chapter on social justice, Hayek sets quotations from Immanuel Kant and David Hume who had been much shrewder on the relation between "desert" and reward than Mill. Both saw that "merit" cannot be defined by general rules. Hume's is particularly sharp:

> So great is the uncertainty of merit, both from its natural obscurity, and from the self-conceit of each individual, that no determinate rule of conduct could ever follow from it.[16]

In other words, what Mill construes as a heavy moral obligation ("should be made in the utmost degree to converge") Hume construes as an irrational pretension. Mill makes "merit" and "desert" sound clear and easy; Hume sees them as highly individual, obscure, and subject to self-centered bias. Mill makes "reason" seem luminous, dispassionate, objective; Hume sees reason as distorted and darkened by passion, ignorance, and bias.

Religious thinkers will here be reminded of Reinhold Niebuhr's sketch of significant differences between the ethics of individuals and the ethics of group behaviors in *Moral Man and Immoral Society*.[17] Niebuhr, of course, was criticizing an individualistic approach to social behaviors, whereas Hume a social approach to individual merit. Both, however, thought certain conceits about reason could be fatal. And so, of course, did Hayek, whose last book was called *The Fatal Conceit*.[18]

Hayek argued that justice is the indispensable foundation and limitation of all law. (He had no difficulty speaking of legal discrimination, segregation, or *apartheid* and the like as "unjust," and in that sense he might employ the term "an unjust society.") But he argued, in the same vein, that the reigning conception of social justice—in part codified by Mill—is an abuse of the term justice, and is rooted in a naive anthropomorphic tendency. The abuse consists in taking the term justice out of the realm in which it properly applies to the acts and habits of individuals, and using it, illicity, to name an abstract standard of *distribution* which authorities ought to enforce—as when Mill speaks of "the highest abstract standards of social justice, towards which the efforts of all institutions, and the efforts of all virtuous citizens, should be made in the utmost degree to converge." Mill here imagines that societies could be virtuous in the way individuals can be. Perhaps in highly personalized societies of the ancient type—under kings, tyrants, or tribal chiefs—such a usage might make sense; in such societies, one person made all crucial social decisions. Curiously, however, the demand for the term "social justice" did not arise in earlier societies, in which it might have seemed appropriate, but only in modern times, when more complex societies operate by impersonal rules applied with equal force to all under "the rule of law."

In ancient societies, however, even kings often made appeal to "reasons of state" to justify behaviors that by the rules of individual ethics would be blameworthy. This is the point Niebuhr had in mind in contrasting the possibilities of "moral man" with the impossibility of "moral society." The term "moral" doesn't quite apply to group behavior. It is a term intended for, and best used for, individuals. Applied to individuals and groups, the term is equivocal.

How, then, shall we judge "impersonal mechanisms" and "market forces" that leave some individuals and groups in situations that evoke pity and a sense of moral outrage? We protest against the "injustices" of nature. Do not storms, plagues, wars, and natural calamities of all sorts sometimes punish the just and unjust equally, often unfairly and even unaccountably? From biblical times, such arguments have been advanced against God Himself by Job, the Psalmist, and others who saw the just suffer and the unjust prosper. Does God Himself lack respect for social justice? Such is our reaction to the ordinary course of nature. It seems only "natural" to extend these feelings to the disappointments and unfair fates we see in the social order. There is a great need in the human breast, Hayek notes, to hold someone accountable, even when in another part of ourselves we recognize that such a protest is absurd:

> Yet we do cry out against injustice when a succession of calamities befalls one family while another steadily prospers, when a meritorious effort is frustrated by some unforeseeable accident, and particularly if of many people whose efforts seem equally great, some succeed brilliantly while others utterly fail. It is certainly tragic to see the failure of the most meritorious efforts of parents to bring up their children, of young men to build a career, or of an explorer or scientist pursuing a brilliant idea. And we will protest against such a fate although we do not know anyone who is to blame for it, or any way in which such disappointments can be prevented.[19]

The birth of the concept of social justice 150 years ago coincided with two other shifts in human consciousness: the "death" of God and the rise of the ideal of the command economy. "Man," Aristotle wrote, "is political by nature." When God "died," men began to trust a conceit of reason and its inflated ambition to do what God had not deigned to do: construct a just social order. The divinization of reason met its mate in the ideal of the command economy; reason (that is, science) would command and humankind would collectively follow. The death of God, the rise of science, and the command economy yielded "scientific socialism." Where reason would rule, the intellectuals would rule (or so some thought); actually, the lovers of power would rule.

From this line of reasoning it follows that "social justice" is given an adequate meaning only in a directed or "command" economy (such as an army) in which the individuals are ordered what to do, so that under "social justice" it will always be possible to identify those in charge and to hold them responsible.[20] For the notion presupposes that someone is accountable, and that people are guided by specific external directions, and not by internalized personal rules of just conduct. The notion further implies that no individual should be held responsible for his relative position. To assert that he *is* responsible would be "blaming the victim" and denying the relevance of considerations of "social justice." For it is precisely the function of "social justice" to blame somebody else, to blame *the system,* to blame those who (mythically) "control" it.

Some who think in terms of social justice seem unable to imagine a non-controlled society, based on spontaneous behaviors, observing universal rules internalized by individuals and flowering in self-government. Society as they imagine it is always under command. If it is not under their command, they see it as under the command of powerful others, who by definition are foes of the party of social justice; hence, oppressors. As Leczek Kolakowski writes in his magisterial history of Communism after many years of faithful service to that party, the fundamental paradigm of Communist ideology is guaranteed to have wide appeal: *You suffer; your suffering is caused by powerful others; these oppressors must be destroyed.*[21]

We are not wrong in perceiving, Hayek concedes, that the effects of the individual choices and open processes of a free society on the fates of individuals are not distributed according to some recognizable principle of justice. The meritorious are sometimes tragically unlucky; the hardworking fail; good ideas don't pan out, and sometimes those who backed them, however noble their vision and their willingness to take risks, lose their shirts; some evil persons prosper; some of the just languish far below their goals; some receive much greater rewards than others for equal or less effort. The free society may run on fairer rules and with more equal chances than any other regime known to the human race, but it does not and cannot guarantee outcomes.

Further, no one individual (no politburo or congressional committee or political party) has any possibility of designing rules that would or could treat each person according to that person's merit, desert, or even need. No one has sufficient knowledge of all relevant personal details. As Hume observed, such work is the work of Solomon, and no one is Solomon in his own case. It is work too obscure for humans. As Kant writes, no general rules have grip fine enough to grab it.

Someone might object that criminal courts assess individual merit and desert all the time. But that objection strengthens Hayek's point. Systems of criminal justice take for granted that the agent is free in his choices, and that there are clear rules that must not be violated. Criminal courts underline the fact of personal responsibility. "If an individual deliberately does violate the law, that is his choice, and it is contrary to the explicit will of the community. The system made me do it" doesn't suffice as an excuse, since no one commands individuals or groups to violate the law, but the opposite. Since the rule-abiding behavior of individuals is essential for its comity, a community can establish rules and pass judgment on violations of them. What it cannot do is imagine, mandate, or guarantee that all free choices of all free citizens, even when they obey all the rules and try hard, will issue in specific outcomes. No one knows all individual outcomes. Too many unforeseen contingencies and unique circumstances enter into each life.

If we wish to live within a system in which people are rewarded for how well they serve their fellow men, it follows that their fellows may not rank their services as high as they expect. The choices of one's fellows are also free, and introduce a major contingency into the most strenuous efforts and best-laid plans. Sometimes people who work hard and play by the rules are not as well rewarded as others, and sometimes their best efforts fail. For the system as a whole, failures by individuals are important, embodying significant negative feedback from which others may learn. A system that values both trial-and-error and free choice is in no position to guarantee outcomes in advance. Not every acorn becomes an oak; laws of probability work in the social order as well as in nature. No one predetermines or controls *who* will fail, but every law of probability says that some will. It is not unjust if some acorns fail to become oaks, and it is not unjust if some free acts fail of their intended outcomes.

> The attribute of justice may thus be predicated about the intended results of human action but not about circumstances which have not deliberately been brought about by men. Justice requires that in the "treatment" of another person or persons, i.e. in the intentional actions affecting the well-being of other persons, certain uniform rules of conduct be observed. It clearly has no application to the manner in which the impersonal process of the market allocates command over goods and services to particular people: this can be neither just nor unjust, because the results are not intended nor foreseen, and depend on a multitude of circumstances not known in their totality to anybody. The conduct of individuals in that process may well be just or unjust; but since their wholly just actions will have consequences for others which were neither intended nor foreseen, these effects do not thereby become just or unjust.[22]

Moreover, it is indispensable to recognize that the term "market" refers to nothing other than the free choices of human beings in exchange: if I sell my house to you, our mutual choosing constitutes "a market." How these choices will work out for each of us cannot be controlled by either of us.[23]

Hayek's vision of the free society is nobler and higher than the vision of those who speak of "social justice."[24] They imagine something like a beehive or a herd or a flock, within which someone is responsible both for giving commands and for outcomes. Hayek thought that a free society has no other model in nature, but is wholly unique to the human species. Furthermore, it has been put into practice only during the past two centuries. Only in recent generations has the economic order been sufficiently distinguished in its principles of operation from the political order, and both of them from the moral and cultural order, for institutions and practices to have arisen that allow individuals unprecedented scope in all three spheres for the actions and habits proper to free persons.

Hayek held that free persons are self-governing, able to live by internalized rules (that is, good habits). For this reason, they need only a fair and open *system of rules* in order to act more creatively, intelligently, and productively than in any other form of society. While the free society will never be able to guarantee the outcomes desired by those who speak of "social justice," it does, Hayek observed, bring more rewards to all, on all reward levels, than any known system. It cannot and will not produce equal rewards for all, only higher rewards for all. Hayek summarizes this position as follows:

> We are of course not wrong in perceiving that the effects of the processes of a free society on the fates of the different individuals are not distributed according to some recognizable principle of justice. Where we go wrong is in concluding from this that they are unjust and that somebody is to blame for this. In a free society in which the position of the different individuals and groups is not the result of anybody's design . . . the differences in reward simply cannot be meaningfully described as just or unjust.[25]

Hayek observed that within any one trade or profession, the correspondence of reward with individual ability and effort is probably higher than is generally supposed. He surmised, however, that the relative position of those within one trade or profession to those in another is more often affected by circumstances beyond their control.[26] In certain fields of endeavor, too, for reasons not related solely to hard work or even ability, rewards are higher, even fantastically higher, than in other fields. He concedes that "systematic" considerations of this sort lead to accusations against the existing order rather than against the luck of circumstances of time and place. Technological change, changes in taste and need, and changes in relative value are also unpredictable, and in that larger sense spring not from the realm of choice but from the realm of luck.[27]

Throughout, Hayek makes a sharp distinction between those failures of justice that involve breaking agreed-upon rules of fairness, and those that consist in results that no one designed, foresaw, or commanded.[28] The first earned his severe moral condemnation. No one should break the rules; freedom imposes high moral responsibilities. The second, insofar as they spring from no willful or deliberate act, seemed to him not a moral matter, but an inescapable feature of all societies and of nature itself. Insofar as labeling these results a "social injustice" leads to an attack upon the free society, in order to move it toward a command society, he strenuously opposed the term for its enormous destructive potential. The historical records of the command economies of Nazism and Communism warranted his revulsion to that way of thinking.

Hayek recognized that at the end of the nineteenth century, when the term "social justice" came to prominence, it was first used as an appeal to "the ruling classes" (as they still were) to attend to the needs of the neglected new masses of uprooted peasants who had become urban workers. To this he had no objection. What he did object to was, first, careless thinking and, second, the imposition on free and creative societies of an abstract conception of justice by coercion.[29] Careless thinkers forget that justice, in the nature of the case, is social; the addition of "social" to "justice," he writes, has the pleonastic force of adding "social" to "language."[30] Such careless thinking becomes positively destructive when the term "social" no longer describes the *product* of the virtuous actions of many individuals, but rather the *utopian goal* toward which all institutions and all individuals are to "the utmost degree made to converge" by coercion. In that case, the term "social" in "social justice" does not refer to something that emerges organically and spontaneously from the rule-abiding behavior of free individuals, but rather from an abstract ideal imposed from above.[31]

Behind Hayek's objections to the careless use of "social justice" lies his unique and powerful insight into the nature of the free society. Hayek recognized that the nineteenth century's addition of the free economy to the eighteenth century's "new science of politics" had liberated women and men as never before. For instance, in lifting the proletariat into the middle class, even Antonio Gramsci had confessed in the 1930s, capitalism was far more successful than Marx and Lenin had predicted; soon there would be no more proletariat in Italy.[32] With great rapidity, in little more than a hundred years, Europe's impoverished, uprooted peasants (Victor Hugo's *Les Miserables*) had been lifted into the middle class and given educations, and were astonishing the world by their talent and creativity.

Hayek believed that the key to these successes of liberty was the rule of law and internalized law-abiding, creative habits, on the one hand, and on the other hand an economic system founded on rules that maximize free decisions, discovery procedures, and feedback mechanisms. Open to contingency, chance and serendipity, such a system was already providing unparalleled universal opportunities. But it could not, and must not be expected to, guarantee outcomes. For any attempt to impose outcomes would force a new foreign architectural principle upon the system; it would strangle the liberty from which invention and discovery bloomed. Recoiling from the dishonesty and destructiveness of the usual arguments for "social justice," Hayek writes:

> I have come to feel strongly that the greatest service I can still render to my fellow men would be that I could make the speakers and writers among them thoroughly ashamed ever again to employ the term "social justice."[33]

"Social Justice" would end up harming most of those whom it putatively intended to help. Its chief beneficiaries would be the political and administrative classes.

HAYEK'S FORM OF SOCIAL JUSTICE

Given the strength of Hayek's argument against and feelings about social justice, it may seem grotesque even to hint, let alone to assert, that he himself was a practitioner of social justice—even if one adds, as one must, "social justice rightly understood." Still, in the sentence just quoted Hayek does offer us a clue: "The greatest service I can still render my fellow men," he writes. This is not the only clue that Hayek saw his vocation as a thinker and writer as a service to his fellow men. He believed, further, that helping others to understand the intellectual keys to a good society, a free and creative society, is to render them a great benefaction. For the free society is an achievement of human wit and enterprise, daring and discovery; and its secrets do not lie upon the surface of things, but must be painstakingly searched out through much trial and error, often at the cost of blood. How terrible to ill-treat these precious insights, then, or to lose sight of them, once gained. That is what repulsed him about "social justice." Used the way the term was being used, it was a betrayal of the free society to its enemies.

Ironically, then, Hayek's war against the misuse of "social justice" was itself a war fought on behalf of his fellow human beings, a service he wanted to render them, an act of considerable consequence for (if I may put it this way) the entire City of Man. Through his intellectual vocation, Hayek *owed* it to his fellow humans to defend the free society and to warn them of dangers against it. His intellectual work was, in this sense, a work of justice. It was also a work aimed at the long-run institutional welfare of the human race. Doing it well was not merely a matter of his own self-interest, narrowly considered, but of significance to the Human City as a whole. It was a work of justice in a plainly social dimension.

I make these brief introductory comments to introduce a conception of social justice that Hayek never considered. It is not a conception widely known. Yet having myself been troubled for many years by the failure, unwillingness even, of Catholic writers in particular to define what they mean by "social justice"—even in the act of devoting whole chapters or entire books to it—I came upon three works that helped me a great deal. One was by an obscure Marianist professor of social ethics at Dayton University, in an obscure pamphlet (today almost impossible to obtain), who won me over by confessing the same discontent with the literature, and then making a practical proposal.[34] The second was an essay by Father Ernest Fortin, who trained here at the University of Chicago.[35] The third was, of course, the challenge presented by Hayek. I didn't need much persuasion from Hayek about the misuses of the term "social justice" or the dishonesty with which the term was employed by socialists or the naiveté of others. But he did help me to mark out with a bright yellow line the unacceptable uses of the term. Fortin gave me my first introduction to the history of the term, later reinforced by looking into Hayek's footnotes.[36]

Here is the way my thinking went. Ethical practices are not merely a matter of acting here and now; they are also a matter of habit, or learned capacity, inclination, skill, or (to use an older term) potency. For a person needs to act well not only once, but again and again, and to be ready to act well, even when caught by surprise. So I was determined to rule out any uses of "social justice" that did not attach to the habits (that is, virtues) of individuals. Social justice is a virtue, an attribute of individuals, or it is a fraud—so I thought. On inspection, I noted that the Popes who introduced the term into the Catholic tradition, Leo XIII (1891) and Pius XI (1931) always spoke of it as a "virtue."[37]

Next, I noted that Leo XIII had as one main intention to ward off socialism, which for nine or ten explicit reasons he found to be both evil and futile (it wouldn't, and couldn't work). In addition, Leo was known as "the Pope of associations." In other words, in thinking of the term "social" he most definitely did not think first of the state; he was opposed to the tide of statism, which he foresaw would end as badly for the poor as for the Church. His alternative was to promote a rich social life, an active civil life, flowering forth in associations and organizations of all sorts. He noted that this was the authentic Catholic tradition, going back to the rich panoply of confraternities, societies, associations, and religious communities that characterized the series of renaissances that began in the eleventh century.[38] There were associations for protecting and maintaining bridges and roads, for beer-making, for burials, for migrant laborers, etc. The great Tocqueville overlooked the medieval precedents for the American habit of association, but he was correct to attach so much importance to the modern need for associations.

Finally, I knew from my own family history that great changes of consciousness inhere in the transmission of a culture from the "old country" to a modern democracy like America. My great-grandparents were serfs of the Austro-Hungarian Empire in the mountainous county of Spiš in Slovakia. My great-grandfather was a game warden for a Hungarian count who possessed one of the largest castles in Europe, or rather the ruins thereof, and the lands around. For some generations, my family had been *subjects* of the emperor, whereas in America they became *citizens;* which is to say, sovereigns. The transition from subject to citizen covers a vast distance, not only psychologically but also morally. The moral obligations of a subject at that time—to oversimplify but not to falsify—were fairly simple and direct: *Pray, Pay,* and *Obey.* If one acquitted such duties, one was in essentials a good subject and a good man. Becoming a *citizen* entails far larger claims on initiative, personal responsibility, imagination, and civic duty. It is much harder to be a good citizen than a good subject; one must exert oneself far more.

Reflections on this transition helped me to grasp why "social justice" is a term that emerged only in the last century, and not before. To be sure, under the term "general justice" the basic concept is as old as Aristotle, and was known to Aquinas. But the term had little utility down the ages—until the end of the nineteenth century. The idea of democracy was shaking monarchies to their foundations, and the new economy of enterprise, investment, invention and factory production was drawing millions from rural areas to cities in search of work. If citizens are not to rally around the unchecked State, as the Communists and Socialists promoted, then what? Leo XIII's answer was: associations. Labor unions, for instance, but also associations of entrepreneurs, associations where both labor and capital could meet, and a host of others. If not the State, civil society.

Father Ferree had put much of this together, although when I had first read his pamphlet years ago I was skeptical. But I didn't forget it. Having learned a bit more about family history and the history of associations, I was ready for it. Here is what I put together, following his lead.

Social justice rightly understood, I came to believe, is a specific habit of justice that is "social" in two senses. First, the specific skills which it calls into exercise are those of inspiring, working with, and organizing others to accomplish together a work of justice. These are the elementary skills of civil society, the primary skills of citizens of free societies, through which they exercise self-government by "doing for themselves" (without turning to government) those things that need to be done. At the time of the American founding, such activities were described as exercises in "civic republicanism." Citizens who take part in such activities commonly explain their efforts as attempts to "pay back" for all that they have received from the free society; alternatively, to meet the obligations of free citizens to think for themselves and to act for themselves. These characteristics establish the habit of such activity as the virtue of justice. The fact that this activity is jointly carried out *with others* gives one justification for designating this activity as a specific type of justice, "social justice," requiring a broader range of social skills than do acts of individual justice.

The second characteristic of "social justice rightly understood" is that it aims at the good of the City, not at the good of one agent only. Citizens may band together, as in pioneer days in Iowa, to put up a school together or to raise roofs over one another's homes or to put a bridge over a stream or to build a church or an infirmary. They may get together in the modern city to hold a bake sale for some charitable purpose, to build or to repair a playground, to clean up the environment, or a million other purposes that the social imagination of individuals leads them to. This is the second way in which this practice of justice is properly designated "social justice." To recapitulate, social justice rightly understood is that specific habit of justice which entails two or more persons acting (1) *in association* and (2) *for the good of the City.* This habit is therefore "social" in two senses: the associative form of the activity and the object of the activity.

One happy characteristic of defining the virtue of social justice in this way is that it is ideologically neutral.[39] It is as open to people on the left as on the right or in the center. Its field of activity may be primarily literary, scientific, religious, political, economic, cultural, athletic and so on, across the whole spectrum of human social activities. Social justice rightly understood is in fact the virtue most proper to civil society, even though the usual usages unmasked by Hayek aim to increase the power of the State, not that of civil society. Still, there is nothing in the concept itself that would prevent democratic citizens from forming associations to get legislation passed, or to block legislation, or for any other political purpose. Persons on the left would certainly organize for purposes from which Hayek would recoil; and some of them would say of Hayek's argument: "I just don't get it; I don't see it that way at all."

In the practical order, the time for argument is not infinite, and people will just disagree. Hayek's argument has a dozen or more steps to it, many of them counterintuitive and most of them running contrary to conventional wisdom in leftwing circles. So there needs to be room to disagree. Thus, the virtue of social justice allows for persons of good will to reach different, even opposing practical judgments about the material content of the common good (ends) and how to get there (means).[40] Such differences are the stuff of politics. Indeed, the free competition of ideas is essential to the free society, including competition among ideas of social justice.

SOME PRECISIONS

If I read Hayek correctly, he would make a much firmer practical stand on the libertarian side of welfare issues than I would, putting up strong resistance to the reasoning and practices of the welfare state. He would certainly do so for reasons of principle. But he might also do so for long-range practical reasons, holding that a premature withdrawal on that flank would result in a weakening all along the front and perhaps even a collapse of the center. In such circumstances, it would be more practical for him—a better service to others—to hold firm, even if he were to be accused of rigidity.

For myself, I believe that there is a strong argument for a modified version of the welfare state, certainly in a large, continental, and mobile society such as the United States. It would be wrong to argue that the welfare state is a desideratum of "social justice," for social justice (rightly understood) is an attribute of citizens, not of states. Social justice is a virtue that can be exercised solely by individuals. Still, one can in a secondary sense speak of a good society—Hayek himself does—and even a just society. By this one means that its laws and institutions respect the moral law governing individuals and do not systematically frustrate that law.

More than that, down the centuries Judaism and Christianity have had a profound effect on Western humanists, such that even secular, anti-biblical thinkers such as Bertrand Russell, John Dewey and Richard Rorty freely admit to borrowing from Moses and from Jesus certain modern liberal principles that they did not learn from Socrates or even the Enlightenment, such as compassion for the weak and the vulnerable; solidarity; and the like. Most Christians, Jews and humanists would not believe that a society that neglects the suffering of the poor and the vulnerable is a good society. They will no doubt argue long into the night about the means best suited to raising the welfare of the poor. Some libertarians would argue that the best means of raising up the poor—by far—is a strong, free, and growing economy. Others might note that this is not always enough, especially in certain hard circumstances; for instance, when people lack the insight or the habits to take advantage of opportunity.

For myself, the bright yellow line between a nurturing and a destructive welfare program must be drawn at those points where welfare creates dependency in otherwise able-bodied and healthy adults, or in other ways corrupts their ability to make practical judgments for themselves and to bear the responsibility for them. For instance, the Homestead Act that opened the American West gave hundreds of thousands of citizens a stake in property, on the condition that they would use their own practical intelligence and labor in developing it. This Act did not create dependency; on the contrary, it helped families establish their independence.

Similarly, for older and more mature women, Aid to Families with Dependent Children has also seemed to work. The vast majority, knocked offstride by a sudden and unforeseen misfortune, use it for one or two years until they regain their independence and then depart from it. But for younger, inexperienced women, AFDC has on the whole been destructive to a very large proportion of their children, whose prognosis for the future is far bleaker than that for other children. Among young American blacks, it seems fair to say that this attempt to be of assistance went seriously wrong and did more damage to the black family than slavery.[41] And now out-of-wedlock births among whites in Iowa, Ohio, and throughout the nation are vaulting inexorably upwards as AFDC becomes a way of life nationwide.[42]

This is not the place for an extended discussion of welfare programs, pro and con. My task today has been to set forth a fresh concept of social justice, as a particular specification of the virtue of justice suited to free, democratic societies; and to defend it in such a way that every person who encounters this concept might see how this virtue can be practiced (is already being practiced) in his or her own life. In a few final words, let me show how I think it was practiced in Hayek's life.

HAYEK'S PRACTICE

One of the great works of mercy is to give sight to the blind. For teachers and writers, this is a metaphor for what they try to do every day: to give understanding where there was darkness; that is, to precipitate those frequent lightbulb insights that give expression to the acute pleasure, "Now I get it!" No one who is reading through the corpus of Hayek's writings can doubt his tireless commitment to communicating the insights necessary to the health and preservation of the free and the good society. Few have worked so hard, or tilled the soil so deeply, or done so with so much originality and passionate instruction. Hayek committed his life to working for the free society—for the sake of all human beings of the future. He worked with as many others as possible to give this work diffusion. He worked for *the good of the Human City;* he worked *with others,* that is, he fulfilled the two conditions that exemplify the habit of social justice.

Yet Hayek did more than write and teach. I have seen his portrait in institutions on practically every continent. He joined with Anthony Fisher and others to launch a set of institutions committed to research and public debate on the foundations of the free society. Mr. Fisher chose a universal name for these institutes that embodied an appropriate metaphor, the Atlas Foundation, for it is ideas and moral commitments that hold up the free society. At considerable personal sacrifice, Hayek was unstinting in his willingness to help these and other institutions committed to liberty by travelling to them for public lectures, making tapes, serving on boards, providing international contacts, even offering shrewd concrete advice. Hayek was an activist as well as a scholar. He was an intellectual *engagé,* as they said two generations ago, a public intellectual, as we say today. To work for the public good is a work of social justice.

The most striking of Hayek's initiatives in this respect was his vision for and leadership of the Mont Pelerin Society, which he launched in 1947, as a prestigious international society of economists, political philosophers, legal scholars, statesmen and others to probe and to discuss the contemporary crisis of the free society, so that after the horrors of World War II the world of intellect would not again rush pell-mell into ideas destructive of liberty. One of Hayek's chief intentions was to draw religious thinkers into reflection on the desperate needs of the liberal society and to pull secular liberals back from unthinking anti-religious prejudices. He believed that the friends of liberty were relatively few, and that those few must not work at cross-purposes. He believed, as well, that the "progressive" bias in favor of the free polity (democracy) while cherishing disdain for the free economy was a betrayal of the liberal intellectual tradition, and he meant to recover the term "liberal" in its classical modern meaning. He at first proposed to call his new society, whose founding members were summoned by Hayek to a meeting in a village near Mont Pelerin, Switzerland, "the Acton-Tocqueville Society." Whereupon a distinguished economist from the University of Chicago is reported to have announced: "I'll be damned if I'll belong to a society named for two Catholics!"[43] A compromise was struck: the name of the nearby mountain was chosen. The Society still prospers, with far more members than ever before.

CONCLUSION

I rest my case. Despite his deep contempt for those concepts of social justice that do injury to the free society, Hayek overlooked a concept of social justice— social justice rightly understood—that put a name to the specific habit of justice of which he was an eminent practitioner. Moreover, if Tocqueville is right, that "The Principle of Association is the first law of democracy,"[44] then social justice understood in this way is the first virtue of democracy, for it is the habit of making the Principle of Association incarnate. This was for Hayek not just an empirical law, but should have moral consequences:

> It is one of the greatest weaknesses of our time that we lack the patience and faith to build up voluntary organizations for purposes which we value highly,

and immediately ask the government to bring about by coercion (or with means raised by coercion) anything that appears as desirable to large numbers. Yet nothing can have a more deadening effect on real participation by the citizens than if government, instead of merely providing the essential framework of spontaneous growth, becomes monolithic and takes charge of the provision for all needs, which can be provided for only by the common effort of many.[45]

In brief, Hayek was something of a model for how a public intellectual ought to practice social justice—tirelessly, with wit, with civility, with gentleness, and with a very deep learning. As I have written elsewhere:

> [Hayek] did write deeply and systematically about ethics and society, about politics and the markets, and above all the kind of laws and institutions indispensable to human liberty. In the sense of working ardently to build a more humane society, he was a great practitioner of social justice.[46]

It might have killed him to say so, but he was in fact a model of the virtue of social justice rightly understood.

NOTES

1. Daniel Bell, *The Cultural Contradictions of Capitalism* (New York: Basic Books, 1976), pp. 3–30.

2. As even the titles of some of his work indicate: Friedrich A. Hayek, *Law, Legislation and Liberty* (Chicago: University of Chicago Press, 1976); and *The Constitution of Liberty* (Chicago: University of Chicago Press, 1978).

3. See Hayek in *The Mirage of Social Justice* (vol. 2 of *Law, Legislation and Liberty*), pp. 62–100.

4. Samuel Gregg and Wolfgang Kasper, "No Third Way: Hayek and the Recovery of Freedom," in *Policy*, Winter 1999, p. 11.

Hayek's economic propositions are rather simple: that human knowledge is far from perfect; that this is at the root of scarcity; and that the finding and testing of useful skills and knowledge is central to economic prosperity. *No* human being, Hayek stresses, can know everything. In this regard, Hayek's greatness as an economist rests on the fact that he restored real human beings to the discipline [of economics], and has raised real questions about economists basing their propositions in the theoretical assumption of perfect knowledge and the fiction that people are anodyne, reactive, automatons who simply maximize and minimize. Hence, the basic supposition of economic planning—that government can know everything required to make correct decisions—is revealed as yet another example of human hubris.

5. Hayek notes expressly that the Roman Catholic Church especially has made the aim of "[s]ocial justice" part of the official doctrine, while "the ministers of most

Christian denominations appear to vie with each other with such offers of more mundane aims" (id. p. 66). Taparelli d'Azeglio in his *Saggio Teoretico di Diritto Naturale,* published in 1840, seems to have introduced the term. Pope Pius XI incorporated "social justice" into official Church doctrine in his encyclical *Quadragesimo Anno.* Oswald Nell-Breuning, S.J., who wrote a major part of this papal document, published a line-by-line commentary, *The Reorganization of Social Economy* (Milwaukee, 1939), in which he treats social justice as both a virtue and a regulative principle. In the subsequent debate, no one generally accepted definition has emerged. The index of the famous post-Vatican II Encyclopedia *Sacramentum Mundi* lists only one reference, a single paragraph alluding to the concept, but no specific entry (vol. IV, p. 204). Rodger Charles, S.J., in *The Christian Social Conscience* (Notre Dame, Ind.: Fides, 1970), does not even mention the term, but relies on the classical distinction between commutative, distributive and legal justice (p. 25). Johannes Messner in his magisterial thousand-page *Social Ethics* (St. Louis: Herder Books, 1965) treats the concept on only one page (pp. 320–21). His understanding, however, is not an example of clarity: "'social justice' refers especially to the economic and social welfare of 'society,' in the sense of the economically cooperating community of the state." Fathers Yves Calvez, S.J., and Jacques Perrin, S.J., in *The Church and Social Justice: Social Teaching of the Popes from Leo XIII to Pius XII,* trans. J. R. Kirwan (London: Burns and Oates, 1961), conclude that "social justice is general justice applied to the economic as distinct from the political society" (p. 153). Cardinal Höffner, in *Christian Social Teaching* (Ordo Socialis, 1983, p. 71), also adopts the position that social justice is legal justice. He suggests calling it "common good justice, a virtue that is exercised only by the state, territorial authorities, professional classes and the Church." Father Ernest Fortin drily summarizes the confusion surrounding the term in "Natural Law and Social Justice," *American Journal of Jurisprudence* 30 (1985).

6. *The Mirage of Social Justice,* pp. 96–97.

7. Id., p. 66: "Even though until recently one would have vainly sought in the extensive literature for an intelligible definition of the term, there still seems to exist little doubt, either among ordinary people or among the learned, that the expression has a definite well understood sense."

8. See Novak, *Catholic Ethic and the Spirit of Capitalism* (New York: The Free Press, 1993), pp. 67–69:

> Yet despite the centrality of the concept of social justice in Catholic thought, precise statements of the concept are exceedingly hard to find; indeed even discussions of the concept are. . . . There is no doubt that Fortin is correct in describing the woolly sloganizing to which "social justice" has become prey. Even the communists found it useful for their propaganda, and socialists use it unabashedly as the generic name for their own purposes. To rescue the term from such ideological misuse is no easy task.

9. For a discussion of the principles of a free society see Hayek in *The Constitution of Liberty,* supra note 2; also Edwin J. Fuelner, Jr., *Intellectual Pilgrims* (Washington, D.C., 1999), especially chapter 2, "Seven Principles of a Free Society."

10. Alexis de Tocqueville, *Democracy in America,* ed. by J. P. Mayer (New York: Doubleday, 1969), pp. 525–28.

11. The main point of my argument is, then, that the conflict between, on the one hand, advocates of the spontaneous extended human order created by a competitive market, and on the other hand those who demand a deliberate arrangement of human interaction by central authority based on collective command over available resources is due to a factual error by the latter about how knowledge of these resources is and can be generated and utilized. As a question of fact, this conflict must be settled by scientific study. Such study shows that, by following the spontaneously generated moral traditions underlying the competitive market order (traditions which do not satisfy the canons or norms of rationality embraced by most socialists), we generate and garner greater knowledge and wealth than would ever be obtained or utilized in a centrally-directed economy whose adherents claim to proceed strictly in accordance with "reason." Thus socialist aims and programmes are factually impossible to achieve or execute; and they also happen, into the bargain as it were, to be logically impossible.

Friedrich A. Hayek, *Fatal Conceit* (Chicago: University of Chicago Press, 1988), pp. 6–10.

12. Hayek writes scathingly in the *Mirage* against "that anthropomorphism or personification by which naive thinking tries to account for all self-ordering processes. It is a sign of the immaturity of our minds that we have not yet outgrown these primitive concepts and still demand from an impersonal process which brings about a greater satisfaction of human desires than any deliberate human organization could achieve, that it conform to the moral precepts men have evolved for the guidance of their individual actions" (pp. 62–63).

13. Leo W. Shields, *The History and Meaning of the Term Social Justice* (Notre Dame, 1941).

14. *The Mirage,* p. 176.

15. John Stuart Mill, "Utilitarianism" (London, 1861), chapter 5, p. 92; in H. Plamenplatz (ed.), *The English Utilitarians* (Oxford, 1949), p. 225.

16. Hume's entire text reads:

> Most obvious thought would be to assign the largest possessions to the most extensive virtue, and give every one the power of doing proportioned to his inclination. . . . But were mankind to execute such a law, so great is the uncertainty of merit, both from its natural obscurity; and from the self-conceit of each individual that no determinate rule of conduct would ever follow from it; and the total dissolution of society must be the immediate consequence.

An Enquiry Concerning the Principles of Morals, sect. III, part II, Works IV, p. 187. Kant's text reads as follows:

> Welfare, however, has no principle, neither for him who receives it, nor for him who distributes it (one will place it here and another there); because it depends on the material content of the will, which is dependent upon particular facts and therefore capable of a general rule.

Immanuel Kant, *Der Streit der Fakultäten,* sect. 2, para. 6, note 2.

17. Individual men may be moral in the sense that they are able to consider interests other than their own in determining problems of conduct, and are capable on occasion, of preferring the advantages of others to their own. They are endowed by nature with a measure of sympathy and consideration for their kind. . . . Their rational faculty prompts them to a sense of justice which educational discipline may refine. . . . But all these achievements are more difficult, if not impossible, for human societies and social groups. In every human group there is less reason to guide and to check impulse, less capacity for self-transcendence, less ability to comprehend the need of others. . . . [I]n part it is merely the revelation of a collective egoism, compounded of the egoistic impulses of individuals, which achieve a more vivid expression and a more cumulative effect when they are united in a common impulse than when they express themselves separately and discreetly.

Reinhold Niebuhr, *Moral Man and Immoral Society* (New York: Charles Scribner's Sons, 1960), p. xi, and also chapter 1, "Man and Society."

18. Hayek, *The Fatal Conceit.*

19. Id., pp. 68–69.

20. Hayek continues:

and any particular conception of "social justice" could be realized only in such a centrally directed system. It presupposes that people are guided by specific directions and not by rules of just individual conduct. Indeed, no system of rules of just individual conduct, and therefore no free action of the individuals, could produce results satisfying any principle of distributive justice. (Id., p. 69)

21. *Main Currents of Marxism,* trans. P. S. Falla (Oxford: Clarendon Press, 1978), vol. 3, *The Breakdown,* pp. 526ff.

22. *The Mirage of Social Justice,* p. 70. Also:

Yet we do cry out against the injustice when a succession of calamities befalls one family while another steadily prospers, when a meritorious effort is frustrated by some unforeseeable accident, and particularly if of many people whose endeavours seem equally great, some succeed brilliantly while others fail. It is certainly tragic to see the failure of the most meritorious effort of parents to bring up their children, of young men to build a career, or of an explorer or scientist pursuing a brilliant idea. And we will protest against such a fate although we do not know anyone who is to blame for it, or any way in which such disappointments can be prevented. (Id., pp. 68–69)

23. Id., p. 73:

It has been argued persuasively that people will tolerate major inequalities of the material positions only if they believe that the different individuals get on the whole what they deserve, that they did in fact support the market order only because (and so long as) they thought that the differences of renumeration corresponded roughly to differences of merit, and that in consequence the maintenance of a free society presupposes the belief that some sort of "social justice" is being done. The market order, however, does not in fact owe its origin to such beliefs, nor was it originally justified in this manner. This order could develop, after its earlier beginnings had decayed during the middle ages and to some extent been destroyed by the restrictions imposed by authority, when a thousand years of vain efforts to discover substantively just prices or wages were abandoned and the late schoolmen recognized them to be empty formulae and taught instead that the prices determined by just conduct of the parties in the market.

24. See Gregg and Kasper, *No Third Way,* p. 12. They summarize four propositions that characterize Hayek's thought:

- The institutions that coordinate society arise largely from human experience, but not human design; hence attempts to design society are fatal to its goodness.
- In a free society, law is essentially found and not made. Law is normally derived not from the mere will of the rulers, be they kings or Rousseau's "General Will," but from the interaction and learning of all citizens.
- The Rule of Law not only is the first and foremost principle of the free society, but is also dependent upon the two previous propositions.
- The Rule of Law requires all people to be treated equally (i.e., with procedural justice), but does not require them to be made equal, and indeed is undermined by attempts to engineer equal outcomes (i.e., "social" justice).

25. *The Mirage,* pp. 69–70.

26. Id., pp. 73–74:

It certainly is important in the market order (or free enterprise society, misleadingly called "capitalism") that the individuals believe that their well-being depends primarily on their own efforts and decisions. Indeed, few circumstances will do more to make a person energetic and efficient than the belief that it depends chiefly on him whether he will reach the goals he has set himself. For this reason this belief is often encouraged by education and governing opinion—it seems to me, generally much to the benefit of most members of the society in which it prevails, who will owe many important material and moral improvements to persons guided by it. But it leads no doubt also to an exaggerated confidence in the truth of this generalization which to those who regard themselves (and perhaps are) equally able but have failed must appear as a bitter irony and severe provocation.

27. Id., pp. 70–71.

28. Id., pp. 73–74:

[T]he competitive price arrived at without fraud, monopoly and violence, was all that justice required. It was from this tradition that John Locke and his contemporaries derived the classical liberal conception of justice for which, as has been rightly said, it was only "the way in which competition was carried on, not the results," that could be just or unjust.

29. Id., p. 79:

> But from . . . an appeal to the conscience of the public to concern themselves with
> the unfortunate ones and recognize them as members of the same society, the con-
> ception gradually came to mean that "society" ought to hold itself responsible for
> the particular material position of all its members, and for assuring that each re-
> ceived what was "due" to him. It implied that the processes of society should be
> deliberately directed to particular results and, by personifying society, represented it
> as a subject endowed with a conscious mind, capable of being guided in its opera-
> tion by moral principles. "Social" became more and more the description of the
> pre-eminent virtue, the attribute in which the good man excelled and the ideal by
> which communal action was to be guided. (Id., p. 79)

30. In *The Fatal Conceit,* Hayek notes that the word "society" in present parlance
not only refers to phenomena "produced by the various modes of cooperation among
man" but it has "increasingly been turned into an exhortation, a sort of guide-word for
rationalist morals intended to displace traditional morals, and now supplants the word
'good' as a designation of what is morally right. Because of this factual and normative
meanings of the word 'social' constantly alternate, and what first seems a description im-
perceptibly turns into a prescription." (p. 114) To illustrate his point he sums up "an instructive list of over one hundred and sixty nouns qualified by the adjective 'social' he
had encountered." (p. 115)

31. Id., p. 69:

> "Social Justice" can be given a meaning only in a directed or "command economy"
> (such as an army) in which the individuals are ordered what to do; and any partic-
> ular conception of "social justice" could be realized only in such centrally directed
> system. It presupposes that people are guided by specific directions and not by rules
> of just individual conduct, and therefore no free actions of the individuals could
> produce results satisfying the principle of distributive justice.

32. *Antonio Gramsci: Selections from Political Writings, 1910–1920,* trans. John
Matthews (Ann Arbor: University of Michigan Press, 1976).

33. See *The Mirage of Social Justice,* p. 97.

34. William J. Ferree, S.M., *Introduction into Social Justice* (Dayton, Oh.: Marianist
Publications, 1948).

35. Ernest Fortin, "Natural Law and Social Justice," *American Journal of Jurisprudence*
30 (1985).

36. See Novak, *The Catholic Ethic and the Spirit of Capitalism,* p. 68.

37. Id., pp. 63–65.

38. See Russell Hittinger's lecture at the Summer Institute, Krakow, Poland, July
1998 (unpublished).

39. Id., p. 79:

> Not all who claim to be acting for social justice, of course, may actually be fur-
> thering the work of justice. Their motives may be suspect, and so may their grasp

of important facts. We would not count "skinheads" or neo-Nazis as doing the work of social justice. So it is with all claims to be practicing a virtue: Those claims must be examined in greater detail. In order to be just, an act must be just in every aspect—manner, timing, motive, accuracy of perception and all the other qualities of action; otherwise, it's defective.

40. Michael Novak, *Free Persons and the Common Good* (New York: Madison Books, 1989), pp. 174–77, especially p. 177.

41. See Michael Novak, *The New Consensus on Family and Welfare* (American Enterprise Institute, 1987), pp. 71–89.

42. Charles Murray, "The Coming White Underclass," *Wall Street Journal,* Oct. 29, 1993.

43. A somewhat less vivid account written by Edwin J. Feulner, Jr., *Intellectual Pilgrims: The Fiftieth Anniversary of the Mont Pelerin Society* (Washington, D.C.: Heritage Foundation, 1999), p. 11.

44. Alexis de Tocqueville, *Democracy in America* (New York: Doubleday, 1969), p. 517.

45. *Mirage,* p. 151.

46. Novak, *The Catholic Ethic and the Spirit of Capitalism,* pp. 62–88.

ECONOMICS, RELIGION, AND MORALITY

"Economics is both a moral and a social art, addressing the proper and just arrangement of social institutions, oriented toward maximizing personal economic creativity, for the sake of the common economic whole."

12

THEOLOGIANS AND ECONOMISTS

The Next Twenty Years

A voracious reader of journals commented recently that during the past four years he has encountered more magazine and newspaper articles on basic concepts of political economy—on tax policy, capital-formation, monetary policy, inflation, infrastructure, employment, the state, the market—than in any period during his lifetime. Whether or not this wry observation is true, to those not formally trained in economics the comprehension of current public discussions has required taking economic questions more seriously and doing more homework on economic matters than at any time in their lives. Religious leaders and theologians, in particular, are awakening to the fact that their own bookshelves and accustomed periodicals have ill-prepared them for this hour. Books on church and state, religion and politics, religion and the arts, religion and psychiatry, religion and (God knows) sex far outnumber books on theology and economics. Moreover, concerning even elementary concepts of economic thought, religious leaders and theologians commonly find themselves without exact and clear definitions. To create a new subdiscipline of theology, "the theology of economics," will take a generation of hard work.

ECONOMICS AND THE POPES

This is not to say that no work has been done. In the Catholic tradition, since Bishop von Ketteler of Mainz (1811–1877) first raised the "social question" in his lectures of 1848, a distinguished line of German scholars, several of them Jesuits, have maintained a vital tradition of critical reflection on the interpenetrations of economic and religious realities. Among the most distinguished names of this tradition are Heinrich Pesch (1854–1926), Oswald von Nell-Breuning (b. 1890), Goetz Briefs (1889–1974), and Franz Mueller (b. 1900). One American scholar, in particular, Father John A. Ryan (1869–1945), quite independently of the Europeans, also created a distinguished body of work (including *A Living Wage, Distributive Justice,* and *The Reconstruction of the Social Order*) which had considerable impact upon the administration of Franklin Delano Roosevelt, as is suggested in the title of Ryan's biography, *Right Reverend New Dealer*. Of the European branch of this tradition, Joseph Schumpeter remarks in his *History of Economic Analysis*:

> Throughout the period, the Catholic Church was on the continent of Europe the object of legislative and administrative attacks from hostile governments and parliaments—in England hostility did not go beyond violent talk about "Vaticanism"—which is what might have been expected in a predominantly "liberalistic" world. What could not have been expected is that these attacks everywhere ended in retreat and that they left the Catholic Church stronger than it had been for centuries. Political Catholicism arose from a renascence of religious Catholicism. . . . But for the purposes of this book another fact is of still greater importance. . . . This concern of the Catholic Church with the conditions of labor was nothing new and only adapted an old tradition to the problems of the epoch. But something that was new developed toward the end of the century, namely, a definite scheme of social organization that, making use of the existing elements of groupwise cooperation, visualized a society—and a state—operating by means of self-governing vocational associations within a framework of ethical precepts. This is the "corporative" state adumbrated in the encyclical *Quadragesimo Anno* (1931).

Since 1891, the Roman Catholic popes have discussed the connections between religion and economics directly in a series of official letters addressed to all Catholics of the world (this is the meaning of the term "encyclical"). Cumulatively, these letters have created a rather substantial and self-conscious tradition of concepts and descriptive analyses, basic principles and prudential judgments, about existing political economies. They form a running commentary on the flow of worldly events during the last one hundred years. Among the basic landmark texts, usually issued on anniversaries of the first, are Leo XIII's *Rerum Novarum* (1891), Pius XI's *Quadragesimo Anno* (1931), John XXIII's *Mater et Magistra* (1961) and *Pacem in Terris* (1963), Paul VI's *Popuiorum Progressio* (1967) and *Octagesima Adveniens* (1971), and John Paul II's *Laborem Exercens* (1981). For the most part, the first two of these focus on the political economies of Western Europe. The later ones assume worldwide perspective and begin to comment upon the problems of development. Since over half the world's Catholics now live in so-called Third World nations, the latter emphasis will most likely continue.

Since 1936, meanwhile, the World Council of Churches has followed the papacy in building a substantial body of reflection on economics and religion. So has the National Council of Churches. In recent years, the Presbyterians, Methodists, and others have maintained high-level study groups on various economic issues. Finally, the evangelical churches, too, are being drawn into fierce public debates that carry them well beyond the traditional individual experience of faith and into activism concerning issues of political economy.

For at least three reasons, moreover, we can expect religious leaders—and lay study groups, universities, and the religious press—to devote yet more attention in the future to religion and economics. First, the continuing struggles of the developing nations will weigh heavily on the consciousness of all, as events and mass communications focus upon them. Second, the twenty or so democratic capitalist nations of the world (some would say "mixed economies" or "welfare states") have had unprecedented success in bringing the great bulk of their populations far above the levels of subsistence known in 1891; this sudden rise to affluence alters the terms of the debate and raises new questions. Third, the "welfare states" themselves seem to have reached the upper limits of the state-guaranteed benefits they can *easily* offer to their citizens. From now on, they may safely be expected to face increasingly difficult choices in which, frequently, one good will has to be traded off for another. For these and other reasons, political leaders will continue to spend a disproportionate amount of their time facing economic difficulties. Citizens will become engaged in intense public arguments concerning taxes and benefits, ends and means. The churches will become, to some extent, activist pressure groups on various economic issues.

For reasons too numerous to detail, many religious leaders and theologians now prefer to focus increasing amounts of their personal and professional energies on the problems of this world: military, political, and economic. This shift in energies is diagnosed and evaluated in many contrasting ways. What can scarcely be denied is that it is a fact and is likely to remain so for at least the near future.

Given the institutional apparatus of the churches, from weekly sermons to instructional classes, from summer institutes to study workshops, from centers of learning to centers of activism, professional economists might therefore come to expect a rising tide of questions, comments, and activities from church people in the United States and elsewhere.

APPROACHING THE PROBLEM

This movement of social forces may or may not proceed with intelligence, civility, and practical wisdom. Surely it will proceed in many different voices and styles. To help establish a workable framework for discussion, three typical habits of mind will here need to be distinguished, since each bears in a different way upon public policy. Let me call these habits of mind the charismatic, the scientific, and the prudential.

The charismatic habit. Often at religious study centers, at some point or another one will hear an appeal from someone on the panel (usually present precisely for this appeal) that all should be "converted" to "peace and justice." This *charismatic* habit of mind deserves the name because of its appeal to conversion, as if from outside-in. The attitude seems to have arisen in Latin America, in the experience of *conscientization*, in which prayerful reflection on their political-economic circumstances (it is said) leads ordinary people to burst into gospel-filled "analysis" of their situation. Whatever its origin, this charismatic habit of mind must be distinguished from the religious habit of mind, in general, since obviously most religious persons do not share it and have to be "converted" into it. It must also be distinguished from another sense of charismatic, increasingly common in evangelical and nowadays in Catholic circles, by which is meant an individual "moved by the Holy Spirit" in a sudden rush of deeply felt experience. Typically, the evangelical sense of the charismatic leads to concern with one's own soul in relation to God and one's neighbors. By contrast, the charismatic habit of mind I have been pointing to is aimed at social activism in political and economic matters: "peace and justice."

The scientific habit of mind. Among professional economists, the scientific habit will need little exposition. It is the habit of disciplining one's perceptions, procedures, and judgments according to established canons of inquiry, in such a way that one's own activities may be replicated by similarly disciplined others. These disciplines are often summed up by the word "objectivity." They make possible the confirmation or disconfirmation of theories in accord with rules for presenting evidence.

The prudential habit of mind. As all political economists have traditionally observed, the scientific investigator employs a habit of mind different from that of the statesman or man of affairs who is an activist in the same field. The statesman faces pressures of time, since he must often act (or fail to act) before a scientific account of the circumstances within which he must act could possibly be executed. Moreover, he must make estimates of how various other free agents may react, if he himself acts thus or so. He must make decisions about human character, current circumstance, and future probabilities, about which science cannot afford him certain judgments in advance. Thus, although the statesman cannot be held to scientific standards, he is not thereby released to standards which take no account of rationality at all. On the contrary, wise decisions are still distinguished from foolish. The standard of rationality applied in such cases has long been called by the classical name of *prudence*. The prudential habit of mind is the acquired skill of recognizing and doing the right thing at the right time and in the right way, so as to be judged by history as having acted wisely rather than foolishly. Since prudence must cover decisions made in all circumstances, under all contingencies, it is not easy to define its workings through some fixed set of standardized procedures. Its presence or absence is, nonetheless, remarked in every human decision.

There is a reason for keeping these three habits of mind distinct. Some but not all of those who are most active in bringing religious judgment to bear on economic matters operate from within the charismatic habit of mind. Sometimes but not always, economists who (as fate would have it) are engaged in argument with them, argue from within the scientific habit of mind. Typically, the issue to be addressed can be wisely approached—that is, in the hope of acting together wisely upon it—only within the prudential habit of mind.

Indeed, in any good argument it is crucial for all participants to find their way into the same habit of mind, so that the rules of discourse and the canons of evidence are clear and mutually agreeable. In the sorts of arguments religious persons are eager to have with economists, this typically means that the argument is not supposed to be *scientific*. The alternative is *not* that it must then become *charismatic* in the sense described above: the proper alternative is that it should become *prudential*. In that case, the economist will not be expected to argue merely as a scientist (although he will be expected not to forget his science), but rather as a statesman or person of affairs: as a prudent person facing concrete cases and the contingent circumstances of decisions about future policies. This seems fair enough. Obversely, the religious leader or theologian must be subject to exactly the same expectations.

DEFINING THE TERMS

The problem is that here, too, there is considerable slippage. On occasion, the *same words* are used, though with *different meanings* rooted in quite diverse intellectual traditions. Four examples of systematic verbal miscommunication may help to clear the air. If participants in future debates are aware of the systematic ambiguities of key words, as they emerge from radically different histories of usage, some progress might be made toward clearer argumentation in the future. The four examples I have chosen from among many others are "self-interest," "acquisitiveness," "profits," and "markets."

Self-interest. When an economist uses these words, he means "autonomous choice." He says nothing at all about the moral content of that choice; in the eyes of the economist, that frame is deliberately kept empty. Self-interest means *whatever* a person has chosen, whether it is sanctity or truth, pleasure or material benefit. The concept is as general and empty as possible, in order to be universalizable.

The very same word, however, has quite different meanings in theology. In Islamic and Jewish traditions, for example, "self-interest" does not typically have negative connotations. It is understood as an elemental commonsense duty to oneself, quite reasonable and basic, as when, in the commandment "Love thy neighbor as thyself," self-love is assumed to be sound. In the Christian tradition, "self-interest" has acquired a pejorative connotation. There are two reasons why this is so. First, Christianity strives to go "beyond the law." Christians often feel obliged to reject (or to disguise) self-interest as too imperfect, too flawed, too self-enclosed. Second, the Christian understanding of love, especially as *agape* (self-sacrificial love), seems to some Christians to be *opposed* to self-interest or self-love. Clearly, "self-interest" is an expression which, in the tradition of Christian symbolic language, has reverberations lacking in the context of economics and in many non-Christian theological traditions. Care must be taken in discussions of religion and economics to unpack the misleadingly simple concept of self-interest, so as to specify its exact moral meaning in each and every context. Without such care, quite conflicting meanings may frustrate understanding.

Acquisitiveness. R. H. Tawney, the socialist historian, was the decisive force in naming the fundamental motive of capitalist economic activity acquisitiveness; he did not do so for friendly reasons. Yet it is not *having* that characterizes the capitalist spirit, in actual fact, but *venturing* and *creating.* Max Weber wrote:

> The impulse to acquisition, pursuit of gain, of money, of the greatest possible amount of money, has in itself nothing to do with capitalism. This impulse exists and has existed among waiters, physicians, coachmen, artists, prostitutes, dishonest officials, soldiers, nobles, crusaders, gamblers, and beggars. One may say that it has been common to all sorts and conditions of men at all times and in all countries of the earth, wherever the objective possibility of it is or has been given. It should be taught in the kindergarten of cultural history that this naive idea of capitalism must be given up once and for all. Unlimited greed for gain is not in the least identical with capitalism and is still less its spirit.[1]

As Weber saw, the goal of the capitalist spirit is not to live sumptuously or even comfortably, as precapitalist persons of commerce did, but to create ever new wealth in a sustained and systematic way. The capitalist spirit appeared to Weber distinctively new because of its emphasis upon the future rather than the past, because of its corresponding "thisworldly asceticism," because of its spiritual rather than materialistic focus. *Acquisitiveness* names this spirit very badly, indeed.

Profit. The semantic confusion is just as great with "profit." Most persons intuitively confuse profit with mark-up. They further intuitively confuse profit with cash taken out of the business by owners or managers. Religious leaders need to understand the ways in which profit is another word for development. By far, the largest proportion of it is reinvested. Usually, only a small proportion of it is used in paying dividends to the original investors (to whom the business is in debt) and in raising salaries. One may say that dividends and salaries go "into someone's pocket," but often that money, too, is reinvested.

The market. In theological circles, the word market has been surrounded by many symbolic overtones. It is treated as a question of faith or ideology, as if some trust "the magic of the marketplace" and some do not. But, of course, there is no one "the market." There are only many particular markets. A market is often imagined as a place, like the "marketplace" of a medieval town. In practice, a market—for home computers, say—is an aggregation of those who want to purchase home computers now and those who manufacture and distribute them for sale. A short while ago, no such market existed. Markets come and disappear; some are large, especially those designed for potentially every family and person, and some are small, especially those for very expensive or highly specialized goods or services. Some markets are easy, some quite difficult, to find or to establish.

To sum up, economists need to know that words they use as familiar coin may strike the ears of religious leaders with echoes economists do not intend. The translation of meaning from one intellectual tradition to another is no easy task.

ADAM SMITH'S LARGER VISION

Not long after Adam Smith completed *A Theory of the Moral Sentiments*, a work on the moral system operative in the culture of Great Britain, he began his *Inquiry into the Nature and Causes of the Wealth of Nations*, his book on the economic system which had not yet been established, but which he hoped would be established, in Great Britain. At his death, he was compiling notes for a volume on the political system. Thus Smith understood implicitly the threefold nature of political economy: its moral–cultural system, its economic system, its polity. Not long after his death, however, economics became—it had for some time been becoming—an independent discipline. No mere philosopher, as he was, could long hope to continue as a professional within it. In short order, the three disciplines which he had combined in his person went three separate ways: moral philosophy, economics, and political science.

Yet what the academy sundered remained one in reality; that social whole comprising the three relatively independent, yet interdependent, subsystems: a democratic polity, a capitalist economy, and a pluralistic (chiefly Jewish–Christian and humanistic) culture. Each of these three had its own proper institutions. The academic disciplines central to each of them each developed its own proper traditions, methods, and canons. It is not too much to say that misunderstandings were inevitable.

During the nineteenth century, religious leaders and theologians often enough defended the *ancien regime* and traditional values, being rather skeptical about political democracy and cultural pluralism. But their hesitations with respect to politics and cultural pluralism were as nothing compared to their virtually unanimous disapprobation of capitalist economics. The so-called liberals—i.e., partisans both of a free market and of political democracy—not unnaturally regarded religion as, on the whole, a conservative force in nearly every sphere. Max Weber argued in *The Protestant Ethic and the Spirit of Capitalism* that certain Protestant conceptions and habits were indispensable to the emergence of the new capitalist ethos. This is quite different from arguing that Protestant (or any other religious) leaders actively promoted the new capitalist ethos in word and book. Few, in fact, did; and Weber could cite only very few. Even those "Catholic liberals" of France like Lamennais who were in favor of political democracy were quite opposed to "individualism" in the economic and cultural spheres. Such religious "liberals" may not have joined the Christian socialists, but most were, in varying degrees, anticapitalist. In England, the motto of the Christian socialists was: "Christianity is the religion of which socialism is the practice." Paul Tillich, one of whose early books expressed his own commitment, said that socialism "is the only possible economic system from the Christian point of view."

This tendency in religious thought, it is worth noting, is sometimes more exactly described as "anticapitalist" than as "prosocialist." Thus, for example, the influential British writers Hilaire Belloc (*The Servile State*) and G. K. Chesterton (*The Outline of Sanity*) opposed both socialism and capitalism, in the name of what they called Distributism. Furthermore, many religious writers employed a *pre*capitalist point of view. While they favored traditional institutions such as private property and free markets, they did not like certain features of the capitalist *spirit*, its ethos, its liberal "philosophy." This is true of Chesterton and Belloc, of many nonmarxist Christian socialists, clearly so of Popes Leo XIII and Pius XI, and probably, as well, if one takes their work as a whole, of such American critics of capitalism, sometimes more or less loosely calling themselves socialists, as Walter Rauschenbusch and the early Reinhold Niebuhr.

If we date the beginnings of the democratic capitalist era from *The Wealth of Nations*, in 1776, it becomes evident that two streams which are analytically quite separate were often in reality intermixed, surely so for those who lived through the period of their gestation. On the one side was the complex reality of the newly emerging social system of political economy. (By parity of designation, this new system is fairly called "democratic" in its political part and "capitalist" in economy.) On the other side was the body of theory—the vibrant ideology, usually called "liberalism"—advanced by those who promoted this system. Quite often the ideology did not match the reality. Yet for those immersed in the movements of that time, the carriers of the ideology were simultaneously the chief activists in shaping the new realities. Pity their opponents. It was not so easy to attack what one disagreed with in the ideology while defending what one agreed with in the new realities. It was easier to attack "Capitalism" (or "bourgeois liberalism") than to make nice distinctions.

Our situation today is rather different. We can more calmly assess the real achievements of the liberal era—of the capitalist economy and the democratic polity—while sharply distancing ourselves from this or that bit of analysis, theory, and philosophy, set forth by way of bringing them into existence. We may take issue, for example, with the extreme individualism of Bentham, with the abstractness of Ricardo, with the sentimentality in parts of John Stuart Mill, and also with particular portions of their economic analysis. In this sense, one can imagine the articulation of a theory of democratic capitalism different from theirs and more closely tied to what actually happened. As artists are often not the best interpreters of their own creations, so activists are not always the best expositors of the realities they helped to bring into being. Today we can distinguish between the realities of democratic capitalism in the nineteenth century and the theories put forward in its promotion.

The anticapitalist tradition by contrast has generally attacked both the reality and the ideology, although not always distinguishing between the two. For example, "possessive individualism" is attacked, often through an analysis of the writings of Bentham or others; but care is not taken to see whether, in fact, persons in democratic capitalist societies *are* actually "possessive" or "individualistic" by comparison with persons in other cultures. The two phenomena are quite distinct. Bentham may have been wrong in his theories. His theories, further, may have been out of tune with the realities of democratic capitalist cultural developments. Again, when Popes Leo XIII and Pius XI attack certain principles of liberal societies, it does not follow either that specific writers actually held the theories ascribed to them or that those theories actually describe the real nature of events. The principles attacked may, indeed, be false. Whether any author actually held them, or whether they were in fact operative principles in historical events, must be shown and not merely asserted. In a word, debates in these matters are sometimes about theories and sometimes about facts. The two sorts of debate must be carefully distinguished.

A PROGRESSIVE ETHOS

On another front, economists must note that the roots of the anticapitalist tendency on religious thought are many. Just as many liberals perceived religious leaders to be, on the whole, conservative, so many religious leaders wished to deny that liberalism—whether in theory or in social reality—represented true human progress. From the beginning questions were raised about the breakdown of community, excessive individualism and "alienation," the proletarianization of the largely rural peasant populations of Europe as they flocked to industrial sites, the breakdown of the family, child labor, the loss of rural independence before the onrush of wage-dependency and the growth of urban slums, and the like. The good that capitalism did or might yet do was discounted; the evil results it brought in its train were denounced.

Perhaps most profoundly of all, the rise of commerce and industry precipitated great changes in the moral-cultural order: in morals, in ways of thought, in aesthetics, and in ordinary behavior. Traditional authorities—whether of the landed aristocracy or of the church, whether in public or in domestic life—seemed plainly to be losing ground. Whereas the traditional ethic might have counseled simple sufficiency, the new ethos counseled each person to try to "better his condition." Whereas the older ethos pictured wealth or the desire for it as the root of all evils, the new ethos taught that the production of wealth is a noble task, even a moral obligation. It is important to recognize that a capitalist economy brings with it—has, perhaps, as its precondition—a novel ethos, a new morality. A capitalist economy is not *merely* a functional relation to production. It has its own *spirit*. It conveys new ideals. It offers a new set of commandments and prohibitions. These imperatives, far from being identical to the received classical wisdom, whether of stoic humanism or of Jewish-Christian provenance, seem, at least intuitively, to run *counter* to most if not all the known and familiar traditional moralities. Some thought of the new morality as liberation. Others found it an abomination.

There is another point. Many of the central propositions of the new political economy of democratic capitalism are counterintuitive. Not only do they run counter to received wisdom; they also seem wrong on their face. From classical times, for example, the main treatise concerning justice dealt almost exclusively with "distributive justice." In a world that had not yet inquired into the cause of wealth, there was no question of "productive justice." The notion that, given the suffering inherent in almost universal poverty, economic development as a moral obligation could not arise. The feeling that an economy is a zero-sum game, in which the wealth of some is a cause of the poverty of others, seemed intuitively sound. Again, the instinct that a free, untrammeled market must necessarily end in anarchy, chaos, abuse, dog-eat-dog acquisitiveness, and the like seemed intuitively as plain as a steeple in the sky. That persons seeking to benefit from a free market will be constrained to attend to the desires and actions of others, and to adapt themselves thereto, had to be arrived at, as it were, counterintuitively, by watching how markets actually work.

To choose a related example: it seems intuitively obvious that the best way for (say) a small nation to avoid waste, concentrate its efforts, and produce efficient results is to allow a group of the most intelligent planners in its midst to set priorities, lay down guidelines, and command multifarious activities. It seems intuitively obvious that a planned socialist economy must be, at the very least, "less wasteful" than a free market economy. (This was, at the turn of the century, one of the socialist arguments most telling even to those who were not socialists.) The lesson that what is intuitively obvious works less well than the counterintuitive principle—that free markets exert their own cooperative disciplines—must be learned through experience.

THE NEXT TWENTY YEARS

In 1983, perhaps, the lessons to be learned from the 160 experiments in political economy now being conducted by the 160 nations of the world render moot certain of the old ideological arguments of past generations. John Stuart Mill, for example, *suspected* that socialist designs would not work out exactly as socialists hoped; his wife, Harriet Taylor Mill, often bade him to be more hopeful. In either case, *he* was in the position of passing judgment on experiments which had not yet taken place. By 1983, many such experiments have passed like water under the bridge. Fact can replace prophecy.

Nonetheless, religious thinkers in the main have not assessed economic history. In few seminaries or divinity schools are courses in economics mandatory although, typically, courses in politics, sociology, and art are. Theologians therefore face two quite different challenges almost simultaneously. First, they need to acquire some of the basic concepts and methods of economic analysis, and to see through some of their intuitively plausible notions which do not, alas, withstand analysis. Second, they must master the rather challenging factual materials concerning both domestic and international economic activities, about which they are concerned to make judgment.

In this task—and this is the main burden of my plea—I would hope that a significant number of economists would turn their attention to the economic questions being raised by official and unofficial church bodies. As religious leaders make more and more pronouncements about economic matters, it is important that they receive prompt and effective feedback. Otherwise, unchallenged assertions will begin to acquire the weight not only of conventional wisdom but also of official tradition. If mistakes are being made, they need to be corrected early, before they become solid and virtually unmovable. For the churches represent not only a legitimate but a reasonably powerful institutional force within democratic capitalist societies. The academic separation of specialized disciplines has its reasons but it also exacts heavy costs in public understanding even among institutional elites. The elites of economics and of religion have weighty responsibilities each toward the other. Both need to acquit these better over the next twenty years than we have during the past twenty.

NOTES

1. See Max Weber's *The Protestant Ethic and the Spirit of Capitalism*, trans. Talcott Parsons (New York: Charles Scribner's Sons, 1958), p. 17. See also chapter 5: "Asceticism and the Spirit of Capitalism." Weber writes: "Christian asceticism, at first fleeing from the world into solitude, had already ruled the world which it had renounced from the monastery and through the Church. But it had, on the whole, left the naturally spontaneous character of daily life in the world untouched. Now it strode into the marketplace of life, slammed the door of the monastery behind it, and undertook to penetrate just that daily routine of life with its methodicalness, to fashion it into a life in the world, but neither of nor for this world. With what result, we shall try to make clear in the following discussion" (p. 154).

13

ECONOMIC RIGHTS

The Servile State

Recently, a theologian friend explained to me the "hurdle" he had to jump before he could accept the concept of "economic rights." He had been raised to believe, he said, that if an able man doesn't work, he shouldn't be fed by others. He could not at first accept the concept that every person deserves income, food, shelter, and other necessities "just by virtue of being born," just because each is a human being. Finally, though, my friend said, he came to accept that right, based upon a new and penetrating insight into human dignity.

It would have been better if this theologian had not made that leap. For if every human being has the right to be given income, and to be fed, sheltered and cared for by the human community, every person who without necessity exercises that right sells himself into dependency. In that way human dignity, far from being gained, is lost. Down that path is reached what anti-capitalist Hilaire Belloc called *The Servile State.*

It is easy enough to understand. Human dignity would seem to require that every human being should have the means necessary to human development. But millions of human beings do not. Therefore, someone should *do* something about this. This argument originates in the modern discovery of a new possibility and a new moral obligation. Given vast stretches of poverty and misery, then if humans *can* raise their standards, they *must*. Human development is a moral obligation.

Questions arise. (1) By what *standards* should the minimal necessities ("basic needs") for human dignity be measured? (2) By what *methods* should they be fulfilled?

The standards of the most developed nations in the late twentieth century are far higher than the standards of preceding centuries. Standards as between nations and regions today vary enormously. So do standards among families and individuals. Is human dignity diminished by life at some standard lower than the highest? That would seem ridiculous. Is there any possible definition of a minimum standard? That would not be easy. In these two examples, though, the concept "human dignity" reveals itself to be equivocal.

In one sense, no human being under *any* earthly conditions loses the fundamental dignity inhering in every human person, made in the image of God and beloved of God. Human dignity, in this sense, is inalienable.

In a second sense, though, "human dignity" does not refer to the transcendent dignity of every human in the eyes of God, but to relative and changing standards of human expectation about what is normative, possible and desirable. Remote but contemporary primitive tribes, living in abominable conditions, may have lower life expectancy, higher infant mortality, and lives more harsh, brutal and short than the better known migrants to the *favelas* of Sao Paulo. By some, the first may be assessed in the light of ancient, the second in the light of modern, standards. Standards of shelter, nutrition, longevity, dental care, hygiene, literacy, education and income have changed dramatically since the liberal project placed the world upon the path of "modern progress" and "development." In the second sense, then, "human dignity"—described in the perspective of "basic needs"—is not a transcendental concept, pointing to the origin of human dignity in the Creator, but rather a goal-centered teleological concept, pointing toward an ideal state of society, which (it is either assumed or argued) human beings ought to strive to attain.

This systematic equivocation in the concept of "human dignity" deserves rigorous scholarly scrutiny. Lying hidden below most debate on the subject, this equivocation has often been employed uncritically.

In order to deal with this systematic equivocation, partisans of economic rights usually make three intellectual moves.[1] Their aim is to include economic rights within the traditional framework of "human rights," in order to gain for the former the prestige won by the latter through the horrors of World War II. Their first move is to weaken the concept of political rights (e.g., by reducing "rights" to "claims"), in order to make them seem analogous to economic rights. The second move is to invest economic goals with moral content, and to describe them in at least a loose sense as "rights." The third move is a "preferential option for the state" as the final and normally the chief bearer of responsibility. Each of these three moves deserves intense intellectual scrutiny, which space here forbids. The first, in particular, represents a disappointing failure to grasp the full power of the American legacy.

Granted that human development is a moral obligation, by what *method* ought it best to be realized? The partisans of economic rights typically perceive those whose "basic needs" are not being met as in need of outside assistance and, ultimately, as wards of the state. Although the elasticity of "needs" is a pitfall Marxist thought has never overcome, concede for a moment that "basic needs" can be defined. Who, then, has the responsibility for seeing to it that such needs can be fulfilled? There are at least three social solutions to this query. Human development and social justice are more likely to be achieved if: (1) The state has primary responsibility for protecting human rights, especially economic rights; (2) other social institutions such as families, churches, villages, neighborhoods, corporations, unions and other associations have primary responsibility; or (3) individuals, especially heads of households, have the primary responsibility. The last is sometimes described as if it represented an individualistic bias. It does not. It is a *social* theory, rooted both philosophically and pragmatically in the centrality of the human person in the human social project.

Obviously, these three models are not exclusive. In fact, it is the genius of the liberal society—the political economy of democratic capitalism—that it includes all three, although in the following order of priority. The primary responsibility for meeting his own/her own basic needs is invested in the individual person; secondly, in mediating human associations and social organizations; thirdly, only as a last resort and with a wary and critical eye, in the state. From human experience, the state is properly regarded as a principal source of abuse of human rights, not only in the political and civil order, but also in the economic order. To be sure, the state is a useful and a necessary human institution. It is far more than simply a "watchman"; its roles are many and indispensable. Its very purpose is to secure "natural rights." Yet it is also a dangerous center of power.

Historically, tyrannies far outnumber genuine democracies; even today, regimes which regularly abuse human rights far outnumber the few that, far from perfect, are systematically restrained from such abuse. Similarly, regimes that stifle economic creativity—and, hence, punitively maintain their peoples far below their potential prosperity—far outnumber those that promote the general welfare through encouraging the creativity endowed in all persons by their Creator. Far from feeding the poor, many states have wantonly caused famine.

The American idea has been that both the political rights and material prosperity of citizens will be best served by a social organization that promotes individual liberty and creativity. This is a *social* vision. It is not a concession to egotism and self-interest run amok. It is a call to a civil, cooperative, republican community, rooted in the mutual respect of persons for each other's liberty and creativity. According to Aquinas, for inert things life is attraction; for plants, growth and flowering; for animals, self-originating motion; for human beings, the liberty of autonomous persons to conduct their affairs through civil conversation and rational persuasion. The liberal society is an experiment testing whether political and civil liberties, and the broadest possible fulfillment of basic (and not-so-basic) human needs, can be met through a constitutional order so defined: *Novus ordo seclorum*. Here is a brief synopsis given by Thomas Jefferson in his First Inaugural Address:

> entertaining a due sense of our equal right to the use of our own faculties, to the acquisitions of our own industry, to honor and confidence from our fellow-citizens, resulting not from birth, but from our actions and their sense of them; enlightened by a benign religion, professed, indeed, and practiced in various forms, yet all of them inculcating honesty, truth, temperance, gratitude, and the love of man; acknowledging and adoring an overruling Providence, which by all its dispensations proves that it delights in the happiness hereafter—with all these blessings, what more is necessary to make us a happy and a prosperous people?

Still one thing more, fellow-citizens—a wise and frugal Government, which shall restrain men from injuring one another, shall leave them otherwise free to regulate their own pursuits of industry and improvement, and shall not take from the mouth of labor the bread it has earned. This is the sum of good government, and this is necessary to close the circle of our felicities.

Catholic critics of the liberal society typically appeal to three alternative intellectual traditions. Historically, the most potent of these is traditionalism: the defense of the preliberal order. In Latin America and elsewhere, traditionalism is a potent force. *("Liberalismo es pecado"* is a cry still heard.) Secondly, the liberal tradition is often opposed by Catholics in the name of the socialist and/or Marxist tradition. Finally, Catholic critics of liberalism frequently appeal, despite its youth, to the nascent Catholic discussion of human rights. As David Hollenbach, S.J., has often candidly pointed out, this Catholic tradition of human rights is barely twenty years old.

This new critical stance wishes to be ecumenical and open, to "forge a new synthesis," and above all to be politically effective in poor countries desperately in need of help. Its attempts to be inclusive bear the signs of eagerness of will rather than of original and sustained intellectual inquiry. It is more syncretistic than distinctive. As a small body of work, its aspirations and sentiments stand out with greater clarity than does its own systematic conceptions.

Meanwhile, the extensive effort under way to commit the Church to "economic rights" has the potential to become an error of classic magnitude. It might well position the Catholic Church in a "preferential option for the state" that will more than rival that of the Constantinian period.

TOWARD PRECISION

A sound theory of human rights is properly rooted in human nature. That nature establishes as the law of human life that each human being is a person, endowed with capacities to inquire, judge, choose, and act. Sharing in such a common nature, under God, is humankind's most powerful bond. This, at least, is the presupposition of both the *philosophia perennis* and what Walter Lippmann called "the public philosophy" of the liberal society. Pope John XXIII captured this consonance well when he wrote in *Pacem in Terris:*

> Any human society, if it is to be well ordered and productive, must lay down as a foundation this principle, namely, that every human being is a person; that is, his nature is endowed with intelligence and free will. Indeed, precisely because he is a person he has rights and obligations flowing directly and simultaneously from his very nature. And as these rights are universal and inviolable so they cannot in any way be surrendered. (para. 9)

It is true that Pope John XXIII wrote, two paragraphs later and still under the heading of "rights and duties," that human persons have a "right" to those things essential to the exercise of that human nature: to income, food, shelter, medical care, and social services. (He did not place these rights under "economic rights," which he treated later, but under "the right to life"; "Welfare rights" might be a more exact name.) But he did not make these rights universal. He confined them explicitly to the person who cannot meet his own responsibilities to provide for these basic needs "through no fault of his own."[2] His clear implication is that human dignity requires that human persons be self-reliant, independent, and able to act out of their own proper intelligence and choice.[3] As the longtime director of the Vatican's Institute for Justice and Peace, Bishop Roger Heckel, made clear in the brilliant pamphlet, *Self-Reliance,*[4] human dignity is not otherwise fully achieved. One would have thought that American theologians, above all, would be quick to see the importance of this point.

Faith itself is rooted in freedom. Freedom to inquire, to judge, to choose and to act is the capacity in humans that leads us to consider each of them, in the phrase of the poet, "immortal diamond," and to treat each of them with that dignity properly called human. To humans, however, freedom to act is not given; it must be achieved through the appropriation of self-reliance and mature independence. The liberal society has been invented precisely to promote a form of community in which as many such persons may emerge as possible, and more than in any other. David Hollenbach, S.J., writes that "the restructuring of the social and economic order in a way that allows genuine communal participation in the corporate life of society is the program of socialist thought."[5] (He forgot the quip: "The problem with socialism is that it would take too many evenings.") He ignores the immense associational energies released and daily at work in the freely chosen communal life of the liberal society. He makes too neat a division (liberal = personal freedom; socialism = communal participation in the corporate life of society). The former affords far more resources for associational life than the latter affords personal freedoms and self-reliance.

Consider again Pope John XXIII's words: "through no fault of his own." No doubt, every person has a right to eat, to find shelter and medical care, etc., at least in the sense that neither the state nor anyone else should *prevent* him from attaining such essential goods. To cause someone to die by so preventing them would be legally regarded as murder. But, supposing a society that allows human beings the freedom proper to their nature, who has the primary *responsibility* for caring for the basic needs of any free, competent and independent person? Why, that very person, of course. Any other arrangement is sheer dependency. Still, sometimes persons "through no fault of their own" cannot meet their own basic needs.

Three different sorts of cases may be distinguished: personal disability, circumstance, and an uncreative system. First, an injury, illness, nervous breakdown or disability may take away a person's capacity for independence. It is self-evident that a person can be held accountable only up to the limits of his or her capacities. Those incapable of helping themselves need the help of others. In their humanity, they make a "claim" upon the community. Should such a claim be called a "right"? In what precise sense? We shall return to this point.

Second, in cases of "circumstances beyond one's control," the moral situation is similar. Flood, famine, fire or war may temporarily deprive even able, independent citizens of their normal means of self-reliance. In such cases, too, a "claim" is made upon (and typically felt by) the community. Here, again, whether this claim constitutes a "right," and of what sort, is in question.

Third, the social system itself may prevent some (or all) citizens from attaining the autonomous self-reliance necessary to human dignity. By this measure, social systems need to be compared with one another, and held to the highest possible standard.

No one can deny that the papal tradition since *Pacem in Terris* does employ the word "rights" for claims of at least two, and probably all three, of these situations. What cannot be claimed, however, is that this word "rights" is unequivocal. Six senses of "right" must be distinguished: the rhetorical, the Catholic, the legal, the constitutional, the Anglo-American, and the Marxist/socialist.

(1) *The rhetorical intensifier.* Sometimes the word "right" is attached to a claim as a means of signalling its emotional intensity. "That's not fair, you've violated my rights," someone says at almost any sense of offense. "I have a right to do that if I want to," another person says, claiming liberty to do whatever. Some dress up even egotistical desires by claiming them as "rights."

(2) *Catholic rights.* During the past twenty years, especially since *Pacem in Terris,* the popes have begun to use the language of rights to designate claims that go beyond claims in charity; these are claims in justice. Thus, the Good Samaritan did not act precisely out of charity, but out of justice due a fellow human being in need, when he assisted the man injured by robbers. This sense of the word "right" goes beyond legal or constitutional senses of "right" and "obligation." It might be called a *moral* right. No matter what the state of the law, this sense of "right" binds humans to care for one another through a sense of common humanity. If this were all that some Catholic authors meant by "economic rights," concurrence might be swift, although some critics would worry that broadening the crucial word "rights" in this sense is but an instance of the rhetorical intensifier.

(3) *Legal rights.* These are rights enforceable in a court of law. In cases of competing rights, brought to a court, the judge (or other official agent) adjudicates. Thus, the "right to a minimum wage" is defined and enforced by the legal system. (This legal right is conceptually and institutionally distinct from the Catholic "right to a living wage." The legal minimum wage may fall far short of the latter.) Some Catholic advocates of "economic rights" *do* mean claims that might be vindicated in a court of law. They have not yet calculated the quantity of litigation or the sheer political divisiveness such a system might inspire.[6]

(4) *Constitutional rights.* These are limits placed upon the powers of government by the U.S. Constitution, with the consent of the governed, to protect certain specified rights deemed to inhere in persons transcendently ("endowed by their Creator"), by nature of their humanity. Constitutional rights are not created by the state; it is prohibited from infringing upon them. The state is formed among men precisely to protect such rights by ensuring that its own agencies do not impede them, and by coming to the defense of those whose rights are infringed by others. The role of the state is strictly circumscribed. Individuals are responsible for their own exercise of these rights. Although the first draft of the bishops' pastoral letter on the U.S. economy was not clear on this point, one assumes that the bishops do not favor the recognition of "economic rights" by constitutional amendment.

(5) *Anglo-American usage.* Behind the rights articulated in the Declaration of Independence and institutionalized in the U.S. Constitution lies a great social achievement: a body of reflection (a) with high social purpose; *viz.,* to inspire a new social order based upon limited government, the rule of law, and the consent of the governed; and (b) based upon a critical analysis of human nature. Against those who would malign this tradition as excessively individualistic, the high social purpose is expressly stated in the Preamble to the U.S. Constitution: "to form a more perfect *union,* establish *justice,* ensure domestic tranquillity, provide for the *common* defense, promote the *general* welfare, and ensure the blessings of liberty to ourselves *and our posterity. . . ."* (Emphasis added.) This long tradition of critical reflection, designed to articulate precisely the special meaning of "natural rights," has seldom been fully appropriated by Catholic theology. Few Americans have followed the initial clues pursued by John Courtney Murray, S.J., in this respect.

This Anglo-American tradition did not only see the state as a crucial threat to personal liberty and to economic prosperity. It also saw the necessity for states to protect natural rights ("To secure these rights, governments are instituted among men. . . ."). The natural rights, in a sense, define what it is to be human; they designate attributes without which human action is frustrated. The Virginia Declaration of Rights affirmed in 1776

> that all men are by nature equally free and independent, and have certain inherent rights, of which, when they enter a state of society, they cannot by any compact deprive or divest their posterity; namely, the enjoyment of life and liberty, with the means of acquiring and possessing property, and pursuing and obtaining happiness and safety.

Flowing from these "natural rights" are the "civil" and "political" rights, specifying the constitutional arrangements through which governments "secure" these "natural rights," on the one hand, and by which governments are limited, on the other.

Natural rights, in practice, can be respected only in a properly constituted civil society; they must be embodied in institutions. Thence the civil, political, and economic rights articulated in the Constitution. That men are not angels, but embodied, is recognized by the care taken to defend the "free *exercise*" of natural powers of rational action, such as in the free exercise of religion, association, speech, and property. As G. K. Chesterton observed: "For the mass of men the idea of artistic creation can only be expressed by an idea unpopular in present discussions—the idea of property. . . . Property is merely the art of democracy. It means that every man should have something that he can shape in his own image as he is shaped in the image of Heaven." Property rights are the condition of economic dynamism because they alone defend personal creativity against the habitual aggrandizement of states and the lawlessness of mobs. By limiting the power of the state, the Anglo-American tradition paradoxically vindicates the state, i.e., the promise of government through the consent of the governed. It has evoked a remarkable love for the institutions of self-governance.

(6) *Marxist and socialist rights.* Both Marxist states and the Socialist International (in its Frankfurt Declaration of 1951) seek, by contrast, to limit individual rights and to cede important rights to the state (conceived of as the preferred expression of community). Here the focus is exactly the reverse of the Anglo-American tradition: to limit individuals, to empower the state. (They cannot be said to inhere in the community, for in that case the state would be limited; it is of the essence of Marxism to make the state supreme, and it is of the essence of the Socialist International to subordinate both individuals and communities to the authority of the democratic state.)

Some Catholic scholars aim to forge a new synthesis of the Anglo-American tradition and the Marxist and Socialist traditions. The intellectual and institutional hurdles faced by this project are insurmountable. The Marxist conception of the state is incompatible both with the Catholic tradition and with the Anglo-American tradition. The Socialist conception of the state, less easy to define, in practice minimizes individual rights and expands the powers of the state. The Socialist International sincerely desires a democratic rather than a totalitarian state. But it has no defense against "the tyranny of a majority," and it has not yet worked out how to move from "the bureaucratic state" of the original socialist vision to the "decentralized state" of the current socialist vision.

Some Catholic scholars make the following argument. The first step is not in dispute: "Rights" (in the Catholic sense) to income, food, shelter, medical care, old-age security and social services flow necessarily from the dignity of the human person. Even absent such goods, the human person does not lose essential dignity. But the full exercise of dignity requires such goods.

The next step, though, is to argue that the Anglo-American concept of rights needs to be expanded from its constitutional declaration of civic, political, and economic rights (property, liberty, enterprise) to include a new table of economic—more exactly, welfare—rights (income, jobs, food, medical care, social services). The crux of the matter is an alleged parallelism between the classic Anglo-American rights and the new economic (i.e., welfare) rights. Proponents argue that, although economic rights are just being recognized, so also civil and political rights emerged late in human history. A public political process formulated the Bill of Rights, and governments are formed to protect such rights. Just so, the political process should now formulate economic (welfare) rights and the government should not only protect them but provide for their fulfillment.

Three major objections tell against this argument. First, the two sets of rights do *not* have a parallel substantive structure. Second, the classic rights limit the state, whereas the new rights tremendously increase the power of the state. Third, the new conception of economic rights confuses "goods" with "rights." Two radically different conceptions of the state and of the human person are involved.

(1) The two sets of rights are substantively disparate. The classic right to free speech does not empower the state to make a person speak. It has the form of a prohibition: "The state shall not . . ." As Joseph Califano, ex-Secretary of the Department of Health, Education, and Welfare, wrote: "The Constitution guarantees many precious rights—to speak and publish, to travel, to worship—but it does not require that the exercise of those rights be publicly funded." By contrast, the alleged new right to food empowers the state to see to it that every person does have food, and to establish conditions qualifying some persons for entitlement to food assistance. And so with other welfare rights.

The classic Anglo-American rights ensure personal liberties from state control. They assign responsibilities to individual persons. These rights and responsibilities are given to the individual directly by the Creator, independently of the state. They are rooted in the nature of the human person. Their exercise cannot legitimately be *prevented* by the state. By contrast, each of the alleged new economic rights meets the human need for income, food, shelter, and social services by transferring responsibility for its fulfillment from the human person to the state. Over time this conception is certain to alter the national ethos and daily practice in the direction of dependency. This would be the opposite of human dignity. Human dignity arises from human liberty and its responsibilities. Economic "duties" (as Pope John XXIII suggested) are prior to economic "rights." Not all the duties of justice are properly defined with reference to rights.

(2) The alleged new rights alter the relation between the person and the state. They tremendously aggrandize the powers of the state and diminish the honor due to the self-reliant person. If, for example, a person is alleged to have a right to a job, which it is the responsibility of the state to provide, the state acquires immense power over the economy in four ways. First, the state must intervene in labor markets so as to create jobs. Second, the state must exact from other citizens sufficient fiscal resources to create jobs. Third, the state must establish conditions defining eligibility for jobs. Fourth, the state acquires the power to assign persons to jobs. In no field of the classical Anglo-American rights are equivalent powers granted to the state.

Further, the actual practice of nations which already recognize economic rights does not reveal admirable outcomes, neither in the Soviet Union and other Marxist states nor in non-Marxist socialist nations that have experimented in this direction. Effects upon personal liberties, upon enterprise and invention, and upon social dynamism are not attractive. The decline of Western European social democracies in recent years ought to sound a tocsin. The declaration of economic rights implies, although its proponents seldom carry their theory through to its practical implications, grave increments in state authority. From such implications serious consequences have followed in other states.

(3) To defend the rights of human persons is to defend their capacity for self-reliance. In making persons dependent upon the state, one diminishes their own sense of earned dignity. When through personal disability or circumstances beyond their control they are unable to fulfill their personal responsibilities, then, of course, others in the human community acquire an obligation in justice to assist them. This obligation *may* be fulfilled through programs administered through the state. It need not necessarily be fulfilled through the state. There are great human costs, moral and political as well as economic, in appointing the state to be the instrument of "economic justice."

The American people of the present generation have apportioned more benefits to the poor, the needy, and the handicapped—largely but not solely administered through the state—than any prior generation in American history. They have done so without thinking of such works of justice in terms of "rights." It is not necessary to employ the language of rights in order to assure the works of justice. Moreover, serious questions must be raised about the costs, inefficiencies, and counterproductive consequences of state action portrayed as justice.

Some Catholic thinkers are fond of saying that the Catholic tradition takes a positive view of the state, since the state is a natural institution. Although this is true, human experience has shown that the powers of the state must be strictly limited if the legitimate powers of other institutions rooted in human nature—the family, the church, free associations, economic institutions, labor unions, the press, etc.—are not to be violated. The Catholic tradition takes a positive view, not of the state *simpliciter,* but of the *limited* state. This implies that those who would aggrandize the power of the state must bear the burden of proof. They must show that every proposed increment to the powers of the state will not injure other basic natural institutions, and that each such increment will, on balance, do more good than harm. The mere assertion that the state is, in any such respect, an instrument of greater rather than lesser justice is not sufficient; consequences must be assessed.

In short, the true conceptual force of the argument in favor of economic rights (to income, food, shelter, a job, etc.) is *not* that the latter are truly "rights" inhering in the nature of human persons, but rather that they are "goods" indispensable to a full human life. Since at present levels of economic development such goods are within human power to provide, one can say unambiguously that they ought in justice to be provided. The bearers of the primary responsibility for providing them, however, are individuals in mature independence and self-reliance; secondarily, human communities and associations; and only *in extremis,* the state. Human persons ought not to be wards of the state. They ought not to be dependent. They ought not to be servile. Nothing less than mature independence and self-reliance is becoming to the dignity of human persons.

Finally, the concept of economic rights (to income, food, shelter, a job, etc.) flies in the face of what John Courtney Murray, S.J., called telegraphically "the American Proposition." That Proposition is in the form of a social experiment, boldly testing whether a system based upon mature independence and self-reliance will produce more in the way of social justice than any system based upon dependency upon the state. That experiment involves a social system rich in the reality of free association, civic responsibility, fellowship, and what Lincoln called the Union (which he conducted history's bloodiest civil war to maintain).

Indeed, commenting on Proverbs 25:11 *("A word fitly spoken is like apples of gold in a setting of silver"),* Lincoln called the Union the "picture of silver," within which "liberty for all"—the "apple of gold"—was framed. And he brilliantly articulated the reason why American prosperity had been attained:

> All this is not the result of accident. It has a philosophical cause. Without the *Constitution* and the *Union,* we could not have attained the result; but even these, are not the primary cause of our great prosperity. There is something back of these, entwining itself more closely about the human heart. That something, is the principle of "Liberty to all"—the principle that clears the *path* for all—gives *hope* to all—and, by consequence, *enterprise,* and *industry* to all.
>
> . . . The assertion of that *principle,* at *that time,* was *the* word, *"fitly spoken"* which has proved an "apple of gold" to us. The *Union,* and the *Constitution,* are the *picture of silver,* subsequently framed around it. . . .
>
> So let us act, that neither *picture,* or *apple,* shall ever be blurred, or broken. That we may so act, we must study, and understand the points of danger.

The points of danger are that, over time, a regime recognizing economic (welfare) rights as a matter of legal disputation will in practice become unable to protect civil, political, and genuinely economic rights. It may well dissolve the national sense of the common good by breeding interest groups attached to their own claims to goods, in a zero-sum competition for power and influence over state decision-making. It may well weaken the morale of those who strive for the dignity inherent in self-reliance, by making dependency upon the state seem to be the easier and more certain course. More profoundly, the deepest danger is that it will irretrievably alter the nature of the American Proposition, setting the United States upon a course foreign to her own originality and historic creativity, a course of tragic and ironical decline.

NOTES

1. See, for example, David Hollenbach, S.J., *Claims in Conflict: Retrieving and Renewing the Catholic Human Rights Tradition* (New York: Paulist Press, 1979) and the collection of essays edited by Alfred Hennelly, S.J., and John Langan, S.J., *Human Rights in the Americas: The Struggle for Consensus* (Washington, D.C.: Georgetown University Press, 1982). John Langan's essay, "Defining Human Rights: A Revision of the Liberal Tradition," is of particular importance in making the case for the new economic (welfare) rights within the liberal tradition. It suffers from its reliance upon John Rawls and Ronald Dworkin for its interpretation of the American human rights tradition.

2. "Beginning our discussion of the rights of man, we see that every man has the right to life, to bodily integrity, and to the means which are necessary and suitable for the proper development of life; these are primarily food, clothing, shelter, rest, medical care, and finally the necessary social services. Therefore a human being also has the right to security in cases of sickness, inability to work, widowhood, old age, unemployment, or in any other case in which he is deprived of the means of subsistence *through no fault of his own.*" John XXIII, *Pacem in Terris,* 11; emphasis added.

3. Under the explicit heading "Rights Pertaining to Economic Life," Pope John XXIII does not mention the new economic (welfare) rights but stresses three rights consonant with the Anglo-American tradition: "Human beings have the *natural right to free initiative* in the economic field" *(Pacem in Terris,* 18; emphasis added). "From the dignity of the human person, there also arises *the right to carry on economic activities* according to the degree of responsibility of which one is capable" (ibid., 20; emphasis added). "The right of private property, even of productive goods, also derives from the nature of man. This right, as we have elsewhere declared, *is an effective aid in safeguarding the dignity of the human person and the free exercise of responsibility in all fields of endeavor*" (ibid., 21; emphasis in original). Incidentally, the pope's reason for stressing the right to private property is to defend the welfare and independence of the family: *"Finally,* [the right to private property] *strengthens the stability and tranquillity of family life, thus contributing to the peace and prosperity of the commonwealth*" (ibid.; emphasis in original).

4. Roger Heckel, S.J., *Self-Reliance* (Vatican City: Pontifical Commission "Iustitia et Pax," 1978).

5. David Hollenbach, S.J., "Global Human Rights: An Interpretation of the Contemporary Catholic Understanding," in Hennelly and Langan, *Human Rights in the Americas,* p. 17.

6. Nor have they calculated another danger, diagnosed by the constitutional scholar Walter Berns:

> We once defined human rights in terms of freedom and the non-material (for even the property right was formulated as a right to acquire). There is a growing tendency to define these rights in terms of equality and the material. Thus, we hear it said that the essential human rights are "freedom from hunger, the right to decent housing, medical care and education regardless of ability to pay, the right to gainful employment, safe working conditions, a clean, nontoxic environment." To secure

human rights in the original sense required government to protect and respect the private realm; to secure the new human rights will require government to intervene in the private realm and eventually to destroy it. Those who now demand as a right the equal distribution of material goods will inevitably come to demand (and in some cases have already demanded) an equal right to the happiness these goods are supposed to bring, not a right to pursue happiness but the right to gain it. To secure this right will require government to declare war on human nature. The well-endowed (with intelligence, energy, beauty, or whatever) cannot be permitted to benefit, nor the unendowed to suffer, from nature's "injustice." Government can secure this new right to equality only by enlisting the assistance of the geneticists. Tocqueville foresaw this development: "I think that democratic communities have a natural taste for freedom; left to themselves, they will seek it, cherish it, and view any privation of it with regret. But for equality their passion is ardent, insatiable, incessant, invincible; they call for equality in freedom; and if they cannot obtain that, they still call for equality in slavery."

Walter Berns, "Does the Constitution 'Secure These Rights'?" in Robert A. Goldwin and William A. Schambra, eds., *How Democratic Is the Constitution?* (Washington, D.C.: American Enterprise Institute, 1980), pp. 76–77. The first internal quotation is from Michael Parenti's essay, "The Constitution as an Elitist Document," in the same volume; the second quotation is from Tocqueville, *Democracy in America,* trans. Harry Reeve, 2 vols. (New York: Vintage Books, 1945), 2:102. See also the critique of John Rawls by Allan Bloom, "Justice: John Rawls vs. the Tradition of Political Philosophy," *The American Political Science Review,* 69 (June 1975):648–662.

14

POLITICAL ECONOMY AND CHRISTIAN CONSCIENCE

I think it best to follow the lead of Richard Neuhaus and Peter Henriot, by at least beginning autobiographically. Cardinal Newman pointed out that the university is a place where persons educate persons; if an education consisted solely in reading the printed word, one could stay at home. Tone of voice, intonation, emphasis, love of and revulsion against certain ideas or materials—all these are communicated in many subtle ways by personal presence. *Cor ad cor loquitur.*

Peter Henriot mentioned that in his formative years as a student he was influenced by many of my writings, including *A Theology for Radical Politics* (New York: Herder and Herder, 1969). Concerning portions of my earlier writings, I do have a lot to answer for! The bulk of that book was written during 1967, but I could not find a publisher interested in it until after the riots at east coast universities in 1968. The book was not published until 1969. If the epilogue is read closely, the first signs of the shift in vision that I was already beginning to experience can be seen. Watching my fellow intellectuals, I was becoming restless with what I saw. I wrote in that epilogue about the electricians, gas-station attendants, and other members of the lower-middle class. I was beginning to become more aware of springing from that class, of being Slavic, and of being increasingly uncomfortable in what I felt was a form of "false consciousness."

Later, particularly in a 1972 essay on Reinhold Niebuhr ("Needing Niebuhr Again," *Commentary* 54 [September, 1972]: 52–62), I began to define more clearly the "new class" into which I had been educated: the class of well-paid, professional persons whose main work is that of communication and organization, including those of us who are professors, journalists, consultants, etc. I became increasingly aware of the special prejudices of that new class, meaning my own prejudices. It had been easy for me, for example, to oppose political leaders like Ronald Reagan, who was just then becoming governor of California, and to look down on capitalism, business, and the corporation, as is evident from many passages of my books and writings of that time. For me and my colleagues, "entrepreneur" was a dirty word.

Those of us trained in the humanities more or less accepted aristocratic values. For us, to call someone a "prince of a man" was to offer a compliment, but to call someone's tastes "bourgeois" was intended as an insult. On reflection, this now seems to be a little odd, since most of the beautiful things of the West—tapestries, cutlery, oaken tables, paintings, statues, etc.—were made by people who were neither peasants nor aristocrats but craftspersons who owned their own homes and were the first city dwellers and, thus, the first of the bourgeoisie. The essay by Christopher Dawson, "Catholicism and the Bourgeois Mind," published in the December, 1986, issue of *Crisis*, next to the Lay Letter, "Liberty and Justice for All," illustrates the antagonism toward "the bourgeois" that most of us were then taught. In any case, already at the end of *A Theology for Radical Politics* I was beginning to take a new direction. This would lead me during 1971 to write *The Rise of the Unmeltable Ethnics: Politics and Culture in the Seventies* (New York: Macmillan, 1972).

At first it was too dangerous a taboo for me to explore the economic implications of my thinking. I needed more time to study economics, so turned my energy to politics. In 1968, Bobby Kennedy had been my political hero, and he has remained so until the present time. He was the only politician in America who could really bring together lower-class Whites and lower-class Blacks, as he showed in Gary, Indiana. Much as I admired Eugene McCarthy, I understood that Jack Kennedy, an earlier hero, had always had opposition on the left, in Adlai Stevenson, for example, and now Bobby Kennedy did, too. I found myself slowly rejecting several elements of the politics of the left. I had noted the ostracism Pat Moynihan had suffered when he raised the issue of "the black family." I noted that when Bobby Kennedy spoke about crime in poor neighborhoods, as he did in Gary, many on the left referred to that aspect of his vision as the "bad Bobby," whereas I thought that was what was good about him. He had a knowledge of life in the streets, and he spoke directly and realistically to the difficulties. However, in those days it was considered bad form for somebody to speak of "crime"; it was as though that were some sort of code word.

In the presidential campaign of 1972, I wrote speeches for Sargent Shriver and George McGovern and tried to get them to talk about crime as Bobby Kennedy had; both were afraid of that "codeword." I felt uncomfortable with the left-wing election workers I met all through that campaign, so full of talk about a "new coalition of blacks, women, and the young," while leaving out the lower-middle class that had always been the backbone of the Democratic Party in urban centers such as Pittsburgh and Philadelphia, without whose votes a Democrat could by no means win the state of Pennsylvania, for example. (To his credit, Sargent Shriver worked very hard to win those voters back to the party; election returns showed how badly we failed.) I became increasingly aware of what struck me as "left-wing racism," perfectly summarized in that dreadful line: "Do not blame the *victim*," as if blacks were to be treated not as responsible persons but merely as passive recipients of the ministrations of others. When you call someone a "victim," you deny him or her any agency and responsibility on his or her own behalf. At that time, as well, welfare began being treated as a "right"—no questions asked, no demands imposed, no obligations or responsibilities attached. This also seemed to me an amoral way of treating people. For a number of reasons, I was beginning to become estranged from the left.

Still, I thought that the left could be persuaded to return to its traditional roots in the homes, families, and neighborhoods of the working class, not least among them the white ethnics of Southern and Eastern European backgrounds, as well as the Anglo-Saxon Protestant poor of the South and the West. However, just as I was rejecting the left, I began to be rejected *by* the left. The reviews of *The Rise of the Unmeltable Ethnics* by several of my friends, notably Garry Wills and Harvey Cox, were quite harsh, and I was all but called a Fascist and a racist by some.

As I continued my studies of American culture, I wrote a book on the symbolic aspects of the American presidency, *Choosing Our King* (New York: Macmillan, 1974); one on the great liturgical ceremonies of American civic life, our games of baseball, basketball, and football, *The Joy of Sports* (New York: Basic Books, 1976); and one on the founding of the United Mine Workers, focused upon a massacre of Slavic workers in Eastern Pennsylvania in 1897, *The Guns of Lattimer* (New York: Basic Books, 1978). That last book taught me how Slavic immigrants in the period of my grandparents kept in mind the experiences they had endured in central Europe, even as they suffered clear injustices in such places as Lattimer Mines. (The best American Slavic writer of that period, Thomas Bell, described in *Out of This Furnace* [Boston: Little, Brown and Co., 1941] the steel towns of Western Pennsylvania, closer to my own roots.) They did not flinch from recognizing injustice, but, in judging America, they also kept in mind a standard I was to find increasingly valuable in my own work: "Compared to what?"

It was only in about 1976–77 that I was ready to resume my studies of economics, and to come "out of the closet" as a capitalist. I had been thinking about socialism for many years, having been brought up to be anti-capitalist, and to sympathize most closely with such democratic socialist writers as Michael Harrington, the editors of *Dissent* magazine, and others of the social-democratic left. One could clearly sympathize with socialist ideals, in faculty and intellectual circles, without drawing any attention to oneself; in religious studies, Tillich and Niebuhr had paved the way. However, if one were to call oneself a "capitalist," one would encounter a fairly hostile reaction, as one still does even today in circles of religious intellectuals. The more I thought about it, the more I realized that I could not, even though I wanted to, be a socialist. The first piece I wrote in this vein was "A Closet Capitalist Confesses" (*Christianity Today* 20 [April 23, 1976]: 34–35).

A later piece, viewing capitalism as the lesser of two evils, was cautiously called "An Underpraised, Undervalued System" (in Irving Kristol, Paul Johnson, and Michael Novak, *The Moral Basis of Democratic Capitalism: Three Es-*

says (Washington, D.C.: American Enterprise Institute, 1980). There was no question that I was making a public renunciation of socialism. The problem was what to put in its place. At that point in my life, capitalism seemed to me to be a system without a moral theory. Reinhold Niebuhr had referred several times to the "inarticulate wisdom" of the American system, better in its practice than in any theory about it. Jacques Maritain made the same point.

In any case, as I experienced it, the rejection of socialism left me temporarily blind. I had not realized how much my own ideas about history and the future were affected by the socialist ideal. We had been taught to think that democracy is noble but that the capitalist part of our system is inferior and would gradually be replaced by something more ideal. Even though some of us did not quite dare to name our dream "socialism," we thought about even capitalism from within a socialist framework. When one rejects socialism, how is one to imagine the future?

I knew I needed a new intellectual framework. Thus, I began to study the texts of the early liberals. In the past, I often had not read these works directly but had been satisfied with the brief refutations of them offered in the many courses I had taken and books I had read. It had not seemed necessary to read Adam Smith, for example. The refutations poked fun at the "invisible hand," *laissez faire*, the "myth" of the free market, etc. Reading it directly for the first time, however, I found Smith's classic far more powerfully argued, more concrete, more vivid, and more complex than I had been taught to believe.

At this stage of my thinking, what most impressed me about the capitalist system, as about democracy, was its very powerful sense of sin. Smith was a moral philosopher. I found his moral philosophy attractive, so far as it went, since it owed so much to the classic traditions, including Roman Catholic traditions, even though it treated many of their basic concepts in what seemed to me a rather diluted and inferior way. Although flawed by comparison with Aristotle or Aquinas, Smith's moral theory was more attractive than I had expected; it was certainly rooted in unselfishness, a sense of fairness, a generosity of spirit, and a strong sense of community. What most attracted me was his insight into unintended consequences, as well as the distinctions he drew between intentions and results and between concepts that seem intuitively clear and concepts that are counterintuitive but closer to everyday practice. In this, his work reminded me far more than I had expected of Reinhold Niebuhr's sense of irony.

Moreover, I had begun to see that a market economy rooted in invention and discovery depended rather more than I had been taught on the idea of humanity's being made in the image of the Creator and, therefore, called to be creative and inventive. To Adam Smith's question—"What is the cause of the wealth of nations?"—the short answer is: creativity, intellect, wit. Instead of the zero-sum world of the pre-capitalist era, Smith envisaged a world in which human beings would pursue the clues left by the Creator so that the wealth of the world could be steadily augmented, much to the relief of the poor. Smith's vision, moreover, was of an interdependent world. Most of his pages are about things he had observed in what today we would call the Third World, including the "colonies" of North America. Smith was arguing against the British system of his time and place. He was arguing for the adoption of a better system, rudiments of which he saw forming in North America and elsewhere. Some of my reflections on these (for me) new materials found their place in *The Spirit of Democratic Capitalism* (New York: Simon and Schuster, 1982) and in other works I produced just before and after it.

I was struck by the extent to which the founders of the United States saw their own problem as how to create a *novus ordo* that would actually work among a world of sinners. Madison pointed out that there was no use building a government for angels. Sin is an abiding reality. To design a political economy that works, the persistence of sin must be taken for granted. The questions that must be faced are how to make sin less destructive and how to make even sin yield elements of creativity.

A second problem that troubled the first liberal thinkers was where to find a model for a genuinely human society. Nature offers no model of a social organism composed of free, autonomous persons. No biological organism fits the need. No form of animal life offers a model. So, how should one design a system for attaining the common good for a society of *free* persons? Each free person has his or her own sense of the good, both the personal good for each and the common good of all. Since each person's vision of the common good will be different, one can no longer think of the common good as something intended by all, as Aristotle and Aquinas had thought of it. One needs an image of the common good that will survive even when free persons have quite different ideas about the common good, but where on earth is there a metaphor or a model on which to conceive of such a society?

Here, as I reconstruct their path in my own mind, liberal thinkers took two steps. The first emerged in dealing with the problem of censorship (in Milton, for example). The justification *for* censorship had always been the common good. Against this, liberal thinkers seized upon the image of the village market. Here was an example of a procedure for achieving the common good, since by the end of the day everyone should be in a better condition than at the day's beginning. Meanwhile, persons could enter the market for its excitement and bustle and fun, and they could make purchases or not, as they chose. Here was an example of the common good's being achieved, without anyone's having foreseen, intended, or directed all the individual outcomes that constitute the common good. Early pioneers of the liberal society used this argument against censorship, praising "the free market of ideas," in which responsible persons would have to grapple with ideas both good and bad, sort them out, and learn to choose for themselves the sound ideas, just as they had learned to distinguish between shoddy and genuine merchandise. (This image survives in theological controversy today, for example, in the Charles Curran case.)

The image of "the free marketplace of ideas" then led to a second use, a century or so later, in trying to imagine an economic order that would not be directed solely by the officials of the state, any more than reading and studying would be directed solely by the censors. Just as for free persons ideas would be better defended in the free market, so also would the production of goods and services. The liberals of the late eighteenth century wanted to liberate the human race from poverty and were looking for a system that held promise for doing so. The metaphor for that system became the village marketplace. Analytically, of course, a world market is far more complex. Many analytic tools had to be developed for dealing with that complexity. The "market economy" and even the "social-market economy" are not simple ideas. Their full, complex development had to come about through trial and error, but Adam Smith, among others (following early intuitions of the Jesuits of Salamanca), got the process of development started—in the world of ideas and in the world of consequences.

I had been in the seminary over twelve years and had thought about joining the foreign missions, as my brother Dick, two years younger, in fact did. Dick was later killed in ethnic-religious rioting in Dacca in 1964. Before and since, the condition of the poor in such places as Latin America and Asia has long been of considerable importance to me. It is perfectly clear, for example, that in Latin America a revolution in the structure of the political economy is needed. Even more than Great Britain before Adam Smith, Latin American countries maintain institutions rooted in the feudal era: large landed estates, with social elites constituted by the landed aristocracy, the military, and the higher clergy. Most of the rest of the people are like the peasants or serfs of the feudal era, and the middle class is rather small. By now, of course, many landholders have turned their original wealth into the ownership of businesses and industries, often as distributors of goods or services invented elsewhere. Since there is little openness in Latin American markets, it is extremely hard for poor persons to enter these markets, to open up businesses of their own, to incorporate legally, and to find credit to help them get started. The upper classes have an almost complete lock upon markets. In short, the markets are not free. The economic system is still in a pre-capitalist mode.

One must recall that even in Jerusalem in biblical days there were markets, buying and selling, private property, and profits. These do not constitute capitalism but the traditional, precapitalist order. The distinctive marks of capitalism are an emphasis upon (1) invention, (2) open entry by the poor into markets, (3) ease of incorporation, (4) the availability of credit to the poor, and (5) other such institutions at the bottom of society. The strength of a capitalist order lies in the swift entrance of the poor into a broad middle class. In a proper capitalist order, wealth wells up from the bottom. It does not trickle down.

In Latin America today, there are about 70,000,000 youngsters under the age of fifteen. Already born, they will begin entering the job market each year from now until the end of the century. Where will they find work? It almost certainly will not come from more employment in agriculture; modern methods mean that there will be fewer persons employed in agriculture. Nor can it possibly come from international corporations, since these in general are cutting back on Latin American operations, and since in any case they employ only a tiny fraction of Latin Americans. Such employment will be found only if there is a vast explosion of entrepreneurship in small businesses. In the United States, the small-business sector produces about eighty percent of the new jobs (over 30,000,000 new jobs since 1970). This is the normal procedure of capitalistic economies. It is small business that is both the seedbed of capitalism and the dynamic sector of the economy. Latin American countries are among the richest in natural resources in all the world, but so far they have been poor in economic activism and in the openness and dynamism of local economic structures.

Once again, then, by another route, I was led to reflect on the experience of my grandparents on arriving in North America. I have often had reason to be extremely glad that they came to North America rather than, as many of their compatriots did, to Argentina or to Brazil. Latin America is probably as rich as, or even richer than, North America in natural resources, but the institutions of North American economic life have been far more favorable to the poor.

Consider the importance of the Homestead Act of the early 1860's, opening up the vast lands of the West to small, private owners, on two principles: (1) that the cause of the wealth of nations is intellect, and (2) that a multiplication of active intellects in the improvement of the land promises the entire nation far greater wealth. Next were the land-grant colleges, also built on the premise that the cause of wealth is intellect. The Extension Service carried new ideas from the universities to every village and farm. Next came the farm credit bureaus and savings and loan institutions, making credit available to small farmers and small businesses. From the beginning, it was easy to incorporate farms and businesses in the United States, giving families legal protection against bankruptcy and loss due to no fault of their own. Even in 1800, there were more incorporated businesses in America than in all of Britain and France together. Finally, there was the system of patents and copyrights, described in Article 1, Section 8, of the U.S. Constitution—one of the most original features of the political economy of the United States. From the beginning, such Americans as Ben Franklin used their wit in inventing new ways to make life simpler and better. The patent and copyright law was designed to encourage this and to give incentives for invention and discovery.

All these were actions on the part of government, designed to empower individual persons and families to act on their own behalf and in their own ways. In short, the democratic-capitalist idea is that government should be active and should help to empower its citizens. In order to empower citizens, government need not dominate them, plan for them, order them around, or otherwise manage their affairs, as socialist governments are wont to do. Government must be active, but there is a way of being active without being socialist. This is the root insight of democratic capitalism as a form of political economy.

I began my professional life (in *A New Generation: American and Catholic* [New York: Herder and Herder, 1964]) by expressing a desire to develop a systematic theology rooted in the experience of North America, that is, drawing upon the experience of North America as earlier generations of theologians had drawn upon the experiences of Jerusalem, Athens, Rome, Paris, and elsewhere. Each culture in Catholic history has contributed its own genius and spirit to the universal church. I wish that North American theologians were as self-conscious as the Latin American theologians of liberation have become in the last twenty years. We share a common hemisphere. I hope that one day we will share a common theology of the American experience, contributing that to the universal vision of our church and of all humanity.

The small book produced in 1984 by the Lay Commission on Catholic Social Teaching and the U.S. Economy, *Toward the Future*, represents a short statement of how some of us, at least, interpret our economic experience as Catholics in the United States and how we hope the future will go as many signs suggest that it is going. Throughout the world, socialism has been discredited as an idea unfruitful for economic development; the lively experiments, even in the socialist world, are in the direction of recognizing human sinfulness, recognizing the long-term social significance of private property as an instrument of the common good, and grasping the creative and ordering principles of free markets. The crucial role of enterprise attentiveness, invention, discernment in generating economic progress is becoming universally recognized. The argument for capitalist institutions is not, in essence, ideological; it is pragmatic and empirical. Its challenge is: Try it and see. Or: Try other methods first, and then see. If there are better ways, it is in the spirit of capitalism (from Latin, *caput*, head) to recognize and to adopt them.

Our shorter letter, "Liberty and Justice for All," published on November 5, 1986, as a commentary on the final draft of the U.S. Catholic bishops' letter, builds on *Toward the Future*. In the latter, we tried to state the proper balance between individual and community, liberty and equality, enterprise and cooperation, and other crucial polarities of political economy—including politics and economics themselves. In our commentary, we concentrated on what we see as imbalances in the bishops' letter. We think, for example, that the bishops emphasize solidarity too much and individual questioning, dissent, and discovery not enough. We also think that their version of economic rights is dangerously formulated, assigning rights without assigning prior responsibilities and obligations. Still, in many ways, we praise the bishops' letter. It is not that it is so bad but that it should have been so much better.

In any case, laypersons have an obligation to be faithful to their own vocations, as we have tried to be. We welcome the civil argument, concerning political economy, to which the bishops have summoned all of us. It is an important argument. Even its nuances have fateful consequences.

15

POLITICAL ECONOMY IN OUR TIME

Catholics, for good reasons and bad, have been taught a certain ambivalence concerning "liberal" philosophy. On the one hand, they have learned to love such institutions as they have come to share in the United States and a few other places on earth. On the other hand, Vatican documents and many polemical or catechetical writings harshly criticize "liberal" philosophies, and tend to use the word "liberal" pejoratively.

LIBERALISM: RIGHT AND LEFT

Oddly, this ambivalence is found among both left-wing and conservative Catholics. From the left, some form or other of "socialist" vision is preferred to a "liberal" vision. In truth, most Catholics who call themselves "socialists"—such as Arthur J. McGovern, and John C. Cort—are plainly *non-Marxist* socialists. They are eager to protect the right to private property, the virtue of enterprise, and the free activities of at least small-scale businesses. Others on the left seem simply anti-capitalist. They cannot bear to call themselves "capitalist," or to admit to being in favor of a capitalist system. They insist upon occupying a position adversarial to the system in which they live. When pressed, however, they supply either reformist notions of what needs correction in it or warmly utopian visions of something better, but ill-defined.

On the other flank, among religious conservatives, there are three further types of anti-capitalist thought. First, especially in the literary world, there are many religious minds of a Tory, aristocratic and agrarian bent who loathe the churning turmoil that capitalism launches into the earlier and tidier order of the precapitalist world. For many such, the eighteenth century (or the thirteenth) represents the high point of humanism. G. K. Chesterton, Hilaire Belloc, George Will, the Southern Agrarians, Russell Kirk, and others are in this number.

Other highly orthodox Catholics, especially those of non-English background, subliminally think that capitalism is infected with English individualism and spiritual "thinness"; that it is insufficiently spiritual and deep; and that it is vulnerable to shallow materialism and the smugness of a satisfying lunch at an all-male club. Overlooking the tacit presuppositions of an English sense for order, good form and social sensibility (queuing up respectfully for a bus) for example, they like to speak of "raw self-interest" and "savage liberalism." Their image of the archetypal liberal is Scrooge—or, perhaps, Lord Beaverbrook. They share the visceral antagonism to the word "liberal" often expressed in papal documents. Their feeling about it has an ethnic dimension. They do not like the Protestant temper. They read Max Weber with morose delight; for them, Calvinism is a nasty word.

The third group of conservative anti-capitalists—having been educated by such eminent anti-capitalists as Christopher Dawson, Matthew Arnold, Irving Babbitt, Charles Beard and Vernon Parrington—have come to despise liberal philosophy both for its aesthetic vulgarity and for, as they see it, its international failings. Although they are by no means socialists, they share many of the socialists' critiques of multinational corporations overseas. They do not like "mass civilization," rock music, jeans and tee shirts. They would like local aristocracies to be more paternal toward and understanding of the poor, and the poor to act with dignity without aspiring to modern acquisitiveness and ugly tastes. Their "option for the poor" does *not* consist in helping the poor to enter the vulgar middle class.

My own dream of undergirding the humaneness of liberal institutions with (as I see it) the more adequate Catholic philosophy of the human person, its deep sense of community, and its long experienced respect for "intermediate associations" or "mediating structures," has been attacked both from the left and from the right. Curiously, the *reasonings* of the left and of the right are often similar. (Left and right have in common their passionate opposition to liberal institutions.)

INSTITUTIONS AND PHILOSOPHIES

Nevertheless, world events are apparently moving rapidly in the direction of liberal institutions, not so much for ideological reasons as because reality is on their side. In order to secure human rights, for example, more and more people are now convinced that liberal *institutions* are indispensable. Why? Because experience teaches that neither "parchment barriers" nor the good will of individual leaders can be relied upon. Again, in order to achieve real economic progress, even General Secretary Gorbachev and Party Chairman Deng Xiaoping publicly confess that liberal institutions are indispensable: chief among them, those that allow and encourage private initiative and creativity.

Institutionally, "liberalization" has become the central word of political economy in our time. The hypothesis undergirding liberal institutions is being daily vindicated in experience. The "system of natural liberty"—i.e., the set of institutions that most favors the flowering of the innate capacities of the human being—really does work for the common betterment of humankind, if not absolutely, at least in comparison to any known alternative. The liberal hypothesis, the liberal *défi* (as the French say), is experimental: Try it and see. Its temper is empirical. Its presuppositions reach deep into the workings of human liberty and creativity.

The axis of my own argument may be stated as follows. There is a difference between liberal philosophies and liberal institutions. Consider an analogy. In the creative arts, there is often a large distance between what an artist has achieved in his work and the interpretation of it given by that artist. One may admire and appropriate for oneself the meaning of a work of art, without accepting (or even knowing) the express interpretation that moved its creator. So also one may cherish liberal institutions, without embracing in all respects the philosophies of the liberal thinkers who first promoted them. Often those institutions have a greater human significance than their first progenitors discerned. Often there was a tacit wisdom in what they did whose full dimensions escaped their own attention. The intellectual resources embodied in institutions, their historical fecundity, their unintended consequences, and their capacities for unplanned adaptation exceed the imaginative capacities of a single generation. When some institutions, like some works of art, have a truly universal dimension, they belong to all the generations and to all human beings.

Failing to grasp this, some commentators have tried to fault my argument in one of two ways. Professor James Haniuck, in the *National Catholic Register,* asserts that John Stuart Mill was a "utilitarian," and surely (he writes with sarcasm) utilitarianism is no philosophy for the Catholic church or anyone else to recommend as a philosophical basis for human rights. Others, such as Peter Steinfels in *Commonweal* and Joseph Walsh in *Catholic World,* make the opposite accusation. I don't pay enough attention, they say, to the institutional, even political, *struggle* that has been necessary to bring about the historical modifications of "liberal capitalism" that they join me in welcoming. Both these types of criticism overlook my main point. The first confirms one side of my thesis: Liberal philosophy *is* often inadequate as a grounding for liberal institutions, particularly as the latter have developed. The second confirms the other side of my thesis: Liberal institutions have grown out of trial and error, out of struggle and conflict, out of the bloody experiences of many generations; but what commends them to our love and admiration is their internal capacity to undergo alteration and reform.

In one sense, then, I am trying to call attention to the way *institutions* have a life of their own in history, an *intelligible* life that permits of growth and genuine development from the germ of earlier intuitions. Institutions are full of tacit and not always articulable wisdom, just as works of art are. They bear study. But they do not yield up all their secrets to any one generation or body of thought—not, at least, if they are consonant with the depths of human personality. In all great achievements of the human race, as in human personality, there is an inexhaustibility that rewards fresh philosophical reflection in every generation. Among human works of art, political and social institutions are most noble. This is especially true regarding institutions of liberty.

In another sense, I am trying to provide a set of insights—a theory, an interpretation—that brings to light the inner intelligibility of liberal institutions, in a way that has never been attempted. Any readers moderately attentive to Reinhold Niebuhr's mature writing on the American experience will recognize here his dictum, expressed in *The Ironies of American History,* that America's basic institutions contain a deeper, truer wisdom than any of the limited and inadequate theories we have about them. Similarly, Jacques Maritain chided American philosophers, noting that we have never articulated an ideology worthy of our institutions. I have always thought that making explicit what is tacit in common experience is a major part of the philosophical vocation.

My interpretation, of course, by no means exhausts the subject. But it is, so far as it goes, a true interpretation, making intelligible in liberal institutions aspects that have not been brought to light before. That at least is its claim.

One aspect of this originality—one only—is that I have taken phrases almost always used pejoratively in Catholic social thought ("liberal," "liberal individualism," "bourgeois individualism," "liberal capitalism," etc.) and shown the limitations of the criticism. In nearly all cases, such locutions in official Catholic social teaching refer to specific philosophical propositions. Those philosophical propositions may well be rejected. But do they adequately describe the tacit wisdom, the inner intelligibility, of liberal *institutions?* I think not. I am certain that they do not.

Is official Catholic social thought opposed to the institutions of religious liberty found in such nations as Switzerland, West Germany and the United States? To such political democracies as are found in the U.S.? To such liberal institutions as the separation of powers? To an independent judiciary? To a free press? To labor unions and other free associations independent of state control? To private universities, independent institutes of study and research, philanthropic foundations? Joseph Cardinal Hoeffner, probably the single most respected scholar of Catholic social thought among the bishops of the world, has written quite explicitly: "The proponents of Catholic social doctrine deem the market economy to be the right basic form for the economic system."

Thus, to repeat myself, my distinction between philosophical propositions and living institutions is vital. Catholic socialists today absolutely rely upon it. When Pius XI said that "No one can be at the same time a sincere Catholic and a true socialist," the pope was condemning, they say, certain propositions of some socialists, but not necessarily the institutional developments sometimes described by that name today. What is good for the goose is good for the gander. If socialists can employ that distinction, so may liberals. Philosophies described as "liberal" have different histories in Italy, Spain and Latin America from their histories in France and Germany; and different histories again in the

United Kingdom and in the United States. I am offering a definition of "liberal" that ties it to specific sets of *institutions.*

Since this point is so basic to my argument, I trust it will not seem immodest to cite Aaron Wildavsky's grasp of it: "To Michael Novak's great credit, he has placed at the center of his analysis a proper appreciation of the combinations of institutions necessary to approximate the disparate visions of Catholic social thought." This emphasis upon concrete institutions is basic.

CHURCH AND SOCIETY

Wildavsky, however, makes a further point, on which we are in some disagreement. He seems to embrace the view that "there cannot be one moral rule for the church and another for society." In other words, a person who favors liberal institutions in the worldly society should also favor them in the church. Wildavsky poses an either/or: either the church will remain hierarchical, and therefore remain uncomfortable with an egalitarian conception of authority; or it will become egalitarian in its concept of authority and more in tune with the patterns of the liberal society.

From my viewpoint, Wildavsky errs in thinking that the secular order and the religious order are better served when both have the same conception of authority. To keep alive the vital tension between two different conceptions of authority seems to me much more fitting to human reality. Indeed, the tension between these two different conceptions of authority is uncommonly fruitful for human creativity. I would not *want* a church that operated with the same conception of authority in the domain of faith and morals that the larger secular society employs. There are many areas of life in which truth is *not* determined by majority rule or individual preference. Scientific truths are not settled that way. Neither are facts. People are entitled to their own opinions. They are not entitled to their own facts.

A democratic, liberal society in particular needs to protect from erosion the fundamental truths by which it lives. For democratic societies (as our Framers knew) are not threatened solely by tyrants; they are vulnerable, too, to temporary majorities that would override reason, virtue and the rights of minorities. The dignity of the human person must be held sacred—not negotiable, not subject to human experience, not vulnerable either to arrogant majorities or to slipsliding changes in public philosophy. Some truths are well held to be absolute, if democracies are not to be destroyed by their own inner weaknesses. I do not say that Professor Wildavsky needs to share my belief in the necessity of grounding the truths that our Framers held to be "self-evident" in an absolute and unshakeable foundation. But he may find it good for democracy that many of us do share such a belief. Many of us *do* believe that democracy is rooted "in the nature of things," truly a "system of natural liberty," and rooted in natural law.

At the same time, I am glad that government is forbidden from making laws about how such truths shall be defined, or by what reasonings they shall be articulated and defended. The state is not equipped, and should not be equipped, to impose truths and values of that sort. Neither may the state forbid minorities, churches, and seekers of truth from articulating, cherishing and defending such truths, or from protecting their foundation in an authority as awesome and as ultimate as the Author of Life, Creator of the World, and Origin of Truth, of whom our fathers did not hesitate to speak openly. In short, the institutions with authority in moral and religious matters need not, and should not, be organized in the same patterns as the civic institutions designed for other worldly matters. Civil society should not be organized as the Catholic church is; the church should not be organized as civil society is. The two different patterns of internal organization can, however, complement one another in ways highly creative for both.

BIBLICAL ECONOMY?

Finally, I have been criticized by some few readers for referring too seldom to biblical texts. They failed to notice, however, that the texts of the Bible have powerful meaning under any and every system of political economy. With the great Jesuit theologian-economist Heinrich Pesch, I am firmly of the belief that no one can deduce a system of political economy from the texts of the Bible alone. In order to discover a system that actually works, to wit, that actually realizes the vision of humankind revealed in the Bible, a great deal of hard institutional discovery and experimentation is required.

Biblical fundamentalism has often been a mischievous force in the story of actual human liberation, leading to murderously utopian policies and justifying dreadful abuses of the rights of dissenters. To read the Bible intelligently, in the light of the best available human disciplines, and with a certain humility concerning one's own capacities for interpretation, is to draw upon far more intellectual disciplines than private meditation alone. One needs to add to study of the Bible a profound study of political philosophy, of social institutions and of economic experiments throughout history. This is especially true regarding practice or, as the Marxists prefer, praxis. One of the central motifs of biblical realism is the pervasive sinfulness of human beings. Partly because of sin, and also for other reasons, one must think clearly about what actually does work to achieve the liberation of peoples and persons. For institutions often work in counterintuitive ways that are best discerned by trial and error. Such is the irony of history. Biblical simplifiers have often before led their followers into tragedy.

Catholic social thought has been moving at first slowly but now with accelerating speed from a solitary emphasis upon "social justice" to the more balanced pairing of "freedom with justice." No justice is worthy of the human person that does not respect the seat of human dignity: human freedom. And the American word "freedom" (which presupposes a culture of "ordered liberty") is a more exact word than the simple Latin-root "liberty," whose Continental cultural presuppositions may include either libertarianism or even libertinism—or both.

16

THE GREAT CONVERGENCE

A New Consensus in Favor of Economic and Religious Liberty

"Less than 75 years after it officially began, the contest between capitalism and socialism is over: capitalism has won."

Robert Heilbroner

"Definition: Liberty is the reign of conscience."

Lord Acton

We are facing a new relation between "the first and second liberties"—religious liberty and economic liberty—as we begin the second hundred years after Leo XIII's *Rerum Novarum* (1891). Religious liberty and economic liberty are intimately connected as two branches of one root; both are inalienably endowed in humans by their Creator. And there are several reasons why, in the twenty-first century, the the disciplines of economics and philosophy/theology will converge in the study of many common materials, especially those of human choice.

Three important intellectual streams bring us to this point. After the collapse of "real existing socialism" in 1989, Eastern Europeans who are emerging from the ruins are rediscovering one by one—and with fresh appreciation—the moral practices of the free society. Secondly, distinguished economists such as James M. Buchanan are predicting that the fall of socialism will be followed by new directions in economic science which will render that science in a certain sense more humanistic than it has been in recent decades. Third, while remaining highly critical of many aspects of Western economies, Pope John Paul II has taken two important steps to bring Catholic social thought into closer contact with the genius of modern economic practice: he has emphasized the role of human creativity, fashioned in the image of God; and he has grasped the importance of the fundamental right to personal economic initiative.

If it can be said that human history is a record of the human race in search of itself, then these are signs that the twenty-first century will be marked by a new approach to the philosophy of humankind, a new vision of the nature and destiny of man.

THE MIRACLE YEAR

Quite impressively, Pope John Paul II entitles one of the chapters of his new encyclical "The Year 1989." 1989 was, indeed, a year of miracles, at least in the sense that the collapse of socialism, although predicted one hundred years ago by Leo XIII in *Rerum Novarum*, surprised the whole world by being both so sudden and so thorough. Quite unexpectedly, the Berlin Wall came down, the Iron Curtain disintegrated, and the Soviet Empire began to implode. The prestige of existing socialism vanished like a puff of smoke.

At the end of the twentieth century, the world is entering a post-socialist era. Those who have turned away from the poverty and misery of the traditional economies of the third world have now joined those who are turning away from the wreckage of existing socialism in Eastern Europe and the USSR. As Nobel laureate James M. Buchanan wrote in a recent issue of *The Economic Journal*: "The post-socialist century will be marked by a convergence of scientific understanding among those who profess to be economists." We are all capitalists now, even the pope. Both traditionalist (third world) and socialist methods have failed; for the whole world there is now only one form of economics.

In a curious way, then, the citizens of the formerly socialist world are awakening like Rip van Winkle from a long slumber. Many reports show them, as it were, rubbing their eyes with wonder and rediscovering the ordinary world of human experience. For example, just this April, a young woman in Leningrad, Nataliya Yeromeeva, legally opened a small housewares shop in Leningrad, and thus became one of the first private shopkeepers in the Soviet Union in 70 years. "It's in people's nature that if something is theirs, it's theirs," she says, "and a person works with a totally different mind set if he has property."

Through such eyes, the foundations of capitalism look quite different than they do to the jaded West. Former socialists see the moral advantages of capitalism. They see its humanistic qualities. Whereas our aristocratic forebears looked down upon commercial activities, those who have experienced the controlled economy see precisely such activities as a moral advance.

Thus, the East is today discovering the moral case for capitalism in the humble events of daily life, as in Mrs. Yeromeeva's discovery of private property. Another example is the simple experience of being a free and adult consumer. A Bulgarian citizen writes:

> Several German intellectuals and politicians had hard words for the fellow citizens who flung themselves on the West German shops as soon as they could. . . . These could only be the words of people who have forgotten, or

never knew, the personal humiliation inflicted by the permanent lack of the most elementary consumer goods: the humiliation of silent and hostile lines, the humiliation inflicted upon you by salespeople who seem angry to see you standing there, the humiliation of always having to buy what there is, not what you need. The systematic penury of material goods strikes a blow at the moral dignity of the individual.

Even the simple access to material things conveys a moral lesson to those who lived under socialism and waited in lines for two to four hours every day.

The overall lesson of the events in Eastern Europe since 1989 is that there is no "socialist economics." In the words of many Eastern Europeans, socialism does not work—and there is no "third way." There is only one form of economics, and it includes markets, private property, incentives, invention, initiative, and enterprise. Haven't Western economists known this all along? Not quite.

As America's most distinguished Marxist, Robert Heilbroner, has written, virtually none of the economists of the left or even of the center predicted the downfall of socialism. It pained him to say so, but the only economists who actually did predict the outcome were such economists as Friedrich von Hayek and Ludwig von Mises, both of whom were treated dismissively by mainline economists in the United States and elsewhere. Where did mainline economists go wrong?

The answer to this question may lead us to a quite new way of thinking about economics. "Why did economists," Professor Buchanan asks, "fail to recognize that incentives remain relevant in all choice settings? Why did economists forget so completely the simple Aristotelian defense of private property? Why did so many economists overlook the psychology of value, which locates evaluation in persons not in goods? Why did so many professionals in choice analysis fail to recognize the informational requirements of a centrally controlled economy in both the logical and empirical dimensions? Why was there the near total failure to incorporate the creative potential of human choice in models of human interaction?"

To a theologian, these questions from Professor Buchanan are quite stimulating. To a remarkable extent, they bring economists into a territory that philosophers and theologians are also obliged to explore. Incentives? Private property? A psychology of value? Persons rather than goods? Creative potential, human choice? These are concepts that have excited philosophers and theologians for centuries; indeed, these are concepts that philosophers and theologians were the first to draw from the mists of human experience.

THE ANTI-CAPITALIST BIAS OF INTELLECTUALS

Professor Heilbroner's questions remind us of the anti-capitalist bias of the intellectuals—and not only of economists, but also of theologians. In 1891, Pope

Leo XIII condemned socialism; he called it "futile" as well as "evil" and "unjust." But he was reluctant to praise "liberal capitalism" as he found it in 1891, and he worked assiduously to reform it.

Why were intellectuals, both secular and religious, so opposed to "liberal capitalism"? Mostly, they saw only its negative features. They feared such dangers as "excessive individualism," "materialism," "acquisitiveness," and "excessive concentrations of economic power," whether in monopolies or in narrow financial circles. They were not wrong to fear such potential dangers and many real abuses. Systematically, however, they underestimated the spiritual resources of real existing capitalist countries, and especially of those in which democratic institutions were powerful, the law was held in high respect, and the religious traditions of Judaism, Christianity, and even a certain ethical humanism remained strong. Over the decades, the original capitalist countries, especially in the Anglo-American world, undertook many forms of social reorganization. In his latest encyclical, *Centesimus Annus*, Pope John Paul II has recognized these internal transformations—and encouraged yet more of them.

One reason why intellectuals overlooked the self-reforming capacities of capitalism, when embedded in powerful democratic and moral-religious traditions, may have to do with the origins of modern intellectual life in certain powerful aristocratic biases. For modern economics was born not in an era altogether neutral regarding commerce, trade, and industry. As the economic historian Jacob Viner has written:

> Among the Greek and Roman philosophers hostile or contemptuous attitudes towards trade and the merchant were common, based in the main on aristocratic and snobbish prejudice, and with no or naïve underpinning of economic argument. Thus Aristotle maintained that trade was an unseemly activity for nobles or gentlemen, a "blameable" activity. He insisted that wealth was essential for nobility, but it must be inherited wealth. Wealth was also an essential need of the state, but it should be obtained by piracy or brigandage, and by war for the conquest of slaves, and should be maintained by slave workers. . . .
>
> The early Christian fathers on the whole took a suspicious if not definitely hostile attitude towards the trade of the merchant or middleman, as being sinful or conducive to sin.

Adam Smith, the inventor of economic science, was a student of theology in his youth and was occupied professionally throughout his life in the teaching of moral philosophy. Nonetheless, theology in his time was deeply embedded in the habits, images, and practices of preceding centuries. Its viewpoint was as rooted in the land as that of landholders and rural peasants; it was adversarial both to commerce and manufacturing; it was aristocratic. The viewpoint of this earlier theology was, on the whole, favorable to inherited wealth (or wealth conferred by royal endowment), but it was quite dismissive of earned wealth, particularly of wealth earned through commerce and manufacturing.

It celebrated the arts of statecraft and war, of entertaining and dining, of magnificence and lavish giving, of ceremony and play. It did not look with equal esteem upon the grubby and sweaty arts of providing goods and services, of buying and selling, and of pioneering in invention and manufacture. It loved the categories of the liberal arts, and looked down upon the "servile" industrial and commercial arts. It called the liberal arts "noble" and the commercial arts "merely useful." The first it commended as a way of "being," while it dismissed the second as crassly "utilitarian." Resenting this rebuff, economists for their part began regarding religious reflection as unrealistic and irrelevant, if not positively harmful to the condition of the poor and to honest empirical inquiry.

RECONCILING ECONOMICS AND RELIGION

The new encyclical of Pope John Paul II, *Centesimus Annus*, issued on May 1, 1991, indicates a strong desire to end the divorce between religion and economics once and for all. Noting the collapse of Marxism, Pope John Paul II completes the efforts begun by Leo XIII a century ago to point to necessary reforms of a democratic, law-abiding, anthropologically sound form of capitalism.

One hundred years ago, Pope Leo XIII won a name for himself as "the pope of associations" because he made free associations central to his social teaching. In a similar way, 100 years from now, Pope John Paul II may be accorded fame as "the pope of economic enterprise" because he made "personal economic initiative" central to his social teaching. In *Sollicitudo Rei Socialis*, the Holy Father declared the right of personal economic initiative to be a fundamental human right, second only to the right of religious liberty, rooted (like religious liberty) in the image of the Creator endowed in every human being. Like their Maker, he suggested, men and women are called to be cocreators in the economic realm.

Perhaps those who have been trained in the disciplines of business life and economics will immediately discern the significance of this theological insight. Schumpeter, Hayek, and Kirzner have taught that the cause of the wealth of nations is invention, discovery, enterprise. In important ways, therefore, human capital is prior to physical capital. Thus, in turning to the creation story of Genesis as a guide to his reflections on economics, Pope John Paul II has found a way to heal the breach between religion and economics from which the West has suffered for 200 years. This move also makes possible a reconciliation of economics and religious reflection, after their long divorce of almost 200 years.

All these moves allow us to look again at the history of the last two centuries, especially the rise of inventiveness. The new order of the eighteenth century—the "commercial republic"—first commended itself to Western civilization by its moral superiority to the old order. In place of brigandage and war, it offered law and consensual contracts. "Commerce and Peace" was the motto of commercial Amsterdam. When the path to wealth was blazed by innovation, industry, and exchange, rather than by plunder, brigandage, and conquest, it was a great moral gain for the West.

To be sure, a new economy was not—is not—enough; we must be *democratic* capitalists, in the sense that a full and thriving form of the free economy requires a sound political system rooted in the consent of the governed, as well as the guidance of a deep, compassionate, and realistic moral and cultural system. Thus, economics will increasingly come to be seen as the study of human choice. Choice will become ever more central in economic analysis. This means the human being will become more central. Now that the world is turning rather more unanimously to forms of political economy which enlarge the scope of choice in the political, economic, and moral/cultural fields, we must deepen the science of public choice. In an important sense, economics will necessarily become more focussed on the human capacity to reflect and to choose, that is, more humanistic.

Exactly these two activities, reflection and choice, the Catholic tradition has long held, constitute the image of God in the human creature. Down the ages, many metaphors have been used of God: God is like the mountains, or like the boundless seas, or like the constant stars, or like the hen taking her chicks under her wing. But the most compelling analogies for God have come from the most complicated form of life found on earth, the human being. No one has seen God, but whatever God is like, He is imagined to be more like the activities of reflecting and choosing—of understanding and loving—than like any other phenomena in the world of human experience. Within the human being, since at least the time of Plato and Aristotle, nothing has been found more godlike than the human capacity for insight and choice: that fire of light and passionate longing for the good, which have so animated Western civilization. Emboldened by Professor Buchanan, I predict that a new vision will take shape around the concept of choice—public choice and private choice.

Already in *Sollicitudo Rei Socialis* the pope had linked religious and economic liberty with the liberty of association and other core liberties:

> The denial or the limitation of human rights—as for example the right to religious freedom, the right to share in the building of society, the freedom to organize and to form unions, or to take initiative in economic matters—do these not impoverish the human person as much as, if not more than, the deprivation of material goods?

The pope added that

> in today's world, among other rights, the right of economic initiative is often suppressed. Yet it is a right which is important not only for the individual but also for the common good. Experience shows us that the denial of this right, or its limitation in the name of an alleged "equality" of everyone in society,

diminishes, or in practice absolutely destroys the spirit of initiative, that is to say the creative subjectivity of the citizen.

TWO CONCEPTS OF LIBERTY

Yet liberty is a concept that begs us to go slowly. It is not the easiest concept to understand. In particular, the tradition of Roman law (and the Napoleonic code) give rise to a different view of liberty than that implicit in the common law. In much of Continental Europe, liberty—the French *liberté*, the Italian *libertà*, and perhaps the Latin *libertas*—seems to embrace the realm of whatever is permitted or not forbidden. Within this horizon, liberty and law are conceived of nearly as opposites: on one side, those things commanded or forbidden, on the other side, those things not covered in the law, concerning which one is free. The Anglo-American conception (the Whig conception) is quite different. Here liberty is conceived of as the inner form of the law. The intelligibility of the free act derives from reason, law, duty, or a well-ordered conscience.

We need to examine this notion further, for it brings religious reflection closer to the economists' notion of "rational choice," while at the same time enriching the economists' notion. This understanding makes plain that "rational" does not mean only "utilitarian" or only "materialistic." Empirically, this notion seems quite sound. After reflection, human beings do frequently act from more than materialistic motives and from motives in no narrow sense utilitarian.

One of the great philosophers on the theme of liberty is the great English Catholic layman and historian, Lord Acton. For Acton, the expansion of human liberty is the key to the design of Providence for human history. And Christianity is the chief historical force in fitting this key to history.

> The Christian notion of conscience imperatively demands a corresponding measure of personal liberty. The feeling of duty and responsibility to God is the only arbiter of a Christian's actions. With this no human authority can be permitted to interfere. We are bound to extend to the utmost, and to guard from every encroachment, the sphere in which we can act in obedience to the sole voice of conscience, regardless of any other consideration.

And conscience, as Acton understood it, is not free-floating or arbitrary, but responsible to reason. He means a rightly ordered conscience. Among other "definitions of liberty" given by Acton, we read: "reason reigning over reason, not will over will" and "reason before will."

> Religious liberty is not the negative right of being without any particular religion, just as self-government is not anarchy. It is the right of religious communities to the practice of their own duties, the enjoyment of their own constitution, and the protection of the law, which equally secures to all the possession of their own independence.

It should be clear from this that the Anglo-American definition of liberty is distinctive. It means liberty *under* law, not liberty *from* law. It means the liberty to do what we ought to do, not the liberty to do anything we feel like. In this respect, liberty in the Anglo-American sense is like the definition of practical wisdom in Aristotle. In Aristotle, prudence is *recta ratio, ordered* understanding (*recta*, that is, directed by a good will), and in American terms, liberty is *ordered* liberty. This is illustrated in the classic and popular American hymn: "Confirm thy soul in self control; Thy liberty in law."

The visual image of this novel insight, captured by its French architects, is presented by the Statue of Liberty: Liberty is a woman (wisdom) with the lamp of reason uplifted in one hand, and in her other hand the book of the law.

THE TRADITIONALIST CONCEPT OF ORDER

In traditionalist religious circles, there are two problems with the idea of liberty. First, traditionalists confuse liberty with libertinism. They do not understand that in the democratic capitalist countries, laws are framed by the consent of the governed, so respect for law is high. And liberty is ordered by law, reason, and conscience. Without law, it is widely recognized that liberty cannot be achieved.

Secondly, traditionalists imagine that liberty must lead to chaos. Where there is liberty, they think, each person will go off in a different direction, at whim, or in pursuit of crass self-interest without order. Only the law, they imagine, or only a strong leader, can hold other wills in check, channel them, and make the trains run on time.

In traditional cultures, this may be so. But in cultures based upon free and dynamic markets, purely centrifugal activities would be self-defeating. For there is one secret to the free society that traditionalists do not grasp. The free market is a centripetal force. Where it is truly dynamic, based upon invention and innovation, the free market obliges those who would succeed in it to pay attention to others, even to their unexpressed wants and desires, and to their longing for basic respect and dignity.

Unlike an aristocratic order, a market order begins on the assumption that all who enter the market are equal, that each has dignity and that each deserves respect. Where these are lacking, something is quite lacking in the market, and its participants will loudly complain. The market's ideal is that every exchange should be based on the full consent of those who take part. In the ideal situation, not only should both parties to an exchange be satisfied; each should think that in a way each has got the better of the deal (given the different immediate needs and concrete situations of the two). Each should be glad to do business with the other again. This is the meaning behind the common axiom, "The customer is always right." If you want your customers to return, they must leave your presence with a certain sense not only of dignity intact, but also of satisfaction obtained.

Thus the insight most lacking to traditionalists is that intelligent and practical persons, acting freely and on behalf of their own practical wisdom, can in their free exchanges generate a spontaneous order, which is superior in its reasonableness to any order that might be planned, directed, or enforced from above. Some traditionalists seem to believe that the only possible order is order enforced from on high. Order, in the traditionalist view, is first an intellectual construct conceived in the mind of the leader, then promulgated, then enforced. In a free society the conception of order is quite different. When free persons try to be reasonable and cooperative, and attempt to enter into reasonable contracts with their fellows, these very efforts give rise to a social order much more alive with intelligence, and more subtly and gracefully ordered, than all the planned and top-down directed orders on earth.

That free markets, under some conditions, produce a superior social order should be treated as an empirical statement. That is, such a statement will be true only if extended social experiments are compared and if the predicted consequences do in fact occur. The prediction of the traditionalists is that a free society will lack all order. The prediction of those who believe in the power of free markets to encourage reasonable and cooperative behavior is that markets will give rise to a more dynamic order, shot through with greater intelligence and a wider and deeper intelligibility, than any known alternative.

DYNAMIC ORDER

The democratic capitalist order is not a static order. New inventions continually disrupt it. Before there was an automobile culture, there was a democratic capitalist culture of horses and carriages. Before there were word processors, there were only typewriters—but typewriters were already a great advance upon quill pens. Before there was an electronic revolution, there was an industrial revolution (characterized by pulleys and pistons and grease). The amazing thing about a civilization built upon choice is that it is a civilization of the most remarkable dynamism. Its order is not the order of static equilibrium, but the order of continual change.

Moreover, this principle of change appears to have a fascinating characteristic: the direction of change does not seem to be random. On the contrary, change fairly regularly occurs in the direction of a purer and more immediate expression of the human mind. If the typewriter seemed obedient to the human mind, the electronic display of the word processor seems to reflect the human mind even more translucently. In the computer screen, the human mind has hardly to think before it sees an expression of itself. The logic built into the computer encourages the human mind again to take flight and to imagine yet more docile machines.

Although we have not come to the end of the series of social experiments to build a social order worthy of the human mind and soul, we have discovered that there are three fundamental orders of liberty: political liberty, economic liberty, and cultural liberty. Even the structure of the famous document of Vatican II on the Church and the world, *Gaudium et Spes*, was conveniently divided into three parts, one part for each of these three spheres of liberty.

Yet, curiously enough, attempts by the modern world to develop institutions that more fully express the human capacity for liberty in all three spheres have resulted in a world more interdependent than ever before. Far from leading to anarchy, ordered liberty leads to interdependence. Far from leading to uniformity, it nourishes cultural variety. Indeed, seldom in history have movements of ethnic, religious, cultural, and linguistic differentiation been stronger. These are normally expressed within and balanced by the powerful centripetal forces of interdependence. In an important way, the motto of such a world might well be *E pluribus unum*.

One may thus imagine that in the twenty-first century philosophers and theologians will acquire a great deal more economic sophistication than they now have. It may also be expected that economists will become ever more skillful in developing humanistic categories—philosophical and theological—adequate to the complex phenomena of human choice which they try to interpret. Fundamentally, the proper subject of both economics and philosophy/theology is the human person and the human community, in their creativity and mutual sustenance.

In the twenty-first century, the disciplines of economics and religious reflection should converge.

17

HOW CHRISTIANITY
CHANGED POLITICAL ECONOMY

What did Jesus Christ add to Athens and Rome that altered the human conception of political economy? The question is a little odd to the ear. It is not a question usually asked. Yet it turns out to suggest, for all its novelty, a fresh way of looking at political history.

Permit me to propose for your consideration the following thesis: At least seven contributions made by Christian thinkers, meditating on the words and deeds of Jesus Christ, altered the vision of the good society proposed by the classical writers of Greece and Rome, and made certain modern expectations possible. Be warned that space is lacking to support each assertion with clinching argument. I present a horizon, a way of thinking to be explored, not an airtight argument in its defense.

It should also be noted that history does not proceed as logic. Many of the implications of the teaching of Jesus—especially the implications for politics, economics, and culture—were not immediately apparent, and some may still not be. Sometimes, as in the case of human rights and even democracy, attention is drawn to these implications not by logical deduction, but by the shocking impact of events arising from outside the Christian community. Catholic social thought proceeds dialectically, that is, by way of reflection on experience as well as logic, and by prudence much more than by logical deduction. Nonetheless, the yeast of Christ's teaching does work darkly in the dough of history even through crooked and contingent byways. Even the devil serves God's purposes.

Be warned, also, that I want to approach this subject in a way satisfying to honest secular thinkers. You shouldn't have to be a believer in Jesus Christ in order to grasp the plausibility of my argument. In fact, Richard Rorty, the self-described atheist and nihilist, opened up this approach in criticizing the Platonism of the revered Czech philosopher and martyr Jan Patočka (1907–1977):

> Jerusalem should share the credit with Athens for making Europe what it has become. The Christian suggestion that we think of strangers primarily as fellow sufferers, rather than as fellow inquirers into Being, or as fellow carers for

194

the soul, should have a larger role than Patočka gives it. The waves of joy of 1989 cannot plausibly be traced to the sense that judgment had been rendered on Socrates' judges, as opposed to the belief that a lot of people who had been humiliated and shamed would now be able to stand up and to speak. Separating out the roles of Socrates and Christ in the history of Europe is a notoriously tricky business, but surely Patočka oversimplifies things when, like Heidegger, he approvingly quotes Nietzsche's comment that "Christianity is Platonism for the people." Might not a sense that charity and kindness are the central virtues have caught on, and helped make Europe what it became, even if some eager Platonists had not grabbed control of Christian theology?

Analogously, in his book, *Why I Am Not a Christian,* Bertrand Russell concedes that, although he takes Jesus Christ to be no more than a humanistic moral prophet, modern progressivism is indebted to Christ for the ideal of compassion.

1. *The first contribution of Jesus was to bring Judaism to the Gentiles, and in at least three key respects, Judaism changed Mediterranean ideas about political economy.* First, from Jerusalem, that crossroads between three continents open to the East and West, North and South, Jesus brought recognition of the One God, the Creator.

Second, the term "Creator" implies a free person; it suggests that creation was a free act, an act that did not flow from necessity. It was an act of intelligence; the Creator knew what He was doing, and He willed it; that is, "He saw that it is good." From this notion of the One God/Creator, some practical corollaries for human action follow.

- Made in the image of God, we should be attentive and intelligent. *Inquire relentlessly.*
- As God loved us, so it is fitting for us to respond with love. Since in creating us He knew what He was doing and He willed it, we have every reason to trust His understanding and His will. Since He made us in His image, well ought we to say with Jefferson: "The God who gave us life gave us liberty." *Trust liberty.*
- At a certain moment, time was created by God, and given a direction toward "building up the Kingdom of God . . . on earth as in heaven." *Understand that history has a beginning, and an end—and that our vocation is progress, in both personal and social pilgrimage.*

Third, then, following from this last point, as many scholars have noted the idea of "progress," like the idea of "creation," is not a Greek idea—nor is it Roman. The Greeks preferred notions of the necessary procession of the world from a First Principle. They viewed history as a cycle of endless return. The idea of history as a category distinct from nature is a Hebrew rather than a Greek idea.

What are the implications for political economy of the fact that history begins in the free act of the Creator, who made humans in His image, and who gave them with their first breath both existence and an impulse toward liberty and communion? In this act of creation, in any case, Jefferson properly located—and it was the sense of the American people—not only the origin of the inner core of human rights (". . . and endowed by their Creator with certain inalienable rights"), but also the perspective of providential history ("When in the course of human events . . ."). The early Americans were aware of creating something "new": a new world, a new order, a new science of politics, a new republic. As children of the Creator, they felt no taboo against originality; on the contrary, they thought it their vocation.

2. *The revelation that God is Three: Father, Son, and Holy Spirit.* When Jesus spoke of God, He spoke of the communion of three persons in one. Unlike the Greeks (Parmenides, Plato, Aristotle), who thought of God or the *Nous* as One living in solitary isolation, the Christian world was taught by Jesus to think of God as a communion of three. In other words, the mystery of community is one with the mystery of being.

Thus, the West wondered at the fact that we are part of a long procession of the human community in time; and that we are, by the grace of God, one with one another and with God. To exist is already something to marvel at; universal communion is even more so.

Recognition of the Trinity is not without significance for the relation between person and community, in political economy as well as in theology. (This is a point frequently made by Catholic writers, but admittedly little noted by Protestant or secular writers.) First, it establishes an ideal of community in which each person is separate, distinct, and independent, and yet one with others. Christians should not simply lose themselves in community, having their personality and independence merge into an undifferentiated mass movement. On the contrary, Christianity teaches us that in true community the distinct independence of each person is crucial.

The communal side of this point taught the West that persons reach their full development only in community with others. No matter how highly developed in himself or herself, a totally isolated person, cut off from others, is regarded as something of a monster. Catholics, Jews, and socialists have emphasized this half of the truth. The personalistic side of this point taught the West that a community that refuses to recognize the personhood of individuals often uses them as means to "the common good," rather than treating persons as ends in themselves. Such communities are coercive and tyrannical. Protestants, Catholic personalists, and liberals have emphasized this half of the truth.

3. *The equality-uniqueness* (not *the equality-sameness) of the children of God.* In Plato's *Republic,* citizens were divided in this way: A few were of gold, a slightly larger body of silver, and the vast majority of lead. The last had the souls of

slaves, and it was fitting that they be enslaved. Only persons of gold are truly to be treated as ends in themselves. For Judaism and Christianity, on the contrary, the God who made every single child gave worth and dignity to each of them, however weak or vulnerable. "What you do unto the least of these, you do unto me." God identified Himself with the most humble and most vulnerable.

Our Creator knows each of us by name, and understands our own individuality with a far greater clarity than we ourselves do; after all, He made us. Each of us reflects a small fragment of God's identity. If one of us is lost, the image of God intended to be reflected by that one is lost, and His image in the entire race is distorted.

Judaism and Christianity grant a fundamental equality in the sight of God to all humans, whatever their talents or station. This equality arises because God penetrates *below* any artificial rank, honor, or station that may on the surface differentiate one from another. He sees past those things. He sees *into* us. He sees us as we are in our uniqueness, and it is that uniqueness that He values. We may call this *equality-as-uniqueness.* Before God, we have equal weight in our *uniqueness,* not because we are *the same,* but because each of us is *different.*

This conception is quite different from the modern "progressive" or socialist conception of *equality-sameness.* The Christian notion is not a levelling notion. Neither does it delight in uniformity.

For most of its history, Christianity like Judaism flourished in hierarchical societies. While recognizing that all humans are equal in this: that each single person lives and moves under God's Judgment, Christianity has also rejoiced in the differences among us. God did not make us equal in talent, ability, calling, office, fortune, or graces.

Equality-uniqueness is not the same as equality-sameness. The first recognizes our claim to a unique identity and dignity. The second desires to take away what is unique and to submerge it in uniformity. Thus, modern movements such as Socialism have disfigured the original Christian impulse of equality. Like Christianity, modern Socialist movements reject the Platonic stratification of citizens into gold, silver, and lead. But their materialistic impulse led them to pull people down, to place all on the same level. This was an ugly program.

4. *Compassion.* It is true that virtually all peoples have traditions of care for those in need. However, in most religious traditions, these movements of the heart are limited to one's own family, kin, or nation. In some ancient cultures, young males in particular were taught to be hard and insensitive to pain, so that they could be sufficiently cruel to enemies. Terror was the instrument intended to drive outsiders away from the territory of the tribe. In principle (though not always in practice), Christianity opposed this limitation by encouraging the impulse to reach out, especially to the most vulnerable, to the poor, the hungry, the wretched, those in prison, the hopeless, the sick, and others. It told humans to love their enemies. This is the "solidarity" whose necessity for modernity Rorty perceives.

In the name of compassion, Christianity tries to humble the mighty, and to prod the rich into concern for the poor. It does not turn the young male away from being a warrior, but it does teach him to model himself on Christ, in order to become a new type of male: The knight bound by a code of compassion, the gentleman. It teaches the warrior to be meek, humble, peaceable, kind, and generous. It introduces a new and fruitful tension between the warrior and the gentleman, between magnanimity and humility, between kindness and fierce ambition. Nietzsche falsely complained that Christianity brought about the feminization of the male. It did bring about the making of gentlemen.

5. *Universal community, incarnate (local) community.* Christianity has taught human beings that an underlying imperative of history is to bring about a law-like, peaceable community, among all people of good will on the entire earth. This was the impulse behind the Holy Roman Empire, however naively conceived that Empire was. For political economy, Christianity proposed a new ideal: the entire human race is a universal family, created by the one same God, and urged to love that God.

Yet at the same time, Christianity (like Judaism before it) is also the religion of a particular kind of God: Not the Deist who looks down on all things from an olympian height but the God of one chosen people and, in Christianity's case, a God who became *incarnate.* The Christian God was carried in the womb of a single woman, among a particular people, at a precise intersection of time and space, and nourished in a local community then practically unknown to the rest of the peoples on this planet. Christianity is a religion of the concrete and the universal. It pays attention to the flesh, the particular, the concrete, and each single intersection of space and time; its God is the God of the "dapple-dawn-drawn" poems of Gerard Manley Hopkins, the "prudence" of St. Thomas Aquinas, and the respect for the *nationes* of the University of Paris. Its God is the God of singulars, the God who Himself became a singular man. At the same time, the Christian God is the Creator of all.

With Edmund Burke, Christianity sees the need for proper attention to every "little platoon" of society, to the immediate neighborhood, to family. At the same time, Christianity directs the attention of these little communities toward ever larger communities. Christianity forbids them to be merely parochial or xenophobic, but it also warns them against becoming premature universalists, one-worlders, gnostics pretending to be pure spirits detached from all the limits of concrete flesh. Christianity instructs us about the precarious balance between the concrete and the universal in our own nature. This is the mystery of catholicity. In this sense, Christianity goes beyond contemporary conceptions of "individualism" and "communitarianism."

6. *"I am the Truth." The defense of intellect. Truth matters.* The Creator of all things has total insight into all things. He knows what He has created. This gives the weak and modest minds of human beings the vocation to use their minds

relentlessly, in order to penetrate the hidden layers of intelligibility that God has written into His creation. Meditation on this theme over many centuries, Alfred North Whitehead suggested, prepared the ground for modern science. Everything in creation is in principle understandable: In fact, at every moment everything is understood by Him, who is eternal and therefore simultaneously present to all things. (In God there is no history, no past-present-future. In His insight into reality, all things are as if simultaneous.)

John Adams, our second president, wrote that in giving us a notion of God as the Source of all truth, and the Judge of all, the Hebrews laid before the human race the possibility of civilization. Before the undeceivable Judgment of God, the Light of Truth cannot be deflected by riches, wealth, or worldly power. Armed with this conviction, Jews and Christians are empowered to use their intellects and to search without fear into the causes of things, their relationships, their powers, and their purposes. This understanding of Truth makes humans free. For Christianity does not teach that Truth is an illusion based upon the opinions of those in power, or merely a rationalization of powerful interests in this world. Christianity is not deconstructionist, and it is certainly not totalitarian. Its commitment to Truth beyond human purposes is, in fact, a rebuke to all totalitarian schemes and all nihilist cynicism.

Moreover, by locating Truth (with a capital T) in God, totally beyond our poor powers to comprehend, Christianity empowers human reason. It does so by inviting us to use our heads as best we can, to discern the evidences that bring us as close to Truth as human beings can attain. It endows human beings with a vocation to give play to the unquenchable eros of the desire to understand—that most profoundly restless drive to know that teaches human beings their own finitude and yet, as well, their participation in the infinite.

The notion of Truth is crucial to civilization. As Thomas Aquinas held, civilization is constituted by conversation. Civilized persons persuade one another through argument. Barbarians club one another into submission. Civilization requires citizens to recognize that they do not possess the truth, but must be possessed by it, to the degree possible to them. Truth matters greatly. But Truth is greater than any one of us. Therefore, humans must learn such civilizing habits as being respectful and open to others, listening attentively, trying to see aspects of the Truth that they do not as yet see. Because the search for Truth is vital to each of us, humans must argue with each other, urge each other onward, point out deficiencies in one another's arguments, and open the way for greater participation in the Truth by every one of us.

In this respect, the search for Truth makes us not only humble but also civil. It teaches us *why* we hold that every single person has an inviolable dignity: Each is made in the image of the Creator to perform such noble acts as understanding, deliberating, choosing, loving. These noble activities of human beings cannot be repressed without repressing in them the Image of God. Such repression is doubly sinful. It violates the other person, and it is an offense against God.

One of the ironies of our present age is that the great philosophical carriers of the Enlightenment no longer believe in reason. They have surrendered their confidence in the vocation of Reason to cynics such as to the postmodernists and deconstructionists. Such philosophers (*Sophists*, Socrates called them) hold that there is no Truth, that all things are relative, and that the great realities of life are power and interest. So we have come to an ironic pass. The children of the Enlightenment have abandoned Reason, while those they have considered unenlightened and living in darkness, the people of Jewish and Christian faith, remain today Reason's best defenders. For believing Jews and Christians ground their confidence in reason in the Creator of all reason, and their confidence in understanding in the One who understands everything He made—and, besides, loves it.

There can be no civilization of reason (or of love) without faith in the vocation of reason.

7. *Judgment/Resurrection.* Christianity teaches realistically not only the glories of human beings—their being made in the image of God—but also their sins, weaknesses, and evil tendencies. Judaism and Christianity are not utopian; they try to understand humans as they are, as God sees them both in their sins and in the graces that He grants them. This sharp awareness of human sinfulness was very important to the American founding.

Without ever using the term "original sin," the authors of *The Federalist* are eloquent about the flaws, weaknesses, and evils to which humans are prone. They designed a republic that would last, not only among saints, but also among sinners.

Christianity teaches that at every moment the God who made us is judging how well we make use of our liberty. And the first word of Christianity in this respect is: "Fear not. Be not afraid." For Christianity teaches that Truth is ordered to mercy. Truth is not, thank God, ordered first of all to justice. For if Truth were ordered to strict justice, not one of us would stand against the gale.

God is just, yes, but the most accurate name for Him is not justice, but mercy. (The Latin root of this word conveys the idea more clearly: *Misericordia* comes from *miseris + cor*—give one's heart to *les miserables*, the wretched ones.) This name of God, *Misericordia,* according to St. Thomas Aquinas, is God's most fitting name. Toward our misery, He opens His heart. "At the heart of Christianity lies the sinner," Charles Péguy wrote.

Judgment Day is the Truth on which civilization is grounded. No matter the currents of opinion in our time, or any time; no matter what the powers and principalities may say or do; no matter the solicitations pressing upon us by our families, friends, and larger culture; no matter what the pressures may be—we will still be under the Judgment of One Who is undeceivable, knows what is in us, and knows the movements of our souls more clearly than we know them ourselves. In His Light, we are called to bring a certain honesty into our own lives, and into our respect for the Light that God has imparted to every human being.

On this basis human beings may be said to have inalienable rights, and dignity, and infinite worth.

SUMMARY

These seven recognitions lie at the root of Jewish-Christian civilization, the one that is today evasively called "Western civilization." From them are derived our deepest notions of truth, liberty, community, person, conscience, equality, compassion, progress, and judgment. These are the most powerful energies working in our culture, as yeast works in dough, as a seed falling into the ground dies and becomes a spreading mustard tree.

18

ECONOMICS AS HUMANISM

For more than a century now economics has been advanced and practiced as a science, on the model of physics and mathematics. It was not always so. From Adam Smith's *Inquiry into the Nature and the Causes of the Wealth of Nations* in 1776 until well after the publication of John Stuart Mill's Principles of Political Economy in 1848, economics was viewed as a branch of moral philosophy astonishingly underdeveloped by earlier philosophers. It seems hardly possible, yet it is true, that before the time of Adam Smith no classic author—not Aristotle, not Aquinas, not Bacon nor Descartes—had asked about the cause of the wealth of nations in any sustained and fruitful way. Such an inquiry may well have been of great social utility, had it been successfully pursued in earlier, poorer centuries. But the problems of political order and the rule of law were of such importance—neither person nor property being safe from marauders, brigands, and feuding princes, whether in Europe or in other places on the planet—that the development of economics required the prior development of politics and law.

During our own century, a school of economics much disdained by the leaders and the general run of professionals in the field (who were more and more attracted to the scientific model, and particularly to the strengths and beauties of mathematics) has restored economics as a field worthy of investigation by moral philosophy. The school is known as the Austrian School, the school of "classical liberals" or, in F. A. Hayek's preferred description, "Whigs." Let me state the accomplishment of these Whigs starkly: As a result of the inquiries of the Austrian School, it has become clear that economics is at least as much a branch of moral philosophy and the liberal arts as it is a science.

This result was the fruit of three investigative strategies favored by the Austrian School. The first strategy was to attend to the *subject* in economic activities as well as the "objective" factors of production. "Why did economists fail to recognize that incentives remain relevant in all choice settings?" asked Nobel Prize-winner James M. Buchanan in 1991. "Why did so many economists overlook the psychology of value, which locates evaluation in persons, not in goods?

. . . Why was there a near total failure to incorporate the creative potential of human choice in models of human interaction?" Taking advantage of cross-cultural studies of the work ethic, social trust, individual initiative, willingness to risk, patterns of cooperation, and other moral habits—together with studies in decision and game theory on the dilemmas that acting subjects typically face—the Whig economists have been able to focus attention on incentives, values, information, and choice, both private and public, including activities of deliberation, reflection, and selection.

The second of the Austrian strategies was to inquire into the concept of human action. The idea was to deepen both our understanding of economic action and its relationships with the other sorts of human actions. Actions begin in choice, and thus Ludwig von Mises opens his classic work *Human Action: A Treatise on Economics*: "Choosing determines all human decisions. In making his choice man chooses not only between various material things and services. All human values are offered for option." But humans not only act, they tend to act in patterns—in economic actions as well as political, religious, and cultural—and the Whig inquiry involved at least rudimentary inquiries not only into atomic human action considered in isolation, but also into characteristic actions or habits or virtues, and thus ultimately into a theory of human character.

The third Austrian strategy was to isolate and highlight the efficient cause of economic activity, the dynamic factor in economics—the habit of enterprise. The source of creativity, invention, even revolution in the way economic activities are carried out, this habit is the engine of change in economic development. Consider the recent experience of Central Europe: Some countries tried to move from socialism to capitalism by abolishing price controls, some began to respect and protect rights to private property, and some even began to permit the private pursuit and accumulation of profit. But even all these together no more constitute an active, capitalist economy than dry wood and air constitute a fire. Socialism inculcates in its people a debilitating passivity, and a formerly socialist people might well have waited for the state to do something else, without doing anything themselves. Capitalism did not properly begin until acting subjects looked around, noticed what could be done, and seized the initiative. In Poland, for example, half a million new small businesses were begun in the first six months after the Revolution of 1989. That is what made the transformation real.

These three Austrian strategies—attending to the human subject, investigating the sources of human actions, and emphasizing the habit of enterprise—have led in the last thirty years to a new focus on "human capital." The term "human capital" calls attention to acts of insight such as the entrepreneur noticing significant points that others fail to see: it thus stresses intellectual skills. But while many people have bright ideas, only some of them have the other qualities necessary for entrepreneurship—the moral qualities, such as boldness, leadership, know-how, tolerance for risk, sound practical judgment, executive skills, the ability to inspire trust in others, and realism. Human capital, even taking into account only matters of economic significance, is a concept of broad moral range. In recent years, in fact, the most interesting developments in the field of economics have come with the new attention paid to moral factors in economic progress. For some generations, so long as traditional Jewish and Christian moral values held sway in the West, such moral factors could operate as silent partners in economic analysis, being everywhere taken for granted. Their current absence has brought to consciousness their earlier unappreciated presence, as economists have rediscovered with a vengeance the moral dimensions of human capital in both cultural and personal contexts.

Two or three decades ago, it was frequently remarked that the systems described as "capitalist" and the systems described as "socialist" were asymmetrical, for socialism named a unitary system in which one set of leaders made all the key economic, political, and moral decisions, while capitalism was the name of an economic system only, capable of being combined with any number of political and moral systems. A man might be willing to die a romantic death defending democracy, but no one is willing to die for an economic system. That would be a confusion of means and ends—and, anyway, there isn't much romantic about capitalism. So it was said.

The truth in the aphorism is that the weakness of socialism lay in its dangerous concentration of power—opening up enormous possibilities for the abuse of power to which many socialist governments succumbed, certainly, but also stripping human capital from private citizens. Pope John Paul II has written that the fatal flaw in socialist anthropology was its atheism, but he had in mind a particular kind of atheism: the atheism that sees man as a flat creature of matter and the will-to-power only, without spirit or soul, and ultimately unfree at his core. Even without theism, many Western classical liberals had an image of human beings as free and self-determining, with all individuals living out a story of weighty moral significance not only for their personal destiny but for the culture as a whole. In short, the ultimate drama in economics is acted out in the arena of human capital.

This humanistic turn in economics, first made by the great Austrian economists of our century, seems to have gone largely unobserved outside of the field of economics, even by humanists. But if economics is not only a science, if it is also a way of looking at reality and a way of thinking (a fact suggested by recent economists' success at borrowing insights and methods from philosophy, law, anthropology, psychology, religion, and even art), then modern economics offers enormous resources for future generations of thinkers—and the possibilities for a new synthesis are immense.

In this light, there seems to be emerging in economics something like a universal science, a science of humans qua humans, in all our variety but also in certain invariant relations to human experience. Every human being on earth is an acting subject, capable of reflection and choice, a spirited animal capable of activities and a range of consciousness no other animal matches, aware of both universal community and unique personal meaning, faced with scarcity and sensing the impulse to inquire, create, trade and barter, and better our condition.

In the twenty-first century, economics has a great deal to teach us, and much of it complementary to the wisdom we have learned down through history. It is the vocation of economics to help us to be better women and men; to make better choices; to see more clearly what our alternatives are, and their comparative costs and advantages; to invest shrewdly in our fellows and in ourselves; and to use our freedom more advantageously and wisely. Economics is a noble vocation. It is also, I am arguing, a humanistic vocation.

THE NATURE AND
RESPONSIBILITIES OF BUSINESS
AND THE CORPORATION

"Half of the pleasure from the business calling derives from a sense that the system of which it is a part is highly beneficial to the human race, morally sound, and one of the great social achievements of all time. The other half is personal—finding purpose and meaning in what one does."

"The system of democratic capitalism brought into prominence a novel social instrument: the voluntary association committed to business enterprise, the corporation. The assumption behind this invention is social, not individualistic. It holds that economic activity is fundamentally corporate, exceeding the capacity of any one individual alone. It requires a social life force which goes beyond the power and the lifetime of one individual. The cooperative principle is essential to a capitalist economic system."

19

A CHALLENGE TO BUSINESS

Just as a whole new class of Americans emerges in such great numbers, there also comes a technology which strengthens their hand. It stems from the establishment and proliferation of nationwide communications media. National news magazines, around since the 1930's, are flourishing. Interpretive columns by nationally syndicated commentators appear in Pittsburgh as they appear in Phoenix, Topeka and Seattle. It is as if each city had the same newspaper; you read the same news everywhere you go. And of course, there are television, radio and cinema. The whole communications industry has a vested interest in reporting conflict and, because the industry feeds very much on the actions of the public sector, it is particularly interested in reporting a war of ideas existing between the new elite and the business elite.

The existence of a strong national communications media gives tremendous advantage to the new class because of the group's strength in articulation, and of its effective use of symbols, myths and ideas. That's the business of the communications media, and that's the business of the consultants, government regulators and members of the helping professions. The function of this group is to straighten out people's ideas, to enlighten them, to teach them to handle their problems, to help them think straight. These are idea people and verbal people. And just as they have become strong in numbers, they have gained a new political instrument—the media—which gives power to ideas and symbols and myths. The result, often, has been a distortion of reality.

A business can produce the greatest product in the world, and it can provide absolutely outstanding service, but if the image gets around that something's wrong or suspect or unhealthy or in some other way damaging or inhumane, that product can be driven from the market. It used to be, that if business provided a good service, or a good product, it didn't have to worry about ideas.

But today, there's hardly anything that can be done without the influence of experts. And not only the experts in production and delivery, but also the experts who can communicate the idea of a product or service, make it understood, have it seen in its proper light. There are a thousand ways of looking at anything, and all of them but one are wrong. Now it's a strange world where the more education you provide, the more unreality there is; the more perspective is important, the more ways of looking at things come to influence judgment. But that's the kind of world we live in and I think it is fair to observe that, by and large, businessmen have not been doing well in the struggle with the new class.

All through the government, all through the media, all through the universities, there are people, thinking night and day, day and night, how to take away the power and the freedom of the business community, and how to acquire that power and freedom themselves. This process is called liberation theology, and it does free people to do all sorts of things. But the one part of American life it does not free, the one it restricts more and more, is the area of capitalistic acts between consenting adults. Those have to be supervised. Those have to be controlled.

A whole new class of people, I'm contending, is strongly interested in finding things wrong with the way life is, in finding things wrong with the leadership of the business elite. They are also interested in developing new standards of values, morality and politics, and in shaping a new culture that will justify taking power from the business community and making decisions at the locations they control, namely within administrative government. The control they exert, further, does not lie in the part of the government that is elected, but in the part which merely administers the law. Or they are in the courts. Both are safe from electoral politics.

It is a magnificent design. It is a way of acquiring power without submitting to the vote of the people and claiming to speak for the people without any way of putting that claim to the test. No practice could be more fundamentally in conflict with the founding principles of this country.

Most young people who go to the universities are, tests show, very much drawn toward what I call "statist" ideas. They become suspicious of free enterprise, business, liberal capitalism—even the West. Considering how few places in the world, at any time in human history, where open criticism has been possible, it is odd that student thought should be so one-sided.

There are other views of campus opinion. One recent survey by Lipsett and Ladd shows that 89 percent of all college professors think of themselves as strongly in favor of capitalism. But that 89 percent certainly does not set the tone. From teaching a recent graduate seminar in socialism and capitalism, I can report exactly what you would expect. The students come to such a seminar terribly suspicious of the claims on one side, and terribly drawn to the claims on the other. That, I think, is a serious problem in a society where the media are so important on a worldwide frame of reference, and in which, on the worldwide scene, ideas are more important to businessmen than they ever were.

Businessmen didn't have to care about culture, about ideas, in any preceding generation. Businessmen believed if you built a better product, ideology would take care of itself. As I've noted, we're learning for the first time that if you build a better product, nobody may ever know it, or it may be so impugned for cultural or ideological reasons that no one will use it.

In the past, corporate executives and managers were chosen because they were doers, not thinkers. They were willing to build a Pepsi plant in Leningrad, or a ball bearing plant in Moscow. They let ideology go. If they put up a better product, they knew the world would respect it and come to their door. But that isn't happening now. For the first time a generation of capitalists faces the need of developing its own theory.

That's the point I'm after. In a time when ideas are more important than ever before, there is no statement of capitalist purpose. Oddly, socialism has a beautiful theory. Most of those who are concerned about the issue get their ideas of socialism from books, and socialist books are beautiful. You read about brotherhood, the new man, the new woman, the new earth, the present—an essentially moral and religious vision.

Only now, more than three decades after World War II, we have seen the effects of thirty years of socialism in 120 countries that call themselves socialist. For the first time, we can compare the vision with the reality. And the vision has been tarnished.

There were no special books or vision about capitalism, only the reality. What students have done is look at the capitalist reality. Slums. Poverty. Inequalities. Inefficiencies. Then compare it to the socialist vision. But now we have a body of information about the socialist reality. And the equation is changed.

What we still lack is a body of capitalist theory. What is our vision? What is our goal? What sort of society do we want to build, and what sort of society do we want to depend on? An economic system like ours is not applicable in every sort of society. Our system is not really an economic system but a trinitarian system, economic and political. It's a market economy and a democratic policy. It's also a cultural system. Of ideas. Images and Practices. Hard work. Discipline. Postponement of gratification. Savings. Investment. Skill. Achievement. Making the best out of yourself that you can.

Those ideas are not held in every society. Cooperation. Teamwork. Nonauthoritation managerial practices. We've had our Vince Lombardis and General Pattons. Every corporation has them; every organization has them. However, a lot of others cherish a model of authority much less directional, more suggestive, more through leading people indirectly, more keeping ears open. Not every culture has that kind of openness, that capacity. It concerns me greatly that we are defending a system—capitalism—that we don't have even one single book about.

We are defending a system which is not only free enterprise, it's democracy. We wouldn't believe in capitalism if it weren't democratic, too. What we defend is democratic capitalism. And we mean a very specific type of market economy and democracy. If the hippies had a market economy and democracy, it would be different from what we want. If everybody just did his thing—no cooperation, no teamwork, no savings, no discipline—our system couldn't survive. So we have a cultural system we need to defend. I think the best name for that cultural system probably is pluralistic, or liberal, in the nonpartisan sense of the word. What we're trying to conserve are cultural attitudes, a cultural system, a morality, a way of dressing, a way of gesturing and so forth. All those things are linked together.

Every time a new elite comes along in history, it soon develops an ambition to make history over in its image. It seeks to develop a new politics, to establish a new style of dress, new attitudes, new values, new morality.

This is the struggle I have been describing. There is a new class. Its great power over the media gives it the power of intimidation over ordinary American life. People who are out of tune with the media feel as though they are "not with it." The "it" that you are supposed to be with turns out to be those members of America's leadership elite who also belong to the new class.

We are in a war of ideas!

The writer Schumpeter said that capitalists would sell the rope to the hangman by which they would be hanged, and that because a new class would develop in the heart of capitalism, this new class would turn capitalism against itself. Therefore, he predicts that in the long run of history, socialism would win out. Freedom is too difficult for the human race to support. But his intention, I believe, was not pessimistic.

I also believe most of the American people remain skeptical about both elites. The future very much depends on which wins this particular struggle; or at the very least there should be a stand-off, a check and balance between them.

As to developing a theory, it's important that corporations begin putting more money and more training into accumulating a cadre of intellectuals who will create the kind of theory, the kind of ideas that now are lacking. Corporations desperately need think tanks, people to think about public policies and where they will be five, ten, twenty years from now. A given organization must decide where it wishes to be versus public policy over, say, the next twenty years.

Corporations can't afford to let the new class set the agenda, define the battle lines, and continue on the offensive. It is terribly important for those who believe in liberty for individuals as well as for corporations to set some of that agenda, to take the initiative in defining the issues. As it now stands, the intellectual elite of the new class have all the advantages. The rest of us are just fighting delaying battles and responding. And that's just not good enough.

20

BUSINESS, FAITH, AND THE FAMILY

Business and the family grew together. Yesterday's "new class" was the rise of the bourgeois family. This is the first theme I wish to introduce. Secondly, in order to understand why that happened and what it meant, you have to grasp the idea of the system which made both of those things possible. Specifically I will discuss those ideas in the "new order" which opened up the path to community and to family life in a way the world had not known before. Finally, I will explain how the family functions with important roles in each of our systems—economic, political and moral.

First, then, is the rise of the free family, of yesterday's new class. When I speak of the new class, I am picking up the contemporary argument about the emergence in the United States since World War II of a new class. The argument, to summarize, goes like this. In 1939, 900,000 students were in college, but in 1979, 13 million. In 1939 about 60,000 professors, in 1979 well over a million professors, laboratory technicians and assistants. This has come to be a substantial class of people. Now the scholars are the experts without whom nothing in the world of business or politics or religion can be done.

My father-in-law, who is a lawyer in Iowa, used to tell me at least twice a year as I was studying history and philosophy, "if you can't do it, teach it." That's a pretty good view of the way America was when he was growing up. People who did things were the movers and the shakers, and the people of ideas were ornaments. That is now reversed. Since World War II, the makers of ideas and symbols are the movers and shakers. Both in politics and in business, people who do things find it exceedingly hard to accomplish very practical things because the world of ideas won't let them.

When I speak of the rise of the new class, I mean the swollen elite. If you define an elite in terms of education, income and status, on all three accounts you must observe the growth. Now 15 percent of the American adult population has at least four years of college. In 1939 the average income of a surgeon or lawyer was $4,500. Only 1 out of 39 Americans paid an income tax, and the average tax paid was $25. Today a full 20 percent of the population by household earns over $30,000 yearly. What's a significant factor, comparatively speaking, is the large numbers with considerable disposable incomes. In terms of status, in the 1970 census 23 percent of the work force had status as managers or professionals in professions that didn't even exist as professions in 1939. Thus, there has to come to be created through this new class, a whole different road to power, influence and wealth.

In most of recorded history there was in Europe and elsewhere, an economy based on land aristocracy. With very little industry to speak of and very little manufacturing, the economy was based on the land. There were few markets and nothing to buy in them. There were few roads. The wealthy, since they had land, raised lots of food. But there being no markets, they had no place to sell it. As a consequence, they raised armies. There was no point in investing in anything because there was nothing to manufacture. You lived from season to season, and off of the profits, built for glory.

By the eighteenth century a new point of view began emerging, with which to look at the aristocracy, the military and the clergy, other than from the position of subservience. There had begun to emerge a new class of artisans and craftsmen and makers of cheese and wine; persons who were no longer serfs.

With the emergence of the business class, constantly being strengthened as new businesses were added, there came to be a great restlessness for greater liberties. There came to be a hunger for political liberty. Why? Political systems characteristically allowed few liberties; they were tyrannical and they taxed you to death. Business people could predict nothing. So there was a move to seek free cities, republican cities in which the government would be elected. Rule would be based not only on birth and status, but on accomplishment, merit and suffrage—election.

A new class was emerging based on a new form of power and wealth with very new ideas, which came to be codified in the expression, "political economy." More and more citizens wanted to participate in making the decisions that affected their lives. It was at this time with the emergence of private property and its importance to the family, that individuals began to take two names. They began to be individualized or personified, and did not simply have a family name.

With the emergence of what was eventually called capitalism, a youngster was no longer imprisoned by birth. A youngster could become of a different politics, or a different religion, or a different art or craft or business. A youngster could forge an identity for himself or herself. This had never been possible before. Then came the movement of what we now know as individualization.

What I want to call your attention to even more dramatically, is the emergence of the family as the central vehicle of civilization. It was for one's children that people normally worked. The butcher can stand the blood all day and the baker can stand the heat all day, in almost all cases, not for himself, but for his family. If it weren't for his family, he wouldn't do it.

The very notion that there could be property had two implications. One, that government could not intrude on you. It was a limitation upon government; that's the first meaning of property. That is why there is the saying "to every man, his home is his castle." When you owned your own home, by the rights of England, the King could not intrude without a warrant. You had a space which politics could not cross.

Also, owning property meant you had a bond on the future. For the first time families had a future for which they needed to take responsibility. John Stuart Mill in his book *Political Economy* wrote in 1864, "We in our generation work far harder than our grandparents or ancestors because they lived for sustenance." People began to live for the future and to work harder in the present so if they themselves couldn't have something, their children would have it. The notion of property had both of these important differences to make; a limitation upon the state and the purchase of the future—both with foundations in the family.

What I mean by democratic capitalism and what the nation has always meant by it, is the system in which the political system plays a very active role. It was the political system that insisted on the Homestead Act, that insisted on the land grant colleges, that built the extension service which eventually provided rural electrification and the Federal Highway Act. You can't imagine development without a very active political system, but the democratic capitalist idea for a political system is one that doesn't attempt to manage everything. We know what happens when governments manage; they've managed from the beginning of time. What's distinctive about the American idea of democratic capitalism is that government must be active and it must promote general welfare. It must promote manufacturing and industry, otherwise democracy will perish.

If we're all farmers without industry and manufacturing, we'll all have the same religion, the same views and we will form a moral majority which will deprive minorities of their rights in spiritual and intellectual matters. To break that up we must have a diversity of industry and commerce. If you multiply the sources of intellect throughout the country, you have a much richer intellectual, inventive life.

I want to conclude these ideas by pointing out that a capitalist and democratic society is dependent upon a distinctive notion of community. Of all the communities which it builds and which it needs, the family is the most important.

Second, the most distinctive invention of this new civilization was not the individual, but the corporation—modeled on monastic law. The first transnational corporation was the Benedictines who made and sold wines and cheeses in multiple locations on a worldwide basis. The notion that this should be applied to the economic order was what was so novel. Two insights evolved; the economic task is too complicated for any one person and too protracted for any one generation. You need a forum which brings many people together, and which goes longer than anyone's lifetime. Thus in 1800 corporate law came to be formulated in the United States, and there were more corporations here than in all of the world combined. We only had four million people, but we had far more corporations than any other nation.

Also, with the invention of the corporation, a new social instrument evolved, a new personality. Democratic capitalist people do not bring up their children to be rugged individualists. In my own case, we have a son and two daughters. In the case of my youngest daughter, by the time she was seven she had already belonged to more organizations, took part in more activities and went to more different group meetings than both my wife or I could drive her to. We don't bring up our kids to be rugged individualists. . . . We bring them up to be the most socially skillful people on earth. That degree of social skill is extraordinary. It is one of the fruits of democratic capitalist societies.

I come now to the third point I wanted to conclude on, namely the role of the family in all three systems. First, in the economic system, without the family there is no way of passing on those skills which make for a vital economy. When I was living on Long Island I met a young man who built a pizza parlor near the beach. Since there were already four other pizza parlors near there, I was curious as to how he had the courage to do that. He wasn't worried. His father had nine restaurants. He'd been taking inventory in these restaurants since he was nine years old. By the time he was 14 years old he had been in charge of some of them. He said he already planned to add 200 more square feet in August, and hoped by the time he was 35 years old, to have four restaurants. Now my family isn't like that, we don't own businesses, I wouldn't know how to take inventory or go to banks and make a proposition to them. In his family, those skills are obviously there, and they're going to be passed on from him to his sons and from them to the next generation. That family has an economic strength that's not comparable to that of other families.

Again, when some successful member of a family moves into a new city or area of life, that becomes an access for the entire family. If you have legal problems, there is cousin Joey, the lawyer. Every family member who blazes a trail into a new area becomes a source of family lure for anybody else in the family who is interested. Much more than we realize, the family is the heart of economic activity, the motivating force of economic activity. Much more than scholars notice, the family is the unit of learning of economic activity. It is the carrier of economic skills. Families that have a complex, subtle set of skills to pass on are way ahead of families who don't.

As a recent study of the American Jewish community over the last 100 years points out, the great tradition of owning your own business, which almost always means a family business, has been wide spread in the Jewish community. In Eastern Europe, Jews were not allowed to own land. They couldn't live as farmers or as peasants. What was their punishment there, became their salvation here. They came here almost all knowing a trade—tinkering, tailoring, baking, merchandising of one sort or another. When they came to the American culture, they already had a tremendous set of skills. This is also true of the Greeks, Italians, Armenians—again, families in very large numbers. Such families suffered much less during the depression than other families. Those who worked for the large companies suffered with those companies, as they are doing even today. They never got terribly far ahead because being paid wages, those wages would rise and fall with inflation. That's all they had. Whereas those who owned their own businesses were not only taking wages, but getting a capital accumulation as their businesses grew. It's not generally known, but the surest way to wealth in the United States is starting your own business. People who work for major corporations get large salaries, but those salaries are taxed at wage rate taxes. It's very hard to accumulate a fortune that way.

The root of wealth and invention in the United States is the family business. The passer-on of economic lure is the family. Almost every family in the United States can tell you of stories of how when things got bad, so-in-so moved in with a cousin, brother or in-law. The family nourished them. Almost everybody can tell you stories about how their own income misstates their own economic situation. When their roof needed to be shingled, they had a cousin who did it. They have another cousin who's an electrician, another who sells cars. From each of these cousins they get a discount. So just from within the family they increase their annual income by $3,000 or $4,000 per year, just through attaining services from family members. Economists make a tremendous mistake when they approach economic reality as though the individual is the unit of analysis. If you take the family as the unit of analysis, you see a lot more of the reality of American economic life. You can't imagine a vital, growing capitalist system without those families.

Second, in the moral system, if I speak simply from experience about the role of the family, I would say it is above all, a learning of realism. If you don't like the truth, don't get married. Your spouse is going to tell you all those things about yourself that you don't want to hear. A spouse will even insist on naming your illusions, and refusing to be bound by them, will not allow you to live as you think proper, but as the spouse thinks is more realistic, more in touch with reality. The same thing is true with your children.

One reason I say this is because capitalism and democracy are systems for adults. Almost all other systems are systems for adolescents. They're systems of ideals. Socialism is for adolescents; it pictures a beautiful society in which people are equal and cooperative and fair. It is the way every adolescent would like the world to be. I tell my children every day that life is unfair and to get used to it.

I want to conclude on this note; small businesses in the United States, although not generally recognized, played a tremendous role in the great achievements of the last ten years. We created 17 million new jobs in this country. The largest number of new jobs in one decade in all our history. And 80 percent of those jobs were created by small businesses, which in almost every case means family business.

When I talk about family business, I want to underline one of the things I mean, and that is—part of the capital for running that business is the contribution of each family member. In Washington, a family of six run a restaurant. All six members work at different hours at the counter, buy the food, prepare it, serve it, and clean up. They pay no salaries, they pay no social security tax on every employee which would normally cost a firm $2,000+ for each one. This family firm doesn't have to pay that. They have capitalized the labor of the family. From that they have bought the restaurant where they are now working. From that they have bought the home where they are now living. From that they have bought the first home for the oldest son. All from the labor of six members. This is an extraordinary achievement. It is the way an extraordinary number of businesses in the United States are started. Seven hundred thousand new businesses were started last year, and this is a record. The rate this year is running ahead of last year. A great many of these will fail, it's true. But the strength and inventiveness of where this country will be twenty years from now disproportionately depend upon these small businesses, and therefore disproportionately depend upon the families of the United States and their capacity for imagination, for invention and for work.

21

TWO MORAL IDEALS FOR BUSINESS

Two years after the end of World War II, Friedrich Hayek assembled a small band of intellectuals in Mont Pelerin, Switzerland, to undertake a long-range reconciliation of liberal and religious forces and to advance the ideals of Western civilization. Along with economists, he summoned historians, philosophers of law, and jurists. "A political philosophy can never be based exclusively on economics or expressed mainly in economic terms," he announced in his opening address (1 April 1947).[1]

Since he wanted to avoid the interests and ideologies of existing governmental machinery, Hayek created a private association, beyond the control of any state or group of states. He wanted to counter the post-war "self-centeredness and nationalist outlook which ill accords with a truly liberal approach." (When Hayek said "liberal," of course, he meant those who favor the rule of law, limited government, the protection of individual rights, the free economy, and the virtues necessary to liberty's defense and fruitful use.) Thus, beyond national interests, he set his association's sights on the common good of all peoples. In this association, he did not want members who accepted liberal views merely by rote. "What we need," he said, "are people who have faced the arguments from the other side, who have struggled with them and fought themselves through to a position from which they can both critically meet the objections against it and justify their views."

Further, Hayek pointed out that liberalism had fallen into the hands of a fierce and irreligious rationalism, which had driven a wedge between it and many who shared its basic values. Many, especially religious persons,

> were repelled by the aggressive rationalism which would recognise no values except those whose utility (for an ultimate purpose never disclosed) could be demonstrated by individual reason, and which presumed that science was competent to tell us not only what is but also what ought to be.

Hayek abhorred such arrogant rationalism. Intellectual humility, he thought,

> is the essence of the true liberalism that regards with reverence those sponta-
> neous social forces through which the individual creates things greater than
> he knows.

This is a lovely phrase: "The individual creates things greater than he
knows." It invites us to regard what we do every day with a certain sense of awe.
What we are about is larger than our imagination's grasp. We set in motion
projects whose effects ripple outward far beyond our ken.

In his last book, Hayek asserted that he was rather tone-deaf on matters of
religion. But as the passage just quoted demonstrates, that was only partly true.
Hayek had an intellectually humble and generous spirit, and was a foe to arrogant rationalism:

> It is this intolerant and fierce rationalism which is mainly responsible for the
> gulf which, particularly on the Continent, has often driven religious people
> from the liberal movement. . . . I am convinced that unless this breach be-
> tween true liberal and religious convictions can be healed there is no hope
> for a revival of liberal forces. There are many signs in Europe that such a rec-
> onciliation is today nearer than it has been for a long time, and that many
> people see in it the one hope of preserving the ideals of Western civilization.
> It was for this reason that I was specially anxious that the subject of the rela-
> tion between Liberalism and Christianity should be made one of the separate
> topics of our discussion.

Hayek even proposed naming his association (today called the Mont
Pelerin Society) for two religious liberals: he wished to call it the Acton-
Tocqueville Society, for Lord Acton of Britain and Alexis de Tocqueville of
France, with perhaps Jakob Burckhardt as "a third patron saint."

During the last months of his life, Hayek enjoyed the great esteem in
which his work was held in Eastern Europe after 1989, and he had the opportunity for a long conversation with Pope John Paul II. There are signs of Hayek's
influence on certain portions of the Pope's encyclical of 1991. "The Hundredth
Year" (*Centesimus Annus*). The realism expressed by Pope John Paul II in Christian terms—recognizing the radical ambiguity in human nature, simultaneously
fallen and redeemed—was respected by the intellectual humility and love for
liberty praised by Hayek. In sections 31 and 32, in particular, "The Hundredth
Year" employs unmistakably Hayekian insights. Indeed, between them, these
two sections offer greater clarity about the ethical situation of human beings
engaged in business than anything yet produced by any theologian or church
body. Nor is the light shed by the Pope's analysis confined to those who share
his religious faith. As I hope to persuade you, there is something here for "all
men of good will." My aim is to present the main texts of these two sections,
which supply the architecture for a practical business ethic today.

THE PROBLEM WITH BUSINESS ETHICS

There is a reason why a new architecture is necessary. So far as I can see, most books on business ethics are not fundamentally about business. They are, in fact, considerations of basic principles of ethics valid in all fields, with barely any special consideration of the ideals and principles of business as a specific practice. Common, kitchen-variety moral standards such as honesty, fairness, sensitivity, and the like command most of the attention. True, concrete cases are studied that derive from perplexities encountered in business. But similar cases also arise in other fields in which employers and employees interact, such as in government, universities, hospitals, and non-profit organizations: hardly any questions apply solely to business. I intend no criticism by calling attention to this deficiency. Case studies taken from real experiences in real organizations (including businesses) are no doubt useful and illuminating. Further, some introduction to general ethics as a philosophical or theological discipline also has its merits.

Nonetheless, unless one understands the ideals inherent in a practice and specific to it, ethical reflection about that practice is bound to be abstract, even uninspiring. It is likely to concern itself with the solution to certain puzzles, dilemmas, or conundrums that arise. This in turn may have the effect of making ethics seem like an intellectual exercise rather than like a guide to a way of life. It may even prevent the crucial ethical question from arising, *viz.*, Which way of life do I wish to choose for myself, among various alternatives, as I commit the larger part of my waking hours to it? What are the ideals inherent in this vocation, that make it special? What are its moral delights? What attracts me to it? What are its moral satisfactions? And specific betrayals?

The aristocratic life of the precapitalist era, for example, had its own specific aspirations, ideals, obligations, and duties. Not a few moral handbooks were written to guide the way of life of princes and other noble families, most of whom, in the beginning at least, made their living from various branches of agriculture, husbandry, forestry, and the management of landed estates. Indeed, it was common for those engaged in such pursuits to be instructed in the proper ethical arts of "the noble way of life." Alexis de Tocqueville in *Democracy in America* has several elegant passages[2] on the differences between the ethos of aristocracy as he knew it in France and the ethos of the commercial republic as he found it in the United States—sometimes to the advantage of the one, sometimes to the advantage of the other.

Yet even now, some eight score years after Tocqueville's magisterial volume, we still lack a well-formed philosophy (or theology) of business life. One reason for this, perhaps, is that philosophers and theologians still think of their own vocations in the light of the aristocratic ideal (no doubt, quite properly so).

Even common speech reveals aristocratic prejudices. For example, if someone says of you that you are a prince of a man, you are likely to feel flattered—no matter that the moral conduct of actual princes in history (murdering their nieces and nephews, plotting and scheming against their cousins) may be, to put it kindly, ambiguous. According to Shakespeare, and even more so according to Machiavelli, princes have seldom been moral giants; they put to death a great many of their own relatives, precipitated many wars of "honor," and employed their armed knights in many countless acts of naked plunder. As a consequence, quite mistrustful of one another, most aristocrats were obliged to live in heavily fortified castles. David Hume remarks in his historical essays that princes are hardly in a position to present the aristocratic era as a shining model of benefits to be reaped by commoners.

By contrast (so powerful is the hold of the aristocratic cast of mind upon our common speech, even today), if someone in a university setting were to tell you that you had bourgeois tastes, you would plainly suspect that you were being disparaged. You would suspect this—and it would be true—despite the fact that almost all the beautiful things that we associate with the aristocratic age (the best wines, the best cheeses, elegant cutlery and glittering armour, fine furniture, draperies, splendid gowns and capes and breeches, paintings, tapestries, and chandeliers) were actually developed, designed, and made by bourgeois craftsmen: that is, by persons who were neither serfs nor nobles but independent enough to have studios, shops, and trades of their own, and whose modest homes were usually clustered together in the towns and small cities that gave them the name "bourgeois." These bourgeoisie were not only not lacking in taste, they created most of the tasteful objects in which the aristocracy took serene pleasure.

Despite such facts, through class prejudice the aristocracy looked down on craftsmen, artisans, and people of commerce. Aristocrats were, or pretended to be, focused on "things in themselves," *noble* things. People of the labouring and commercial classes were concerned merely with *utility*, with means rather than ends, and for the sake of vulgar profit. Besides, they often sweated, and exhibited rude and lowly manners.

Alas, this aristocratic bias also infected the Christian moral tradition (but not, I think, the Jewish).[3] Jacob Viner made this point succinctly in one of his notable essays on the history of economic thought:

> It was a commonplace of Greek and Roman thought, destined to be absorbed in the Christian tradition, that trade was either by its inherent nature, or through the temptations it offered to those engaged in it, pervasively associated with fraud and cheating, especially, according to Cicero, if it were "small," or retail trade. Horace decried trade as "unnatural" and "impious."
>
> ... For the early Christian Fathers, as for the pagan philosophers, it was the element in trade of the pursuit of a middleman's profit which they found specially objectionable, as demonstrating "avarice," and therefore "sin." ... Underlying this condemnation of trade was an implicit economic analysis which failed to see any possible counterpart in service to the buyer or the community for the gain of a merchant selling at a higher price than that at which he had bought. This came nearest to being made explicit in a passage of St. Jerome, destined to have a lasting influence: "All riches proceed from sin. No one can gain without another man losing."[4]

Needless to say, Marxist and socialist economic thinking owes not a little to this anti-commercial strain in both Christian and aristocratic thought. Even thinkers who are in their best moments in favor of democracy and capitalism, given the sorry alternatives, have not entirely broken free from these prejudices. Terms like *money, wealth, profit,* and *entrepreneurship* still somewhat embarrass them.

There are cultural reasons, in short, reasons of history, why we have been slow to reflect more profoundly on the transformation of values wrought in Western history by the replacement of the aristocratic ideal with the—dare I say it?—"business ideal." We have not been in a position to speak confidently of a "business ideal." We tend to think that business lacks ideals, is merely utilitarian, concerned mainly with vulgar profit, and ranks considerably below a humanistic or Christian vocation. We tend to think of business, in short, as if we were aristocrats. This is false consciousness. It is also an anachronism. As Machiavelli coldly observed, aristocrats were not at all lacking in self-interest. Nor is anyone else. "Self-love," the great reforming monk St. Bernard taught his fellow monks, "dies fifteen minutes after the self." If it is so in monasteries committed to the pure love of God and fellow man, it is no less so outside the monastery walls.

I have sketched elsewhere, following David Hume and Adam Smith,[5] the great moral transformation in Western ethical reality—a transformation, they thought, for the better, especially from the viewpoint of ordinary people and the poor. It is quite important to grasp this moral transformation, if you wish to understand how business came to be regarded as the cutting edge of human progress. In seeking to establish the rule of law, liberty, and self-government, as well as to liberate the human race from immemorial poverty, writers since Montesquieu have looked to the business world to show the way. I cannot enlarge upon that historical background here; all I can do is summarize its relevant lessons.

I am entirely in favor of the democratic project, by which I mean limited government, the rule of law, and the protection of individual and minority rights. Without an active business community, this democratic project is not empirically sustainable.[6] Without an active business community, national wealth can hardly be created or broadly distributed. Without an active business community, opportunities for employment—jobs—must necessarily be few and low-paying. Without an active business community, vital moral habits necessary to republican self-government—the virtues of civic republicanism—are highly unlikely to flourish.[7]

Those on the American left, Democratic presidential candidate Paul Tsongas said in 1992, "would like to believe that they can create employment without employers. They're wrong." Let that commonsense warning serve as our transition. Business provides crucial services to the free society. That is its utility. But what are its internal moral ideals? We would be in a better position to develop a business ethic nourished, guided, and corrected by those ideals, if we actually knew what those ideals were.

THE FIRST IDEAL

Pope John Paul II has recently written quite eloquently about two ideals internal to the business vocation. No doubt, other ideals might be discerned, since it is not unusual for different personalities to be attracted to a specific vocation by different facets. Needing and drawing upon a broad range of talents and temperaments, the business vocation is rich with possibilities and opportunities. For our purposes today, however, it will suffice to make a beginning in the large task before us by limiting our attention to the two ideals singled out by John Paul II. The first of these is creativity; the second, community.

Most of us first learned to think about the ethic of capitalism by way of the analysis given by Max Weber in *The Protestant Ethic and the Spirit of Capitalism*.[8] It was Weber's great achievement to bring to consciousness the fact that cultural, specifically *religious*, forces are essential to the definition of capitalism: capitalism is not a system solely about *things*, but about the human spirit. Nonetheless, there is some question whether Max Weber actually caught the spirit of capitalism in his sights. I think it more exact to say that he scored a near-miss.[9] The target he hit was calculative rationality, which would confine human spontaneity within an "iron cage." He seemed to have in mind the huge industrial enterprises of the turn of the century, and dreaded the (as he saw it) coming spirit of bureaucracy. In all this, he missed something much closer to the heart of the matter: discovery, invention, serendipity, surprise—what my colleague Rocco Buttiglione of the International Academy of Philosophy in Liechtenstein calls "the Don Quixote factor," the romance of risk and enterprising.

At the very heart of capitalism, its dynamic core, as Friedrich Hayek, Joseph Schumpeter, and (in far greater detail) Israel Kirzner have shown, is the creative habit of enterprise.[10] Enterprise is the inclination to notice, the habit of discerning, the tendency to discover what other people do not yet see and, in addition to that, the capacity to *act* on insight, so as to bring into reality things not before seen.[11] As John Paul II observed:

> It is precisely the ability to foresee both the needs of others and the combinations of productive factors most adapted to satisfying those needs that constitutes another important source of wealth in modern society. . . . Organizing such a productive effort, planning its duration in time, making sure that it corresponds in a positive way to the demands which it must satisfy, and taking the necessary risks—all this too is a source of wealth in today's society. In this way, the *role* of disciplined and creative *human work* and, as an essential part of that work, *initiative and entrepreneurial ability* becomes increasingly evident and decisive.[12]

Many academic writers seem never to have imagined the sheer fun and creative pleasure involved in bringing a new business to birth. Such creativity has the stamp of a distinctive personality all over it. In the pleasure it affords its creator, it rivals, in its way, artistic creativity.

To verify this, one only has to visit a business in the presence of its builder. It is quite possible that no *diva* was ever so pleased with what she has sung as an entrepreneur is with what she has built. (And I should add quite explicitly that a rapidly increasing proportion of entrepreneurs in this country, in Latin America, and worldwide is female; enterprise is a vocation made-to-order for newcomers into the market.)

As he approaches the question of creativity in section 32, the Pope has just finished explaining how in history two factors—*work* and *the land*—are to be found in every society:

> At one time *the natural fruitfulness of the earth* appeared to be, and was in fact, the primary factor of wealth, while work was, as it were, the help and support for this fruitfulness. In our time, *the role of human work* is becoming increasingly important as the productive factor both of nonmaterial and of material wealth.[13]

Note that the Pope linked work more and more with knowledge. *And this is the crucial switch.* Unlike Marx, who developed "the labour theory of value," the Pope links value to knowledge: "Work becomes ever more fruitful and productive to the extent that people become *more knowledgeable* of the productive potentialities of the earth and more profoundly *cognizant* of the needs of those for whom their work is done.[14] The cause of wealth is knowledge. This cause lies in the human mind.

"What is the cause of the wealth of nations?" This is the question that Adam Smith was the first to raise in 1776; Pope Leo XIII alluded to it in *Rerum Novarum*.[15] Pope John Paul II has his own crisp reply:

> In our time, in particular, there exists another form of ownership which is becoming no less important than land: *the possession of know-how, technology and skill.* The wealth of the industrialized nations is based much more on this kind of ownership than on natural resources.[16]

The cause of wealth is intellectual capital. If the wealth of nations is based much more on intellectual property and know-how than on natural resources, then we can understand how some nations that are very wealthy in natural resources (such as Brazil) can still remain poor, while other nations which have virtually no natural resources (like Japan) can become among the richest in the world.

In this respect, the Pope differentiates the late twentieth century from two earlier periods:

> There are specific differences between the trends of modern society and those of the past, even the recent past. Whereas at one time the decisive factor of production was *the land* and later capital—understood as a total complex of the instruments of production—today the decisive factor is increasingly *man himself,* that is, his knowledge, especially his scientific knowledge, his capacity for interrelated and compact organization, as well as his ability to perceive the needs of others and to satisfy them.

These are exactly the factors in which Japan is preeminent—knowledge, scientific knowledge, a capacity for compact organization, and ability to perceive the needs of others and to satisfy them. Through these factors, the Japanese, who are extremely poor in natural resources, have made themselves preeminent.

Of course, natural resources are still important. But if human beings do not see their value and figure out ways to bring them into universal use, natural resources may lie fallow, forever undiscovered and unused, just as oil lay beneath the sands of Araby for thousands of years unused and treated as a nuisance, until human beings developed the piston engine and discovered the process of converting crude oil into gasoline. It is human beings who made useless crude into a "natural resource." In this sense, inanimate things are not the deepest, best, or most inexhaustible resource. The human mind is, as Julian Simon puts it, "the ultimate resource."[17]

It is not the things of earth which set limits to the wealth of the world. On this matter the Club of Rome made an elementary mistake. Many of the things of this earth are useful at some times and not useful at other times (e.g., whale oil), depending on the value the human mind sees in them. In this sense, the mind of human beings is the primary source of wealth. And no wonder: It participates from afar in the source of all knowledge, the Creator. Thus, the Pope says:

> Indeed, besides the earth, man's principal resource is *man himself*. His intelligence enables him to discover the earth's productive potential *and* the many different ways in which human needs can be satisfied.

The Pope sees three ways in which human knowledge is a source of wealth. First, "It is precisely *the ability to foresee* both the needs of others and the combinations of productive factors most adapted to satisfying those needs that constitutes another important source of wealth in modern society." Second, "Many goods cannot be adequately produced through the work of an isolated individual; they require *the co-operation* of many people in working toward a common goal." This second kind of knowledge entails knowing how to organize the large-scale community necessary to produce even so simple a thing as a pencil.[18]

It does not ordinarily occur to theologians, but it is a matter of everyday experience to businessmen, that even so simple an object as a pencil is made up of elements of graphite, wood, metal, rubber, and lacquer (to mention only the most visible, and to leave aside others that only specialists know about) which come from vastly separated parts of this earth. The knowledge and skills needed to prepare each one of these separate elements for the precise role they will play in the pencil represent a huge body of scientific and practical knowledge, which is almost certainly not present in the mind of any one individual, but is widely dispersed among researchers, managers, and workers in factories and workplaces in different parts of the world. All these factors of production—materials, knowledge, and skilled workers—must be brought together before anyone has a pencil in his hands.

For such reasons, the Pope recognizes admiringly this second kind of wealth-producing knowledge:

> Organizing such a productive effort, planning its duration in time, making sure that it corresponds in a positive way to the demand which it must satisfy, and taking the necessary risks—all this too is a source of wealth in today's society.

Thus far, the Pope has discerned two kinds of knowledge at work in human economic creativity: accurate insight into the needs of others and practical knowledge concerning how to organize a worldwide productive effort.

But there is also a third kind: the painstaking effort "to discover the earth's productive potential."[19] Consider briefly three such discoveries whose diffusion has done so much to change the world since Pope John Paul II first became Pope in 1978: the invention of fiber optics, which in so many places are replacing copper (and thus contributing to the difficulties of Chile's copper industry); the invention of the word processor and of electronic processes in general (which are doing so much to shift the basis of industry from mechanical to electronic technologies); and the use of satellites and electronic impulses to link the entire world in a single, instantaneous communications network. All three of these breathtaking discoveries are the fruit of "man's principal resource," his own creative intelligence. Man the discoverer is made in the image of God. To be creative, to cooperate in bringing creation itself to its perfection is the human vocation.

In this light, we see that it is no accident that a capitalist economy grew up first in the part of the world deeply influenced by Judaism and Christianity. Millions of people over many centuries learned from Judaism and Christianity not to regard this earth merely as a region of taboos, never to be investigated or experimented with, but rather as a place in which to exercise human powers of inquiry, creativity, and invention. The philosopher Alfred North Whitehead once remarked that the rise of modern science was inconceivable apart from the habits human beings learned during their long centuries of tutelage under Judaism and Christianity. Judaism and Christianity taught humans that the whole world and everything in it are intelligible, because all things—even contingent and seemingly accidental events—spring from the mind of an all-knowing Creator. This teaching had great consequences in the practical order. The belief that each human being is *imago Dei* was bound to lead, in an evolutionary and experimental way, to the development of an economic system whose first premise is that the principal cause of wealth is human creativity.

COMMUNITY

In section 31, Pope John Paul II had already noted that, nowadays, "It is becoming clearer how a person's work is naturally interrelated with the work of others. More than ever, work is *work with others* and *work for others*: it is a matter of doing something for someone else." From the very beginning, the modern business economy was designed to become an international system, concerned with raising "the wealth of nations," *all* nations, in a systematic, social way; it was by no means merely focused on the wealth of particular individuals. In section 32, Pope John Paul II picks up this line of thought: "Mention has just been made of the fact that *people work with each other*, sharing in a 'community of work' which embraces ever-widening circles." The Pope then notes that "many goods cannot be adequately produced through the work of an isolated individual: they require the cooperation of many people in working toward a common goal." And so again he comments: "It is man's disciplined work in close collaboration with others that makes possible the creation of ever more extensive *working communities* which can be relied upon to transform man's natural and human environments."

In a word, the businessman is constantly, on all sides, involved in building community. Immediately at hand, in his own firm, he must build a community of work. Next, for its practical operations this firm depends on a larger community of suppliers and customers, bankers and government officials, transport systems and the rule of law. In the third place—as we saw in the example of the pencil—modern products derive from every part of the planet. The modern business system expresses the interdependence of the whole human race. In all three ways, then, business is a community activity. Capitalism is not about individualism. It is about a creative form of community.

Indeed, even in making a point about the role of profit (in section 35), the Pope shows that in its internal composition the business firm is primarily a community of persons. He writes:

> In fact, the purpose of a business firm is not simply to make a profit, but is to be found in its very existence as *a community of persons* who in various ways are endeavouring to satisfy their basic needs, and to form a particular group at the service of the whole society.

Precisely because even the business firm should be understood primarily as a community, the Pope is able to write that

> The Church acknowledges the legitimate role of profit as an indication that a business is functioning well. . . . But profitability is not the only indicator of a firm's condition. It is possible for the financial accounts to be in order, and yet for the people—who make up the firm's most valuable asset—to be humiliated and their dignity offended. Besides being morally inadmissible, this will eventually have negative repercussions on the firm's economic efficiency.

In brief, the institution which is capitalism's main contribution to the human race is the private business corporation, independent of the state—and the main thing to notice about it is that it is a new and important form of human community. It is a community one of whose main social purposes is to make a profit, that is, to create new wealth beyond the wealth that existed before it came into being. The Pope notes this aspect with approval: "When a firm makes a profit, this means that productive factors have been properly employed and corresponding human needs have been duly satisfied."[20] In other words, through the exercise of knowledge, the business firm uses the productive factors of the earth properly; it well discerns and satisfies human needs. By this path, it is "at the service of the whole of society." The economic and the ethical point of a business corporation is to serve others. So even in itself the business firm represents a novel but important form of human community.

In fact, in section 32 the Pope goes to quite daring lengths in describing the modern business process. He sees that the modern business process "throws practical light on a truth about the person which Christianity has constantly affirmed," and for this reason "it should be viewed carefully and favorably." The truth he sees reflected is this: *The person working in community with other persons, and for the sake of other persons.* This creative community is the greatest transformative power of the earthly order: "It is man's disciplined work in close collaboration with others that makes possible the creation of ever more extensive *working communities* which can be relied upon to transform man's natural and human environment."

THE CAPITALIST VIRTUES

Immediately after this last quoted passage, the Pope goes on: "Important virtues are involved in this process," and then he names them:

> such as diligence, industriousness, prudence in undertaking reasonable risks, reliability and fidelity in interpersonal relationships, as well as courage in carrying out decisions which are difficult and painful but necessary, both for the overall working of a business and in meeting possible setbacks.

At first glance, these virtues sound like a list taken from Max Weber's famous book, *The Protestant Ethic and the Spirit of Capitalism.* But one sees on reflection that the context and meaning are utterly different. Max Weber saw the roots of capitalism in the negative attitude held by Protestants toward creation: in their sense of self-denial, their asceticism, and their sense of the depravity of natural man. By contrast, Pope John Paul II sets these ordinary, kitchen-variety virtues in the context of the basic goodness of creation as it springs from the hands of the Creator, and in the light of the *imago Dei* impressed upon man's nature. These virtues are not negative, repressive, or ascetic—or at least not primarily so—for they entail invention, serendipity, surprise and the sort of romance that leads many to risk their shirts.

This is quite a considerable contrast. And thus one might speak, quite accurately, of "the Catholic ethic and the spirit of capitalism." This is the new ethic that the Pope recommends for the Catholic nations of the world, from the Philippines through Latin America and on into Central and Eastern Europe—all those nations that are just now beginning to make the transition from a socialist or precapitalist, Third World economy to a capitalist economy.

CONCLUSION

These, then, are the two basic ideals around which the Pope orients his approach to business ethics: creativity and community, and of course the virtues involved in them. These two are extremely demanding principles. They will require great changes in the workings of the economy. They especially require change in all those economies that do not yet promote the right to personal economic initiative among all citizens, universally.

Every single person, no matter how poor or unlearned, is made in the image of God. Each has a right to exercise his or her own personal economic creativity. Therefore, existing economic systems that repress the right to personal economic creativity must be reformed, since they abuse the image of God endowed in all. They abuse that image by making the incorporation of small businesses prohibitively difficult; by failing to provide sources of cheap credit to poor people (while credit is the mother's milk of new enterprises); by failing to provide universal education, particularly in the creative and practical skills of economic activity; and by not cherishing human capital and intellectual property as the primary sources of wealth. Indeed, to fulfill the Pope's vision of a genuine ethic of capitalism, a peaceful but profound revolution will be necessary throughout much of the Third World. In the developed world, too, great changes will be necessary, particularly in the moral and cultural area; but that is another and larger subject than the foundations of business ethics.

The implication of the Pope's argument is that true development must begin from the bottom up. It must be universal. It must allow every person, no matter how poor or unlearned, to participate in economic activism. Thus, every free society must examine all its institutions to see whether they are promoting or repressing human creativity. The test of a business system is what is happening among the able-bodied poor. Here in this country, we must ask ourselves, are we doing enough to draw the poor into business activities, to include them? Are current government programs, *intended* to help the poor, actually an aid to the poor—or an obstruction?

Centesimus Annus is a marvellous and revolutionary piece of work. It is original, clear, and compelling. It sets before us a huge agenda. It offers no grounds for complacency. It does what no other religious document has done before: It grasps the interiority of the life of business, the excitement of it, the idealism of it, the challenge of it.

Men and women of business *enjoy* creating something that did not exist before. In Pope John Paul II business leaders have at last found an ecclesiastical leader who sees clearly what moves them, speaks of that spirit affirmatively, and sets great challenges in front of them. There is nothing business leaders like better than challenges. So it would be surprising if men and women of business are not stimulated by the Pope's words to become more creative than ever, and to lead the way to the revolution in the world's economy that the Pope envisages.

For Pope John Paul II, business ethics means a great deal more than obeying the civil law and not violating the moral law. It means imagining and creating a new economic order, based on the principles of individual creativity, community, and the special virtues of enterprise. It means respecting the right of the poor to their own personal economic initiative and their own creativity. It means fashioning a culture worthy of free women and free men—to the benefit of the poor, and to the greater glory of God.

NOTES

1. Opening Address to a Conference at Mont Pelerin, in *Studies in Philosophy, Politics and Economics*. London: Routledge & Kegan Paul, 1967, pp. 148–59.

2. See especially Book III, Chapter 2, "How Democracy Renders the Habitual Intercourse of the Americans Simple and Easy," and Book II, Chapter 19, "What Causes Almost All Americans to Follow Industrial Callings."

3. See Irving Kristol, "The Spiritual Roots of Capitalism and Socialism," in Michael Novak (ed.), *Capitalism and Socialism: A Theological Inquiry*. Washington, D.C.: AEI, 1979, pp. 1–14.

4. Jacob Viner, "Early Attitudes towards Trade and the Merchant," in Douglas A. Irwin (ed.), *Essays on the Intellectual History of Economics*. Princeton University Press, 1991, pp. 39–40.

5. This development is traced in Michael Novak, *This Hemisphere of Liberty*, paperback ed., Washington, D.C.: AEI, 1992, Chapter 7, "Wealth and Virtue—The Development of Christian Economic Teaching," pp. 63–88.

6. In Peter Berger's formulation, "Capitalism is a necessary but not sufficient condition of democracy. . . . As to falsification of the above hypothesis, the most convincing one would be the emergence, in empirical reality rather than in the realm of ideas, of even one clear case of democratic socialism." (*The Capitalist Revolution*, New York: Basic Books, 1986, p. 81.)

7. For a full consideration of the civic dimension of Adam Smith, see Jerry Z. Muller's *Adam Smith in His Time and Ours*. New York: Free Press, 1993.

8. Max Weber, *The Protestant Ethic and the Spirit of Capitalism*, trans. Talcott Parsons. New York: Charles Scribner's Sons, 1958.

9. My appreciation and critique of Weber is developed at greater length in *The Catholic Ethic and the Spirit of Capitalism*. New York: Free Press, 1993, esp. pp. 1–14.

10. The most developed treatment of this point is to be found in Israel Kirzner, *Discovery and the Capitalist Process*. Chicago: University of Chicago Press, 1985.

11. For a fuller treatment of enterprise, see Michael Novak, *This Hemisphere of Liberty*. Washington, D.C.: AEI, 1992, "The Virtue of Enterprise," pp. 25–35.

12. *Centesimus Annus*, No. 32.

13. *Ibid.*, No. 31.

14. *Ibid.* Emphasis added.

15. For a discussion of this point, see Oswald von Nell-Breuning, S.J., *Reorganisation of Social Economy*. New York: Bruce Publishing, 1939, pp. 131–32.

16. *Centesimus Annus*, No. 32. (Hereinafter, unidentified quotations in the text are found in No. 32.)

17. Julian L. Simon, *The Ultimate Resource*. Princeton, N.J.: Princeton University Press, 1981.

18. See Leonard Read's classic essay of 1958, "I Pencil," reprinted in *Imprimis*. Hillsdale, Michigan, June 1992.

19. *Centesimus Annus*, No. 32.

20. *Ibid.*, No. 35.

22

SEVEN PLUS SEVEN

The Responsibilities of Business Corporations

Viewed in the long run of history, the business corporation is a fascinating institution. It is a *social* institution, independent of the state. Its legal existence is transgenerational; it goes on even when its progenitors die; and it may endure across many generations. Its members come to it voluntarily. They do not give it all the commitment and all the energies of life; it is not a "total institution." They may well commit more of their time and energy to it, on a sustained basis, than to any other institution of their lives, except possibly their families.

The business corporation is also a "mediating structure," that is, a social institution larger than the individuals who make it up, but smaller than the state. An institution both voluntary and private, it stands between the individual and the state, and is, perhaps (after the family), the crucial institution of civil society.

Civil society is composed of all those associations, freely chosen or natural (such as the family), through which citizens practice self-government independently of the state. Through the institutions of civil society and its mediating structures, citizens pursue their own affairs, accomplish their social purposes, and enrich the texture of their common life. Civil society is a larger, more basic, and more vital component of social life and the common good than the state. The state is a servant of civil society. This is caught in Lincoln's classic phrase: "government of the people, by the people, and for the people."

The private business corporation is a necessary (but not sufficient) condition for the success of democracy. This insight is one of the crowning achievements of this nation's founders, who inherited parts of it from Montesquieu. They saw quite clearly that democracy would be safer if built upon the commercial and industrial classes than if built upon the military, aristocratic, clerical, or landed classes, on which most regimes of prior history had been built. Our founders offered several reasons for this view, which here need not detain us.

Furthermore, the founders of this nation looked to commerce and manufacture as essential keys to economic prosperity. In Article 1, section 8 of the

233

Constitution, they looked to the private business corporation for the advancement of the arts and practical sciences—they looked to invention and discovery—and saw in *ideas* a new form of property far more significant than land. Only in this one place in the body of the Constitution did they use the word "right," to protect the "right" of authors and inventors to the fruit of their original ideas. In mind, they saw, lies the primary cause of the wealth of nations. To genius of mind they added, as Lincoln admiringly noted, the "fuel of interest." To mind they gave incentives and, later, in the land grant college act, a basis of institutional support through the research of an entire array of state-funded universities.

BUILDING COMMUNITY

One of the most striking features of early American life, according to Tocqueville, was the delight Americans took in forming associations, in cooperation, and in teamwork. (It is little wonder that the only sports to attract universal acclaim in the early United States were team sports—baseball, football, and basketball.) A major preoccupation of the early centuries was building communities—entire cities where none before had existed. This entailed learning to work together under private auspices, while keeping the state both as weak and as strong as is consistent with self-government.

In this climate, the private business corporation became a prime model of public association, common motivation, mutual dedication, widespread optimism and the "can do" spirit. "The impossible takes a little longer," is the sort of motto that members of enterprising institutions like to exchange. (Professors, with their professional interest in ambiguity, have always shown discomfort in the face of the rhetoric of business leaders; the latter like to get past ambiguity in order to act successfully. Typically, the temperaments of the professor and the businessman diverge—and the two tend toward genial enmity toward one another.)

Despite its obvious importance, until recently it has been difficult to find theological or religious writing on the business corporation that meets two conditions: that it is not positively hostile to business; and that it is not merely patronizing, but fair and sympathetic. Sections 32, 33 and 42 of Pope John Paul II's magnificent encyclical of 1991, "The Hundredth Year," meet these tests. They are, by far, the most religiously helpful passages that people involved in business are likely ever to have found. These passages are so apt that it is less useful to paraphrase them than to allow them to be heard directly:

> Many goods cannot be adequately produced through the work of an isolated individual; they require the cooperation of many people in working toward a common goal. Organizing such a productive effort, planning its duration in time, making sure that it corresponds in a positive way to the demands which

it must satisfy and taking the necessary risks—all this too is a source of wealth in today's society. In this way the role of disciplined and creative human work and, as an essential part of that work, initiative and entrepreneurial ability becomes increasingly evident and decisive.

At this point, the Pope makes a startling claim. Speaking of the process of organizing the productive effort, the Pope writes: "This process . . . throws practical light on a truth about the person which Christianity has consistently affirmed," and "should be viewed carefully and favorably."

Please note these words. Pope John Paul II recommends that we study the *business corporation* in order to gain "practical light on a truth about the person." We should study this example "carefully and favorably." Indeed, the Pope himself immediately highlights some of the lessons for "the Christian truth about the person" that become evident in the life of the business corporation:

> Indeed, besides the earth, man's principal resource is man himself. His intelligence enables him to discover the earth's productive potential and the many different ways in which human needs can be satisfied. It is his disciplined work in close collaboration with others that makes possible the creation of ever more extensive working communities which can be relied upon to transform man's natural and human environments. Important virtues are involved in this process such as diligence, industriousness, prudence in undertaking reasonable risks, reliability and fidelity in interpersonal relationships as well as courage in carrying out decisions which are difficult and painful, but necessary both for the overall working of a business and in meeting possible setbacks.

Pope John Paul II also has a sound word on profit:

> The church acknowledges the legitimate role of profit as an indication that a business is functioning well. When a firm makes a profit, this means that productive factors have been properly employed and corresponding human needs have been duly satisfied. . . . In fact, the purpose of a business firm is not simply to make a profit, but is to be found in its very existence as a community of persons who in various ways are endeavoring to satisfy their basic needs and who form a particular group at the service of the whole of society. Profit is a regulator of the life of a business, but it is not the only one; other human and moral factors must also be considered, which in the long term are at least equally important for the life of a business.

The private business corporation is, then, an extraordinary institution. It is a practical model for the Christian church to reflect on, "carefully and favorably." "Carefully"—since, after all, "The first moral responsibility is to think clearly." The corporation is not a church, not a state, not a welfare agency, not a family. A corporation is an economic association with specific and limited responsibilities. In this light, seven corporate responsibilities may be said to constitute its *primary* moral duty.

SEVEN CORPORATE RESPONSIBILITIES

Some who work in the field of business ethics were trained first in ethics, with a liberal arts background, and tend to think of business corporations as morally naked, unless hung with baubles and jewels from ethics to disguise that nakedness. In other words, they do not see the ethical dimensions *inherent* in business activities. As a consequence, one detects a certain dualism in many discussions of business ethics: on the one side is business, and on the other side are all those other responsibilities that business needs to add on in order to be, or to appear to be, ethical. In an analogous way, parents sometimes try to impose on one of their children an ideal of behavior that seemed appropriate to their other children. Sometimes it is necessary to listen for a while to the distinctive being of a child, in order for the parents to detect a lifetime ideal rather different from any they have known before, and yet altogether proper to that child. It is wrong to impose on one child the ideals that worked very well for another.

Thus, it is of considerable importance to discern, first of all, the moral ideals inherent in business *qua* business. A business corporation is not a church; it is not a state; it is not a welfare agency; it is not (except rarely) a religious association; it is not a political association; it is not a "total institution" (Erving Goffman). It is an economic association, which in several ways serves the common good of the community simply by being what it is. Accordingly, among the corporate responsibilities of business that spring from its own nature are at least these seven:

1. *To satisfy customers with goods and services of real value.* This is not so easy as it seems. Some three out of five new businesses fail—perhaps because the conception their founders have concerning how to serve the customer is not sufficiently realistic, perhaps in the conception itself, perhaps in the execution. Like other acts of freedom, in the beginning launching a new business is an act of faith; one has to trust one's instincts and one's vision, and hope that these are well enough grounded to build success. In the end, the customers decide.

2. *Make a reasonable return on the funds entrusted to the business corporation by its investors.* It is more practical to think of this responsibility in the second place, rather than in the first, where some writers place it, because only if the first is satisfied will the second be met.

3. *To create new wealth.* This is no small responsibility, because if the business corporation does not meet it, who else in society will? Probably more than a third of American citizens who are employed receive their salaries from non-profit institutions. But non-profit institutions receive their funding from the benefactions of others, which in the end come from the new wealth created by the business corporations. It is also from this new wealth that the firm finds it possible to pay a return to investors, in addition to returning their principal. From this new wealth, provision must also be made for the future, including a fund to underwrite all those failed projects which are certain to happen along with some successes. If a company is not creating new wealth, it is spinning its

wheels or going into debt or consuming its seed corn; such a process is self-destructive. On the other hand, the steady, incremental creation of new wealth is the road to what Adam Smith called "universal opulence," the condition in which the real wages of workers keep growing over time until even the poor live at a level, with new technologies and other benefits, that even kings and dukes did not enjoy in 1776.

4. *To create new jobs.* It is better to teach a man how to fish than to give him a fish, and in the same way it is far better to provide all willing citizens with jobs rather than with government grants that keep them permanently dependent and in the condition of serfs. This is one of the great social responsibilities for whose accomplishment democracies look to business corporations, and in particular to new entrants into the field. The rate of small business formation is usually a very good index of the general health of society, and not only its economic health, but also its morale, hopefulness, and spirit of generosity toward others. When economic horizons close down, and when large masses of people are unemployed, divisive and self-destructive passions such as envy, leveling, and *ressentiment* multiply.

In South America, where there are nearly 110 million persons fifteen years old and under, youngsters enter the labor force cohort by cohort with every year that passes, looking for employment, with little employment to be found. In the future, surely there will be fewer agricultural workers in Latin America, and perhaps even fewer working in large industrial factories. Unless there is a rapid expansion of the small business sector, in firms employing from two or three to one hundred workers, it is not easy to see how economic health will come to Latin America. The creation of jobs is a very high priority, but you cannot create employees without creating employers. Like other societies, Latin America will have to look to its small business sector for a realistic hope of liberating the poor.

5. *To defeat envy through generating upward mobility and putting empirical ground under the conviction that hard work and talent are fairly rewarded.* The founders of the American Republic recognized that most other republics in history had failed, and that the reason they failed was envy: the envy of one faction for another, one family for another, one clan for another, or of the poor toward the rich. If a republic is to have a long life, it must defeat envy. The best way to do this is to generate economic growth through as many diverse industries and economic initiatives as possible, so that every family has the realistic possibility of seeing its economic condition improve within the next three or four years. Poor families do not ask for paradise, but they do want to see tangible signs of improvement over time. When such horizons are open, people do not compare their condition with that of their neighbors; rather, they compare their own position today with where they hope to be in three or four years. In this way, they give no ground to envy. The realistic hope of a better future is essential to the poor, and this hope is made realistic only through the provision of universal chances for upward mobility such that hard work, good will, ingenuity, and

talent pay off. When people lose their faith in this probability, they become cynical. For this reason, a dynamic economy is a necessary (although not sufficient) condition for the survival and success of democracy. If they do not see real improvement in their economic conditions, people in the formerly communist countries of Central Europe, for example, are not satisfied merely with the opportunity to vote very two years.

6. *To promote invention, ingenuity, and in general, "progress in the arts and useful sciences"* (Article 1, Section 8, the U.S. Constitution). The heart of capitalism is *caput;* the human mind, human invention, human enterprise. Pope John Paul II puts it well: "Indeed, besides the earth, man's principal resource is *man himself.*" And again: "Today the decisive factor is increasingly *man himself;* that is, his knowledge, especially his scientific knowledge, his capacity for interrelated and compact organization, as well as his ability to perceive the needs of others, and to satisfy them." The great dynamo of invention, discovery, and ingenuity is the business corporation. To repeat Abraham Lincoln's formulation, the property in ideas made possible by the patent and copyright clause of the Constitution "adds the fuel of interest to the fire of genius." The Constitution gives an incentive to discover new practical ideas, and to bring them to the realistic service of one's neighbors. Perhaps no other practical device in history has so revolutionized the daily conditions of life and actually brought about a higher level of common good than any people ever experienced before.

7. *To diversify the interests of the Republic.* One of the least observed functions of the business corporation is to concretize the economic loyalties of citizens, and to sort out their practical knowledge into diverse sectors of life. The interest of the road-builders is not that of the canal-builders nor of the builders of the railroads nor of the airline companies. The sheer dynamism of economic invention makes far less probable the coalescing of a simple majority which could act as a tyrant to minorities. The economic interests of some citizens are, in an important sense, at cross-purposes with the economic interests of others, and this is crucial to preventing the tyranny of a majority.

All seven of these *economic* responsibilities need to be met by a nation's business corporations. All seven are crucial to the health of the state and, more important, to the health of civil society, the master social reality. But there are also other responsibilities, inherent not so much in business qua business as in the convictions of its practitioners.

SHOULD THE CHRISTIAN BUSINESSMAN BE DIFFERENT?

Romano Guardini once wrote that you should be able to tell a Catholic even from the way he climbs a tree. For the cult of the Catholic Church is culture-forming. The liturgy is intended to inspire a distinctive style of life. Thus, while the business corporation has a set of inherent responsibilities, proper to itself, these do not exhaust the responsibilities of the Christian whose vocation calls him to the business world. Without intending to be exhaustive, and in a kind of shorthand, one might discern seven further sets of moral responsibilities proper to the business worker *qua* Christian. I have taken pains to state them in a way that shows their relevance to business, and makes them analogously compelling to those who are not Christian. Among these responsibilities are another seven:

1. *To establish within the culture of the firm a sense of community and respect for the dignity of persons,* including a respect for the standards, the discipline, the motivation, and the teamwork that brings out the best in people, and helps them gain a sense of high achievement and human fulfillment.

2. *To protect the political soil of liberty.* Since free business corporations are permitted to operate freely only in a minority of countries on this Earth, those involved in business must come to see how fragile their activities are—how they can be crushed by war, revolution, tyranny, and anarchy. Most people on Earth today, like most in history, have suffered from such devastations. Many individuals have hardly ever (or even never) experienced that peace, stability, and institutional environment that supports the daily activities and long-time hopes of business. Businesses do not grow in any soil at all; they depend on specific sorts of political environments. People in business, therefore, have a responsibility to be watchful over the fate of their political society, even as a matter of self-survival. It is no accident that they have had reason to learn to love liberty as ardently as any others in history, and indeed, have often been forerunners of free societies.

3. *To exemplify respect for law.* Business cannot survive without the rule of law. Long-term contracts depend for their fulfillment upon respect for law. Often in America we take the rule of law for granted, and hardly appreciate how fragile it may be. In any case, hardly any institution is so much at risk as the business corporation, and hardly any is so dependent on the reliability, speed, and efficiency of the daily operation of the rule of law. Thus it is doubly scandalous for people in business to break the law. It is wrong in itself, and it is also suicidal, since to the extent that the law falls into disrespect, the life of corporations is rendered insecure if not impossible.

4. *To win the allegiance of the majority.* Since the survival of business depends on the survival of free institutions, the responsibilities of people in business go well beyond their strictly economic responsibilities. A look at the top twenty percent of American society—i.e., its elite, defined in terms of income, education, and status (professionals, managers, the self-employed vs. employees)—shows that our elite is roughly divided into two parts. Call one part the "Old Elite," whose income and status depend upon the expansion of the private sector, particularly the business sector. Describe as the "New Class" those who see their own income, power, and status as dependent upon the expansion of the state. These two rivals vie for the allegiance of a democratic majority. A society simultaneously democratic and capitalist benefits when these two perennial

rivals are of roughly equal strength, so that the free political system and the free economic system are in healthy equilibrium. (Given the tendency of the state to amass power and even coercive force, however, a society is probably closer to healthy equilibrium when at least a slight majority favors economic liberty.)

5. *To overcome the principle of envy.* Benjamin Franklin and Thomas Jefferson ransacked the libraries of London and Paris, respectively, in an attempt to understand what brought about the downfall of earlier republican experiments. Virtually all republics failed, often after only a few generations. Typically, the cause of failure was envy and the division it caused between rich and poor, family and family, dynasty and dynasty, or one section of the Republic and another. No vice is deeper and more destructive than envy, not even hatred. Hatred is visible, and everybody knows it is wrong. Envy is typically invisible, like a colorless gas, and normally it presents itself under a beautiful (but deceptive) name, such as "justice," "fairness," "equality," or even "social justice." All these are good names, and often envy for this reason hides behind their skirts. Envy is so pervasive among the human race that in the Ten Commandments, under the name "covetousness," God forbade it seven times.

What people in business need to learn from this is that envy, once mobilized in society, can strangle the open society. They need to be on the alert to defeat envy. For this reason, they should avoid some things which are otherwise innocent in themselves. Conspicuous privilege, ostentation, and other forms of behavior, even when not necessarily wrong, typically provoke envy among others. Unusually large salaries or bonuses, even if justified by competition in a free and open market (since high talent of certain kinds is extremely rare), may offer demagogues fertile ground on which to scatter the seeds of envy. It is wise to take precautions against these eventualities.

6. *To communicate often and fully with their investors, shareholders, pensioners, customers, and employees.* A business firm represents ever-widening circles of people, and it is much to its advantage to keep all of them informed about its purposes, needs, risks, dangers, and opportunities. In a democratic society, the corporation needs the support of a great many, and it is of itself—especially over against the omnivorous administrative state of the late twentieth century—exceedingly fragile.

7. *To contribute to making the surrounding society, its own habitat, a better place.* It is much to the advantage of the business firm that the republican experiment in self-government should succeed; and that also, therefore, there should be an active private sector as an alternative to the state. The business firm does well to become a leader in civil society, and to contribute to the good fortune of other mediating structures in the private sector, whether in areas such as education and the arts, healthful activities for youth, the environment, care for the elderly, new initiatives to meet the needs of the homeless and the poor, or other such activities. The business corporation cannot take primary responsibility for these things; it is not, in itself, a welfare organization. Nevertheless, it does well to strengthen the networks of civil society, and to strengthen those of its allies who

provide an alternative to government. Government is not the enemy of business, nor of the citizens; on the other hand, it has been, historically, a fertile source of tyranny, corruption, the abuse of rights, and plain arrogance of power.

In sum, the business corporation is, in its essence, a moral institution of a distinctive type. It imposes some moral obligations that are inherent in its own ends, structure, and modes of operation. Other obligations fall upon it through the moral and religious commitments of its members. Thus, those who labor within the business corporation have many moral responsibilities and a richly various moral agenda, of which the fourteen responsibilities mentioned here are basic but not exhaustive.

Those academics (and journalists) who do not take the high moral responsibilities of business with due seriousness are making a serious mistake, on two different levels. First, they are guilty of intellectual blindness or, perhaps, professional prejudice. Second, since a capitalist economy (indeed, a healthy, thriving capitalist economy) is a necessary condition for the success of democracy—including the rule of law, the protection of the rights of minorities, resistance against the voracious power of the state, and a flourishing of civil society—this error is in the long run self-destructive.

23

IS BUSINESS A CALLING?

Not many years ago, a friend of mine who had grown up in Gary, Indiana, went home to visit some old high school buddies, one of whom was the owner and manager of an old family factory that was being forced to lay off a couple score of workers.

In his office, stony-faced, the manager explained to his old friend why this was sad but necessary, the pressures he was under, the bottom line, what was happening all around the country in the machine-parts business he was in. There is no alternative, he said, it's tough, but that's business. My friend was sympathetic, even admired the kind of asceticism the manager had to live under, and found himself wondering whether he, a journalist, often a freelancer, would be able to summon up the discipline to fire almost fifty people.

Then, afterward, to talk about old times, the two of them retired to a neighborhood bar. Over beers, the manager started going over the same ground, the firings. His whole mode of speech changed. He began reciting names and telling when they had begun to work with him, who had kids in college, whose wives were sick, how uncomprehending most of them were about what they would do next. Before long, tears were coming down his face.

It was as though he had to live two lives, one as a professional, the owner and manager, who could talk tough about the bottom line, the other as an old buddy talking about what was now bothering him. The two quite different languages coming from the same man was what most struck my friend. Not as though one were a private language, a language of sentiments, and the other a professional language, the language of necessity, although that was certainly part of the picture. Rather, a strictly economic business language has grown up without including within itself the moral, religious, even humane language appropriate to its own activities.

For various historical reasons, economics and business faculties have often pictured their disciplines as more like the sciences, or more like the *useful* arts, than like the liberal arts.

They have been complacently concerned almost exclusively with *means* rather than with *ends*—which, often enough, they have been quite content to leave to ministers, bishops, confessors, moralists, and other (as they see things) more woolly-headed thinkers. "*We'll* tell you *how* to get there, the costs and the benefits, but as for the ends, goals, purposes, values, that's up to you. Talk to your chaplain." We all know where that leaves the chaplain.

Worse still, experience teaches, religious leaders speak inadequately about business. Their professional vocabulary, for the most part, so misses the point that it is painful to listen to them. Some of them, of course, have been misled by the kind of leftist sentiments uttered by the great Harvard theologian Paul Tillich, who, long before the collapse of socialism in 1989, wrote: "Any serious Christian must be a socialist."

Others of them speak of economic behavior in an ancient aristocratic language, looking down on "vulgar mammon."

THE ANTI-BUSINESS SKEPTICS

Many persons educated in the humanities (with their aristocratic traditions) and the social sciences (with their quantifying, collectivist traditions) are uncritically anticapitalist. They think of business as vulgar, philistine, and morally suspect.

The most unthinking in this regard, as Michael Medved shows in *Holly-wood vs. America* (HarperCollins), are post-1960s Hollywood filmmakers. Prior to 1965, television shows portrayed businessmen as good guys twice as often as bad guys. In the 1970s, this ratio was reversed—two villains for every good guy.

Today, big business has become television's favorite villain. Medved quotes an exhaustive analysis of prime-time television by the sociologists Richter, Richter, and Rothman that concludes: "By 1980 a majority of the CEOs portrayed on prime time committed felonies." Respectable businessmen were by then committing 40 percent of the murders on prime-time television and 44 percent of vice crimes like drug trafficking and pimping. All this is far removed from Hollywood's Golden Age in the '30s and '40s, when Lionel Barrymore played a dignified shipping magnate in George Cukor's classic *Dinner at Eight,* and in the all-time favorite *It's a Wonderful Life,* Jimmy Stewart played a humane, compassionate, and (believe this or not) *likable* banker.

So it is easy these days, even against the prompting of common sense, to let pass without resistance repeated images that a life spent in business is probably immoral, or criminal. In actual fact, we usually expect people in business, especially in large corporations, to be buttoned-down and traditional in their moral lives—far from being fans of permissiveness or promoters of the "new morality." Beyond the Hollywood pretense that people in business are morally derelict, the other criticism most often heard from artistic and academic types is that they lead morally *boring* lives. Which is it?

Three accusations, in particular, came up among strangers and friends when I asked them about the subject. The first was based on such matters as Calvin Klein ads and Time Warner's distribution of brutal, worse-than-pornographic "gangsta rap." It was usually phrased this way: In pursuit of profits, won't business act immorally whenever necessary?

The second typical accusation was as follows: Aren't executive salaries out of line? Isn't dramatic inequality wrong?

The third accusation deplored downsizing: Isn't it wrong to subject workers and middle managers in their mature years to so much insecurity? Isn't it wrong to let people go abruptly and without a parachute?

My general position on these three questions has two parts. First, business is a morally serious enterprise, in which it is possible to act either immorally or morally. Second, by its own internal logic and inherent moral drive, business *requires* moral conduct; and, not always, but with high probability, violations of this logic lead to personal and business disgrace.

In the examples mentioned above, both Calvin Klein and Time Warner backed down, precisely because they saw harm being done to their businesses. Deviations from the public moral code invite retribution. In Time Warner's case, there are indications that even personal shame was involved. When William Bennett and C. DeLores Tucker asked the top officers of the corporation, around a table, to read aloud the lyrics of the rap songs in question, the officers refused to do so.

To return to the general point: It *is* possible for people in business to do moral wrong, even though such wrongdoing sooner or later injures both the business in question and the moral reputation as a whole. Immoral acts do occur in business. But to behave immorally is neither necessary to nor conducive to business success. One may get away with immoral behavior for a while, but sooner or later it is highly likely to catch up with the perpetrator and the firm.

WANTED: MORAL LEADERSHIP

To return to the three specific questions raised above:

1. Yes, some people in business do have lax moral standards, and others think that the sole driving force in business (and the only morally legitimate one) is making profits. Still others occasionally, even if not often, are guilty of moral lapses. Business is a morally serious enterprise, however, and persons of suspect moral character cannot and will not escape moral judgment, sometimes from their own consciences, sometimes by the moral disapprobation (private or public) of others, and in the end by the Judge of all of us. That there is such a Judge (or at least a transpersonal standard) we all testify when we exclaim that certain actions—even if they go unpunished by law and public opinion—morally *stink*.

An indication that such a moral dynamism is at work, even among some who violate it, is that business practices, over the generations, keep being held to higher standards. Some things done without shame in the nineteenth century are today regarded by business leaders as morally primitive and impermissible. Thus, even if individuals (or an entire generation) are for some time blind to them, moral standards slowly make their presence felt, sometimes by way of shocking abuses that stir the public. (Of course, over time moral standards may *decline,* too, thus setting the stage in a later era for a moral reawakening. Our own era seems to be at the beginning of such a reawakening.)

2. There are two sound responses to the question of stratospheric executive compensation. The first is that the most destructive passion in any free society is envy. Anything that incites envy—or seems to support the arguments of those moved by envy—is a danger to the free society. Even the *appearance* of excessive compensation, seemingly far beyond the bounds of common sense, injures both democracy and capitalism.

With James Madison, I hold that the passion for absolute equality is wicked and self-destructive. Except in terms of equal standing under the rule of law, equality is not a morally acceptable social ideal. Yet, observation shows that business executives are blind to the social destructiveness of current levels of compensation. Current practices give the appearance of cozy collusion, in which executives on one another's boards of trustees scratch each other's backs, heedless of the sacrifices others in their firms are making. For the sake of the moral reputation of business, executive belt-tightening is desperately needed, and moral leadership from somewhere in business must step forward. If the whole country is tightening its belt, to be morally credible business leaders must also be seen to do so.

The second argument does not invalidate the first but sets it in context. The extraordinary skills required to manage a large modern firm are extremely rare, and the competition to attract top talent pushes their market value to unprecedented heights. Finding just the right top talent may be worth scores of millions of dollars to a large corporation. A single inspired business decision by the right CEO is likely to mean far more to a firm's future earnings than his total earnings over the five or so years that he is likely to be at the helm (the average service of a CEO is about that of a professional football player).

The skills required by a business executive today are many, varied, and not often found in combination. Among them are the ability to grasp the possibilities of new technologies, to understand complex market forces, to master financial questions complicated by instantaneous international transactions, and to provide moral and intellectual leadership for a large (and often widely dispersed) corporation, while attending to crucial matters of personnel.

When I asked Gerard R. Roche, a leading headhunter for executives at Heidrick and Struggles in New York, about this, he told me that "Everyone wants a Jack Welch, but there're not many of his caliber. The truly great talent is extremely rare." There are too many buyers chasing too few great talents; no wonder the market price goes up. "Everyone wants a great operating officer who is also great on vision and strategic change," Roche says. "There are few enough who are great on one of these counts, but on two? Not enough to fill the demand out there."

Moreover, except for the inventors of new technologies or new business concepts who are also owners of their company's original stock (such as Bill Gates and Sam Walton), most business leaders are likely to be less well-paid than stars of the entertainment industry such as Oprah Winfrey, Michael Jordan, Robert Redford, and Bill Cosby. If a market test is considered fair for entertainers, why is it unfair for creators of new wealth through business? My answer is that it may not be unfair but that, for the first reason mentioned above, it may destroy moral esteem for the business system.

3. One of the structural and inherent moral weaknesses of capitalism is that the creativity, inventiveness, and questioning spirit that make it dynamic have a moral downside and impose a heavy human cost, sometimes even on top executives and investors. The great economist Joseph Schumpeter called this characteristic of the system "creative destruction." Many new technologies make old technologies—and the industries and firms based upon them—obsolete. In addition, firms not living up to their wealth-creating potential are subject to being bought out by value-seekers, who see ways to turn existing assets to better economic use. In both cases, many persons are subject to losing their jobs—sometimes from the top of the firm to the bottom, but most often at levels below the top. Many personal tragedies may result.

This is not a morally commendable aspect of capitalism. Its best defense is that the known alternatives are worse.

HOW TO TELL IF YOU'VE BEEN CHOSEN

The famous author M. Scott Peck, M.D., tells the story of a young enlisted man in Okinawa who served under him as a practicing therapist. Peter was unusually good at his assignment, and Peck tried to get him to enter graduate school on his return to the United States. "You're a fine therapist. I could help you get into a good master's program. Your GI Bill would pay for it."

The young soldier said he wanted to start a business. Peck admits to being "aghast."

As Peck began reciting the advantages of a career in psychotherapy, he was stopped cold by the young man: "Look, Scotty, can't you get it in your head that not everyone is like you?" Not everyone wants to be a psychotherapist.

Callings are like that. To identify them, two things are normally required: the God-given ability to do the job and (equally God-given) enjoyment in doing it because of your desire to do it.

How can you tell if you have a calling? First, each calling is unique to each individual. Not everyone wants to be a psychiatrist, as Peck discovered. Nor, for that matter, does everyone want to work in business. Each of us is as unique in his calling as he is in being made in the image of God. (It would take an infinite number of human beings, St. Thomas Aquinas once wrote, to mirror back the infinite facets of the Godhead. Each person reflects only a small—but beautiful—part of the whole.)

Second, a calling requires certain preconditions. It requires more than desires; it requires talent. Not everyone can be, simply by desiring it, an opera singer, professional athlete, or leader of a large enterprise. For a calling to be right, it must fit our abilities. Another precondition is love—not just love of the final product but, as the essayist Logan Pearsall Smith once put it, "The test of a vocation is love of drudgery it involves." Long hours, frustrations, small steps forward, struggles: Unless these too are welcomed with a certain joy, the claim to being called has a hollow ring.

Third, a true calling reveals its presence by the enjoyment and sense of renewed energies its practice yields us. This does not mean that sometimes we do not groan inwardly at the weight of the burdens imposed on us or that we never feel reluctance about reentering bloody combat. Facing hard tasks necessarily exacts dread. Indeed, there are times when we wish we did not have to face every burden our calling imposes on us. Still, finding ourselves where we are and with the responsibilities we bear, we know it is our duty—part of what we were meant to do—to soldier on.

Enjoying what we do is not always a feeling of enjoyment; it is sometimes the gritty resolution a man or woman shows in doing what must be done— perhaps with inner dread and yet without whimpering self-pity. These are things a grown man or woman must do. There is an odd satisfaction in bearing certain pains. The young men who died defending the pass at Thermopylae, Aristotle intimates, died happy. But he was not describing their feelings, only their knowledge that they did what brave young Spartans ought to do to protect their city, no matter the taste of ashes in their mouths.

A fourth truth about callings is also apparent: They are not usually easy to discover. Frequently, many false paths are taken before the satisfying path is at last uncovered. Experiments, painful setbacks, false hopes, discernment, prayer, and much patience are often required before the light goes on.

Business people who have found their calling will recognize all of these things, if only tacitly. Against sometimes dreary opposition, they know their calling to be morally legitimate, even noble. The point of business is to "accomplish something collectively," "to make a contribution to society," "to do something which is of value," "to provide something unique," "to test a person's talents and character," "to build community." This is unambiguously moral language that reflects moral reality.

ANATOMY OF A "CALLING"

A career in business is not only a morally serious vocation but a morally noble one. Those who are called to it have reason to take pride in it and rejoice in it.

But what is a "calling"? Sociologist Max Weber wrote of "Politics as a Vocation." "Calling," however, seemed the more common word in English. The best way to grasp the concrete meaning of these synonyms, in any case, is through examples.

Business is a demanding vocation, and one is not good at it just by being in it or even by making piles of money. The bottom line of a calling is measured by pain, learning, and grace. Having a good year in financial terms is hard enough; having a good year in fulfilling one's calling means passing tests that are a lot more rewarding. The difference is a little like being drafted into the army and, instead, volunteering for the Green Berets. Doing anything as a calling—especially doing something difficult—is a lot more fulfilling than merely drifting.

24

EXECUTIVES MUST BE
ALLOWED TO EXECUTE

Like a proud frigate, the American business corporation is sailing confidently into the twenty-first century. But a cannonade has already erupted off port, and off starboard, rockets' red glare, bombs bursting on "corporate governance" and "economic fairness." The corporation—the most successful institution of our time, flexible and adaptable beyond all others, maintaining its way in white-capped seas while others founder—is suddenly a ship that others want to capture. They want to reform it into something it is not. There is a lot of ruin in today's cries for reforming corporate governance.

Most of today's reformers are quite sophisticated. They are no longer socialists, they say. They want to "humanize" the corporation, not to expropriate it. Some even quote a passage Adam Smith wrote about the corporation in 1776 [*An Inquiry into the Nature and Causes of the Wealth of Nations*] well before the nineteenth century arrived. Smith feared that the corporation, that then-new beast, slouching toward who knows what city, that oddly contrived thing that separated ownership from management, could not possibly work. He gave three pretty good reasons why:

> The directors of such companies, being the managers rather of other people's money than their own, it cannot well be expected that they would watch over it with the same anxious vigilance with which the partners in a private copartnery frequently watch their own. Like the stewards of a rich man, they are apt to consider attention to small matters as not for their master's honor, and very easily give themselves a dispensation from having it. Negligence and profusion, therefore, must always prevail, more or less, in the management of the affairs of such a company. It is upon this account that joint stock companies for foreign trade have seldom been able to maintain the competition against private adventurers. They have, accordingly, very seldom succeeded without an exclusive privilege, and frequently have not succeeded with one. Without an exclusive privilege they have commonly mismanaged the trade. With an exclusive privilege they have both mismanaged and confined it.

Adam Smith was analytically clear and prescient; the problems he described dog us still. But as a predictor of the corporation's future, he was uncharacteristically wrong.

In Adam Smith's day, the business enterprise was essentially a small owner-managed affair. As late as 1820, in all of France there were not more than several dozen business enterprises (factories) employing as many as twenty persons in one building. As Smith foresaw, the device of splitting ownership from management required by the growth of great stock associations shifted the flows of motives, interests, and passions. When the executive manager was no longer the owner, he was in charge of spending someone else's money. (His compensation may be chiefly in stock ownership, but that does not make him the owner—far from it.) He might well feel comfortable with a handsome salary and enjoy the prestige of being boss, while losing the singular mark of the original owner—the willingness to be imaginative and take risks. The original owner, meanwhile, might have qualms about risks taken with his money by new managers, more qualms than he once had about risks he used to take lightheartedly for himself. As a thinker who paid a great deal of attention to men's passions, interests, and motives, Smith may have been the first to worry about future problems of corporate governance. He was not the last.

PIRATES!

In the 1980s, financiers like Carl Icahn, Michael Milken, and many others began to make an analysis of the problems of corporate organization not unlike that of Adam Smith. They judged that many corporate managers were not doing nearly as well as they could with the value under their stewardship. Armed with new financial methods of their own devising for assembling large amounts of capital, they began buying and reshaping corporations to bring out overlooked values. No good deed going unpunished, these laser-eyed analysts were treated like pirates preying on Spanish galleons that had gold hidden in their holds. "Corporate raiders" they were called—and worse—and they terrorized an entire ocean of slowly moving companies.

Alarmed and awakened, corporate executives and corporate boards began trimming ship and preparing either to repel the Blackbeards or outsail them. Disapprove of them or not, we owe these "pirates" a debt. They were not alone in issuing a stirring wake-up call—worldwide economic competition arrived simultaneously—but they certainly got everyone's attention.

And they left us with a lingering problem. What if corporate management is comfortable and content with "good enough"—or worse? What should be done, and who should do it? All may agree that corporate managers are not the most important owners, only somewhat more so than mere employees—for, even as employees, most of their compensation comes as stock ownership, much of it in options that give them longer-term interests than many ordinary stockholders. But, insofar as they are employees, who is it that really employs them? Legally, it is the board of directors that has that responsibility, along with several other responsibilities, such as the strategic direction of the company and provident forethought about its resources, needs, and future contingencies. But what if the board is in the pocket of, or in collusion with, the corporate managers, some of whom also sit on the board? What if the board loses dispassionate objective distance?

RATIONALLY IGNORANT

Besides, who are the owners of the contemporary corporation? Who are they in whose name the board of directors acts as steward? In a publicly owned company, the rightful owners may be scattered all over the stock market. More likely, though, large portions of the shares of any major company are held by specific mutual funds, pension plans, and other institutional investors, acting as proxies for hundreds of thousands of individual owners, most of whom are likely to be, in the term of art, rationally ignorant—that is, poorly informed and willingly uninvolved—concerning an individual corporation's practices and prospects.

Both the directors of mutual funds and the directors of pension plans want to invest in corporations that produce high returns. They are competing against their peers in seeking higher returns; they demand "performance." Managers of corporations that "perform" admirably year after year become market favorites. As their corporations attract investors, the wealth of their stockholders increases.

Thus, when someone writes or says that Wall Street likes or does not like a particular company, we need to remind ourselves that the active intelligence that first reaches such judgments is probably working in a pension plan office in Sacramento or Albany or Eugene, Oregon, or in a new, quick-to-the-draw mutual fund in Denver, Santa Fe, or Fort Lauderdale, or in the small and unpretentious offices of financial legends in Menlo Park or Omaha. Wall Street has been decentralized. One result is that corporate managers dare not become lazy and self-satisfied. They have powerful incentives to seek out untapped resources within their own companies and to turn these to creative use. Money managers all around the country are watching them like hawks, competing with one another to spot hidden strengths or weaknesses before others do.

Moreover, the directors of pension plan funds and other investors have learned by experience that they can, if necessary, vote a chief executive officer out of office by taking over the board of directors of his corporation. They have already done so at GM, American Express, IBM, and Westinghouse. Boards have power to hire and fire, and boards are themselves elected (usually for renewable three-year terms) by stockholders. Large stockholders cast weighty votes. So large stockholders have begun throwing their weight around.

LOOKING FOR THE RIGHT STUFF

Conversely, money managers are learning the hard way that their bread is buttered by corporate managers with vision, steadiness, talent, and guts—in short, with what used to be called "the right stuff." That means character, wedded to a precise talent, a talent for figuring out the right thing to do and for doing it the right way and at the right time. Today there are a lot of people competing fiercely to find the few persons in the whole world not only capable of being great CEOs but already in place in the right companies. Corporations are executive enterprises. That is of their essence. In business, the quality of the people in charge determines nearly everything else.

On the brink of the twenty-first century, therefore, the environment within which corporate governance operates is drastically different from what it was even twenty years ago. The performance of CEOs is under much greater scrutiny. Investment flows are instantaneous and worldwide. Moving beyond traditional watchdogs of business such as banks and regulatory agencies, money managers at newly powerful institutions such as mutual funds and pension funds have gained an upper hand over corporate managers through computer-driven tools of analysis and boldly employed voting clout.

Today every corporate manager in his right mind knows that his perch is insecure. Unless he is employed by a firm that he himself or his family founded (and not even that will always protect him), he can expect the average length of his tenure to be about that of a linebacker in the National Football League, a little less than six years. He faces very little danger from boredom, laziness, or complacency. What Judge Learned Hand in the 1950s called in a famous monopoly case "the quiet life" is no longer the CEO's lot. He will be lucky to have the freedom of spirit to make time for solitude and soul. He will be lucky not to make a mess of his family relationships, especially with spouse and older children.

A WELL-LIGHTED PLACE

Once you grasp the need for energy in the executive and note the new competitive conditions prevailing in the corporate environment, much of the hullabaloo about corporate governance seems radically misplaced. According to most of the analysis, the problem is that of finding checks and balances and otherwise borrowing from the power-limiting institutions of republican government. But the problem of corporate governance is not to check power—that is already done today by unprecedented dimensions of competition—but rather to summon up and channel power. Checks enough abound: the explosion of financial information and analysis—not only in the number of financial television channels, the Internet, and the proliferation of financial newsletters but also in the institutional power of independent professional analysts representing large shareholders—has made the business corporation quite suddenly a well-lighted place.

Thus, what Adam Smith feared about the stock association—that in zeal its managers would be inferior to its owners—is not likely to happen today. In fact, today's publicly owned firms run by hired managers may be far more performance-oriented than privately owned and managed firms of yesteryear. There are now many more ways to keep chief executive officers on their toes than there were two decades ago. Investor checks and balances are very strong, indeed.

The great problem of corporate governance today, therefore, is not how to create checks and balances against power. The great problem is how to govern corporations internally to overcome the great cultural tide of envy and "political correctness" that bids fair to swamp them in syrupy, corrosive sentiment.

Argument over governance is often designed to avoid the main subject: governors. Since the point of business is to get things done, argument over governance must not be allowed to suggest the opposite of action—restraint on action or, even worse, process of the sort that pours molasses into the machinery. Reforms of governance must protect sufficient energy in the executive. This freedom to act, in turn, poses new tests for executives in our generation.

"TWO FEET OF PEANUT BUTTER"

Oversight, collective consultation, information gathering, and some division of responsibility—these will always be needed, for reasons rooted in human ignorance, partiality, passion, and fallibility. Intelligent executives, therefore, may well decentralize decisionmaking and rely on decision teams rather than solely on themselves. Their paramount concern is to be in constant touch with reality, and this requires as many eyes and ears, as many dispersed agents of practical wisdom, as possible. But the point of these safeguards is to protect the purposiveness of the corporation. Any scheme of governance that sinks executives in two feet of peanut butter violates the nature of executive institutions: Executives must be allowed to execute. They must be helped, strengthened, fully informed, corrected, and reinforced; but, in the end, they must be propelled to step forward to create new wealth.

Today's leading revolutionary force is not the state but the business corporation, turning the mechanical industrial age into the electronic age. Since 1980, corporation-produced miracles such as computers, word processors, fax machines, satellite transmissions, fiber optics, genetic research, and medicines heretofore unseen have transformed the world.

Under Democrats as well as Republicans, the great American job machine has continued to turn out more jobs, and higher-paying jobs, than this country has ever known: more than 50 million new jobs since 1970. Great experiments have also been launched (and already once or twice revised) in corporate structures, management reorganization, work groups, and internal entrepreneurship. Who today can doubt that the most dynamic institution in the world is the business corporation?

Thus, whatever new steps are still to be taken in reforming corporate governance, such steps must protect the inimitable creativity of the business corporation as a unique form of social organization. Its freedom and flexibility are the envy of other institutions. These must be protected, under any and all new schemes for reorganization. If this freedom and flexibility are not protected, the entire society will suffer.

THE POOR'S BEST FRIEND

Only in periods of dynamism and creativity do ever greater numbers of the poor rise out of poverty and discover their own talents for accomplishment. In finding a route out of poverty, second only to small businesses, public corporations are the poor's best friend. That is the main reason why healthy business corporations are the sine qua non for the success of democracy.

Corporate leaders often lose sight of the fact that the most important secondary effect of what they do—not what they aim at, perhaps, but what their actions lead to—is to raise the poor out of poverty and to offer unparalleled opportunities for the development of human talents. Their further great effect is to animate civil society, that huge, bustling arena of the world's grand experiment in self-government. These two signal achievements, raising up the poor and energizing civil society, provide powerful moral claims for business corporations. Corporate leaders should take care that new schemes for corporate governance do not jeopardize these achievements nor distort their one main purpose: to create new wealth for the whole society.

THE INTERNATIONAL SCENE

" To establish the moral, philosophical, and religious case for wealth creation is one thing; to find the practical institutions that reach all of the destitute, poor, and vulnerable on this planet and include them in the creative economy is yet another."

"We need to think hard and with practicality about how to include the poor of Ghana, Bolivia and many other Third World nations within systems that concentrate on developing their innate human capital. We need to put in place institutions that liberate and empower . . . creativity: private property, access to markets, ease and rapidity of incorporation, access to credit, practical tutorials in the elements of creative economic practice, and a logical system structured to spread opportunity to the poor rather than (as at present) to protect the advantage of the rich."

25

THE AGE OF ENTERPRISE

How Small Business Became the World's Biggest Business

In 1989 the Berlin Wall came down. Three years later, most people still haven't begun to imagine the implications of that one crucial fact. For small business, the implications are enormous. The early part of the twenty-first century should see the biggest explosion in small business in the history of the world.

Consider: three of the largest regions of the world—Central Europe, Eastern Europe (and via Russia, all the way to the Pacific Ocean), and Latin America—are just beginning to open themselves to the capitalist revolution, and that means especially to small business.

And all this is still not to mention the growth of small business in the United States, Britain and other mature capitalist societies.

Entrepreneurship is sweeping the world. The dominant virtue of the late twentieth century and the beginning of the twenty-first is enterprise—that settled habit or disposition of *seeing* new needs and services to be supplied and having the practical *follow-through* to make sure they are supplied. Our era is likely to be known to historians as the Age of Enterprise.

DEMOCRACY AND SMALL BUSINESS

Since 1989, the people of the formerly Communist lands have already learned two powerful unmistakable lessons.

• They have learned, first, that no one is going to be happy with democracy if all it means is the chance to vote every two years. The people of Central and Eastern Europe want desperately to see their material conditions improve. If they are to love democracy they will have to see steady economic progress. And since great investments in large-scale corporations are not likely—and, in any case, would employ far fewer workers than the antiquated, overstaffed Communist industries—that leaves only one practical hope: the rapid expansion of millions of new small businesses.

This first lesson may be summarized as follows: *Economic growth is a necessary condition for the success of democracy.* (A necessary condition, but not sufficient.) Without the rapid growth of small businesses, like the first shoots of prosperity after the long winter of Communism, democracy will not make poor people happy. The latter do not ask for paradise; they have had too many false promises of it. But they do rightfully ask for tangible signs of improvement in the condition of their families.

• Second, the people of the formerly Communist lands have learned that they cannot get the millions of small businesses they need without a major moral revolution. If these newly free citizens continue to act as they have for the last 40 to 70 years (that is, merely waiting passively for the state to take care of them), then absolutely nothing will happen. The Communist state no longer exists. Even if it did, it is broke and totally inept at inspiring the virtues necessary for dynamic growth.

Suppose, for example, that the Polish *Sehm* (Parliament) declares that, henceforth, private property will be respected in law and that free market exchange will no longer be criminalized but officially sanctioned. Still, unless millions of individuals start to look around them to see what needs to be done and to begin doing it themselves, nothing whatever will happen. Zilch. Silence. Inaction.

The citizens of the East are learning, quickly, that capitalism is not constituted by external forms, such as private property, market exchange and the legitimacy of profit; such externals do not capitalism make. Capitalism arises only through a moral revolution. Citizens must cease regarding themselves as passive—as objects of the actions of others—and start regarding themselves as acting persons. They must begin drawing upon their own internal creativity; begin determining for themselves which goods need to be supplied and which services their fellow citizens need; learn how to meet these needs themselves—and how to do so in a way that improves their own condition.

Suddenly, throughout Poland, as the *Wall Street Journal* reported (May 18, 1992), the quickest of these entrepreneurs were buying small automobiles—the number of autos owned by Polish citizens rose by some 500,000 during 1991 alone. Homes were going up. Builders, surmounting incredible problems, were doing a booming business. A new dream—buying a mortgage for a home of one's own, to be paid off over twenty years—was rapidly replacing the recent practice of moving into the small apartment of one's in-laws for the first twelve years of marriage while waiting for a cramped flat.

The needs of most people in Central and Eastern Europe are many, simple, basic and immediate—exactly the sort of needs that small businesses (builders, electricians, farmers, household suppliers, carpenters and others) best supply. The amount of work to be done is vast; the armies of the unemployed and underemployed are legion. Enter the creative entrepreneur to match these two together: work to be done and workers eagerly searching for paychecks.

Another example is available in Latin America, where today there are more than 90 million persons under the age of fifteen. Where will these 90 million youths find jobs? To make a dent in Latin America's fearful unemployment, 20 million new small businesses will be needed, each employing five to ten new workers. But here, too, signs are favorable.

Attention is at last being given in Latin America to "decriminalizing" small business. At present, most poor Latin Americans work as *illegales,* unable to get the business licenses that would allow them to work legally. Very few sources of legal credit are open to those who start new businesses—like those who today supply 95 percent of the public transportation available in Lima, Peru, and build 66 percent of Peru's housing. The entrepreneurship of Latin America's *illegales* is formidable; that their energies are repressed by the heavy hand of government is inexcusable, and now widely seen to be so.

The truth is that human beings are born with the talents to meet these challenges. Max Weber has taught us that hard work, a worldly asceticism, and enterprise are part of the "Protestant ethic." So perhaps a sign of how universal this ethic has now become may be seen in the recent words of Pope John Paul II, in his encyclical letter of May 2, 1991, *Centesimus Annus,* noting that the Creator made every woman and every man in His own image: to be creators.

More appreciative words for the virtue of enterprise have seldom been given by religious authority: "It is precisely the ability to foresee both the needs of others and the combinations of productive factors most adapted to satisfying those needs that constitutes another important source of wealth in modern society," the Pope wrote.

"Besides, many goods cannot be produced adequately through the work of an isolated individual; they require the cooperation of many people in working toward a common goal. Organizing such a productive effort, planning its duration in time, making sure that it corresponds in a positive way to the demands which it must satisfy and taking the necessary risks—all this too is a source of wealth in today's society. In this way the role of disciplined and creative human work and, as an essential part of that work, initiative and entrepreneurial ability become increasingly evident and decisive."

It is probable that overall world opinion will see the following:

- Democracy with all its flaws is the best practical defender of individual human rights;
- A dynamic creativity-based economy is the best hope of reducing poverty in this world; and
- Undergirding both is a necessary moral (and even religious) transformation.

A crucial role in rebuilding new societies must be played by entrepreneurs—by ordinary people using their creative gifts in the economic sphere, discerning the secrets of wealth in the world around them. "Man's chief resource," the Pope insists, "is *man himself:* his knowledge, especially his scientific knowledge, skill, and know-how." This is the secret, he and others point out, that best explains the wealth of the advanced countries. It is not so much natural resources that make nations rich but human know-how, without which natural resources lie undis-covered, idle, and without effect.

RESTRUCTURING THE "ADVANCED WORLD"

The revolution of enterprise and small business is sweeping the advanced world, too, every bit as much as it is sweeping the formerly Communist world and the Third World. Of the 22 million new jobs created in the United States from 1980 to 1990, 80 percent were supplied by new small businesses employing 25 or fewer persons. Even many of the great corporations have been "downsizing," farming out many of their functions to small entrepreneurs. Typically, their food services, security forces, cleaning crews and certain internal business services (accounting and payroll, pension plan maintenance, information services, etc.) have been turned over to independent operators. These smaller operations can do more cheaply and efficiently what corporations used to do internally.

In many ways, then, "smaller" is turning out to be more efficient and of higher quality than "bigger." Even "synergy" is giving way to "exergy" (a newly coined word), as concentration on a few essentials and emphasis on excellence via intensive quality control come to the fore.

There is at play in all this a recognition of certain essential features of human nature. Even in ancient times, the most practical argument for private property was that human beings are so made that they pay closer attention to what is their own, and closer to them, than to abstract considerations that do not include them in the immediate picture. Long ago, the Romans noted that when property was held in common, individuals were more careless with it, shirked responsibility, and watched what others did rather than took charge for themselves.

The same sort of insight governs the new emphasis on smallness. Give individuals a stake in what they do, bring the business close to their own concerns—and watch the quality of their work improve. In small circles, peo-ple see their work as an expression of themselves, which puts their own creative endowment into play.

In the end, human nature always wins out. That is the one great reason why one can safely predict that the current mania for "downsizing" is not just another trend: It is in line with human nature. It was exactly on this ground that experts diagnosed the collapse of socialism: It misread human nature; it was based on a mistaken "anthropology." God made humans to be "creative subjects," the Pope says, and endowed them with a "fundamental right to personal economic initia-tive." We pour ourselves into our work, which is an expression of ourselves. A wisely constructed social system must allow for this "subjectivity."

Subjectivity is the essential reason that small business (or even a not-so-small business allowing for this expansion) is inherently *more satisfying* to human nature. But, today there are also technological reasons why this aspect of human nature can be given far greater economic leeway than ever before: the electronic, computer and communications revolutions.

Immense factories were first built by large corporations, in an age when communications were poor, to bring many people close together for highly organized cooperation. At a time when communications were primitive, standardization was essential, since directions for small differences could not be intelligently passed along. Without standardization, chaos would have resulted. Now, however, given the massive precision of detail made possible by computerization, and at virtually instantaneous speed, detailed instructions can be enacted immediately, and even at planet-circling distances. No longer is it necessary to mass all relevant factors in one place. Without losing synergy, a manager today can add to his or her repertoire all the advantages of drawing on the higher quality achieved by widely dispersed local units. At these smaller locations, more people are personally involved in the perfection of what they do.

GOVERNANCE AND SPIRIT

Even the world's political shape is being transformed by the quiet revolution in communications technology. Just as the European community was rushing blindly into a political union of Europe's diverse cultures, Margaret Thatcher held up a warning hand and cautioned against an inept pursuit of "yesterday's tomorrow." Why *political* union? she asked. Why not stop at economic openness? The opening of economic frontiers, the reduction of tariffs and other forms of economic openness are clearly mandated, the former Prime Minister said; but not so political union. Today, even the smallest cultural groups are demanding greater recognition, autonomy and scope. Politicians must recognize the legitimate demands of smallness and local enterprise. *Tomorrow's* tomorrow must allow for the uniqueness of cultures and nations, as well as of individuals.

Indeed, one of the marvels of our present circumstance is that two great historical movements are conjoining: the obvious growth of world interdependence, clashing with the equally obvious longing for cultural differences. The first is a centripetal force drawing together the human race in a kind of solidarity never before so starkly visible. The second is a centrifugal force demanding greater scope for smaller cultures, local agencies, and creative individuals. The human race can now have the best of both of these forces. Global interdependence is here to stay. But so is the demand of human nature for personal autonomy, personal expression, and creativity.

Another evidence of the same movement is the downsizing of government—the worldwide movement to privatize state-owned corporations and yesterday's nationalized industries. In addition to this, governments are also privatizing many functions that past bureaucracies used to manage: New Jersey towns are contracting for private sanitation services; job training programs are contracted out to local entrepreneurs; in Great Britain, privatization is being introduced into some aspects of the National Health Service; in Chile, even social security has been privatized.

Bureaucratic, homogeneous uniformity is losing its appeal. Far from being seen as the best path to efficiency, uniformity is now thought of as contrary to human nature. Diversity, smallness, individual creativity are at last getting their due. The individual person, social by nature, is more than ever seen to be (in the words of the French philosopher Jacques Maritain) "the glory of the universe." Drawn to associate with others and to cooperate freely with them in associations that now girdle the world, the individual human person remains the dynamic source of human progress. And personal initiative launches new businesses.

This new vision is the fundamental force behind the surge of small business now sweeping the world. Interviews with the founders of small business consistently reveal that their driving motivations are independence, autonomy, self-expression, the chance to work for themselves and the pleasure of creating something new. Far down the list, more as a requisite of continued existence than as a dominant motivation, is making a profit. To be sure, for some, "going it alone" means a chance for much greater profit than can be gained by punching a clock for somebody else. But risks are also greater, and the bottom line is their desire to put themselves to the test. Many millions would rather give vent to their own nature as personal creators than earn far more money working for a large corporation.

This human longing for personal enterprise is a force that cannot be stopped, given today's technological possibilities and immensely pressing world needs. And it is gathering strength just in time, too. The fate of democracy rests very much on its success. If small businesses fail in their worldwide creative tasks, democracy will also fail, because the necessary condition for successful democracy is a dynamic economy. And that dynamism can only be supplied by an enormous number of successful small business entrepreneurs enlivening every small neighborhood on earth.

Look around your own neighborhood: you'll see the spirit of enterprise growing. You just might be next.

26

THE INTERNATIONAL VOCATION
OF AMERICAN BUSINESS

Not long ago, the business school of Wheeling Jesuit University printed up a T-shirt for its annual gathering, inscribed as follows:

**The Calling of Business
Is to Support
The Reality and Reputation of
Capitalism, Democracy, and
Moral Purpose Everywhere
And Not in Any Way to
Undermine Them**

Permit me to borrow that quotation from a T-shirt as a starting place.

PRESUPPOSITIONS

Behind that quotation lie six presuppositions, whose validity was established by *Business as a Calling.*[1] We might as well start out by making them as clear as the snowy peak of Mont Blanc against a cold blue sky:

(1) A life committed to business is a noble vocation.

(2) The moral structure of the corporation is propelled by important moral ideals (creativity, community, and practical wisdom) and nurtures many virtues (such as teamwork, honesty, a willingness to serve others, disciplined work, sacrifice, vision, and strength in confronting hard decisions).[2]

(3) Without specific moral virtues and respect for moral law, neither democracy nor capitalism can long endure.

(4) A person in business works in a form of human community which at its best exemplifies a relation between person and association that Christian teaching has always tried to inspire.[3]

(5) Business firms operate within a system that is usefully named "capitalism" (from *caput*, L., head) because it is law-governed, mind-centered, creativity-driven, rather than merely being named a "free enterprise" or "market" system. For an inventive, creative capitalism is a necessary (but not sufficient) precondition for the emergence and healthy development of democracy.[4]

(6) Business is also the primary support (on the material side) of the associations and organizations of civil society.[5]

Until a few years ago, these six solid premises were being widely ignored, under the spell of unreality cast on many social thinkers by the dream of socialism.[6] Those of you still undecided about one or more of these premises may consult an array of studies.[7]

Few today believe that socialist economics is the wave of the future. But most nations still find it difficult to root themselves in capitalism, democracy, and moral purpose. Most have little experience under the rule of law. Most of the countries of the former USSR, most of Asia (emphatically including China), much of the Middle East, and most of Africa lack many of the cultural and political habits (and institutions) required for a successful capitalist system. What, then, is the proper conduct for U.S. businesses with respect to such countries? Let us invent a composite, fictional nation called Xandu, and do a case study.

A TEST CASE: XANDU

Suppose that a graduate from the Notre Dame business school went to work for Kavon (a fictional, new electronics firm), and suppose that Kavon was scouting out the possibility of launching an operation in Xandu. The general rationale for these projects is that "constructive engagement" is the only way in which Xandu will be brought into the circle of democratic, capitalist, and law-governed nations. No doubt, that rationale has merit. But will its premises be realized? What must be done to make sure that they are?

The political system in Xandu is still a narrow, closed, paranoia-feeding system, whose elites remain in power only by maintaining total political and psychological control over their population. These elites are intelligent and have come to see that capitalist methods deliver abundance where socialist methods deliver scarcity.

But the Xandunese leaders have studied recent history and found that many societies that first pursued economic growth then awakened demands for political democracy. That was the sequence in Greece, Portugal, Spain, South Korea, and the Philippines; from Chile and Argentina in South America's southern cone northward throughout Latin America; and in Kenya. They can see that a system of economic liberties generates a desire for political liberties. The social mechanism seems to be as follows: Successful entrepreneurs learn by experience that they are smarter and in closer touch with some realities than political commissars.[8] They resent being badly governed. They begin to demand republican institutions—that is, institutions of representative government.

Thumbnail sketch: In the year 1900, there were only four democratic regimes on earth, but by the year 1998 there were at least seventy.[9] All are characterized by capitalist economies, and many followed the path from economic to political liberty.[10]

In the Xandunese diagnosis, therefore, the business corporation is the camel's nose under the totalitarian tent. They know that they need Western corporations, at least for the next twenty years. But they discern the essentially moral character of business, and its subversive effect, since the corporation embodies principles of limited government, the rule of law, and high internal ideals of person and community. Through the practices of business corporations, these ideas spread like a "disease," which Xandu wants to keep in quarantine. The Xandunese need the technical and moral *culture* of the corporation—the technology, the skills, the methods, the training. They do *not* want the *political* culture to which it gives rise. They hope that by redoubling their efforts at control, they can quarantine liberty within the economic sphere. They want at all costs to prevent the principle of liberty from gradually seeping into the political life of Xandu.

By seven or eight favorite devices, the Xandunese leaders attempt to control the efforts of Kavon and all the other foreign companies now bringing their factories, know-how, and new technologies to Xandu.

First, the Xandunese insist that all employees of some new foreign firms be selected and "prepared" by a Xandunese personnel company. This company will be run by the Xandunese National Party, and this Party will insist on having an office on the site of the foreign firm to mediate any labor problems. From that office, it will also maintain strict political control over the work force.

Second, to the extent that labor unions will be represented within the foreign firm, these will be limited to official Xandunese National unions and will also be used as instruments of political control.

Third, some foreign firms will be required to provide information about the behavior of their employees. For instance, signs of religious practice or having children beyond the mandated minimum or reading certain political materials are matters about which the labor monitors want to be informed.

Fourth, foreign entrepreneurs who own small firms will be obliged to enter into "partnerships" with Xandunese firms—firms owned either by the government or by freelancing officials. From time to time, in fact, a recalcitrant foreign entrepreneur has been arrested and thrown into jail, his assets seized and communication with the outside world entirely cut off. One such imprisonment has already been known to last six years. Larger foreign firms will be expected to turn a blind eye.

Concerning the government, there is no rule of law. Even one or two large firms have been bilked out of large sums—$50 million in one deal, $100 million in another—when Xandunese partners (government officials or their proxies) walked away from losses caused by their own behavior.

Fifth, foreign firms are sometimes expected to accept suppliers assigned to them. Factories in Xandu, unhappily, are very often staffed with slave labor maintained in appalling conditions and forced to toil for years for the sole benefit of the ruling party elite. To say that standards of nutrition, sanitation, and living quarters in the Xandunese labor camps are primitive is too weak. They are intended to humiliate and to intimidate. Details have been confirmed in texts smuggled out by survivors.

Sixth, Kavon and other high-tech companies will be requested, cajoled, and compelled to share with their counterparts in government firms important secrets of U.S. satellite, missile, metallurgic, or computer technology. (Obviously, they will also have to share these secrets with their own Xandunese work force, put in place by the party.) Xandunese engineers, scientists, and technicians learned enormous amounts from their American counterparts, particularly when their own rockets, hired to carry aloft U.S. satellites, blew up and when, to avoid more such heavy expenses, U.S. technicians coached the Xandunese in the details of more advanced rocket technology. The latest Xandunese rockets are now being sold to at least three sworn enemies of the United States.

Seventh, the government of Xandu regards religions of the Creator (such as Judaism, Christianity, and Islam) as threats to its own total power. Because the leadership is obscurely aware that respect for the individual arises from belief in a Creator Who transcends the power of governments, the government of Xandu regards personal acts of religious piety as dangers to the regime. It discreetly watches over Xandunese employees of international firms for signs of religious deviation. It especially persecutes Christians.

Under conditions such as these, the mere presence of American firms in Xandu will not necessarily lead to social change for the better. "Constructive engagement" that is complicit in the practices described above can be a delusion. If American businesses blindly, unintelligently, and uncritically collaborate with leaders who implicate them in barbarous practices, they will destroy the reputation of capitalism, democracy, and their own declared moral purposes.

If, on the other hand, American firms are fully prepared for techniques such as those listed above, and armed with countermeasures and a firm insistence on living up to their own international standards, they might well use their bargaining power (Xandu needs their know-how) to creative moral purposes.

A handful of American firms, for instance, are led by evangelical Christians with a strong commitment to following the practice of Jesus by taking their efforts to the whole world, no matter how unsavory the reputation of the regime. Even such firms will need to have procedures in place to protect themselves against complicity and scandal, lest they be taken advantage of. So also will other firms whose interests are predominantly economic. There may be some firms whose leaders are so cynical that they make it a practice not to raise moral or political questions about potential business activities. Yet even they will need to take precautions against the sort of abuses listed above, lest large sums be lost in crooked dealings.

Corrupt government officials are found all around the world. Some firms know better than others how to draw a bright line around the edges of their own dealings and to instruct their agents clearly to live by U.S. company standards. They do not enter negotiations expecting Sunday school, but they are prepared to spot and to avoid abuses in advance.

No doubt, few are the governments that *in the full range* of their attitudes and practices manifest all the behaviors ascribed above to this fictional country of Xandu. Yet even within countries whose record on the whole is good, there are rogue operations that need to be checked.

Thus, in planning their operations in Xandu, the executives of Kavon might wish to consult a checklist of all the abuses of sound business ethics that have been reported in various countries. They should certainly prepare defensive tactics. They will need an ongoing capacity to gather accurate information about their business contacts. They will also need to be on guard against contractual provisions for any practices about which they would not wish the world to know. They also need a set of positive proposals to suggest *in the place of* those they find objectionable.

Having looked briefly at a concrete (albeit fictional) case, let us now return to some of the underlying substantive issues.

THE MORAL AMBIGUITY OF HUMAN FREEDOM

As a set of practices, business is an inherently moral occupation—rooted in free creativity, dependent on and nourishing an important form of cooperative association, and inculcating humble realism. But if business is an inherently moral occupation, then in the very practice of its craft, practitioners are capable both of moral and immoral acts. Again and again, every day, they must choose whether to fulfill their own firm's moral ideals, presuppositions, and tendencies—or to betray them. Since the practice in which they are engaged is inherently moral, they are held to high standards. Should they betray those standards, they injure not only their firms and themselves but the reputation of the entire business system. Those three betrayals—of their firms, themselves, and the business system—inflict an enormous loss on a great many human beings, especially the poor, whose economic welfare depends upon a successful business system.

Moreover, betrayals by business are certain to be noticed. Many members of the literary class—journalists and moviemakers as well as novelists, poets, cultural critics, and historians—have inherited a literary culture steeped in anti-business sentiment. Such sentiments flow abundantly from two reservoirs—one socialist, the other aristocratic. Both tories and socialists teach that "economic liberalism" is a sin—in Spanish, *Liberalismo es pecado*. Both are inclined to hold that business is immoral; even worse, that it is *amoral* (i.e., nonhuman). Business, in the view of socialists and aristocrats alike, is irretrievably *vulgar*. It is concerned with the *cash nexus*, the *almighty dollar, filthy lucre, greed*. It overlooks such noble things, such ends-in-themselves, as beauty, truth, and compassion. This view is wrong, of course, but it is deeply entrenched in literary culture and among historians.[11]

Hence, it is that we often meet in literary productions the figure of the humanly misshapen businessman, whose callous misdeeds (those of Scrooge, for instance) are employed as an indictment of an entire profession, even an entire economic system. I ask you point-blank: Can you think of a novel, play, poem, or essay in literary criticism that does not portray business in terms of moral inferiority?

For such reasons, people in business must anticipate that every moral failing of theirs will not be discounted merely as a personal lapse. It will be magnified as evidence of the moral corruption of the entire system in which they spend their lives.

Really good people, it is sometimes suggested even in serious universities, even Christian universities, would not go to business school. Serious Christians, in particular, called to lives of compassion for the poor, and service to a Divine Master who lived in such poverty that he had not whereon to rest his head, should want more out of life than merely to make a buck. Going to business school, hoping to make a lot of money, expecting to live well and constantly to better one's position—such things are held to sit uncomfortably with the Gospel of Jesus Christ.

We know from the history of Christian reflection on business that such derogations from the vocation of business represent neither moral reality nor true Christian belief. If you remember that in fine textiles, design, fashion and other fields, northern Italy has for centuries been one of the most entrepreneurial regions of the world, it should not surprise you that popes from northern Italy have often envisioned a large and creative social role for entrepreneurs, as in this text from Pius XII in 1956:

> Every exchange of products, in fact, quite apart from satisfying definite needs and desires, makes it possible to put new means into operation, arouses latent and sometimes unexpected energies, and stimulates the spirit of enterprise and invention.[12]

Almost ten years later, Pope Paul VI told men and women in business that he saw in them reflections of the divine:

> You represent a splendid development of the faculties of man, which, as used by the leading masters of your calling, have given proof of vast and superb capabilities. Indeed, they have further revealed the divine reflection of the face of man and displayed still more the traces of a transcendent and dominant thought in the cosmos that has been opened by scholars for new explorations and by yourselves for new conquests.[13]

There should be no doubt in our minds. The vocation of business is inherently noble.

An historical example from the early economic development of the West may deepen our insight. From the fourth century onward, Benedictine monasteries were the first outposts of civilization. Around their walls, and taught by their learning, the wandering barbarian tribes of Europe learned for the first time how to live above the level of subsistence and how to establish towns for many new civilizing pursuits around the monastery libraries and centers for the arts. Invention and discovery flourished.[14] The monasteries also became the first multinational business corporations. By organizing long-term economic systems for efficient, lawlike, and rational production,[15] the monks were able to invest in the construction of institutions of higher civilization and take some of their own profits in the form of leisure for prayer and contemplation.

Today, the high hopes of the poor depend on a widespread fulfillment of the business vocation. When national economies are in freefall, in recession, or in decline, it is difficult even to imagine raising up the poor from poverty; the creation of new jobs, new wealth, and open opportunity; the strengthening of civil society and its nonprofit sector; the economic growth that inspires confidence in democracy; and leisure for contemplation and the pursuits of civilized living. Under conditions of scarcity, depression, or economic stagnation, such goods are threatened. Social well being depends upon at least some measure of creative business activity.

Yet none of these potential contributions removes from business endeavors the fateful ambiguity that inheres in all human freedom. None of these good fruits of business activity flows automatically, ineluctably, necessarily. Being in business is a morally serious vocation, freighted with grave consequences for nations and civilizations.

An index of this ambiguity is found in the opinions of the American founding fathers. The problem of the international vocation of American business is not, at the end of the day, much different from the burning question posed for the founders of our republican experiment in the beginning—whether to foster an ethos of active commerce. We should not forget that North America was the original "underdeveloped country." By comparison, South America was awash with gold and silver and blessed by abundant and easily plucked supplies of food. The decision whether to promote commerce and invention in North America was a fateful decision.

THE COMMERCIAL REPUBLIC OF
THE FOUNDING FATHERS

The American founders held that each type of political regime influences the habits of its people, but each in a different way. Aristotle had noted long before that, under occupation by a foreign power, some people become sycophantic and corrupt, while others resist corruption heroically. In other words, the individual does not mature in isolation, but in a particular city. Each individual is a child of his *polis*: Man is a political animal. Ethics, properly understood, is a branch of politics: The character of the *polis* shapes the *ethos*.[16] This *ethos*, in turn, impresses the sentiments and habits of individuals.

This insight was familiar to the founders; it was part of their own world view. A republican form of government, they believed, would form a better type of citizen than a monarchy. A monarchy forms *subjects*; a republic would form *citizens*. As the character of the *polis* is different, so also the *ethos*.

For instance, in a letter written to Mercy Warren six months before the Declaration of Independence, John Adams took up the fundamental Aristotelian principle: "It is the Form of Government which gives the decisive Colour to the Manners of the People, more than any other Thing."[17] Since Adams believed a republic demands a high ethical standard from its citizens, he at first believed a republic would *not work* in America:

> Virtue and simplicity of manners are indispensably necessary in a republic among all orders and degrees of men. But there is so much rascality, so much venality and corruption, so much avarice and ambition, such a rage for profit and commerce among all ranks and degrees of men even in America, that I sometimes doubt whether there is public virtue enough to support a republic.[18]

Nonetheless, Adams had no doubts about the comparative effects of a republic and a monarchy upon moral character:

> But a Republic, altho it will infallibly beggar me and my Children, will produce Strength, Hardiness, Activity, Courage, Fortitude and Enterprise; the manly noble and Sublime Qualities in human Nature, in Abundance. A Monarchy would probably, somehow or other make me rich, but it would produce so much Taste and Politeness, so much Elegance in Dress, Furniture, Equipage, so much Musick and Dancing, so much Fencing and Skaiting, so much Cards and Backgammon, so much Horse Racing and Cockfighting, so many Balls and Assemblies, so many Plays and Concerts that the very Imagination of them makes me feel vain, light, frivolous and insignificant.[19]

Yet even after Adams became convinced that republican self-government was morally better, he was deeply worried that the *commercial* spirit would undercut republican virtue.

> I sometimes tremble to think that, altho We are engaged in the best Cause that ever employed the Human Heart yet the Prospect of successes is doubtful not for Want of Power or of Wisdom but of Virtue.
> The Spirit of Commerce, Madam, which even insinuates itself into Families, and influences holy Matrimony, and thereby corrupts the morals of families as well as destroys their Happiness, it is much to be feared is incompatible with the purity of Heart and Greatness of soul which is necessary for an happy Republic.[20]

Thomas Jefferson, Adams' lifelong friend and correspondent, shared similar fears: "Our greediness for wealth, and fantastical expense has degraded and will degrade the minds of our maritime citizens. These are the peculiar vices of commerce."[21] The spiritual strength of a nation, Jefferson held, lies in the *proportion* of its citizens who husband the soil, and he believed (like many of the ancient poets such as Horace and Virgil) that manufacture and commerce introduce rot into the body politic.[22]

For Jefferson, the corruption of morals that arises from commerce is

> the mark set on those, who not looking up to heaven, to their own soil and industry, as does the husbandman, for their subsistence, depend for it on the casualties and caprice of customers. Dependance begets subservience and venality, suffocates the germ of virtue, and prepares fit tools for the designs of ambition.[23]

Some of these are powerful arguments. Even today, we see some evidence on their behalf.

Montesquieu, whose *The Spirit of the Laws* was well known to the American founders, is usually regarded as the progenitor of the new American ideal of the "commercial republic." His basic insight was that every regime is centrally constructed around one social class: the royal family and its aristocracy; the military; the clergy; men of manufacturing and commerce; or the lower classes (hunters or cultivators). In Montesquieu's time, the freest country in the world and the most mildly governed was Britain, and Britain was manifestly a "nation of shopkeepers." In this, Montesquieu saw an important connection:

> Commerce is a cure for the most destructive prejudices; for it is almost a general rule, that wherever we find agreeable manners, there commerce flourishes; and that wherever there is commerce, there we meet with agreeable manners.[24]

Is Montesquieu right about this? We may test his thesis against contemporary examples. Under communism, shops in Eastern Europe were run by state bureaucrats; customers expected to be ignored and insulted. In the same shops a few years later, under the spirit of commerce, agreeable manners slowly returned. In Washington, D.C., to go to city hall for a driver's license and to shop in a private store are two quite different experiences. Commerce *does* seem to encourage agreeable manners, more so at least than government agencies.

Next, Montesquieu adds another testable observation about building democracy on commerce:

> True it is that when a democracy is founded on commerce, private people may acquire vast riches without a corruption of morals. This is because the spirit of commerce is naturally attended with that of frugality, economy, moderation, labor, prudence, tranquility, order, and rule. So long as this spirit subsists, the riches it produces have no bad effect. The mischief is, when

excessive wealth destroys the spirit of commerce, then it is that the inconveniences of inequality begin to be felt.[25]

In America, Tom Paine used an even stronger argument against the fears about commerce expressed by Adams and Jefferson:

> I have been an advocate for commerce, because I am a friend to its effects. It is a pacific system, operating to unite mankind by rendering nations, as well as individuals, useful to each other. . . . If commerce were permitted to act to the universal extent it is capable of, it would extirpate the system of war.[26]

Alexander Hamilton's observations from his own upbringing in Jamaica also brought him to lessons almost opposite to those of Jefferson. Hamilton argued that men do not work well in uncongenial fields; in nations, therefore, the larger the variety of occupations, the more abundant the flowering of human talent.

> To cherish and stimulate the activity of the human mind, by multiplying the objects of enterprise, is not among the least considerable of the expedients, by which the wealth of a nation may be promoted. Even things in themselves not positively advantageous, sometimes become so, by their tendency to provoke exertion. Every new scene, which is opened to the busy nature of man to rouse and exert itself, is the addition of a new energy to the general stock of effort.[27]

In direct opposition to Jefferson, Hamilton adds that the spirit of enterprise "must be less in a nation of mere cultivators, than in a nation of cultivators and merchants; less in a nation of cultivators and merchants, than in a nation of cultivators, artificers [manufacturers] and merchants." In a nation in which enterprise multiplies the fields of activity, the tyranny of a majority is less likely.[28]

Finally, Alexis de Tocqueville also praises the spirit of commerce in America; he sees both its dangers and its positive advantages. At first, he seems to give a sharp rebuke to Jefferson: "Democracy not only multiplies the number of workers. . . . It gives them a distaste for agriculture and directs them into trade and industry."[29] Still, Tocqueville makes only modest claims for commerce. It does not produce high virtue, but it prepares the soul for it:

> The doctrine of self-interest properly understood does not inspire great sacrifices, but every day it prompts some small ones; by itself it cannot make a man virtuous, but its discipline shapes a lot of orderly, temperate, moderate, careful, and self-controlled citizens. If it does not lead the will directly to virtue, it establishes habits which unconsciously turn it that way.[30]

The inner structure of commerce, in fact, encourages many garden-variety virtues:

in democracies the taste for physical pleasures takes special forms which are not opposed by their nature to good order; indeed they often require good order for their satisfaction. Nor is it hostile to moral regularity, for sound morals are good for public tranquility and encouraging industry.[31]

A little later, though, Tocqueville sees an opposite danger:

> Carried to excess, however, the taste for pleasure destroys the vigilant protection of rights. When the taste for physical pleasures has grown more rapidly than either education or experience of free institutions, the time comes when men are carried away and lose control of themselves at sight of the new good things they are ready to snatch. Intent only on getting rich, they do not notice the close connection between private fortunes and general prosperity. There is no need to drag their rights away from citizens of this type; they themselves voluntarily let them go.[32]

Yet, while success in commerce may breed moral laxity:

> There is a closer connection than is supposed between the soul's improvement and the betterment of physical conditions. A man can treat the two things as distinct and pay attention to each in turn. But he cannot entirely separate them without in the end losing sight of both.[33]

The human being is an embodied spirit. Concern for one's own body cannot be entirely separated from care for the interior life of one's soul. Each without the other lacks an essential side of one's being. This seems to me a sound Christian point.

But here is a third argument for commerce: To invest in the future is to give up consumption in the present. Parents or even an entire generation must sacrifice their pleasures for the benefit of those to come in the future. It is a condition of business that people are able to transcend their own immediate gratifications.

> That is why religious nations [Tocqueville observed] have often accomplished such lasting achievements. For in thinking of the other world, they had found out the great secret of success in this. . . . As soon as they have lost the way of relying chiefly on distant hopes, they are naturally led to want to satisfy their least desires at once; and it would seem that as soon as they despair of living forever, they are inclined to act as if they could not live for more than a day.[34]

The font and origin of business, in other words, lie in the human spirit. But a total preoccupation with commerce—or with physical pleasures—dries out the soul; the cistern cracks, and there is no living water.[35]

In short, the life of commerce is more closely related to the life of the spirit than its critics often suppose.

To summarize this section: Despite the ambiguities inherent in founding a republic upon commerce, the founders soberly considered commerce the best of available foundations. Commerce increases diversity, the diffusion of power and wealth and talent, and the healthy multiplication of interests, in such fashion that no one faction can become tyrannous.[36]

And yet a man of solely commercial interests and commercial purposes may lose sight of larger purposes. He may stultify his soul. He may lose his taste for eternal life and, thus, his sense of the immortal dignity of every human being, the very ground of human rights.

This ambiguity, inherent in the commercial republic, is a fact of human life. It is not an ambiguity unknown to other types of regime. Yet, in the commercial republic, facing it squarely is even more important than in other regimes. For the commercial republic depends on a doctrine of rights and, therefore, on a doctrine of the incomparable worth of the human person.

THE BUSINESS CORPORATION IN XANDU

Let us now return to our main theme. Earlier, we noted seven or eight ways in which Xandunese authorities have asked Western firms to carry out certain political activities on behalf of the government. Some major American corporations have refused to go along with these demands, and in those cases, the Xandunese authorities have let the matter drop. One can imagine the surprise and contempt that the Xandunese authorities must feel toward those companies who, without any sign of resistance, simply comply with their demands.

The chief justification for encouraging American businesses to invest in foreign societies such as Xandu is to help to build up an international civil society. If and when business corporations indulge in activities that injure or destroy civil society, then they commit a fourfold evil: (1) They do things *evil in themselves*; (2) they distort and damage the *internal moral structure* of the corporation; (3) they injure the moral *reputation* of their firm; and (4) they defile the model of the *free society* to which they swear allegiance, and in whose name they justify constructive engagement in the first place.

By such practices, some companies *have* injured the moral reputation of capitalism around the world. They have acted as if all they were interested in was their own financial gain. They have allowed observers to infer that they were indifferent to the plight of human beings and to the immoral and oppressive structures of the lawless nations in which they operated.

It is *because* business organizations are economic organizations, rather than political or moral organizations, that they are allowed to function in totalitarian countries, while moral and political institutions are not. Nonetheless, business corporations are not *merely* economic institutions, for they develop to normal growth and in normal ways only within certain kinds of political regimes, and only in certain kinds of cultural ecology. In this sense, corporations are fragile plants; they grow only in certain kinds of soil. Corporations, therefore, cannot shed their commitment to law, liberty, and moral purpose as snakes shed their skin. (Unless, of course, some *are* snakes.) Commitments to law, liberty, and moral purpose are part of their inner constitution.

What should corporations do in countries like Xandu? Let us suppose that in recent years a number of prison labor camps have been identified in Xandu. Support that these camps were built both for political and religious dissidents. In these labor camps, torture is a frequent practice. Punishment is meted out daily, and indoctrination and "moral reeducation" are daily aims. In these labor camps, goods are produced that are offered for sale to Western and other corporations. Some American corporations may already have participated unknowingly in buying goods from slave labor camps. This would be evil stuff.

First, if such happenings became known, such purchases would be impossible to justify before the world. Trade in goods made by the sweat and blood of slaves is an abomination.

Second, Western companies themselves have a stake in the rule of law. Some foreign authorities already treat Western companies capriciously, seize their assets, change unilaterally the terms of contracts earlier signed. The abrogation of the rule of law, in short, imposes heavy costs.

Third, absent an active civil society, there will be no associations or groups within Xandunese society to protest against abuses. Naked authority will rule nakedly. This would not be a long-term environment for productive commercial activities.

In such circumstances, it is crucial for American and other Western firms to maintain their moral self-respect. They must become acutely conscious of their own moral and political identity, determined not to sell themselves as less than they are. Business corporations truly are the *avant-garde* of free societies. They represent the first wedge of the development of healthy civil societies, the rule of law, and the new birth of activities, associations, and organizations independent of government.

NEW RULES OF ENGAGEMENT: PRACTICAL STEPS

The first practical step for Kavon and other companies is to recognize that some rare nations may, for a time, under a certain regime, be so bad that it would be a blunder for any self-respecting firm to collaborate with them. Such decisions are easier when international sanctions (or even national laws) prohibit trade and investment. They are more difficult when companies must reach decisions in hard cases without political guidance. Today, of course, sanctions are too profligately and unsystematically used; the U.S. currently exercises sanctions against some seventy countries. This renders long-range investment planning useless.

Still, the long-range good of the human race depends on bringing *all* nations, even rogue nations, back within the circle of law-abiding and tolerably moral behavior. The leaders of nations are not choirboys, and the morality of nations is in some ways more gross and less observant than the morality of individuals (although in some ways it can also be nobler and higher).[37] Still, there are four powerful reasons why the executives of Kavon and other companies must support the rule of law and sound moral codes:

- Trade, investment, and commerce depend on the rule of law and on clear standards of morality.
- Companies have a long-term interest in promoting international moral and legal standards and in making sure that these standards are framed with economic development in view.
- Misguided standards set by antibusiness elites both at home and abroad could do a lot of harm, and careless behavior by companies strengthens such elites.
- Internally, business corporations need high standards themselves, in order to gain moral authority to take the lead in international activities.

The second practical step is for some enterprising business school to launch a major research project outlining new "rules of engagement" for our new international era. This project would consist in two closely related surveys. The first survey would develop a list of fifty or so of the most common abuses of ethics or human rights by governments or firms around the world—a kind of checklist of pitfalls that alert managers ought to have in hand. Such a list should include the seven or eight abuses enumerated in this paper, plus others such as bribes, secret fees, kickbacks, hidden shares in profits, and sweetheart deals, whether demanded by local officials or offered by competitors.

The second survey would generate a parallel list of practical strategies and tactics for successfully defeating all attempted abuses. A corporation whose field officers are fully trained and amply armed with the relevant authority to foil anticipated abuses would have in hand, as it were, clearly stated "rules of engagement," by which to report and to repel outside attempts to compromise the home company.

Internal rules of behavior (it goes without saying), including conditions of immediate dismissal for specified acts of wrongdoing, would guide internal corporate initiatives and practices. The cleaner the ethical principles within the company, the easier decisions are for executives in the field. They know in advance which sorts of behavior will receive moral support from the home office and which will end in reprimand or dismissal. In business as in football and other contact sports, energy is more swiftly channeled when the rule book is clear.

Negatively, then, businesses must avoid those activities that injure or destroy the moral structure of civil society. *Positively*, they must proactively seek out ways—quiet ways—to nurture the political and moral soil that the universal growth of commerce requires.

For instance, using due prudence, modestly and without fanfare, they might instruct employees in the rule of law and the corporate code and teach them the elementary history of liberal political and economic institutions, so that employees might understand the ethos of the firm. Obviously, companies should avoid proselytizing for a particular political party or engaging in domestic politics, local or national. Nonetheless, they should import reading materials and introduce the literature of liberty to their own executives and employees, as well as into schools and libraries in the host country. For practical reasons, they need to regard themselves as teachers. They should be forthright in recounting the history of their firm, telling the stories of its heroes, explaining its corporate ethos, and defending the cultural and political presuppositions on which its being depends. They should always conduct themselves as full-fledged carriers of the thinking and morals of the free society. To do less would be to lack self-respect.

If they fail these responsibilities, they will win disdain from the very foreign tyrants who will welcome them like prostitutes bought and paid for. And they will not deserve to be honored by their fellow citizens back home.

By contrast, when firms fulfill their responsibilities to their own full identity, they strengthen commerce, and commerce is the foundation of a free polity. Commerce is the "commercial" half of "the commercial *republic*" envisioned by our founders. Commerce multiplies human opportunity and generates economic growth and thus opens upward pathways for the poor. Commerce promotes inventions and discovery. As new talents rise, and obsolete technologies die, commerce constantly stirs the circulation of elites. Commerce helps to establish a complex system of checks and balances. Further, commerce makes resources available for projects outside the orbit of state activities and thickens social life while subtracting from the power of the central state. It gives incentives to enterprise and character and inculcates an important range (but not the full range) of moral virtue, especially the virtues necessary for prudent living and the rule of law.

Let me summarize: The success of many new businesses from the bottom upward is crucial to economic growth. The success of these businesses is crucial to the success of democracy, especially where large majorities are poor.

All these goods belong not solely to Americans but to all people on earth. To help set in place the preconditions for the achievement of these great social goods—to help break the chains of worldwide poverty—is the international vocation of American business.

Being a business leader today, then, is a highly moral profession. The bad news is that one can fail. The good news is that one can succeed.

That is the human drama.

That is the suspense.

NOTES

1. The T-shirt was created by Prof. Edward Younkins; quotation from my *Business as a Calling* (New York: Free Press, 1995), p. 175. This lecture builds on, and goes beyond, the argument of *Business as a Calling*.

2. *Centesimus Annus*, #32.

3. *Centesimus Annus*, #32:

Important virtues are involved in this process [the work of firms], such as diligence, industriousness, prudence in undertaking reasonable risks, reliability and fidelity in interpersonal relationships, as well as courage in carrying out decisions which are difficult and painful but necessary, both for the overall working of a business and in meeting possible setbacks. This process, which throws practical light on a truth about the person which Christianity has constantly affirmed, should be viewed carefully and favorably.

4. Peter Berger, *The Capitalist Revolution* (New York: Basic Books, 1986), pp. 78–81.

5. *Business as a Calling*, p. 136.

6. "Socialism is the name of our dream!" wrote Irving Howe in the premier issue of *Dissent*. Fortunately, the Catholic Church never fell into that dream. Pius XI taught definitively in 1931 that "'Religious Socialism,' 'Christian Socialism' are expressions implying a contradiction in terms. No one can be at the same time a sincere Catholic and a true socialist." *Quadragesimo Anno*, #120 in *The Church and the Reconstruction of the Modern World: The Social Encyclicals of Pius XI*, ed., Terence P. McLaughlin, C.S.B. (Garden City, NY: Image Books, 1957), p. 261.

Leo XIII had seen, 40 years earlier, that socialism is not only against nature, inhumane, and evil, but also unrealizable:

The *Socialists* may do their utmost, but all striving against nature is vain. There naturally exists among mankind innumerable differences of the most important kind; people differ in capability, in diligence, in health, and in strength; and unequal fortune is a necessary result of inequality in condition.

Rerum Novarum, #9 in *Seven Great Encyclicals*, ed., William J. Gibbons, S.J. (New Jersey: Paulist Press, 1963), p. 158.

7. See, e.g., Peter Berger's *The Capitalist Revolution*; Irving Kristol's *Two Cheers for Capitalism* (New York: Basic Books, 1978); my own *The Spirit of Democratic Capitalism* (Maryland: Madison Books, 1991), and *The Catholic Ethic and the Spirit of Capitalism* (New York: Free Press, 1993); Richard John Neuhaus, *Doing Well and Doing Good: The Challenge to the Christian Capitalist* (Garden City, New York: Doubleday, 1992).

8. Berger, *op cit.*, pp. 78–81.

9. *World Survey of Economic Freedom 1995–1996*, Freedom House, ed. Richard E. Messick (New Brunswick: Transaction Publishers, 1996).

10. This progression from economic to political liberty is noted on p. 10:

With few exceptions, countries the *Survey* rated economically "free" during 1995 also earned a "free" rating on political and civil liberties.

11. Friedrich A. Hayek, *Capitalism and the Historians* (Chicago: University of Chicago Press, 1954).

12. Cf. also: "One would rather compare such activity to a scientific invention or to an artistic work sprung from a selfless inspiration directed to the whole human com-

munity, which it enriches with new knowledge and with more powerful means of action." Address of Pope Pius XII to the Italian Federation of Commerce, *The Pope Speaks*, vol. 3, no. 1, Spring–Summer 1956, p. 46.

13. Address of Pope Paul VI to the Christian Union of Employers and Executives, *The Pope Speaks*, vol. 10, no. 1, Autumn 1964, p. 17.

14. See David S. Landes, *The Wealth and Poverty of Nations: Why Some Are So Rich and Some Are So Poor* (New York: Norton Books, 1998).

15. Randall Collins, *Weberian Sociological Theory* (Cambridge: Cambridge University Press, 1986), p. 52.

16. *Nicomachean Ethics*, Book I, Chapter 2, in *The Basic Works of Aristotle*, ed. Richard McKeon (New York: Random House, 1941), p. 935.

17. John Adams to Mercy Warren, January 8, 1776, in *The Founders' Constitution*, vol. 1., ed. Philip Kurland and Ralph Lerner (Chicago: University of Chicago Press, 1987), p. 669.

18. *Ibid.*, p. 669.

19. *Ibid.*, p. 670.

20. *Ibid.*

21. Letter to John Adams, May 17, 1818, *The Founders' Constitution*, p. 670.

22. *Notes on the State of Virginia*, Query 19, 1784: The proportion which the aggregate of the other classes of citizens bears in any state to that of its husbandmen, is the proportion of its unsound to its healthy parts, and is a good-enough barometer whereby to measure its degree of corruption. p. 675.

23. *Ibid.*

24. *The Spirit of the Laws,* XX, 2, trans. Thomas Nugent (New York: Hafner Press, 1949), p. 316. On the same page, he adds: "The spirit of trade produces in the mind of a man a certain sense of exact justice, opposite, on the one hand, to robbery, and on the other to those moral virtues which forbid our always adhering rigidly to the rules of private interest, and suffer us to neglect [private interest] for the advantage of others."

25. *Ibid*, V. 6, p. 46.

26. Thomas Paine, *Rights of Man*, Part 2, 1792, in *The Founders' Constitution*, p. 140.

27. Alexander Hamilton, *Report on Manufactures*, December 5, 1791, in *The Founders' Constitution*, p. 140.

28. This argument, against the tyranny of a majority, is picked up by Tocqueville in *Democracy in America*, ed. J.P. Mayer (New York: Doubleday, 1969), pp. 250–254.

29. *Ibid.*, p. 552.

30. *Ibid.*, p. 527.

31. *Ibid.*

32. *Ibid.*, p. 540.

33. *Ibid.*, p. 546.

34. *Ibid.*, p. 547.

35. Jeremiah 2:13, *The Bible* (Revised Standard Version): "For my people have committed two evils; they have forsaken me, the fountain of living waters, and hewed out cisterns for themselves, broken cisterns that can hold no water."

36. See *Federalist* #10 and #53.

37. See Reinhold Niebuhr's *Moral Man and Immoral Society* (New York: Charles Scribner's Sons, 1932), *Man's Nature and His Communities* (New York: Scribner's, 1965), and my essay on Niebuhr, "Moral Society, Immoral Man," in *A Time to Build* (New York: Macmillan Company, 1967).

27

THE SILENT ARTILLERY
OF COMMUNISM

AIMS

For seventy-two years, Communism in Russia waged a silent war against the human soul. Sometimes screams were heard from torture chambers deep in prisons and in detention centers but, mostly, the war was fought with ideas and incessant public propaganda. Below the surface, it eroded foundations. Out of sight, it taught people to have a low opinion of themselves, as if they were incapable of nobility of soul. It ridiculed the soul's capacity for discernment and for truth. Year after year, its silent artillery leveled the inner landscapes of the soul.

My aim in this paper, after certain introductory remarks, is to pull two forgotten themes from the rubble of the fall of Communism. The collapse of Communism in 1989 was one of the greatest events of human history—one of the most sudden, unexpected (although Wojtyla was not surprised), dramatic, and utterly transformative. We are too close to it to be certain how to read it. Yet one characteristic of Communism proved to be decisive. It is, furthermore, very easy to overlook. I mean, its particular form of atheism, and the long-term effect of this atheism upon the morale of the people and upon their economic performance.

These last two themes reward attention: atheism's effect upon the soul, and its effect upon economic vitality.

INTRODUCTORY POINTS: ON HUMAN CAPITAL

A more secular way to speak of these things is to say that Communism set out to destroy human capital. It set out, for instance, to eradicate centuries of learning, habits, cultures—to erase what it chose to call "bourgeois culture," and to salt it as Carthage was salted, and to plow it under, and even to pour oceans of sludge on top of it: lies, propaganda, agitprop. In the process, in one generation,

281

and then in two, and three, and almost four, Communism destroyed the simple habits of economic life. It wounded enterprise, investment, innovation, even the ability to distinguish between profit and loss (since in the end the State didn't care, and paid whatever it wished to pay). It wounded, as well, simple habits of honesty and trust, self-reliance and the honor of being faithful to one's word. More deeply still, it dulled the most distinctive human mark: the soul's primordial endowment of creativity, its sense of personal responsibility, its knowledge of itself as a *subject*.

I need to linger on this last point a moment. The denial of the dignity of the individual, the reduction of the human being to merely material elements, erases the awareness humans have of themselves as persons who reflect and who choose, who launch new and creative actions into history, and who accept responsibility for their actions. Not to be misunderstood, this is the meaning I attach to *subject*. Unlike a horse or a cow, a human being is an acting person, an active agent—inquiring and understanding, deliberating, judging, deciding. In precisely these ways, a human is made in the image of God. Therein lies both his unparalleled glory and the probability of his tragic and often bitter falls.

Communism aimed to objectify everything and everybody. Its fundamental premise was materialism. Human beings are—meat. Animated for a time, perhaps, but essentially no more than a *sachetto* of chemicals. Instruments. Means. The "dialectical" part of "dialectical materialism" belonged to a dynamic class position. The "materialist" part describes human beings. (Truly, it is hard to believe that anybody really believed this, but some did.) The individual should *expect* to be expended, sacrificed, used up, like a thing. Like the steel girders he could see rusting, unwanted and unused, outside the mills of Nowa Huta.

Sacrificed—in this last respect, Communism traded on deep symbolic resonances emanating from Judaism and Christianity. Among these are the long expectation of a New Jerusalem, and the sacrifice of self for others like the ritual lamb, or in the image of the Savior. Communism's materialistic theory, in and of itself, had no such resonance. Mere things do not make sacrifices for noble purposes. Mere things do not consider sacrifice a noble act. Communism's deepest sentiments were borrowed.

THE VIA NEGATIVA

It is well-known that belief in God can lead to torture, as in the awful scrutinies of heresy tribunals. It is less well-known that atheism of a particular kind also leads to torture. The two routes to torture are quite different. The temptation of believers comes from moral arrogance or its mirror image, as in the case of Dostoevsky's Grand Inquisitor, who was moved to torture by "pity," a foolish belief that most people are not as wise as he, so that it was his "duty" to keep them from liberty. This route begins in moral debility. With atheists of the Communist kind it is quite different. Here torture flows from its fundamental premises about the human being. No human has any worth apart from contributing to the Cause—to the Dialectic, to the triumph of the Party (the Vanguard of History, the Custodian of human fate). If a man will not contribute willingly to History or (it comes to the same thing) the Collective Will of the Party, he is without value and may be disposed of—indeed, may be a threat to the Party, and *should* be disposed of. Still, though, some utility may be squeezed from him. If necessary, squeeze.

The bile that rises to our mouths when we contemplate the record of believers who administered torture or committed devout dissenters to the flames is informed by our belief that they were hypocrites, profoundly betraying the example of their Teacher and all His deeper lessons. They were traitors, hypocrites, betrayers, the more to be despised because the level of the teaching they purported to protect was so high. Importuned to be meek and humble, they were arrogant and swollen mightily with pride until their eyes were blinded to the horror of their deeds. One thinks: "They ought, at least, to have been faithful to the faith that they professed." *They deserve to be condemned in the light of their own beliefs*, because those beliefs did *not* lead logically to the torturing of others; quite the opposite. Such men snaked circuitously to that place, held close to the earth by pride.

The case was altogether different with the Communists. Some of them, of course, never really believed their philosophical indoctrination. For various motives, however, good Party members *acted them out*. Against Communists who are torturers, one cannot appeal to the figure of Christ or to the commandments of God. One cannot appeal to natural law or moral law or "bourgeois illusions." They have their orders. History has a certain logic. They can be quite well trusted to overcome their own feelings, and do what is required to turn a man into a means for the Party's ends. Their feelings, also, can be trained, as can their minds. What is an individual man, after all?

Countless memoirs from survivors tell us in detail the logic of the Gulag, and how it worked. We have the testimony of Sakharov and of Scharansky. We have the memoirs of Mihailo Mihailov and Armando Valladares. We have Arthur Koestler's *Darkness at Noon*. We have scores of thousands of windswept camps, millions of graves. Not the mechanics, not even the "logic," but rather the underlying vision of the human being interests us now.

I am certain that I have read more eloquent literary statements than the following. But for clarity and economy of speech I have encountered nothing equal to it:

> The fundamental error of socialism is anthropological in nature. Socialism considers the individual person simply as an element, a molecule within the social organism, so that the good of the individual is completely subordinated to the functioning of the socio-economic mechanism. Socialism likewise maintains that the good of the individual can be realized without reference to his free choice, to the unique and exclusive responsibility which he exercises in the face of good or evil. Man is thus reduced to a series of social

relationships, and the concept of the person as the autonomous subject of moral decision disappears, the very subject whose decisions build the social order. From this mistaken conception of the person there arise both a distortion of law, which defines the sphere of the exercise of freedom, and an opposition to private property. A person who is deprived of something he can call "his own," and of the possibility of earning a living through his own initiative, comes to depend on the social machine and on those who control it. This makes it much more difficult for him to recognize his dignity as a person, and hinders progress towards the building up of an authentic human community.

This text, of course, is from *Centesimus Annus* (para. 13). Here Wojtyla does something quite unusual for a Pope; he employs an encyclical, a formal tool designed for teaching the Gospel to the entire circle of nations (hence "encyclical"), for the purpose of interpreting one single historical event; the whole of its second chapter is given to the meaning and causes of the extraordinary year, 1989. *C.A.* is an astonishing encyclical. It is much too neglected in Europe.

The Pope's point is philosophical; one does not have to be a believer to grasp it. If at the core of man's being nothing "calls" him in a way that demands a response—a free and uncoerced exercise of his personal responsibility, in the secret depths of his heart—then the "dignity" attributed to him for some centuries now is without reality. That call to "respond" engenders *responsibility*, which in the vastness of these galaxies grounds our dignity.

Certain types of Western atheists have an analogous point of view. They also recognize human responsibility—to truth, to reality, perhaps to justice and even to love. It is just that they lack the talent for, the gift of, recognizing God. When they look, they "see" nothing there. Yet as they do not believe in God, neither do they believe that human liberty is just a neural reflex. They have known in themselves a willing exercise of reflection, deliberation, and the sort of choice that is a commitment, on which others can count. They are atheists for whom "truth," "honor," and "courage" are not empty words. (I myself have met many such. As readers of *Belief and Unbelief* and *The Experience of Nothingness* will know, I have sometimes wondered why I should not include myself among them.) For one reason or another, such men and women cannot bring themselves, even when they try, to be at peace in accepting belief in God; they simply do not see. To the extent that they are atheists, so far as they are aware, this is because they are not internally compelled by evidence to the contrary. (Sometimes, they confess, there are hidden desires impeding their will to see, which they have not the inclination to override.) In most other crucial human respects, they share with the theist a sense of a transcendent order that is not made by man, but to which a man can only respond as honestly and courageously as he (or she) knows how. As I once wrote: "Atheists who are not nihilists know that they are bound by conscience, which they find in their own reason and in the judgment of their fellows down the ages. And if despite their beliefs, there is a God, they expect that reason is in accord with the judgment of God. No one escapes."

The fact that there are many such atheists led me to speak above of "the particular kind" of atheism found in Communism. By contrast, Communist atheism denies any transcendent dimension to being, any "call" to which humans must freely respond, any standard of truth, evidence, moral integrity and goodness by which humans are every moment being judged. For the Communist, all is nothingness except the Dialectic of History, before which and in whose name he prostrates himself. The Communist borrows from Christians and Jews an improper comfort, viz., that his prostration places him on the side of an idealistic justice and compassion for workers, in which his premises forbid him to believe. Respecting moral principles, he can have only one: the Collective Will of the Party. All else can be done in that name: murder, torture, imprison, exterminate, assassinate. No other moral question can be scientifically raised. Respecting moral comfort, the Communist is a thief.

For Communism, there is in man no internal source of dignity. Personal liberty and personal responsibility cannot be honored in theory, although of course they continued to live on. In theory, these realities were dismissed as bourgeois affectations.

Paradoxically, the Communist system of imprisonment, torture, and public confession constituted, despite itself, a *via negativa* that led a great many of its victims to God, and to a fresh sense of being an *individual* who possesses *dignity*. For under torture they discovered evidence for the presence of God at the core of their own being. The prison literature of our time is full of such instances.

The typical pattern, if I am not mistaken, went like this. The KGB handbooks listed more than twenty different degrees of torture, more or less scientifically studied and refined. At some point in the proceedings, the torturer would tell his victim that there is no point in resisting, why put everybody through the pain? "No one will ever know what happens here. It has no significance. Neither resistance nor confession, really, will affect the outcome of History. Just be pragmatic. Tell me what I wish, write what I request, and do it sooner rather than later. Why not? Bourgeois prejudices? You are too intelligent for that. No one is ever going to know what you or I will do here. It will be locked up in files with millions of other files, and a thousand years from now when Socialism is truly consolidated, people will never even notice. Consider yourself a forgotten man. Be practical. Sign now rather than later. There is no such thing as truth. It is only a matter of making a decision. It is a matter of will. Write down what you know is fact. I will even help you. The sooner I can go home the better for me—and for you. It is a matter of will. Be practical."

And then the light would go on in the victim's head: "My torturer is telling me that he has all the power. But he is actually confessing something else. There is something he wants from me that he does not have. So he does not have *all* the power. What he needs is this: that I should conform. He needs my will. He needs my denial that there is any such thing as truth. Only then will his philosophy be confirmed.

"As long as I remain faithful to my own intellect and will, as long as I refuse to be complicit in his lie, then my existence unsettles him. *I will not tell a lie.* As long as I can hold out for that principle, then my existence shows him that his philosophy is false.

"Of course, he will overpower me. He can break me with pain. He can take away my mind and my liberty with drugs. But the real power in this relationship is mine. He cannot get what he wants unless I freely give it to him. It is not enough for him to force me, to destroy me—that would be only an instant's work. I am totally in his power. Except for the sanctuary of my consciousness, my fidelity to the light. He will strip me of everything but honesty and naked will. These I cannot give him. He will have to destroy me, and then he cannot have them. Death is now my friend. I will be no use to him—or his precious Party—dead."

Along this way, very much like the way that St. John of the Cross marked out in *The Dark Night of the Soul*, thousands of victims came to know themselves at a depth they had never experienced before. They began to distinguish among the movements of their own souls—memory, imagination, desire, dread, understanding, will.

Moreover, when their bodies ached with pain from beatings, and from the application of electrical current, and from being contorted and held for hours in positions of excruciating pain, they learned something else. They learned that the light inside themselves, to which they were trying to be faithful, the light of truth (or at least the will not to be complicit in any lie), cannot properly be said to be *part of themselves.* That was, of course, their first awareness, that they were being faithful to themselves, clinging to their own minds and wills. When the pain becomes intense enough, however, one sees that one is not really suffering this for oneself. If that were so, why would one not just surrender and make the pain go away? Why wouldn't one be pragmatic?

Rather, it certainly seemed as though, in being faithful to the truth, and in calling up his stubborn courage of will, a man was answering to something that did not belong to himself, something that called (although it had no voice) from outside his own mind and will, something at any rate not reducible to his own mind. His own mind and will were focused in a direction running contrary to everything good for his body and his comfort and his peace. But why? Why was he running from his own self-interest, narrowly considered?

On the matter of self-interest, his torturer was certainly correct. In fact, the torturer's insistence on self-interest suggested the one line of thought that explained why the torturer was wrong.

The light in my mind (before which I am trying to be honest) is, as it were, something I *participate* in, and it is not reducible to me. This light approves of my liberty and grows brighter with my own acts of responsibility to it. This light seems very like what people mean—the people an atheist couldn't earlier understand—when they speak of God. And yet (as St. John of the Cross insists) in the place where we would like God to be, "no one appears." Only silence.

Emptiness. Nothingness. Yet from emptiness strength emanates, and from it one feels constantly stronger. And more comforted, despite the wracking pain and weariness and tedium, than by anything one has ever before experienced. And one feels *true*.

I did my best to express this in my Templeton Address:

> To obey truth is to be free, and in certain extremities nothing is more clear to the tormented mind, nothing more vital to the survival of self-respect, nothing so important to one's sense of remaining a worthy human being— of being no one's cog, part of no one's machine, and resister to death against the kingdom of lies—nothing is so dear as to hold to truth. In fidelity to truth lies human dignity.
>
> There is nothing recondite in this. Simple people have often seen it more clearly than clerks.

This is the plain insight that Aleksandr Solzhenitsyn expressed, and also Silvester Krcmery—a man who may have endured solitary confinement, without breaking, longer than any living man—in his magnificent memoir, *Breakpoint* [Herder and Herder, 1999].

In the *via negativa*, the voyager sees nothing, hears no divine voices, feels no mystic "presence." As it were, he has before him no more "evidence" concerning God than he did when he called himself an atheist. But he can no longer call himself that. He has come to know that he is no longer accurately described as an atheist. He has been led to the threshold where God dwells, by a dark and obscure knowledge that carries with it a warrant unmistakable to those who have participated in it. He may or may not be ready to say that he believes in "God," but now he has had the experiences that allow him to know what others have been talking about. Not that these are "experiences" that can be isolated, or that they are a kind of "special knowledge" given to some but not to others. Rather, something much more simple.

In the act of fidelity to the light—the resolve not willingly to be complicit in any lie—a man has become aware of a dimension of his being he had never glimpsed before in such stark clarity. In this awareness, he is aware of a powerful personal dignity. What impresses him is its inalienability. Unless he is simply destroyed, it cannot be taken away from him without his consent. It is true that later he may weaken and give in. But he does not have to fight *later*, only now. He needs only to concentrate during this staccato second, one second at a time, on the dark light within. Silvester Krcmery simply concentrated on repeating the words of the Gospel of St. John, the whole of which he had committed to memory. Too broken sometimes to think of *meanings*, he found even the effort to recite the mere words nourishing. And, of course, the meanings when he had strength to grasp them illuminated what he was enduring.

The term *dignus* is a precious term in the vocabulary of the West. That single word helps to explain why we attach so much importance to the millennium—rather, the *second* millennium. For it was Jesus Christ, bringing the Torah to the Gentiles, who taught humankind that Plato was wrong to teach that the lowly have slavish souls, souls of lead, whereas their superiors have souls of gold and silver. Even the children, even the poor, even the outcasts, every one of God's children, Jesus said, as the Torah also taught through the prophets, is *dignus*. The world has never been the same.

That term attaches great worth, nobility, immortal and incommensurable value to every woman and every man, each of whose names, the Pentateuch tells us, the Creator knows and calls. The Bible assigns humans this status as *dignus*, as it does to no other creature, for reasons that, strictly, we do not need revelation to reveal: because of our capacity for ordered liberty, for the exercise of responsibility, for living in the truth. That term *dignus* made possible the rise of modern science, by raising even the poor in their own estimation, and calling upon their enormous, hidden talents, and instructing all humans that fidelity to truth is in touch with the way things are, and giving all the vocation to inquire in the light of truth. Fidelity to truth is a way of participating in the life of God. Truth and Light are among the names God gives Himself in the biblical record.

In a way too little reflected upon, Wojtyla the philosopher has articulated a crucial point: the close relation between atheism and the disappearance of individual dignity, and between theism and the inner experience of dignity. But I hasten to add again, there are "atheists" of fidelity to truth and goodwill who have also experienced their own dignity in acts of responsibility and reflective liberty. As Albert Camus once wrote, there are atheists in our time who lack nothing but churchgoing to distinguish them from believers. In *Belief and Unbelief*, I show how in the darkness the inner life of both the serious believer and the serious unbeliever can also be quite similar, except that for the believer perhaps it can be less comforting. The atheist, after all, says he expects the darkness.

To that last point, however, honesty forces me to add that for Jews and Christians, truth is not merely a property of propositions or even a term for fidelity to the light. It is a personal name, the name of a Person. So that participation in fidelity to truth is, in the eyes of faith, communion with a Beloved. But to say this much takes us beyond the *via negativa*. I will say no more than that faith does not take away the experience of emptiness, of *nada*. Clouds of witnesses have so testified.

Let me return speedily, therefore, to the first part of my argument. This anniversary of the fall of Communism forces us to confront one of the deepest lessons to be gleaned from a seventy-year Plague upon the human race. Even in the emptiness, the sheer willingness not to turn away from the light, not to be complicit in a lie, leads to an experience of the emptiness in which God darkly dwells. Receptivity is all. It is as though our inquiring souls are already God-shaped. Silently formed in His image. So that when we try to be honest and brave, try to hold a steady light, that obscure light is already a form of participation.

For seventy-two years, Communism leveled its silent artillery upon this image in the human soul. Its aim was to level the soul's grandeur, thus to make it more pliable as an instrument of the Collective Will. In such a system, torture is not an accident. Torture expresses its essence: The human individual has no worth.

And yet, ironically, the experience of this torture upon their own flesh led many thousands of ordinary people to an extraordinary recovery. In the recesses of their own being, they witnessed the hidden action of God. By this *via negativa*, those determined to cleanse the world of God were divinely outmaneuvered. Trying to drive God out of the soul, they tormented the soul into abandoning everything else, there by negation to find Him.

THE DESTRUCTION OF HUMAN CAPITAL

Before Communism collapsed in 1989, it had also lowered its silent artillery on the human capital of its people, especially the human capital that suited them for personal economic initiative. (Communism forbade capitalist acts between consenting adults, in some circumstances under penalty of death.) In defining the nature of capitalism, however, Karl Marx made an egregious mistake. He thought that capitalism is constituted by three institutional arrangements: (1) private property; (2) a market system of exchange; and (3) the private accumulation of profit. These three institutions, however, are all *pre*-capitalist. They are found even in the biblical period (and earlier), whereas scholars hold that "capitalism" is something very new, modern in fact, and quite different from the traditional system based on private property, markets, and profit. Max Weber dated the birth of capitalism after the Protestant Reformation (also a mistake, but indicative of the timing). During the years after 1775, Adam Smith, David Hume and others in Scotland and England were arguing for a *new* system, a system that did not yet exist except *in nuce*. They made, as O. E. Hirshman puts it, "arguments for capitalism before its arrival."

The defining dynamic of the new system is *invention* and *enterprise*. Capitalism applied imagination and practical intelligence to creating new goods and services not provided by earlier systems, agrarian, feudal and mercantile. Adam Smith opened his *Inquiry into the Nature and Cause of the Wealth of Nations* (1776) with a description of the invention of the pin machine that made it possible to produce thousands of pins with less labor and expense than it had earlier cost to produce a dozen pins. Before, only duchesses could afford pins; afterwards, every poor girl in the kingdom had them. In the nineteenth century, the real income of the poor in England rose by 1600 percent.

In the United States in 1787, the U.S. Constitution included an article granting to "authors and inventors" for a limited time the right to the profits from their own inventions; in other words, *constitutional* protection for patents and copyrights. In the penetrating words of Abraham Lincoln not quite a century later, this patent system "added the fuel of interest to the fire of genius." Like a spark, this law changed the social position and meaning of wealth. For it shifted the focus of the pursuit of wealth off *land* and placed it upon *enterprise*, invention and discovery; away from the physical and material, and toward ideas. It took the focus of the will-to-power, that ineradicable fact of human life after the Fall, away from the generals and national glory, and wooed it toward those who could create new wealth and international connectedness (now called globalization). What had three thousand years of generals and national glory done to raise the condition of the poor? David Hume asked. Only the spread of manufacturing and commerce could do that. *Commercium et Pax* was the wise motto of Amsterdam.

So it happens that nearly all business corporations (and even unincorporated businesses) in the United States today are based upon creative ideas for new goods and services or new ways of providing them. The virtue of *enterprise*, in short, is the essence of capitalism; enterprise is the new dynamic in the world. Until enterprise is present in sufficient density, capitalism cannot even begin. In Poland in 1990, for example, after laws were reestablished protecting private property, restoring the market system of exchange, and allowing for the private creation of wealth, the question remained, Whether the Polish people had lost all habits of initiative under forty years of Communist passivity? Would the new system simply die of inertia? As it happened, in the first six months of 1990, 500,000 new small businesses were formed. This spirit of enterprise provided lift-off. It has only grown stronger since.

In this respect Max Weber was correct (as against Marx), that the explanatory factor in the new system lies in the realm of the spirit rather than the material order. Capitalism is most of all a set of human habits—virtues, in the old-fashioned sense, natural and learned dispositions. For example, the virtue of enterprise consists, like the classical virtue of prudence, in both an intellectual habit and a moral habit. The intellectual habit is to *notice*, often before others do, new creative economic opportunities, new goods to create or new ways to create them; to *innovate*; to *invent*. The moral habit is to have the realism, the practicality, the know-how, and the stubborn obstinacy *to turn ideas into realities*; that is, *to make ideas work*. Not everybody who has one of these two habits has the other. Enterprise requires both. Enterprise is not unlike the creative habit of the artist, who also makes to be what never was. People in business are not infrequently as vainglorious about their creations as any diva of the opera.

Thus, contrary to Max Weber, it is not precisely "hard work" or "asceticism" that creates new wealth, although both of those factors are highly supportive and almost always necessary. Rather, it is often the factor of serendipity, the gift of the act of creation, sometimes occurring suddenly in the ready mind as if inspired by a Muse, that ignites "the fire of invention." The creative act is what Rocco Buttiglione once called the "Don Quixote" factor.

The great sociologist Max Weber stressed what he called "the Protestant virtues," and I do not want to underestimate their importance. Actually, however, the *creativity* and élan of what I call "the Catholic virtues"—the zest for invention, a love for surprise and for wonder, and a sense that life is as much a gift as a result of hard work—are in actual practice closer to the mark. Creative people do not always work by schedules and routines. Thus, Northern Italy has been a creative precursor of capitalist activity for at least five centuries, and today is one of the top ten entrepreneurial hot spots in the European Community. Catholics make too little of their own genius for enterprise. A political affection for social democracy among Catholics smothers this widely distributed genius; the long agrarian history of Catholicism predisposes many to "organic" theories, and dulls the vision of the capacity of enterprise to open opportunity to the poor. The British left shares this same bias, which Tony Blair's "Third Way" is meant to correct.

Contrary to Amintore Fanfani's famous book on capitalism, *Catholicism, Protestantism and Capitalism*, Catholic theology, freshly considered, throws a more illuminating light on the essence of capitalism than Max Weber and "Protestant ethic" did, and better explains the course of economic history. As David Landes of the Massachusetts Institute of Technology makes clear in his 1998 study of economic history, *The Wealth and Poverty of Nations*, one main cause of the economic leadership of the West lies in the "joy of discovery" taught to Jews and Christians, through the teaching that each woman and each man is made in the image of God, the Creator, and is called to be a creator, too.

It goes without saying that Communism tried to eradicate this image in the human soul, and to strip away from society every social support that over the ages had been brought to its flourishing. Economic initiative was forbidden. The good Socialist system was expected to be receptive to the Collective Will and to submerge individual creativity within it. Private property was abolished. (As late as 1986, along the banks of the dark river in the center of Moscow, huge red letters blazed at night: THE ESSENCE OF SOCIALISM IS THE ABOLITION OF PRIVATE PROPERTY.) The system of market exchange as old as Jerusalem in the biblical period—for Jerusalem was nothing if not a marketplace at the crossroads of three continents—was replaced with a system of national planning. "Experts" had the task of setting prices each month for more than 20 million different items; they had to *fantasize* these "correct" prices, make them up out of whole cloth, *invent* them, with no reference to the costs, desires, or efforts expended by individual buyers or sellers; and they had to do so each month. The epistemic problem of knowing such things is beyond any team of mere mortals, as Ludwig von Mises had predicted in the 1920s. No wonder the Socialist economy had a Mickey Mouse quality; epistemically, it had the realism of a comic strip.

As if that weren't bad enough, Communism cut the tie between economic effort and reward. It forbade private accumulation, and settled instead for rewarding its most faithful ones with political favors (including living quarters, dachas, automobiles, and "official" stores).

Not only this. Communism set out to abolish the ancient traditions, customs and habits of law and morality. It wanted to dirty, distort and bury the past so that it would be irrecoverable. It tried desperately to replace "bourgeois morality" (in reality, the morality of Judaism and Christianity, more dear to the poor perhaps than to the affluent) with "Socialist morality," a morality of means and ends, in which the human person is never an end but always a means. It taught disregard for critical thinking, personal judgment, and a love for truth, in order to make room for Party ideology and propaganda.

As a final affront, it withheld even the humblest goods—toilet paper, meat, oranges—so that humble citizens would have to spend hours in line every week just in order to live. In this way, they might come to feel grateful for the smallest triumphs. They would also learn to hold themselves in contempt, as unworthy of anything at all except what was allotted them. Shortages demean people, and Communism used them as a means of social control. (Those who too facilely oppose "being" to "having" have not reflected on the close relation, not only lexical, between the terms *proprius* and property, and between the self and dominion over necessary and convenient things. Communism's war against the self traded on this distinction.)

Thus it is that after seventy-two years of Communist "moral education," the legal and moral traditions of Russia are today in a shambles. The human capital built up over centuries of religious and humanistic striving was bleached out of each successive generation—one, two, three, four generations in all—and nothing was put in its place but cynicism. Means and ends. Instrumentalism.

In such a moral and legal environment, neither democracy nor capitalism can take root, let alone flourish. Democracy and capitalism are, both of them, sets of moral and intellectual habits before they are anything else—even before they are institutionalizations of these habits. "Democracy," Alexis de Tocqueville wrote, "is a long education." It is learned by experience, and must be internalized. Like any fragile plant, however, it will grow only under a limited set of ecological conditions. There is an "ecology of liberty," as vital as the ecology of the biosphere—*more* vital. Communism tried for seventy-two years to raze that ecology, to plow it under, as the Romans plowed Carthage under: *Carthago Delenda est.*

Few commentators have noticed this aspect of Communist destructiveness. In destroying the heritage of religion and law, and in destroying the very idea of evidence-based truth (independent of preference or Party, aimed squarely at an accurate assessment of reality), Communism destroyed, or perhaps gravely injured, the "social capital" on which all human progress in liberty depends. The loss of social capital is an incalculable loss for individuals, for one person alone does not make a free society. Even if the ecology of liberty in a particular society is healthy, it takes a degree of heroism to act virtuously, when others are not doing so. But when the whole ecology of the society frustrates your actions at every turn, trying to act virtuously in solitariness seems futile, and one must struggle daily against the temptation to despair. (This is perhaps why the Pope keeps preaching, "Be not afraid!" and why he lays so much stress upon the desperate social need for hope, in our time especially.)

A metaphor for the Communist destruction of human capital was suggested to me in the spring of 1990 by a brilliant priest in Prague, Tomaš Halík. Looking at the Socialist skyline of Prague he said wryly: "Forty years of Communism will be remembered for not one piece of worthy architecture. Look!" More than that, he pointed out to me that for forty years the Communists plowed not a korona back into capital maintenance of the existing buildings, except upon a few Potemkin facades. The plumbing, wiring, and plaster were left as they had been in 1948, which meant in most cases as they had been in 1938 when the Nazis rolled into Prague. The Communists created little new capital, and spent down the old. "It will take decades to bring these properties back to the condition in which the Communists confiscated them." Communism was like a tapeworm, devouring the capital, social, human, and even architectural, of its captive nations from within. One hears in Eastern Europe many wry jokes about this aspect of Socialism.

In sum, Communism was not merely an alternative to democracy and a dynamic, free economy. It destroyed the human capital on which a free economy and polity are based. It poisoned the ecology of liberty. Detoxifying it will require years of patient work in the moral and cultural sphere. Most Western economists, alas, have little or no comprehension of how much they take this sphere for granted.

THE WESTERN BLIND SPOT

Before concluding, let me tell a parable to exemplify this blind spot among Western economists, a parable I learned (and hereby adapt for present purposes) from an economist at George Mason University, Jennifer Roback. She describes an American couple who adopted a young boy of three or so from Rumania, one of those orphans brought up mass-production style, never held in human arms, fed by a bottle put in place by a mechanical apparatus. Isolated from human closeness with adults until he left the orphanage, the child is grown now, handsome, smart, winning in his ways—but absolutely incapable of forming a human relationship, only capable of seeking his own will and his own pleasure. He fears close contact with adults, only pretending to affection so far as is necessary. Cleverly narcissistic, he lies, steals, cheats, whatever he needs to do to obtain whatever he desires. And all the while, smiling, he charms people by his seemingly open manner. He has already been arrested once for shoplifting, and his teachers at school, for a time in love with him, have reluctantly had to report the times he has stolen things from his classmates.

This engaging boy has learned precisely how to deceive. His parents, serious and devout people, are in despair about his behavior. For he is certainly heading for self-destruction and may, they fear, charm innocent and inexperienced people into accompanying him thereto. Professor Roback explains that the totally self-centered impulse that moves this child, the total preoccupation with his own physical self-interest, at the expense of all other more noble interests (except insofar as pretending to these helps him to achieve his own purposes), sounds remarkably like what the economists conventionally discuss as "economic self-interest."

Professor Roback has even written a lecture to this effect, daring other economists to tell her in what respect the conduct of this warped and totally narcissistic (almost emotionally autistic) young man *differs* from the behavior of their theoretical "economic man." This challenge infuriates the economists, she has found, but they only sputter and do not answer it. When they have had time to reflect upon it, however, they may find that, *more than they explicitly recognize in their published theories*, the "man" they assume to be acting in their theories is a highly developed humanistic person, of Jewish and Christian provenance, or of some correlative tradition. For when they write "rational," they also mean "law-abiding" and at least minimally "honest," "trustworthy," and "morally reliable." They emphatically do *not* mean a crook, cheat, liar, manipulator, or narcissist with whom it is impossible to have a rational relationship. A deal has to be a deal. A partner one cannot trust brings a high cost in efficiency, and a high probability of eventual disaster. The true anthropology of capitalism, the only premise on which it can work, encodes a far richer morality than is exemplified by that unfortunate orphan.

Analogously, an unfortunate orphan brought up until the age of three without human contact, warmth, or emotional involvement is not a fair metaphor for the ordinary people who endured the imposition of amoral Communism upon them for seventy or (in Eastern Europe) forty years. But it *is* a fair metaphor for the aims and practices of Communism. Our parable describes a human being rendered emotionally autistic by being treated as an object, raised like a little animal in a large stable (mechanically, without maternal embrace or touch), made over into a rational calculator of means and ends, evacuated of genuine and reliable *subjectivity*. Where there ought to be a "self" in him, there is a cipher. This child learned to determine his direction by vectoring around any resistance he meets to getting what he wants, like a robot bumping and bouncing away, incapable of internal self-government. Like the "Eveready Bunny," he never stops calculating and driving onward. Within his own personal history, there is a dialectic of resistant objects that have marked out the paths forced upon him: a kind of miniature Dialectical Materialism, blind and irresistible.

Also inhuman.

CONCLUDING REMARKS

Long before World War II ended, a group of economists and philosophers in Germany began thinking about the *novus ordo* that would have to replace

Nazism, once Hitler came to the end of his line. They recognized that if they were to build a humane society they would have to reconstruct a new political order, a new economic order, and a new moral/cultural order. To construct any *one* of these orders is a herculean job, but to be obliged to construct all *three*—and to be obliged to do so almost simultaneously (although not instantaneously)—is virtually superhuman. The hope of these "*Ordo* economists," as they called themselves, was that Germany had not suffered total cultural and moral damage under Nazism, given that the regime had lasted only twelve years. They further hoped that there were strong remnants of the humanistic past that could again be drawn upon, but in a more careful way. Their philosophy, and their vision of a "social market economy," became the practical guide to the "miraculous" success of Germany during the years 1945–1999. Their great success shows that it is not impossible to construct the three interdependent social systems—political, economic, and moral-cultural—that constitute the free society, in which free persons and free communities can flourish, and even to do so within a relatively short time. This success gives heart to all who must achieve something similar, even if more difficult.

Such a task, moreover, is never fully done once and for all, but must often be recapitulated. For later generations need to rediscover the reasons why the free society is constructed as it is, and why it demands so many sacrifices and so much unrelenting effort. The price of the free society is unceasing reformation.

The free society is moral, or not at all. That is why it is so precarious. Any one generation, deciding that it is not worth the cost, can throw it over.

But the moral situation of the formerly Communist countries is far more desperate than the situation of Germany in 1945. For the moral destruction that Communism wrought in Russia during seventy-two years had time to plow far deeper into the primordial soil of the human spirit, and to be far more destructive of traditional institutions, practices, and associations. The damage to human capital was incalculable.

When my plane landed in St. Petersburg on September 10, 1991 (I had bought my ticket for "Leningrad" but when I landed it was "St. Petersburg"), the white, red and blue flag of Russia was flying over the city for the first time in decades, in place of the red flag of Communism. People in St. Petersburg were still exhilarated by their own heroism in standing for hours outside the Winter Palace in defense of the new Constitution, surrounded by tanks and Party photographers snapping their pictures for future prosecution. "Now we feel," a philosopher at the university told me in his apartment that night, "like normal people. We stood for our liberty just as Americans once did. We did it! You can't imagine how it felt, in front of the Winter Palace."

Later, in a more sober mood he told me, poking his finger up and down into my chest: "Next time they try an experiment like Socialism, they should try it out on animals first. Humans it hurts too much!"

He was brave and hopeful that night. I often wonder what his thoughts are now.

This much we know. Even under the best of conditions, it is extremely difficult to construct a free society that works, that endures, that is self-correcting. The silent artillery that Communism leveled at the human spirit and at every internal nerve of human capital for more than seventy years had its effect. The transition from Communism to a free society is consequently a severely demanding moral task. It requires a transition from a monistic system to a three-fold system, that is, to three relatively independent yet interdependent systems. It is a transition to a society free from torture, assassination, extortion and tyranny in its political system; nourishing orderly and creative enterprise, and liberating the poor from poverty in its economic system; and through its cultural system rewarding the habits that make a free economy and a free polity both possible and worthwhile.

How that transition goes is perhaps the greatest drama of our time. Everything depends upon the use that humans make of the liberty with which each is endowed, while there is still time to affect the outcome. We are the *subjects* of this drama, not the *objects*.

Thomas Jefferson, no orthodox believer, put it this way: "The God who gave us life gave us liberty at the same time." It is no hindrance to our purposes to understand that liberty is the Creator's jewel, favored by Providence. Theism is no hindrance to personal dignity. On the contrary, it is its source.

In sum, the twin themes of my paper are not so disparate as at first glance they may appear. By its simultaneous hostility both to the human soul and to personal economic initiative, Communism testified to their connection.

28

SOLIDARITY IN A TIME OF GLOBALIZATION

The Best of Times for Catholic Social Thought

"Be not afraid!" is the favorite injunction of John Paul II to the peoples of the world. "Be not afraid!" And those of us who were privileged to be present at the Second Vatican Council during the years 1961–1965 (including the antepreparatory session) will never forget Pope John XXIII's injunction to turn away from "the prophets of gloom."

In this spirit, I would like to address the formidable array *rerum novarum* that goes by the name of "globalization." (Exactly one month ago I heard John Paul II address this theme at Castel Gandolfo, and again he said: "Be not afraid!")[1]

My thesis is easy to state simply, but difficult to unpack completely in a short space of time. The thesis is this: Now is the best of times for the credibility of the basic themes of Catholic Social Thought, and the worst of times for those described by *Ecclesia in America* as "neo-liberals."

I want to unpack this thesis under five headings: *materialism* or, rather, the primacy of the spirit; *solidarity*; the *subjectivity* of society (that is, the liberty, initiative, and creativity of the human subject); *subsidiarity*; and *breaking the chains of poverty*. Many of you will notice that each of these terms plays a central role in John Paul II's masterpiece of Catholic Social Thought, *Centesimus Annus*.

MATERIALISM

The Synod of America described "neo-liberals" as materialists concerned solely with market processes, profits and efficiency, to the neglect of the human spirit, human values, and human rights.[2]

In the new economy of today, however, it is very difficult to be a materialist. Consider your last purchase of a new disc, or a new program for your computer. You hold it in your hand and recall that you paid $200 for it. But how much *material* do you actually have in your hand? About eighty cents' worth of plastic. What you actually paid for is almost entirely composed of *mind*, the fruit of the human spirit, information in a design created by human intelligence.

All around us, the mechanical revolution is being replaced by the electronic revolution. All around us, matter matters less and less, and intelligence (or spirit) matters more. Even the nuclear physicists have developed such a new notion of "matter" that the old gap between "spirit" and "matter" seems as oldfashioned as the horse and buggy. The seemingly solid stuff of material objects is analyzed into tiny particles—molecules, atoms, neutrons, quarks—that evanesce into something like imperceptible units of energy or light, nearly as refined as what was once imagined as "spirit."

As John Paul II explains, the cause of wealth *used* to be explained in largely material terms: At one time, the major form of wealth—in Latin America, say— was *land*. At a later time, especially for Marxist thought, it was *capital*, conceived of as large inert investments in factories and huge machines. In our time, however, economists affirm that the chief cause of the wealth of nations is not material at all, but *knowledge, skill, know-how*—in short those acts and habits of discovery, invention, organization and forethought that economists now describe as "human capital," located in the human spirit and produced by the spiritual activities of education and training and mentoring.[3] Human capital also includes moral habits, such as hard work, cooperativeness, social trust, alertness, honesty, and social habits such as respect for the rule of law. The one factor, more than any other, that makes the rich countries rich is their investment in and development of human capital. A nation's greatest single resource, economists say, is its people.[4]

Put another way, it is not material resources that make a nation rich. Some of the nations richest in natural resources are among the world's poorest nations. Some of the nations with virtually no natural resources are among the world's richest nations. The cause of wealth cannot be said, today, to be material.

These days, on all fronts, materialists face hard times. All the evidence of physics and other sciences, and economics too, seems against them.

On the other hand, no principle is as basic to Catholic Social Thought as the primacy of spirit. Everywhere today that principle seems to be vindicated: in care for the physically and the mentally ill, in overcoming drug abuse and alcoholism, in turning from a life of crime, in moral formation, in economic development, in nourishing among a people the rule of law and a civic spirit, in encouraging people to act with unimpeachable honesty even when no one is looking, and in engendering confidence in the future even in the face of great obstacles. Empirical research seems to confirm the primacy of spirit, and to disconfirm merely materialistic accounts of human behavior.[5]

SOLIDARITY

When Leo XIII described in *Rerum Novarum* (1891) the tumultuous changes then churning through the formerly agrarian and feudal world of pre-modern Europe, he saw the need for a new sort of virtue (a reliable habit of soul) among

Christian peoples, lay people especially, and he wavered between calling it *justice* or *charity, social justice* or *social charity.*[6] By the time of *Centesimus Annus* (1991), one hundred years later, John Paul II had brought that nascent intuition into focus in the one term *solidarity*. By this term, he did not mean the great Polish labor union which contributed so much to bringing down Communism—although no doubt the worldwide fame of the term *Solidarnosc* added helpful connotations to what he intended—but rather the special virtue of social charity that makes each individual aware of belonging to the whole human race, of being brother or sister to all others, of living in *communio* with all other humans in God. Solidarity is another way of saying globalization, but in the dimension of communal interiority and personal responsibility. Solidarity is not an impersonal habit of losing one's self in group-think, disappearing into a collectivity. Solidarity is exactly the reverse of what socialists meant by collectivization, for it points simultaneously to the personal responsibility and initiative of the human subject and to communion with others. Solidarity awakens, and does not lull, individual conscience. Solidarity evokes responsibility and enlarges personal vision and connects the self to all others.[7]

And in these days of "globalization," even when that "new thing" is described in merely economic terms, it is almost impossible for any intelligent human being to imagine the self as an unencumbered, detached, solitary individual, unlinked to others. In fact most attempts to define globalization fail. Globalization is not merely a dramatic drop in transportation and communication costs. It is not only the shrinkage of a formerly vast realm of distant and remote nations into one small "village," linked in instantaneous communications. Nor is it merely the centripetal energies of a single global market interconnected by internet and satellite and cellular phone and television. Globalization is not the mere geometric increase of "foreign direct investment" [FDI] and cross-border trade. Although of course globalization today is all these things,[8] globalization also has an interior dimension. External, economic globalization has changed the way individuals experience themselves and the way they think.

Thomas Friedman, for instance, describes a Jordanian friend of his, a political journalist, telling him with satisfaction one day that CNN had just begun to include Amman in its reports on the day's temperatures and weather forecasts; because that means that Jordan now *exists* in a way it had not before. Shortly thereafter, an Israeli businessman explained to Friedman that he and his associates no longer think first about local economic conditions and what they will produce, and then about some possibilities for export on the side. Rather, they now find themselves thinking about the whole planet, and about what they might be able to export, and then they think about how to produce it. We have become different sorts of persons, the man explained; we think of ourselves in a new way. A planetary way.[9]

Is this not a major step in the direction of the realities of solidarity? Are human beings not planetary creatures, one another's brothers and sisters, members of one same body, every part serving every other part?[10]

These are the best of times for those committed to solidarity, and pinching, painful times for those committed to a view of themselves as solitary individuals—pinching like shoes that do not fit.

If a Catholic cannot feel confident in a time of globalization, what is the point in bearing the name "Catholic," which is another name for global? (The imperative for globalization began with the commission, "Go preach the gospels to all nations," which turned Christianity away from being the religion of one tribe or one people only, and commanded it to see the whole human race as one people of God.) Globalization is the natural ecology of the Catholic faith.

THE SUBJECTIVITY OF SOCIETY

The theme of subjectivity in Pope John Paul II has been much overlooked in conventional expositions of Catholic Social Thought. This theme grows out of the Pope's reflections on what makes the human person different from a cat or a dog or any other creature in the world of nature. It grows out of the young Wojtyla's dissatisfaction with merely reciting "the human person" as if it were an incantation. What *is* a human person?[11] And how would you make this clear to a Marxist, a materialist, who thinks that human beings are mere parts in a social system? To someone who thinks that human individuals are mere members of a collective, like sheep in a flock or bees in a hive or animals on a farm? Marxists, Wojtyla found, reduce humans to their social relations.[12] Here is where Wojtyla found that phenomenological methods add a new dimension to Thomism, a dimension of interiority and psychological analysis that is closer to lived reality.[13]

To state the matter briefly, anyone who has a pet in the house knows that animals *behave*; they cannot do other than follow the laws of their own nature. One's own children, however, do not always "behave," they imagine new futures for themselves, invent new projects and new trajectories for their personal development. In part they invent themselves. In the long run, they must become provident over their own identity, responsible for choosing who they will become. In short, children must learn to reflect, to deliberate, to choose, to take initiative and to accrue responsibility for their own actions. Unlike the other animals, they *can* choose against the laws of their own nature, or they can choose to walk in those laws.

To summarize, whereas the other animals *behave*, the human person *acts*. The human person is *the acting person*.[14] Action flows from the interior life of insight, reflection, and decision—acts that only persons can perform, acts that humans have in common (analogously) with angels and with God, but with no other known creatures.

John Paul II began using this conceptual framework in his very first encyclical, *Laborem Exercens* (1981), and he returned to it again in *Sollicitudo Rei Socialis* (1988) when contrasting the view of man as a cog in a machine, a part of a collective, with the unmistakable "right of private economic initiative."[15] By the time he wrote *Centesimus Annus*, the Pope had come to distinguish between "the subjectivity of society" and "the subjectivity of the individual," both canceled by "Real Socialism."[16] He then pushed his earlier thought to the new insight that the capacities of the human being for creative action are the cause of the wealth of nations, and the most important form of capital from an economic point of view.[17]

This concept enabled the Holy Father to talk about solidarity in terms of personal responsibility and initiative. Correlatively, the concept of solidarity enabled him to talk about the individual subject in terms of universal *communio*.

Without the integrity of the human subject, there is no genuine communio. Without communio, there is no whole human subject.

Without solidarity, subjectivity degenerates into unencumbered individualism. Without subjectivity, solidarity degenerates into mushy and mindless collectivism.

Ours is a very good time for grasping the complementarity of these two conceptual tools, in ways that earlier generations could not so broadly and so unmistakably experience. For during our lives we have experienced excesses of both collectivism and individualism alone. We have lived through the failures of both socialist and liberal materialism.

By contrast, we have seen stunning examples of the fullness of solidarity and subjectivity in one person, the singular determination and courageous initiatives of John Paul II, acting as universal pastor and worldwide pilgrim, in each site gathering around himself the local college of bishops and the local people—at times, seemingly, the whole people, millions in one place—have crystallized before our eyes a liturgical representation of the concepts he articulates analytically in his encyclicals.[18] What he writes, he also enacts. In more than one sense he has been a dramatist. He has shown us an acting person both in interior solitude and in worldwide solidarity.

SUBSIDIARITY

Simultaneously with the great rushing power of economic and legal globalization there has also arisen a powerful set of local demands for greater local autonomy and a stronger role for intermediate institutions and mediating associations. In other words, from outside and from within, the nation state is under great pressures. These pressures are all the more acute since, at least since the time of Hegel, the nation state has been thought to be the mythical embodiment of the *Geist* of a whole people. One can read the history of the last two centuries as an enactment of the myth of the benevolent nation state, caring for its people as the nanny for her children, rendering them secure and happy. From Lenin to Hitler, Mussolini to Peron, Mao-tse Tung to Castro, Kim Il Sung to Qaddafi, dictators have loved this myth. They have portrayed themselves as personifications of the Popular Will. Various forms of socialism, social democracy, and the liberal welfare state have all embraced other versions of the same mythic impulse. The twentieth century has predominantly been the story of the nation state, at the expense of every other institution—family, church, mediating institution. The nation state has proved inadequate, however, to its own boasts. It has over-promised and under-achieved. Great pressures from outside and from within are bursting through its governing myths.

Catholic Social Thought itself has invested a great deal of its conceptual weight in a theory of the state, especially the welfare state, which has not met the tests of reality. A massive rethinking is needed, and quickly.

The need for this rethinking is obvious in the international dimension. The Pope and the Synod of the Americas call plaintively for new international institutions to "guide" the new energies of globalization.[19] But much of the rethinking must attend to the intra-national dimension, the vitality of the smaller institutions *within* states that the hyperactive states of the last one hundred years have repressed and suppressed. Whole regions, ethnic peoples, cities, townships, villages have been neglected. Yet today many diverse local forces are stirring and coming again to life.

The defense of the civic association by the church is at least as old as Innocent IV's defense of such "corporations" as cities, cathedral chapters, and guilds, independent of the state,[20] and the defense of the human rights of the members of mendicant orders such as the new Franciscans and Dominicans by Thomas Aquinas at the University of Paris.[21] But the Catholic doctrine on "subsidiarity" appears to have been given a great boost by the Swiss and the American experiments in confederation and federalism, respectively. Abraham Lincoln gave a succinct formulation of the theory before Leo XIII or Pius XI did.[22] Lord Acton identified federalism—that is, one form of subsidiarity—as one of the great achievements in the history of liberty.[23]

The basic justification for subsidiarity is epistemic. Decisions taken closer to the concrete texture of reality and the immediate interests of the decision makers are likely to evince a higher degree of practical intelligence, not to say wisdom, than decisions taken at a higher, more abstract remove. Practical wisdom tends to demand hands-on, experiential knowledge, the sort of knowledge Jacques Maritain identified as "knowledge by connaturality," a kind of knowledge by "second nature."[24]

The Catholic Church itself, as a universal body whose daily life is intimately concrete and immediate, immersed in local languages and cultures, is a historic embodiment of the principle of subsidiarity. Pope John Paul II kisses the local soil in every place he visits. Localities are, as it were, almost sacramental—as is the Holy Land of the Bible. The God of Abraham, Isaac, Jacob and Jesus is not abstract, but identified with a concrete history, and yet withal universal and the Creator of all things. Bishops are the embodiment of practical wisdom for their local churches, even while they are rightly jealous of their communion with Peter and all other local churches.

In any case, I can recall no time in history in which allusions to the doctrine of subsidiarity have become so common outside theological circles, part of the daily speech of theoreticians and practical people alike. This is a good time for the principle of subsidiarity.

BREAKING THE CHAINS OF POVERTY

Still, with all this discussion of doctrine, it is well to remind ourselves of our main task in the Americas: That task is to arrange our institutions so that all the poor of the hemisphere may exit from poverty. In the last 150 years we have made tremendous strides in that direction. In 1850, as many as 350 babies out of 1,000 died within the first year of childbirth.[25] Poor habits of hygiene and sanitation, ignorance of germs and viruses, and lack of vaccinations and medicines led to such early deaths that, the average age of death throughout this hemisphere, as throughout the world, was about 20. Today, infant mortality has been reduced to about 20 out of 1,000. Many formerly mortal diseases have been eradicated or drastically reduced. In the more highly developed countries, average mortality has soared from 24 to 78 years. Even in the poorest countries of the Americas average mortality has nearly tripled since 1850, to about 61 years. This improvement, economists say, is the most dramatic in the human condition since the beginning of time.

A graph of average mortality in France and China hovers in an almost straight line in the low 20s from about 6000 B.C. to about 1910. At the right side of the graph, that line shoots straight up to the low 70s.[26] Why has population increased so dramatically during the past century? Because (1) infant mortality has been driven down mightily, and (2) 40 or 50 years have been added to the average lifespan. It is not so much that a larger number of children is being born to each mother; on the contrary, women are having far fewer children today. It is that children, once born, are living longer. That is a great victory over poverty, a victory not even secured for kings and queens in earlier ages.

Nonetheless, although about three-quarters of the population in our hemisphere have escaped from dire poverty and mere levels of subsistence, still about 78 million persons live on an income of less than $1.00 per day, and 182 million live on less than $2.00 per day (in PPS US dollars).[27] Their longevity may be far greater, but their living conditions are still unnecessarily harsh. Enough is known about how to create new wealth on a systematic basis—and many entire nations have moved their peoples out of an equally dire poverty during the last fifty years—so that we know well that the poverty of these 182 million is unnecessary, even scandalous. It makes us ashamed. It fires our determination to alter their circumstances.

Our goal must be to eliminate this last large pocket of poverty in this hemisphere during the next two generations, by say 2040. We know that human capital is the most important form of capital. Therefore, education is the most crucial form of economic development, the *sine qua non* of all others. The good news is that adult literacy around the world has jumped from about 48 percent in 1970 to about 72 percent in 1997.[28] That is a good gain in less than thirty years. In the next 15 years, we ought to push this number above 90 percent. Nothing would better reduce poverty than this increase in human capital.

But to education must also be added job creation.[29] There cannot be new employees if there are not new employers, that is to say, new businesses. The creation of an atmosphere, a legal system, and a banking system favorable to the creation of many new small businesses is an urgent matter for the liberation of the poor. Business formations depend upon the exercise of the creativity and the desire for serving others with honest goods and useful services that the Creator has instilled in every woman and man. (As it happens, in Latin America in particular, women excel in launching new small businesses.)

Until now, theologians and bishops have not had to extend a great deal of thought to economic and business matters. If they must do so today, it is for the sake of the poor. Better than to give the poor bread is to help them launch bakeries and other firms, through which they might serve others, as a way of providing for their own families, and in an independent, honorable, and prideful way.[30] In no other systemic and practical way can the poor be brought "into the circle of development."[31]

Through such work the formerly poor, like others, will exhibit in their lives the primacy of spirit, solidarity, the subjectivity of society, and subsidiarity. And they will live out their vocations as lay Christians, responsible citizens, in free and prosperous societies. So also they will bring before the altar of the Lord "bread the earth has given, and human hands have made."

NOTES

1. For an account of the event that captures the spirit of the Pope's lecture well see, *Il Sole 24-ore*, 12 September 1999, "Il Papa: Sbagliato Condannare la Globalizzazione." An English version of the Pope's speech was published in *L'Osservatore Romano*, N. 38 - 22 September 1999, also on the Holy See website (www.vatican.va), letter dated 11 Settembre 1999 (09/23/1999 8:51 AM).

2. *Ecclesia In America*, #58:

More and more, in many countries of America, a system know as "neoliberalism" prevails, based on a purely economic conception of man, this system considers profit and the law of the market as its only parameters, to the detriment of the dignity of and the respect due to individuals and peoples. At times this system has become the ideological justification for certain attitudes and behaviors in the social and political sphere leading to the neglect of the weaker members of society. Indeed, the poor are becoming ever more numerous, victims of specific policies and structures that are often unjust.

3. See *Centesimus Annus*, #32; e.g.,

Whereas at one time the decisive factor of production was *the land*, and later capital—understood as a total complex of the instruments of production—today the decisive factor is increasingly *man himself*, that is, his knowledge, especially his scientific knowledge, his capacity for interrelated and compact organization, as well as his ability to perceive the needs of others and to satisfy them.

4. Amatrya Sen, for instance, and the other authors of the 1999 *Human Development Report* (*http://www.undp.org/hro*, visited 10/07/1999, 9:11 AM), p. 1, citing the 1990 development report: "The real wealth of a nation is its people. And the purpose of development is to create an enabling environment for people to enjoy long, healthy and creative lives. This simple but powerful truth is too often forgotten in the pursuit of material and financial wealth." See also Gary S. Becker, *Human Capital: A Theoretical and Empirical Analysis, With Special Reference to Education* (Chicago: University of Chicago Press, 1993).

5. For an interesting survey, see Patrick Glynn, *God: The Evidence: The Reconciliation of Faith and Reason in a Post-Secular World* (Prima Pub, 1999)

6. See *Rerum Novarum*, ##11, 16, 17, 19, 27, 45.

7. *Sollicitudo Rei Socialis*, #38:

On the path toward the desired conversion, toward the overcoming of the moral obstacles to development, it is already possible to point to the *positive* and *moral value* of the growing awareness of *interdependence* among individuals and nations. . . . It is above all a question of *interdependence*, sensed as a *system determining* relationships in the contemporary world, in its economic, cultural, political and religious elements, and accepted as a *moral category*. When interdependence becomes recognized in this way, the correlative response as a moral and social attitude, as a "virtue," is *solidarity*. This then is not a feeling of vague compassion or shallow distress at the misfortunes of so many people, both near and far. On the contrary, it is a *firm and persevering determination* to commit oneself to the *common good*; that is to say to the good of all and of each individual, because we are responsible for all. This determination is based on the solid conviction that what is hindering full development is that desire for profit and thirst for power already mentioned. These attitudes and "structures of sin" are only conquered—presupposing the help of divine grace—by a *diametrically opposed attitude*: a commitment to the good of one's neighbour with the readiness in the Gospel sense, to "lose oneself" for the sake of the other instead of exploiting him, and to "serve him" instead of oppressing him for one's own advantage. The exercise of solidarity *within each society* is valid when its members recognize one another as persons.

8. See the discussion in *Human Development Report, op cit.*, p. 3; and for a page with table summarizing some of these trends on p. 26.

9. Thomas Friedman, *The Lexus and the Olive Tree* (New York: Farrar, Straus & Giroux, 1999), pp. 8-9.

10. *Centesimus Annus*, #10:

[W]e nowadays call the principle of solidarity, the validity of which both in the internal order of each nation and in the international order I have discussed in the Encyclical *Solicitudo Rei Socialis*, is clearly seen to be one of the fundamental principles of the Christian view of social and political organization. This principle is frequently stated by Pope Leo XIII, who uses the term "friendship," a concept already found in Greek philosophy. Pope Pius XI refers to it with the equally meaningful term "social charity." Pope Paul VI, expanding the concept to cover the many modern aspects of the social question, speaks of "civilization of love."

In #32:

Moreover, it is becoming clearer how a person's work is naturally interrelated with the work of others. More than ever, work is *work with others* and *work for others*: it is a matter of doing something for someone else. Work becomes ever more fruitful and productive to the extent that people become more knowledgeable of the productive potentialities of the earth and more profoundly cognizant of the needs of those for whom their work is done.

In #33:

Even in recent years it was thought that the poorest countries would develop by isolating themselves from the world market and by depending only on their own resources. Recent experience has shown that countries which did this have suffered stagnation and recession, while the countries which experienced development were those which succeeded in taking part in the general interrelated economic activities at the international level. It seems therefore that the chief problem is that of gaining fair access to the international market, based not on the unilateral principle of the exploitation of the natural resources of these countries but on the proper use of human resources.

11. On Wojtyla's philosophical thinking, see my article "The Philosophy of John Paul II," in *America* (October 1997), and the discussion in George Weigel, *Witness to Hope* (New York: Harper & Row, 1999).

12. *Centesimus Annus*, #13:

Continuing our reflections, and referring also to what has been said in the Encyclicals *Laborem Exercens* and *Sollicitudo Rei Socialis*, we have to add that the fundamental error of socialism is anthropological in nature. Socialism considers the individual person simply as an element, a molecule within the social organism, so that the good of the individual is completely subordinated to the functioning of the socio-economic mechanism. Socialism likewise maintains that the good of the individual can be realized without reference to his free choice, to the unique and exclusive responsibility which he exercises in the face of good or evil. *Man is thus reduced to a series of social relationships, and the concept of the person as the autonomous subject of moral decision disappears, the very subject whose decisions build the social order.* (Emphasis added.)

13. "Thomistic Personalism" and "The Person: Subject and Community" both in: Karol Wojtyla, *Person and Community*. Transl. Theresa Sandok, OSM (New York: Peter Lang, 1993), pp. 165-177 and pp. 219-261, respectively.

14. Karol Wojtyla, *The Acting Person* (Dordrecht: Reidel Publ. Company, 1979).

15. *Sollicitudo Rei Socialis*, #15:

> It should be noted that in today's world, among other rights, *the right of economic initiative* is often suppressed. Yet it is a right which is important not only for the individual but also for the common good. Experience shows us that the denial of this right, or its limitation in the name of an alleged "equality" of everyone in society, diminishes, or in practice absolutely destroys the spirit of initiative, that is to say *the creative subjectivity of the citizen*. As a consequence, there arises, not so much a true equality, as a "leveling down." In the place of creative initiative there appears passivity, dependence and submission to the bureaucratic apparatus which, as the only "ordering" and "decision-making" body—if not also the "owner"—of the entire totality of goods and the means of production, puts everyone in a position of almost absolute dependence, which is similar to the traditional dependence of the worker-proletarian in capitalism. This provokes a sense of frustration or desperation and predisposes people to opt out of national life, impelling many to emigrate and also favoring a form of "psychological" emigration.

16. *Centesimus Annus* ##13-14. From the mistaken conception of the person described in note 12 arises

> [b]oth a distortion of law, which defines the sphere of the exercise of freedom, and an opposition to private property. A person who is deprived of something he can call "his own," and of the possibility of earning a living through his own initiative, comes to depend on the social machine and on those who control it. This makes it much more difficult for him to recognize his dignity as a person, and hinders progress toward the building up of an authentic human community.
>
> From the Christian vision of the human person there necessarily follows a correct picture of society. According to Rerum Novarum and the whole social doctrine of the Church, the social nature of man is not completely fulfilled in the State, but is realized in various intermediary groups, beginning with the family and including economic, social, political and cultural groups which stem from human nature itself and have their own autonomy, always with a view to the common good. This is what I have called the "subjectivity" of society which, together with the subjectivity of the individual, was canceled out by "Real Socialism."

17. *Centesimus Annus* #31-32:

> In history, these two factors—*work* and *the land*—are to be found at the beginning of every human society. However, they do not always stand in the same relationship to each other. At one time *the natural fruitfulness of the earth* appeared to be, and was in fact, the primary factor of wealth, while work was, as it were, the help and support for this fruitfulness. In our time, *the role of human work* is becoming increasingly important as the productive factor both of nonmaterial and of material wealth.

In our time, in particular, there exists another form of ownership which is becoming no less important than land: *the possession of know-how, technology and skill.* The wealth of the industrialized nations is based much more on this kind of ownership than on natural resources.

18. See Margaret Melady, *The Rhetoric of Pope John Paul II: The Pastoral Visit as a New Vocabulary of the Sacred* (Praeger 1999).

19. *Centesimus Annus*, #58:

Today we are facing the so-called "globalization" of the economy, a phenomenon which is not to be dismissed, since it can create unusual opportunities for greater prosperity. There is a growing feeling, however, that this increasing internationalization of the economy ought to be accompanied by effective international agencies which will oversee and direct the economy to the common good, something which an individual state, even if it were the most powerful on earth, would not be in a position to do.

20. Randall Collins, *Weberian Sociological Theory* (Cambridge: Cambridge University Press, 1986), pp. 51-52.

21. St. Thomas Aquinas, *Contra Impugnantes Dei Cultum et Religionem* (1256). St. Thomas presents here the first known defense of associations, cited by Leo XIII in *Rerum Novarum* (#37) as the *locus classicus* on associations. Also Russell Hittinger's lecture at the Summer Institute, Krakow, Poland, July 1998 (unpublished).

22. *Sacramentum Mundi*, Karl Rahner ed. (New York: Herder and Herder, 1970) Vol. VI, p. 115. "The legitimate object of government is to do for a community of people whatever they need to have done but cannot do at all, or cannot do so well for themselves in their separate and individual capacities. In all that people can individually do as well for themselves, government ought not to interfere."

23. See especially "The Influence of America," in section II, "The Anglo-American Tradition of Liberty" in J. Rufus Fears (ed.), *Essays in the History of Liberty, Selected Writings of Lord Acton* (Indianapolis: LibertyClassics, 1985), pp. 198-212.

24. Jacques Maritain, *Man and State* (Chicago: University of Chicago Press, 1951), p. 91; see also Maritain's *Approaches to God* (Greenwood Publishing Group, reprint ed. June 1978).

25. See Julian Lincoln Simon (ed.), *The State of Humanity* (Blackwell Publ., 1996), especially the introduction, pp. 1-28, and chapter 2, "Human Mortality Throughout History," by Samuel H. Preston, and chapter 3, "The Decline of Mortality," by Kenneth Hill.

26. *Id.*, pp. 8 and 35.

27. See http://www.worldbank.org/povery/data/trends/income.htm (visited 10/07/1999 12:11 PM). The total population of Latin America and the Carribean is estimated at 504 million people. (http://www.popin.org/pop1998/4.htm, visited 09/16/1999 9:31 AM)

28. *World Development Report, op. cit.*, p. 25.

29. In the World Labor Report unemployment was estimated for this area at about 59.6 million (see http://www.ilo.org/public/english/80relpro/publ/wlr/97/annex/tab8.htm, visited 10/07/1999 9:39 AM). Youth unemployment rates are usually double

the national average and women's unemployment rates are 60 percent higher than men's rates. Overall employment in Latin America increased on average 2.9 percent between 1990 and 1998, but this was not sufficient to absorb the annual 3.3 percent expansion of the labor force. (See http://www.ilo.org/public/english/235press/pr/1999/26.htm, visited 10/06/1999 11:36 AM).

    30. *Centesimus Annus*, #32:

> It is precisely the ability to foresee both the needs of others and the combinations of productive factors most adapted to satisfying those needs that constitutes another important source of wealth in modern society. Besides, many goods cannot be adequately produced through the work of an isolated individual; they require the cooperation of many people in working toward a common goal. Organizing such a productive effort, planning its duration in time, making sure that it corresponds in a positive way to the demands which it must satisfy, and taking the necessary risks— all this too is a source of wealth in today's society. In this way, the *role* of disciplined and creative *human work* and, as an essential part of that work, *initiative and entrepreneurial ability* becomes increasingly evident and decisive. This process, which throws practical light on a truth about the person which Christianity has constantly affirmed, should be viewed carefully and favorably. Indeed, besides the earth, man's principal resource is *man himself*. His intelligence enables him to discover the earth's productive potential and the many different ways in which human needs can be satisfied. It is his disciplined work in close collaboration with others that makes possible the creation of ever more extensive *working communities* which can be relied upon to transform man's natural and human environments. Important virtues are involved in this process, such as diligence, industriousness, prudence in undertaking reasonable risks, reliability and fidelity in interpersonal relationships, as well as courage in carrying out decisions which are difficult and painful but necessary, both for the overall working of a business and in meeting possible setbacks.

    31. *Centesimus Annus*, #34:

> It is a strict duty of justice and truth not to allow fundamental human needs to remain unsatisfied, and not to allow those burdened by such needs to perish. It is also necessary to help these needy people to acquire expertise, to enter the circle of exchange, and to develop their skills in order to make the best use of their capacities and resources.

AN AUTOBIOGRAPHICAL
AFTERWORD

"Having begun life in the bosom of a good family in an out-of-the-way steel town, best known for the tragedies it has endured by flood in 1889, 1936, and 1977; having had an excellent classical education in philosophy, literature, and theology; having from the start declared my intention to create a philosophy of the distinctively American experience; having begun by seeking a 'third way' between capitalism and socialism, as a result of the typical anticapitalist biases of the humanities (not least in Catholic thought); having long looked for this 'third way' in the direction of socialist thought and radical politics—after all this, during my forties, I came to find the socialist and radical paths destructive of truth, and signs of bad faith. And I came back to re-discover the power of the American idea, 'man's best hope' as Jefferson called it in his First Inaugural. I came back, in short, to the tradition of Aristotle, Cicero, and Aquinas; of Madison, Hamilton, Jay, Jefferson, and Lincoln; of Montesquieu, Smith, Burke and Acton—i.e., to the Whig tradition."

29

CONTROVERSIAL ENGAGEMENTS

On March 19, 1998, the young social historian Eugene McCarraher delivered a portion of his doctoral thesis as a lecture at the Cushwa Center of the University of Notre Dame. His subject was Michael Novak, "The Technopolitan Catholic." Though the lecture was highly critical of Novak's work, especially after his "rightward turn," it also stressed the continuities in his thought. The Cushwa Center invited Novak to respond the following autumn, and on October 6, 1998, he delivered an account of his career from which the following article was adapted.

—Editors, First Things

I

I was born in Johnstown, Pennsylvania, in 1933, and lived briefly in two other cities in western Pennsylvania towns, (Jimmy Stewart's) Indiana and (Andy Warhol's) McKeesport. At fourteen, I entered the Little Seminary on the campus of Notre Dame University for my high school years, graduating in 1951. From there I went to the novitiate of the Fathers of the Holy Cross in North Dartmouth, Massachusetts, took simple vows, completed my undergraduate degree in philosophy and English literature, and was sent to Rome for theological studies. After two happy years I nonetheless began to believe that my vocation was as a layman. My superiors advised me not to make so weighty a decision on foreign soil, and brought me back to Washington to complete my theological studies at Catholic University. After eighteen months of great darkness but also inner peace, I became certain that I should not be a priest.

Thus, in early January 1960, after twelve years in religious life, having had a profound experience of religious and intellectual community, I found myself in a garret apartment in New York City working on the manuscript of a novel. I had one hundred dollars that my father had given me, plus a determination not to go to work at any job except writing. I was budgeted at $35 a week (rent took $10), and so I had three weeks to find the next check. Luckily, an assignment for a book review or an article kept arriving each month. The manuscript I was working on was not my first novel, but in June of 1960 Doubleday accepted this one for publication. The advance seemed to me a fortune. I believe it was $600, with a matching check when I would hand in the completed manuscript.

Meanwhile, I had also applied to graduate schools for further study in philosophy; naively, I sent applications only to Yale and Harvard. Yale offered me tuition but Harvard added a supplement for living expenses. I preferred Harvard for other reasons, and was there for election night of 1960 and inauguration day of 1961 when in the Law School dining room, surprised by tears gathering in my eyes, I watched on television as John F. Kennedy was sworn in as the first Catholic president. I had sent in drafts of speeches to his campaign, copies of speeches I had prepared for a young lawyer running for Congress in northern New Jersey, including one on "The New Frontier." The Democratic pols in Newark had mocked my speech when my candidate started giving it, but once JFK used the theme in his acceptance speech at the convention they said it was brilliant.

In the spring of 1961, Robert Silvers of *Harper's* asked me to write the article on religion for an issue on universities to appear that fall. That article, "God in the Colleges," though it caused a lot of discussion, left my professors at Harvard not at all pleased. It was reprinted several times in various New Left publications a few years later, since in some ways it anticipated the Port Huron Statement (the founding document of the New Left) in 1964. What I wrote in that article—about the death of humanism under the onslaught of the Enlightenment—has been a permanent theme of my work, and I have reprinted that essay in later books in 1964 and 1994. These are its closing lines:

> "God is dead. . . . What are these churches if they are not the tombs and sepulchers of God?" Nietzsche asked. But much of Western humanism is dead too. Men do not wander under the silent stars, listen to the wind, learn to know themselves, question, "Where am I going? Why am I here?" They leave aside the mysteries of contingency and transitoriness for the certainties of research, production, consumption. So that it is nearly possible to say: "Man is dead. . . . What are these buildings, these tunnels, these roads, if they are not the tombs and sepulchers of man?"

The greatest event of my Harvard years was meeting my wife, a painter who was then teaching at Carleton College in Minnesota, an Iowan herself, who had studied with Kokoshka in Austria and Lasansky at Iowa City. She came to Boston to paint for a year during her sabbatical, and despite serious competition from two lawyers I prevailed upon her to marry me. We took part of our honeymoon as a working autumn in Rome for the Second Vatican Council, beginning from late August 1963 until mid-January of 1964.

In late November I unexpectedly received a contract for *The Open Church*—an existing contract that the *Time* correspondent could not fulfill. Taking Lord Acton's report on the First Vatican Council in 1870 as my model, I wrote with great intensity for the seven weeks that the contract allowed me after the Council closed in early December. It was a bitterly cold winter, and the marble rooms in our pensione had no central heating. Wearing gloves to grip my pen (for revisions) and my dictating machine (for reporting speeches at the Council), I kept as many as three secretaries busy—one transcribing dictation, one deciphering my handwriting for typing, and the third typing the revised versions of the work of the preceding day. Although I was supposed to be studying for my comprehensive exams at Harvard, I nonetheless completed the manuscript by the January 18 deadline.

My second nonfiction book, which was also published in 1964, was a collection of essays called *A New Generation: American and Catholic.* In it I laid out my dissatisfactions with the various philosophies of the Enlightenment that had been my diet at Harvard, and announced my intention to pick up and develop the ancient and more capacious pragmatism and empiricism of Aristotle and Aquinas. I declared that in solving the crucial problems of Americans and Catholics in America, one needs "a consistent point of view, [one that is] empirical, pragmatic, realistic, and Christian." To this day, I think I have been faithful to that vision.

Although I have published versions of this story before, certain persistent misreadings of my intellectual biography make it seem judicious to give a short account of a half-dozen of the main continuities, the undergirding, of my intellectual life these past fifty years, before turning to those areas where my thoughts have changed significantly.

II

Most Americans seem to believe that every single human life has value and worth. But, I wondered from the beginning, is that really true? Is that how hurricanes, cancer, Hitler, and communism have treated human beings? During my lifetime, nearly one hundred million persons have died by violence, making life seem cheap. When I was eleven years old I saw the first movie reels from Auschwitz. What if this planet is as empty of meaning as it sometimes seems? I was struck very deeply by this at least apparent meaninglessness, and I took very seriously the challenge of Albert Camus that any philosophy of the future, any ethic, must originate within it, or risk not being credible. To build a new civilization on the ashes of Auschwitz would take much hard thought.

Most of my colleagues and friends didn't share my problem. It is not that I didn't believe. My faith never flagged. It was only that I felt nothing, I was empty, and I could not see how to answer the problems put by Auschwitz—and by explicit nihilists, including defenders of Hitler and Stalin, not to mention by nice atheists like some of my professors at Harvard.

Some of my friends could say with Pascal, "The heart has its reasons which the reason knows not of." Others could say: "Faith is a leap; you just have to let go and leap." In my case, I have known my own heart to have many bad reasons, and to be a great deceiver. So I didn't like these two existentialist dodges. Regarding the first, I admire but I don't quite trust "reasons of the heart." Regarding the second, I appreciate why others are content with a "leap" of faith, but it has always seemed to me that creatures blessed with the sort of minds God gave us should be able to give a better account of the why of our faith than that.

In other words, even accepting the Christian account on its own terms, we should from within it be able to find the way out of meaninglessness. We should be able to take in the worst this century has had to offer, and show why it is reasonable to find God also in that. I put the emphasis on *reasonable*. Many people I have talked to over the years think that that is asking too much. But if God really does want the worship of free men standing erect (and He does), then that much we have to achieve. *Fides quaeret intellectum.*

The second continuity in my work has been an experience of the dark region wherein God dwells. God is best understood to be *caritas*, a dark and terrible form of realism best symbolized by the Cross on which He willed his Son to die. God is best understood to be Love, but not in the types of love associated with the English word "love." Latin has at least five words for love—*amor, affectus, dilectio, amicitia, caritas*—and then the Greek *agape* adds a nuance, as do certain Hebrew words such as the one we usually render "compassion" but which more literally means "moved to the very bowels." Even when we cannot see God, we can turn our wills and intellects toward Him, aim them like arrows bound to fall short, and in effect say *Fiat*. The fundamental prayer to God is only one word, in the teeth of any storm: yes. Ivan Karamazov swore he could never say that. Not in a world in which so many children go to sleep in tears and alone.

The greatest continuity in my work is this affirmation that the basic energy, power, and force in creation is *caritas*. In this otherwise vast and possibly empty series of silent galaxies, the Creator made humans in order to have at least one creature able freely to respond to Him—either with love or not. *Caritas* is the one energy that matters. In it, we are first related, before we are solitary. We first receive, before we act on our own. We are first empowered, before we take responsibility for our own acts. We are first endowed, before we have rights. In all these things, all humans are linked together. Creatures depend. That is the great "intuition of being" that Jacques Maritain talked about.

In 1979 I gave a lecture at Notre Dame I have never forgotten—not, at least, the reaction of the audience. It was my first public defense of capitalism. In that context, I began with the presence of *caritas* within all of us. "Through the work of our minds and hands," I said,

> the life of the triune God expresses its own love and truth and healing power, not all at once, imperfectly and in the darkness, but yet effectively. We build up the social institutions by which human history is slowly, very slowly, transformed into God's own image. As our God is triune—a communal God—so is our vocation communal.

I gave the lecture at a conference occasioned by a Declaration by Chicago Laypersons fourteen years after Vatican II on the continuing neglect of the laity in the Church. After setting forth my theological vision of the action of the Trinity in this world, and on the need to reconstruct the social order, I spoke of the need to transform our approach by grasping capitalism's *religious* possibilities. The capitalist system, after all, was the system in which most Notre Dame graduates would work. There could not be a realistic theology of the laity, or theology of work, without a theology of capitalism. When the lecture period adjourned for dinner, no one would speak to me. I had violated an important Catholic taboo. Those last few moments of that lecture—the capitalism part—admittedly marked a great discontinuity in my work. And that meant, of course, that I had excommunicated myself from the Catholic left.

The third most important continuity in my work is the theme that supplies the philosophical root that unites the first two themes: our unlimited, unquenchable drive to ask questions, the eros of inquiry. This is the organ of our appetite for transcendence, the point in us where our union with the communion of persons of the Trinity is joined, like two fires becoming one. We do not see God, but we thirst for Him. We seek Him. Our relentless drive to inquire is present in every act of our awareness. Thus, in every act, the transcendence of God is present to us (by reverse image, as it were). Furthermore, to pursue this unlimited drive within us is the best way to discover the multiple aspects of our duty on earth to build up the Kingdom of truth, liberty, justice, and love. The light that emanates from this drive to understand suffuses all we do. Issuing in *caritas*, it is the dominant dynamic of civilization.

A fourth crucial continuity is my emphasis on the incarnational dimension in theology. Some Catholics commit their lives to an eschatological witness, some to an incarnational witness. The former (Thomas Merton, Dorothy Day) believe that the world is sinful, broken, even adversarial, and they choose to light within it the fire of the love of God, while having as little to do with the things of this world as they can. Those who choose the incarnational witness try to see in every moment of history, in every culture, and in every place and time the workings of divine grace, often in ways that are hidden like the workings of yeast buried in dough. And they lend their energies to altering that world in its basic institutions, even if ever so slightly, in the direction of *caritas*. Both traditions are legitimate.

Early in my life, as I will recount later, I was sorely tempted by the witness of Dorothy Day and by Baroness de Hueck with her Friendship Houses, and even by the Benedictines. I was also drawn toward becoming a missionary. Yet I gradually realized that my own vocation lay in working in the world, in intellectual life, preferably in environments in which Catholics were few. Early in this pursuit I inclined toward a vocation in political action. By 1968, teaching in Cuernavaca, Mexico, that summer with Peter Berger, I came to see that economics was an even more neglected field in Catholic thought. By about 1976, I at last recognized that a capitalist system was not in fact what I had been taught it was; that no system is, in practice, more likely to raise the poor out of poverty than capitalism; and that capitalism is a necessary (but not sufficient) condition for democracy. I began to see that grace works also in economics.

Thus, it slowly dawned on me that, just as Jacques Maritain had recognized in American political institutions the yeast of the Gospels working in history, so also Max Weber had dimly seen that the original impulses of capitalism spring from Christianity, too. These impulses had been systematically neglected by economists, who had abandoned religious and even philosophical considerations in order to model their discipline on the physical sciences. In this way, economists had lost sight of the spirit of capitalism, and neglected the human habits on which its survival depends. Simultaneously, nearly all theologians had become as adversarial toward capitalism and business as Europe's aristocrats were; they looked down upon economic activities as vulgar and crass, if not evil. In other words, I came to see the need for a reconstruction of the world's understanding of capitalism and, beyond that, a reconstruction of capitalism's realities.

We need to think of capitalism in a larger and deeper way than the economists and business schools typically think of it. We need to think of it in a Catholic way. This is what Pope John Paul II does in *Centesimus Annus*. He describes the business corporation as a community that is a model for truths Christianity has always attempted to teach about the human person and community.

Note, however, that the underlying continuity I am stressing here is theological. I am stressing the incarnational emphasis in general, not my particular judgment about capitalism. Whatever the present model of political economy, it will not measure up to the height and depth of the Kingdom of God. It will always be inadequate. The city of man will never be the city of God.

Just the same, it is important that there be Christians who go out into this city, whatever its stage of moral and religious development, and try to incarnate the Gospels in it as Jesus incarnated God in history. No doubt, this will often enough be by the way of the Cross and rejection, as it was for Jesus. But it is only thus that great Christian civilizations have been reared in the past. In any case, the "liberal popes" from whom we learned so much—for that is how scholars in my youth described the social teaching of Leo XIII, Pius XI, and Pius XII—called millions of us precisely to this task of "reconstructing the social order."

In my earlier years, I thought the best model for this reconstruction lay in a blend of democracy with some form of socialism. Later, I came to believe that socialism in any of its forms would be futile and destructive. I saw greater hope in a more realistic effort to reform and reconstruct society through the unique combination of capitalism and democracy that we have been lucky enough to inherit in America. But my point, to repeat, is that my own strategic vision, which is incarnational rather than eschatological, has been constant throughout my life.

The fifth continuity—related to the incarnational theme just mentioned—is a sense of the importance to Christian thought of the body, the flesh, the senses. No other religion promises the resurrection of the body. No other is so lavish in its evocations of the senses, as a holiday Mass in St. Peter's Basilica dramatizes. Catholicism, G. K. Chesterton once wrote, is a thick steak, a glass of stout, and a good cigar. He wrote this not because he was a materialist, or blind to wit and spirit, but because turning away from the body weakens our grasp of the Incarnation. That is why an important theme of the Catholic Renaissance during the past hundred years has been a recovery of the theology of the body. In the Catholic America of my youth, this recovery was badly needed. One saw it in renewed emphasis on poetry, fiction, sound, smell, and texture. One saw it especially in the early liturgical renewal. I felt it keenly in my own struggles to learn the craft of fiction.

The sixth fundamental theme in my work has been "intelligent subjectivity." By this concept, beginning with Belief and Unbelief, I have always protected the role of the tacit, the inarticulable, the well-ordered senses and passions and emotions and heart at the very center of our acts of insight and judgment. But I have also tried to show how these are, properly, acts of reason.

Some critics mistakenly read my use of "intelligent" and "rational" as if my intellectual roots were utilitarian, post–Cartesian, and merely concerned with skill or *techne*. In fact, my primary concern has been that "knowledge by connaturality," that "wisdom," which my parents exemplified for me, and which Jacques Maritain and Michael Polanyi first taught me how to express. To make myself understood at Harvard on these matters, then a bastion of Quinean logic where Maritain and Polanyi were rejected (or simply disregarded), I needed to spell out the working of a form of "subjectivity" that is intelligent, reasonable, and empirically present in every act of reasoned judgment. That was the main effort of *Belief and Unbelief, The Experience of Nothingness,* and *Ascent of the Mountain, Flight of the Dove.*

These six continuities—and there are others—are plainly interrelated. Every one of my books had a place in the journey whose route I announced in *A New Generation* in 1964, and I have never deviated from it. I do admit plenty of errors, oversights, hasty judgments, and wrong turns. According to Winston Churchill, consistency is like a helmsman in a small boat amid thirty-foot waves; the only way to keep going is to lean hard first to one side, then to the other. That is not inconsistency. That is prudent sailing. Whatever the storms of my time, from Auschwitz to Vietnam, from the fall of the Berlin Wall to welfare reform, this particular Michael has always hoped, in the end, to row his boat ashore.

III

The great discontinuity in my life occurred when I decided, from much evidence, that the economic and social thought of the left which I had long supported—working for John F. Kennedy, Eugene McCarthy, Robert Kennedy, George McGovern, and Henry "Scoop" Jackson—was turning out, despite our good intentions, to be injurious to the poor of the world, including the poor among whom I had grown up in Johnstown during the 1930s. It was my rule—inculcated in me by my father—never to forget where I had come from and who my family was. But I owe a lot, as well, to my "second family," the Congregation of the Holy Cross.

I can hardly give enough credit to the Holy Cross seminaries for what they taught me between 1947 and 1959 about *caritas*, the drive to understand, and an incarnational humanism. There my soul became in a sense a child of France. I learned to love the Jacques Maritain of *Integral Humanism*, François Mauriac, and Albert Camus. From the French I learned the desire to write both philosophy and fiction. I also began an intense study of the life and work of St. Thérèse of Lisieux.

St. Thérèse (1873-1897) is *the* teacher of the Church about the everyday exercise of *caritas*, in ways so humble that they mostly cannot be seen, even though their effects may be subjected to the tests of the gospel. She taught me the importance of thinking small and honoring the humble things that I at first tended to despise. For the theology of the laity and the theology of work and the theology of daily institutional life, her work has been described—by no less an authority than Hans Urs von Balthasar—as revolutionary.

The influence of Thérèse is most often visible in my work when I refer to the transformation that St. Thomas Aquinas wrought in Aristotle's philosophy of human action. Aristotle organized his thought around the conception of *phronesis* or practical wisdom; Aquinas saw the potential in this concept to support a new mode of *caritas*. This transformation shapes the horizon within which I placed the work of Reinhold Niebuhr, on whom I had intended to do my doctoral thesis at Harvard. (I wrote and published *Belief and Unbelief* instead, to clear away a conceptual obstacle to understanding the theology of the person and community, by way of "intelligent subjectivity.")

By 1965, I had accepted an assistant professorship at Stanford—the first Catholic ever to be hired in the religion department—and my duties and purposes there took my writing in more practical directions. I attempted to read every word that Maritain and Niebuhr had written, including as much of their occasional journalism as I could lay my hands on. How they applied their vision to the practicalities of lay life in the world interested me greatly, but so did their theoretical framework.

As mentioned above, early on in my life, mainly through the subscription to the *Catholic Worker* that my father brought into our home, my heroes were Dorothy Day, Baroness de Hueck, and (later) Michael Harrington. While I was at Catholic University (1958–59), the radical writings of the sociologist Paul Hanly Furfey were added to these influences. Nonetheless, I hesitated about declaring myself a democratic socialist or social democrat, because I was unclear about the implications of that allegiance. I resolved to study economics more carefully, and to clarify in my mind questions about poverty and wealth, economic development and religion. I devoured Weber, Tawney, Fanfani and others, as well as magazines such as *Dissent*. I thought it morally correct and religiously satisfying to be something of a socialist and a tart critic of capitalism. I tried hard.

It was during my years at Harvard, 1960–1965, that I first heard the term "WASP," and had to ask its meaning. At the Divinity School, I learned how loftily "mainline" Christians looked down on the vast majority of evangelicals in America. When Billy Graham came to lecture, most went to jeer (at Harvard this means making dry jokes), although some said later he did much better than expected.

One exception to the general climate was James Luther Adams, a great defender of what others at Harvard referred to as "the garbage bin of the Reformation," the Anabaptists and all the free churches that sprang from them, who eventually became the largest number of Protestants in America. Adams held that the free churches, more than any other social movement, taught America the practice of association that Tocqueville later described as "the first law of democracy." Leo XIII had won the sobriquet "the pope of associations," and this link to an entire world of Protestantism, a world I had never before clearly distinguished in my own mind from the Philadelphia–New England "mainline," gave me a new conceptual tool. From then on, the principle of association became a golden thread in my analysis of society, democracy, capitalism, welfare policy, and civil society. It is at the heart of my conception of the open society and the open church.

The theology of *caritas*, the Catholic tradition of personalism and community, and now the principle of association—all these helped me to break the horizon of left-wing socialism in which I had been formed. "A Catholic boy like you has to be a Democrat," our high school advisor, Father Peverada, had told me in the fall of 1948, when he caught me making counterarguments in favor of Thomas E. Dewey. (I have always been, in discussions, a counterarguer. My friends purposefully used to advance arguments they had first learned from me, in order to trap me into arguing against my earlier self—and I always fell for their deception.) Similarly, I remember Maritain writing about wanting always to be "a man of the left." (Though in France, "right," and therefore "left," mean something very different from anything in America.) Paul Tillich added that "Any serious Christian must be a socialist." Practically everyone concurred. It took me many years to begin questioning this magnetic pull, and to figure out whence its power came.

When I found myself questioning my own left-wing commitments, which had been somewhat influential in the "radicalization" of other liberals, I was frightened. I thought something must be wrong with me. As Kathie McHale Mulherin noted in *Commonweal*, my turn to the radical left in politics was a matter of intellectual conviction, against my own conservative temperament; she had been my research assistant and watched it happen. Her comment surprised me when it appeared, but I came to admit that she was right. The radicals, temperamentally, were not my sort of people. When they said "power to the people," the last thing they meant was the workers of Joliet and Johnstown, the white ethnics of Mayor Daley's Chicago, or the Moral Majority. They did not have the good of my Uncle Emil in mind.

I need to say a word about Uncle Emil. He was my father's oldest half-brother, by an earlier marriage of my grandfather. He was a big, rough, hearty man who was missing one whole finger and part of another from accidents in the steel mill, and his language was goodhearted, loud, punctuated by laughter, and not at all suited for Sunday School. He made his own wine. His Slovak was as rough as his English. Around his humble frame house, which even then seemed like an antique in a mining town, he grew hollyhocks and a grape arbor, of exactly the sort I was later to see in Slovak mountain villages in the Tatra mountains whence our family came to America about 1885. He was a boisterous supporter of FDR, the Democrats, and the unions. In all my memories, Emil seems to be in a sleeveless T-shirt, although I must have seen him squeezed uncomfortably into a suit, shirt, and tie at one or another funeral or wedding.

Somewhere along the line at Harvard, I got the idea of submitting every generalization I heard about "the Americans" to a test: Did that sentence fit my Uncle Emil? For instance, 1968 newpaper reports that "Catholic ethnics support Wallace." I could agree that Emil might have admired the guts of George Wallace in his presidential run in 1968, when Wallace took on the "pointy-headed liberals." But I am certain that the Wallace crack about "running over protestors" would have disgusted Emil; and compared to Wallace, Hubert Humphrey was the proven union man. Humphrey was Emil's kind of Democrat. Many political writers and sociologists, in those days, seemed not to know of Uncle Emil. They confused him with the migrants from the South who migrated north into the mills, and did support Wallace. Ethnicity confused them.

In the autumn of 1970, I took a leave of absence from Stanford to accept an invitation from Sargent Shriver during his campaign to elect Democrats to Congress around the country. We visited some thirty-nine states, and spent nearly every day from August through November on the road. Years later I wrote that by election day,

> I had a far better grasp of the diverse neighborhoods of America than I had ever had before. I had seen at first hand the true significance of ethnicity and localism in American life. . . . Words that I had written about the American majority—complacently drinking beer in front of television—in *Toward a Theology of Radical Politics* now made shame color my cheeks. I met the American people in the flesh; my literary imagination had been calumnious. But this had not been my vision only. In rejecting it, I was rejecting the leftist vision of America (or Amerika), the anti-Americanism so common among my intellectual colleagues.

This thought weighed on me as time passed. I saw many analyses of American politics and social needs go wildly wrong about the actual texture of American social reality, and decided I must write *The Rise of the Unmeltable Ethnics* (1972, 1996). Later, I followed up with an account of a crucial but almost totally neglected union struggle among Slavic miners in eastern Pennsylvania, *The Guns of Lattimer* (1978, 1996). It remains my ambition to tell the story of my grandfather's immigration and the great Johnstown flood of 1889, which took more lives than the battle of Gettysburg.

There is one minor continuity in my work that I should mention here. In every period of my life, I have come back to the "gap" in our society between the intellectuals and the people. I make a sharp distinction between two halves of the American elite: those who choose to support the growth of a larger, supposedly more compassionate state, and those who choose, because it is actually better for the poor, to support the growth of the private sector. I define "elite," roughly, as the top 20 percent of the population as sorted out by three measures: income, years of education, and professional status. Since World War II, about half of this elite has found a new route to power, wealth, prestige, and influence through the promotion of a larger, more activist state. The others see a better route for themselves and the country through the promotion of a limited state, and a larger, more compassionate civil society. I call the first of these "the new class" and the second "the old elite." It is good for America to have a divided elite, of roughly equal size, so that the two elites check and balance each other. In terms of political economy, the new class tends to favor the political solution, while the old elite tends to favor the free economy, a reformed welfare state (toward which we have begun to move), and a civil society with the state "off its back."

Once I started criticizing the errors of the left, I was en route to becoming a "neoconservative," a term that I at first hated. The term was invented as a sign of excommunication by the Catholic socialist (and my good friend) Michael Harrington. Harrington, who began with the *Catholic Worker,* committed himself to the left; he became a socialist in the way that some people become Catholic. Socialism became his religion, not only his politics. He meant the term to signify a way of life, a horizon, a way of seeing things, an ethos, an ethic, a dream, an ideal goal. He called those of us who were beginning to question the premises of his faith "neo," to suggest "pseudo" or "imitation," and he called us "conservatives," knowing full well the judgment of Louis Hartz and Lionel Trilling that "there is no conservative intellectual tradition in America." For a socialist to call someone a conservative is the meanest name he can think of. It means outside the moral pale—greedy, money-grubbing, narrow-minded, bigoted, troglodytic—you get the picture.

Breaking ranks with the left is a phenomenon that deserves its own study. I lost the company of formerly good friends, received some letters from friends who severed all contact with me or pleaded with me not to continue in my horrible mistake. I had articles returned from magazines that had once begged me to write for them, and watched hostile and ad hominem reviews replace the glowing notices of just a short time earlier. But this has been a common experience among ex-leftists; some had it far worse. I took comfort from noting that Paul Johnson had just made the same break with the socialist left in England, and Irving Kristol and Norman Podhoretz had done so in New York. There seemed to be a growing band of us: "We few, we happy few!" (The literature on, by, and about neoconservatives is by now quite extensive.)

What we had in common was a past on the far left—not necessarily at the Communist extreme, but well to the radical side of Arthur Schlesinger's "vital center"—and a powerful intellectual conviction that the left was wrong about virtually every big issue of our time: the Soviet Union, the North Vietnamese regime, economics, welfare, race, and moral questions such as abortion, amnesty, acid, and the sexual revolution.

In my experience, people join the left out of idealism. Once they see through the deceptions of the left, and break with its powerful set of internal controls, including censorship, they come to hate it. One must fight this hatred in oneself, and try hard to remember how one fell for the left because of one's own uncritical ideals. What defectors come to hate in the left is its pervasive lack of honesty—the constant use of euphemism and linguistic deception (in public, socialists call themselves liberals and liberals call themselves moderates), its black-and-white vision of the world, its intolerance of any questions about its own principles.

It has been said before that a neoconservative is a radical who has begun to understand economics. In studying economics, one begins to grasp why socialism cannot possibly work in practice, and why it is especially damaging to the poor. In the days of my left-wing idealism, I thought the left would help the poor. I favored the War on Poverty. But then I watched what actually happened: A 600 percent increase in births out of wedlock (especially among the poor), a 600 percent increase in violent crime (especially among the poor). Once you begin to judge the fruits of programs inspired by a socialist analysis of social reality, not as dreams but as realities, disillusion begins. I watched the most liberal city in America, New York, slide into social and financial bankruptcy, becoming less civilized and more dangerous with every year that passed. I watched North Vietnam after the war was over, and noted what happened in the prison camps and reeducation centers, and wondered where now were my friends from the antiwar days who once said they cared so much about the Vietnamese people.

Nonetheless, the great intellectual utility of being a leftist, a utility I at first missed, is that you have a clear compass for interpreting every day's events: If x undermines business, corporations, and capitalism, x is good. If x strengthens the central state, x is good. Using this template, you can detect instantly what the proper "progressive" line is. For cultural critics and journalists, as well as activists, having such a template is a great advantage. In cases of serious doubt, you have only to wait for your favorite left-wing journal to put out the correct line.

Well, you can see why my first articles reflecting a fundamental change of mind on political and economic matters seriously disturbed my former friends. Some were accustomed to looking to me to see where the progressive line lay; in the past, I had sometimes seen it before others. They were used to regarding me as one of their minor leaders. Then, in about 1976, I published two quite tentative articles, but only after I had estimated the probable incoming fire. One was called "A Closet Capitalist Confesses," in which I expressed shame that I could no longer, try as I might, desire to be a socialist. I couldn't find, anywhere in the world, one single example of socialism that worked in practice, in a form that I could admire. Even when I pulled photos of Sweden out of my desk drawer, I wrote, Sweden no longer held any attraction for me. Neither did Cuba. Nor any other of the romantic options held out by the left. I didn't even admire the British health service.

My wife didn't want me to announce this disgrace in public, but I had to be honest: Once I thought about it, it was clear to me that capitalism had been better for my Uncle Emil and other poor folks than what had befallen those in our family who were still in the Slovak Socialist Paradise or had migrated anywhere else on earth.

The other article, at greater length, was not yet ready to become positive about capitalism, but its title announced its thesis well enough: "Capitalism, An Underpraised and Undervalued System." I did not renounce my former criticisms of many aspects of capitalist reality. Admittedly, it *is* a bad system, except, as Churchill noted about democracy, that all other known systems are worse.

When an intelligent person loses his or her confidence in socialism, what he or she most misses is the North Star it placed in the sky, its guidance system. Once you stop believing, you feel the ideological vacuum keenly, and recognize its moral hazard. Never again do you want anything else so totalistic to take its place. Irving Kristol in his book *On the Democratic Idea in America* argued that the American experiment, rooted in Aristotelian prudence and a sense of human fallibility and evil, is a bracing corrective to the ideological and utopian thinking of Europe. Hannah Arendt and others have pointed out that the American experiment is the most intellectually neglected social reality. Nowadays, almost no one grasps its originality or can articulate its specific moral vision, its table of virtues. The American tradition teaches a modest and humble way of thinking, close to earth, anti-utopian. It is also internally conflicted. Its tendencies toward liberty are at war with its tendencies toward a broad egalitarianism. To begin explaining this *novus ordo seclorum,* my first neoconservative book properly so called was *The American Vision* (1978).

By the late 1970s, I realized that it is worse for the poor of America (and around the world) to rely upon the state and to pin its main hopes on political measures. And it is better for the poor of America and the world to support a limited state, in which the conditions are favorable to the growth of business (especially small business), and to prefer opportunity rather than handouts from the state. Characteristically, neoconservatives favor the welfare state for those really unable to care for themselves, but try to break the corrupting bond between the central state and the welfare function. There are better ways to provide welfare than what we have constructed since 1965. About the specifics of such matters, persons of good will can argue long into the night. Politics is about argument.

In brief, my conversion from a mildly socialist way of viewing reality to a more distinctively American (that is, enterprising) way did not occur all at once. I can't quite determine whether foreign or domestic experiences generated my first doubts about the leftism I effortlessly acquired with an excellent education. After all, for at least a century the humanities have been anticapitalist for traditionalist reasons, and the social sciences have been anticapitalist for socialist reasons. Against the pressures of my education, one experience after another during the 1970s made me a Reagan Democrat even before Reagan became President. In fact, a set of themes I articulated in an article in 1978 about why I still remained a Democrat, even while moving away from statism in my principles, was field-tested by Richard Wirthlin and adopted by Ronald Reagan as his election slogan: work, family, neighborhood, peace, strength.

The collapse of communism between 1989 and 1991 persuaded even many of its former adherents of the failure of socialism. As the people of the world gradually learned the condition of the mass of people under the Soviet Union, they learned what Gorbachev had already admitted: Under a first-world military establishment, the USSR hid a third-world economy. Socialism was a fraud. This did not surprise those of us who had learned from Hayek and von Mises why socialist economics is irrational and unworkable, and from Leo XIII why a socialist anthropology is both evil and futile.

Let me return, in closing, to the theological development, the "open church," that corresponds most closely to my developing appreciation of America.

The "open church," like Karl Popper's "open society," is utterly different from the idealized "secular city" (which even Harvey Cox has now disowned). Its dynamism springs from a fidelity to the drive to understand, in all its workings throughout human life. The gospel is best preached when it uses this dynamism, since here the divine purpose in creation and in history works its way out.

My book *The Open Church* was a report, both journalistic and theological, on the second and most crucial session of the Second Vatican Council, where the nature of the Church was the focus. Unlike the secular city, this open church has a vicar of Christ as its visible head, the Pope, and a highly visible body of bishops around the world in communion with the Pope. The open church, therefore, does not lack a center and a hierarchy and a visible symbol of worldwide communion. Its reason for being is to form a community around the Eucharist and the Word of God. Against the widespread urges to tamper with doctrine in the years since the Council, the criterion of the open church is analogous to that of the open society, as described by Karl Popper: the falsification principle. New proposals must be submitted to rigorous tests.

The Second Vatican Council took care to preserve an important check-and-balance. The bishops in collegiality, including the Bishop of Rome, are the authenticating body of last resort—yet with an important twist. Even all the bishops of the world together, if without the Pope, do not suffice for authentication. The Pope must concur. On other occasions, he is bound to teach and confirm the brethren, even when alone. All are bound by the Word of God as held by the whole Church at other times and places. No mere majority vote suffices.

In writing *The Open Church,* I did not foresee such an exemplary Pope as John Paul II. I did not foresee most of the things that would happen between 1968 and 1999. But I did suggest that they would be ironic, and that at the conclusion of the Council the jesters of the Roman fountains would be laughing at yet another generation passing through that eternal city, with high and unrealistic hopes. "All things human," was the inscription on the fly leaf of that book, "given enough time, go badly." The progressives who have dominated the American Catholic Church since that time have not yet drawn up a realistic accounting of their own failures.

A future generation may find it hard to believe that so many theologians of his time failed to see the greatness of Pope John Paul II and the precious gifts he gave the open church. During the darkest years he helped throw the Polish church open to all comers—believers and unbelievers—for intensely vital civil discussions. He encouraged associations of all sorts to press forward with their work. The Polish church met in factories, in homes, in the private quarters of professors. There were underground newspapers, theaters, printing presses, universities, catechetical centers, liturgies. There was little that I imagined in *The Open Church* that Archbishop Wojtyla did not try.

It gives me no small pleasure when I look back at my life of battles and controversies to find that, at least intellectually, I have ended up trying to further the great work of Karol Wojtyla.

APPENDIX

A Reader's Guide to Michael Novak's Works on Democratic Capitalism

ARTICLES AND LECTURES

"A Closet Capitalist Confesses." *The Washington Post*, March 14, 1976.

"A Closet Capitalist Confesses." *Christianity Today*, April 23, 1976.

"An Exchange on Socialism, Confessions of a Closet Capitalist." *New America*, July 1976.

"The Closet Socialists." *The Christian Century*, Feb. 23, 1977.

"An Underpraised and Undervalued System." *Worldview*, July/Aug. 1977.

"Capitalism, Socialism, and Democracy." *Commentary*, April 1978: 63–64.

Introduction to *The Denigration of Capitalism*, ed. by Michael Novak. Washington, D.C.: AEI, 1979.

"New Questions for Humanists." In *The Denigration of Capitalism: Six Points of View*, ed. by Michael Novak. Washington, D.C.: AEI, 1979.

"Productivity and Social Justice." In *Will Capitalism Survive? A Challenge by Paul Johnson with Twelve Responses*. Washington, D.C.: Ethics and Public Policy Center, 1979.

"Seven Theological Facets." In *Capitalism and Socialism: A Theological Inquiry*, ed. by Michael Novak. Washington, D.C.: AEI, 1979.

"A Challenge to Business." *Dravo Review*, Spring 1979.

"In Praise of Democratic Capitalism." Paper presented before the Conference on Contemporary Political Thought. Florence, Italy: April 1979.

"Making the Case for Capitalism." *Commonweal* 106, June 22, 1979: 366–69.

"Changing the Paradigms: The Cultural Deficiencies of Capitalism." In *Democracy and Mediating Structures: A Theological Inquiry*, ed. by Michael Novak. Washington, D.C.: AEI, 1980.

"God and Man in the Corporation." *Policy Review*, Summer 1980.

"Religion and Public Policy: The Need for Theory and Vision—The Religious Foundations of Democratic Capitalism." From Seminar on Religion at AEI, 4th Annual Public Policy Week, Dec. 10, 1980.

"On the Governability of Democracies: The Economic System." 1980–81 Franklin Foundation Lecture Series, vol. 2, ed. by Carl A. Bramlette, Jr.

Introduction and Editor's Postscript to *Liberation South, Liberation North*, ed. by Michael Novak. Washington, D.C.: AEI, 1981.

"The Moral-Religious Basis of Democratic Capitalism." In *Christianity and Politics, Catholic and Protestant Perspectives*, ed. by Carol Griffith. Washington, D.C.: Ethics and Public Policy Center, 1981.

"The Vision of Democratic Capitalism." *Public Opinion*, April/May 1981.

"Democratic Capitalism." *National Catholic Reporter*, May 22, 1981.

"The Spirit of Democratic Capitalism." *Creative Living*, Summer 1981.

The Economic System: The Evangelical Basis of a Social Market Economy." *The Review of Politics*, July 1981: 355.

"Race, Culture, and Economics." *Fortune*, Oct. 1981.

"Democratic Capitalism: Formulate a Defense." *The News World*, Nov. 23, 1981: 15A.

"The Cultural and Moral Roots of Democratic Capitalism." In *Freedom, Order, and the University*, ed. by James R. Wilburn. Malibu, Calif.: Pepperdine University Press, 1982.

"Failure of Socialism." *National Catholic Reporter*, Jan. 15, 1982.

"Why Latin America is Poor." *The Atlantic Monthly*, March 1982.

"Economics and the Public Interest." A paper delivered for conference on "The Promise of American Politics," at Wake Forest University, April 6, 1982.

"Mediating Institutions: The Communitarian Individual in America." *The Public Interest*, Summer 1982.

"Is America Still The Land of Opportunity? A Conversation with Michael Novak and Robert Lekachman." *Public Opinion*, June/July 1982.

"The Judeo-Christian Values Which Characterize Economic Freedoms." In *The Economic System of Free Enterprise: Its Judeo-Christian Values and Philosophical Concepts*, ed. by Paul C. Goelz. San Antonio, Tex.: St. Mary's University Press, 1983.

"Religion and Public Policy: The Need for Theory and Vision—The Religious Foundations of Democratic Capitalism." From Seminar on Religion at AEI, 4th Annual Public Policy Week, Dec. 10, 1980. (Also printed as "The Judeo-Christian Values Which Characterize Economic Freedoms" in *The Economic System of Free Enterprise: Its Judeo-Christian Values and Philosophical Concepts*, ed. by Paul C. Goelz. San Antonio: St. Mary's University Press, 1983.)

"Mediating Structures and Democratic Capitalism." *Economic Impact* 1, 1983.

"Theology and the Business Corporation." Lecture at the University of Southern California, Feb. 7, 1983.

"The Spirit of Democratic Capitalism." Keynote Address, April 21–22, 1983, Charleston, W.V. Sponsored by the Humanities Foundation of West Virginia.

"Business, Faith, and the Family." *Loyola Business Forum*, Summer 1983.

"Helping the Poor." *Center Journal*, Summer 1983.

"The Wisdom of Madison." *Free Inquiry*, Summer 1983.

"The Spirit: Corporate Bonds." *Bell Telephone Magazine*, no. 3–4, 1983.

"Capitalist and Proud of It." *Imprimis*, Oct. 1983.

"On Democratic Capitalism." Seminar lecture, Oct. 19–21, 1983, at Gardner-Webb College.

"Creation of Wealth, Not Redistribution, Needed." *Presbyterian Journal,* Nov. 2, 1983.

"The Catholic Anticapitalist Bias." An introduction to *Catholicism, Protestantism and Capitalism,* by Amintore Fanfani. Notre Dame: University of Notre Dame Press, 1984.

Introduction to *The Church and the Social Question* by Franz H. Mueller. Washington, D.C.: AEI, 1984.

"Theologians and Economists: The Next Twenty Years." *This World,* Winter 1984.

"Saving Distributism." *The Chesterton Review,* Feb. 1984.

"Public Theology." *This World,* Spring/Summer 1984.

"Michael Novak on Democratic Capitalism." Series of four talks on democratic capitalism given in Munich, July 1984.

"On Democratic Capitalism." Lecture given in The Netherlands, Aug. 1984.

"The Ideal of Democratic Capitalism." In *Is Capitalism Christian? Toward a Christian Perspective on Economics,* ed. by Franky Schaeffer. Westchester, Ill.: Crossway Books, 1985.

Introduction to *Speaking to the Third World: Essays on Democracy and Development,* Peter L. Berger and Michael Novak. Washington, D.C.: AEI, 1985.

"Democratic Capitalism: A North American Liberation Theology." *Transformation,* Jan./Mar. 1985.

"Economic Rights: The Servile State." *Crisis,* Oct. 1985.

"Democracy and Capitalism." From United States Information Agency Television and Film Service Worldnet, Oct. 3, 1985.

"Corporation Support for Democratic Capitalism." *St. Croix Review,* Dec. 1985.

"Income-Tax Burden Is Shifting away from the Poor onto the Rich." *Los Angeles Herald Examiner,* Feb. 23, 1986.

"The Moral Spirit of Capitalism." *Success,* March 1986.

"Poverty down, Inequality Up?" With Gordon Green in *Public Interest,* Spring 1986.

"Breaking with Socialism." *Integer,* Summer 1986.

"The War of Ideas: The Spirit of Democratic Capitalism." Lecture at the Fund for an American Renaissance Capital Forum, July 16, 1986.

"Free Persons and the Common Good." *Crisis,* Oct. 1986.

"Is There Virtue in Profit: Reconsidering the Morality of Capitalism." Discussion with Michael Novak, Robert Lekachman, Walter Wriston, Peter Steinfels, *Harper's,* Dec. 1986.

Introduction to *Liberation Theology and Liberal Society,* ed. by Michael Novak. Washington, D.C.: AEI, 1987.

"The State and the Economy: Can They Live Together in Freedom?" *Servant or Tyrant,* 1989, from lecture June 2–4, 1987.

"Political Economy and Christian Conscience." *Journal of Ecumenical Studies,* Summer 1987.

"Freedom, Justice, and Morality in Economic Organization." Florida State University Conference, March 1988.

"Political Economy in Our Time." *Freedom at Issue,* Nov.–Dec. 1988.

"Economics and the Public Interest or Liberty, Equality and Democratic Capitalism." In *The Promise of American Politics,* ed. by Robert L. Utley, Jr. Lanham, Md.: University Press of America, 1989.

"A Christian Perspective of Economics." In *Christian Perspectives on Economics,* ed. by Robert N. Mateer. CEBA [Contemporary Economics and Business Association], 1989.

"The New Capitalism: A Civilizing Vision." Confindustria Conference, Santa Margherita Ligure, Italy, June 9–10, 1989.

"The Future of Democratic Capitalism." Conference on International Perspectives, Sydney, Australia, July 11–13, 1989.

"Boredom, Virtue, and Democratic Capitalism." *Commentary,* Sept. 1989.

"Capitalism Is Moral." In *Soviet-American Debate,* 1990 Annual Opposing Viewpoints Sources. San Diego, Calif.: Greenhaven Press, 1990, pp. 15–18. Reprinted from *Commentary,* Sept. 1989.

"Freedom, Justice, and Morality in Economic Organization." *The Political Legitimacy of Markets and Governments,* ed. by Thomas R. Dye. Greenwich, Conn.: JAI Press, 1990.

"Morality, Capitalism, and Democracy." London: IEA Health and Welfare Unit, 1990.

"Wealth and Virtue: The Development of Christian Economic Teaching." In *The Capitalist Spirit: Toward a Religious Ethic of Wealth Creation,* ed. by Peter L. Berger. San Francisco: ICS Press, 1990, pp. 51–80.

"The Morality of Wealth Creation: Ten Modest Clarifications." Lecture delivered at Attitudes to Industry in Britain, Christianity and Wealth Creation, St. George's House, Windsor Castle, Sept. 28–30, 1990.

"Wealth, Poverty, and Human Creativity." *Social Action,* Oct. 1990: 6–7.

"The Church and Capitalism." *On the Issues,* April 15. Forest Hills, N.Y.: AEI, 1991.

"Countering the Adversary Culture." In *The Making of an Economic Vision,* ed. by Oliver F. Williams and John Houck. Lanham, Md.: University Press of America, 1991, pp. 99–120.

"Free Persons and the Common Good." In *Liberty/Liberati: The American and French Experiences,* ed. by Joseph Klaits and Michael H. Haltzel. Washington, D.C.: Modern Writers Center Press, 1991.

"How to Make a Republic Work: The Originality of the Commercial Republicans." In *"The Constitution of the People": Reflections on Citizens and Civil Society,* ed. by Robert E. Calvert. Lawrence: University of Kansas Press, 1991, pp. 85–112.

"Transforming the Democratic Capitalist Revolution." *International Journal of Value-Based Management* 4, 1991: 9–56.

"Capitalism Rightly Understood: The View of Christian Humanism." *Faith and Reason* 17, no. 4, Winter 1991: 317–52.

"Democratic Capitalism: Moral, or Not at All." *Freedom Review,* May–June 1991: 12–14.

"The Pope Preaches the Market, but within Limits." *International Herald Tribune,* May 9, 1991.

"The Pope Sends a Strong, Free-Market Message." *The San Diego Union,* June 9, 1991: C-4.

"Novak on Capitalism." *Commonweal,* June 14, 1991: 386.

Contribution to "The Pope, Liberty, and Capitalism: Essays on *Centesimus Annus.*" *National Review Special Supplement,* June 24, 1991: S11–S12.

"Socialism's Last Stand." *AEI on the Issues,* from *Forbes,* Oct. 28, 1991.

"The Great Convergence: A New Consensus in Favor of Economic and Religious Liberty." *Crisis* 9, Dec. 1991: 28–33.

"Culture First: The Democratic Capitalist Revolution Transformed." In *Being Christian Today,* ed. by Richard John Neuhaus and George Weigel. Washington, D.C.: Ethics and Public Policy Center, 1992: 251–84.

"The Economic Preconditions of Democracy." In *Ethics in the Russian Marketplace: An Anthology,* ed. by Mark R. Elliott and Scott Lingenfelter. Wheaton College: Institute for East-West Christian Studies, 1992, pp. 21–26. Excerpted from *This Hemisphere of Liberty: A Philosophy of the Americas.* Washington, D.C.: AEI, 1990.

"The Big Economic Lie." *First Things* 21, March 1992: 14.

"The Age of Enterprise: How Small Business Became the World's Biggest Business." *Creative Living,* Autumn 1992: 3–6.

"Wealth and Virtue: The Moral Case for Capitalism." *Word and World,* Fall 1992.

"Foreword." *Capitalism versus Anti-Capitalism: The Triumph of Ricardian over Marxist Political Economy.* New Brunswick, N.J.: Transaction Publishers, 1993: ix–xi.

"Eight Arguments about the Morality of the Marketplace," section I. In *God and the Marketplace: Essays on the Morality of Wealth Creation.* London: IEA Health and Welfare, 1993, pp. 8–29.

"The Crisis of the Welfare State." Lecture given at the Center for Policy Studies, May 25, 1993.

"Two Moral Ideals for Business." *Economic Affairs,* Sept./Oct. 1993.

"Seven Plus Seven—The Responsibilities of Business Corporations." *Crisis,* July–Aug. 1994.

"How Christianity Changed Political Economy." *Crisis,* Feb. 1995.

"Is Business a Calling?" *Across the Board,* July/Aug. 1996.

"The Future of Civil Society." *Crisis,* Oct. 1996.

"Executives Must Be Allowed to Execute." *Directors and Boards,* Fall 1997.

"Economics as Humanism." *First Things,* Oct. 1997.

"The Judeo-Christian Foundation of Human Dignity, Personal Morality, and the Concept of the Person." *The Journal of Markets and Morality,* Oct. 1998.

"The International Vocation of American Business." Lecture given Nov. 12, 1998, at the University of Notre Dame.

"The Silent Artillery of Communism." In *The Collapse of Communism,* ed. by Lee Edwards. Stanford: Hoover University Press, 1999.

"The International Vocation of American Business" (shortened version). *Religion and Liberty,* July/Aug. 1999.

"Controversial Engagements." *First Things,* April 1999.

"Hayek: Practitioner of Social Justice." *Social Justice Properly Understood* (Celebration of Friedrich Hayek's 100th Birthday), Oct. 28, 1999.

BOOKS

Capitalism and Socialism: A Theological Inquiry. Washington, D.C.: AEI, 1979.
The Denigration of Capitalism: Six Points of View. Edited by Michael Novak. Washington, D.C.: AEI, 1979.
The Spirit of Democratic Capitalism. New York: Simon & Schuster, 1982 (paperback, 1983). Reprint with new afterword, Lanham, Md.: Madison Books, 1991.
Freedom with Justice: Catholic Social Thought and Liberal Institutions. New York: Harper & Row, 1984. Second edition with a new introduction and concluding chapter, retitled *Catholic Social Thought and Liberal Institutions,* New Brunswick, N.J.: Transaction, 1989.
Will It Liberate? Questions about Liberation Theology. Mahwah, N.J.: Paulist Press, 1986. Paperback with a new introduction, Lanham, Md.: Madison Books, 1991.
Free Persons and the Common Good. Lanham, Md.: Madison Books, 1989.
This Hemisphere of Liberty: A Philosophy of the Americas. Washington, D.C.: AEI, 1991.
The Catholic Ethic and the Spirit of Capitalism. New York: Free Press, 1993.
Awakening from Nihilism: In Preparation for the Twenty-First Century—Four Lessons from the Twentieth. Washington, D.C.: Crisis Books, 1995.
Business As a Calling: Work and the Examined Life. New York: Free Press, 1996.
The Fire of Invention: Civil Society and the Future of the Corporation. Lanham, Md.: Rowman & Littlefield, 1997.
On Cultivating Liberty: Reflections on Moral Ecology. Edited by Brian Anderson. Lanham, Md.: Rowman & Littlefield, 1999.
In Praise of the Free Economy: Essays by Michael Novak. Edited by Samuel Gregg. Center for Independent Studies, 1999.

MONOGRAPHS

The American Vision: An Essay on the Future of Democratic Capitalism. Washington, D.C.: AEI, 1978.
Toward a Theology of the Corporation. Washington, D.C.: AEI, 1981. Revised edition with new introduction, 1990.
Morality, Capitalism and Democracy. Lecture at the Queen Elizabeth II Conference Center, June 1990. London: IEA Health and Welfare Unit, 1990.
The Crisis of the Welfare State: Ethics and Economics. Lecture for the Center for Policy Studies at Church House, London, May 25, 1993. Center for Policy Studies, 1993.

INDEX

About the Author

Michael Novak holds the George Frederick Jewett Chair in Religion, Philosophy, and Public Policy at the American Enterprise Institute in Washington, D.C., where he is also director of social and political studies. In 1986, Mr. Novak headed the U.S. delegation to the United Nations Human Rights Commission in Geneva. Mr. Novak has won the Templeton Prize for Progress in Religion, the Anthony Fisher Award, the Wilhelm Weber Prize, and the International Award of the Institution for World Capitalism, among others. The author of more than twenty-five books on philosophy, religion, politics, economics and culture, he is also a cofounder and former publisher of *Crisis* and has been a columnist for both *National Review* and *Forbes*. His most recent books are *Tell Me Why: A Father Answers His Daughter's Questions about God*, written with Jana Novak; and *On Cultivating Liberty*, a collection of his essays edited by Brian C. Anderson. He lives in Washington, D.C., with his wife, Karen. His books have been translated into every major language.

About the Editor

Edward W. Younkins is a professor of accountacy and business administration in the Department of Business and Technology at Wheeling Jesuit University and the founder of the university's degree program in political and economic philosophy. His articles and reviews have appeared in *The Journal of Markets and Morality, Ideas on Liberty* (formerly *The Freeman*), *The Social Critic, Free Life, The Individual*, and many other publications.